Singing Archaeology

MUSIC / CULTURE

A series from Wesleyan University Press

Edited by George Lipsitz, Susan McClary, and Robert Walser

Published titles

JOHN RICHARDSON

Singing Archaeology

PHILIP GLASS'S *AKHNATEN*

WESLEYAN UNIVERSITY PRESS

Published by University Press of New England

Hanover & London

WESLEYAN UNIVERSITY PRESS
Published by University Press of New England, Hanover, NH 03755
© 1999 by John Richardson
All rights reserved
Printed in the United States of American 5 4 3 2 1
CIP data appear at the end of the book

Illustrations from Wallis Budge, *Tutankhamen: Amenism, Atenism, and Egyptian Monotheism* (New York: Dover, 1991 [1923]), and from L. Austine Waddell, *Tibetan Buddhism* (New York: Dover, 1972 [1885]), are used by permission of the publisher.

The thirty-four excerpts from Philip Glass, *Akhnaten, Satyagraha, 1+1, Two Pages,* and *Einstein On The Beach,* which appear throughout this book as "Examples," are used by permission of Dunvagen Music Publishers, Inc., New York.

Contents

Illustrations

Acknowledgments

This book would not exist had Susan McClary not taken an active interest in this project in response to a letter I wrote to her in the summer of 1994. At the time, I was having trouble finding outside evaluators for my doctoral dissertation who were both versed in recent approaches to music criticism and sympathetic—or even neutral—in their attitude toward Philip Glass's music. I wrote in my letter to McClary that her writing on Glass and other postmodern musicians revealed "an intuitive and deeply-felt understanding of the way this kind of music works." She wrote that she would be happy to "fly to my defense"—which she did. A year later (in 1996) I flew to Los Angeles, where I spent a little over a year working as a postdoctoral research fellow in the department of musicology at UCLA. The many challenging and inspiring conversations I shared with McClary and other members of the faculty as well as graduate students during my tenure at that university have had an enormous impact on many aspects of the book as it now appears.

Philip Glass himself also had a hand in the success of this project, both directly, by giving of his time in two interviews conducted during the early stages of my research, and indirectly, by any part he may have played in the policy of his publishing company, Dunvagen Music, toward this research, which has seldom left anything to be desired. The staff at Dunvagen— Gary Schuster, Jim Keller, and Ramona Kirschenman—have consistently, over the five years I have been working on this project, been both efficient and obliging, occasionally going to extraordinary lengths to help me to track down important items of research material.

Matti Vainio, chair of musicology at the University of Jyväskylä, Finland, has been a great supporter of my work, particularly while I was writing my dissertation; he was also a congenial landlord during the two years I and my family lived in his house. Drafts of various versions of this book or sections of it have been read by the following people: Anne Sivuoja-Gunaratnam, Susan McClary, Raymond Monelle, Juhani Nuorvala, Peter Rabinowitz, Pekka Toivanen, and Robert Walser. All of these readers had some influence on what you are reading here, and, needless to say, I am greatly indebted to each one of them. Nuorvala, moreover, provided tapes and transcripts of his own interviews with Philip Glass, which, supplemented with the material I collected myself, provide a substantial body of original interview material, much of which addresses issues the composer has not, to my knowledge, dealt with in as much detail in other publications. Monelle, in his facility as an evaluator of my dissertation, offered numerous concrete suggestions for improving my work, many of which have been taken up here. His contribution is greatly appreciated. Corresponding and collaborating with Sivuoja-Gunaratnam over several years has on many occasions and in very tangible ways reminded me of the importance of community in scholarly work. The same can be said of James Westby, with whom I shared an office at UCLA, and whose friendship and irrepressible sense of humor did much to make my time at that institution an extremely enjoyable one. Individuals who are deserving of thanks for other reasons include Marcia Herndon, Liz Ihre (Transatlantic Films), David Ingram, Petri Kuljuntausta, Erkki Salmenhaara, Steve Taylor, and Jeff Todd Titon. Institutions that are deserving of thanks include the University of Jyväskylä, Finland, the Academy of Finland, Brown University, and the University of California at Los Angeles.

Michael Freeman proofread my dissertation, which although different from this book in terms of its general orientation as well as in other significant respects, is sufficiently similar to be considered an early draft of it. Timothy Mennel did a very thorough job of copy-editing the book. I am grateful to both for their very important contributions. I would also like to thank the staff of Wesleyan University Press and University Press of New England for their work on this project.

The biggest thanks of all go to Ulla, however, who has stuck by me through thick and thin during one of the most demanding times in both of our lives. This book is dedicated to our daughter, Liselotte.

Introduction

If, like myself, you were not a part of New York's downtown artistic movement in the late 1960s to 1970s, and did not belong to a small group of musician, critics, and aficionados of avant-garde music around the world who were in the know, Philip Glass may have seemed to have appeared out of nowhere in the 1980s. Indeed, this composer's strangely haunting harmonies and busy, pulsating rhythms did in a sense seem to come from nowhere, to be strangely unattached from what had come before, but at the same time to resonate with music one already knew, be it from the classical repertory or with its roots in popular culture. It is this paradoxical mixture, of a present aware of but not indentured to the past, of musical experience that seemed not just to be about remembering but also *remembering* that you are remembering, that for this listener at least made Glass's music stand apart from so much of what was going on in musical life at the time. At the same time, however, it was precisely this orientation that tied it in with a new cultural tendency of questioning existing wisdom regarding the relationship between the present and the past.

"Singing Archaeology"—a phrase coined by Shalom Goldman, the archaeologist who worked with Glass on *Akhnaten*—was chosen as the title of this book because it seems to encapsulate the subject matter of this particular opera; but also because it becomes a particularly apt metaphor both for the approach to music theater Glass and artists like him were pursuing in the 1980s, and for other more general tendencies in postmodern culture at that time—as exemplified by Foucault's influential "Archaeology of Knowledge."

This book was born out of the desire to get to the bottom of what was and still is so appealing to me in Glass's music. As a musician my first reaction upon hearing this music, apart from wanting to hear more, was to want to play and write music like it myself. Although I have now largely overcome the desire to imitate this music, it would be dishonest of me were I not to admit that it has profoundly influenced much of what I do today in and about music as well as the way I listen to much of the music I listen to—even music that was composed long before Glass and I were born. My connection with this music has, since the first time I heard it, been powerful and intuitive—a kind of magnetism is probably the best way of describing it. The arguments put forward in these pages may at times seem elaborate and intellectually driven, but it is important to stress that what initially drew me to this music was definitely not the elegance of an abstract aesthetic position; nor was it the desire to profit in some way from the latest musical trend. Rather, the tracks I have left for the reader in the pages that follow are my attempts both to explain to myself and to relate to others the extraordinarily powerful musical affects I myself have experienced when listening to this music. Many other motivational factors may have come into play at a later date, such as the desire to learn how to be a better musician/composer/writer myself, the desire to get a Ph.D., the desire to establish myself in my chosen career, and the desire to respond to some of the unjust criticism Glass has received. I will not deny that those factors have all had some influence on what you are reading now, but I have, throughout the research and writing process, attempted to remain true to my initial responses to the music; responses which I have had no trouble rekindling over the five years it has taken to write and rewrite this book, and which I hope I have managed to impart to the reader in some, at least, of what I have written.

This book is a personal and subjectively colored vision of Glass's music as I myself have experienced it. It is not a documentary on how the composer went about putting *Akhnaten* together; nor is it a descriptive analysis of the entire musical score. What I have written may or may not match other listeners' experiences of this music. I have attempted, however, to ground the observations made here in the inter-subjective experiences of the composer, performers, audiences, critics, and musicologists—a move that is sufficient in my mind to situate this study firmly in the scholarly domain and, further, to take it beyond the abstract and often circular argumentation of theorists. In this respect, the approach is in keeping with a large number of recent studies in critical musicology, or (academic) music criticism, with recent research on opera, and with certain studies in the semiotics of music. This study addresses a musicological readership, but is not, I hope, restricted to such a readership. The idea of a musical intelligentsia that exists in isolation from and is largely oblivious to—or is even openly antagonistic toward—the broader music listening public is one that I, like Glass, emphatically resist. Most of this book is intended to be accessible to the general (educated) reader. Some passages of the text *do* attempt to shed light on specific music-analytical problems—particularly chapter three, which can, if necessary, be skipped over by readers with little musical training. The passages in question are not an end in themselves, however, but serve to illustrate how musical procedures construct and are reflective of affective and other discursive realities as experienced: realities that most listeners at least intuitively know exist, but that the dominant formalist tradition in musicology has until recently been reluctant to take seriously. When I have deemed it necessary to don a more overtly music-analytical cap, I have done so for the above reasons, but also in order either to correct pervasive misconceptions that have arisen in discussions of this music or to illustrate as graphically as possible the ways in which it is distinctive.

One of the main misconceptions I address is the assumption that the music composed by those musicians who have either rightly or wrongly been labeled as minimalists is a music without a past. A central concern here is to examine the complex and often troubled relationship between this music and earlier musical practices; this is related to the more general concern to shed further light on perceptions of the past in recent postmodernist thought. *Akhnaten* would seem to be ideally suited for this task; both in its music and in its subject matter it makes more overt reference to historical practices than any previous or, arguably, subsequent work by Glass.

Although I often attempt to tackle large, apparently abstract issues, mine is in actual fact a (very) close reading of the opera intended to reveal that what is at stake in works of the imagination such as this could hardly be more personal and concrete. A central assumption I make is that works of art are more than entertaining diversions from the vicissitudes of everyday life; they become meaningful precisely because they are experienced as addressing some of the most fundamental inter-subjective, social, and psychological concerns we are faced with as human beings in our day to day existence. Given this assumption, it is easy to see why artists like Glass become controversial; if what is at stake are really such fundamental issues, when someone comes along who challenges an existing musical point of view, it is not solely the musical language that is being challenged but the myriad underlying assumptions that go along with it. Without being drawn into the polemical debates surrounding Glass's music, this study does attempt to answer the question: why do the people who like Philip Glass's music like it? Implicitly, as well, it addresses the more complex question of why certain parties within the musical establishment have had so much trouble in accepting it. The second is treated only as a peripheral concern, however; I have no desire to participate in a virtual mud-slinging match with unfriendly critics, nor would anything be achieved by my doing so. Considerably more is to be gained by concentrating on my own positive and constructive but also critical experiences as well as those of others.

The layout of the book is largely self-explanatory. The first chapter discusses the genesis of *Akhnaten* as well as examining the history of the ideas Glass and his collaborators drew on when constructing the opera. Chapter 2 provides a contextual springboard for the more specific discussions of the music and drama in later chapters. In this chapter, Glass the theater composer is discussed from various separate and overlapping cultural and ideational perspectives. Chapter 3 looks back at the genealogy of Glass's musical language as it touches on the musical language of *Akhnaten*. This chapter is concerned with the palette of techniques and affects the composer drew on when composing this opera as well as examining the ways in which this palette was utilized in specific musical passages. Chapters 4 to 7 are a thorough, critically grounded discussion of the opera. These chapters are arranged according to broad thematic categories, although in many places I have found it congenial to follow the overall structural schema of the piece. This reflects my concern to adequately account for the way the opera is put together musico-dramatically. I found that the best way to illumine Glass's unique conception of narrative structure in this work was to systematically work my way through the piece addressing specific critical concerns when they arise. The chapters do, nonetheless, focus on distinct clusters of ideas. Chapter 4 deals with the Brechtian idea of alienation and its application to music; and with the related concern of how the composer goes about representing ideas he considers either oppressive or outmoded—those of the so-called "old order." Chapter 5 explains how the "new order" is represented in music and drama, identifying specific musical procedures that are marked in the music as more "progressive" as well looking at the ways in which even the new order is found wanting, both musically and ideologically. Chapter 6 is about Akhnaten's religious credo and its representation in music. Some fundamental questions are asked here about issues of representation and religion as they relate to musical texts. Questions of exoticism and ethical questions pertaining to the representation of other cultures are also addressed in this chapter. Chapter 7 returns to more general considerations of musical narrative and ends with a short general discussion. Chapter 8 discusses the reception of *Akhnaten*. In addition, some tentative conclusions are drawn concerning the position of Glass vis-à-vis his musical antecedents as well as the relevance of both this opera and subsequent works as we approach the new millennium. This is, in conclusion, a complex and many-sided exposition of the subject at hand; under such circumstances, the best place to start is at the beginning.

Singing Archaeology

CHAPTER ONE

Oedipus and Akhnaton
Of Origins and Archaeologies

Glass's Opera Trilogy:
A Present-Day Gesamtkunstwerk?

The idea of an opera trilogy initially took root in a meeting between Philip Glass and Dennis Russell Davies in 1979. Davies, the recently appointed musical director of Stuttgart's State Opera, wanted to mount a production of Glass's second major theatrical work, *Satyagraha*, but was also interested in commissioning from the composer a new opera. With performances of two Glass operas planned, it was not difficult to construct a rationale for production of the composer's first opera—the avant-garde classic *Einstein on the Beach* (henceforth *Einstein*)—by proposing a thematic linking of the three operas. Riding in the slipstream of two major box-office successes—with European and North American productions of his first two operas having elevated his status to that of a contemporary-music phenomenon—Glass was clearly no longer the young upstart who just a few years earlier had driven a New York City taxicab and fixed plumbing in Greenwich Village lofts in order to make ends meet. Seen by some as a Dickensian whippersnapper-made-good, by others as the personification of the American dream, and by others as the Prodigal Son returning home to take what he might not deserve, Glass was, perhaps for the first time in his career, in a position to take stock.

It is probably pointless to speculate on the extent to which Glass's motivation in making his third full-scale music theater work the third part of an operatic trilogy—thus transforming the earlier pieces a posteriori into trilogy works—was pragmatic and the extent to which it was artistic. Suffice it to say that both factors seem to have entered into his equations. Artistic considerations notwithstanding, tying the three operas together would help to ensure performances of the earlier works, while at the same time playing on the taste for the monumental that the nineteenth-century tradition of grand opera, most notably Richard Wagner's mammoth Ring tetralogy, has instilled in opera audiences.[1] Glass's standing was unlikely to suffer unduly from the association. And the Stuttgart audiences that attended the 1984 premiere of *Akhnaten*, and that several years later witnessed performances of the entire trilogy, could hardly have failed to recognize the allusion, as the composer himself has quite rightly observed.[2]

To be sure, there are those who object to postmodern spectacle on the grounds that it constitutes nothing more than a return to the overblown rhetoric of Romanticism. Worse still, critics contend, such spectacle appears totally oblivious to the political ramifications of such a return. Glass's account of the genesis of the trilogy seems, however, to suggest an engagement with his operatic antecedents, and with the genre itself, that is at odds with the historical blinkeredness of which he has been accused.

That the sheer magnitude of Glass's trilogy invites comparisons with Wagner is undeniable. The issues seem to be whether such an association is ipso facto problematic, as Andreas Huyssen seems to find the work of Glass collaborator Robert Wilson; whether Wagner is an appropriate yardstick by which—without undue concern for the historical ramifications of the association—to measure Glass's greatness, as *New York Times* critic John Rockwell has done; or whether Glass, as well as many of his downtown New York contemporaries, is seen as emerging from a somewhat different tradition that acknowledges Wagner but sees him through the lens of a distinctly post-Brechtian, postmodern theatrical sensibility.[3]

As Huyssen rightly points out, the reemergence of the Wagner cult in recent years might well be "a symptom of a happy collusion between the megalomania of the postmodern and that of the premodern on the edge of modernism."[4] One might go further still and attribute partial responsibility for the contemporary Wagnerian movement to Glass. Arguably, no composer has done more in the second half of the twentieth century to demonstrate the viability of music theater as a genre. Rockwell's position is also tenable, however. His intention was, of course, to pay tribute to Glass, although the compliment is not necessarily one with which the Jewish-born composer might feel altogether comfortable.[5] Huyssen, while agreeing on the suitability of the analogy, evidently disagrees on the conclusions to be drawn from it. Both positions rest on the assumption that there is much that is similar in the serial operas of Wagner and Glass, and it is difficult to deny that the scale of Glass's trilogy is Wagnerian. I will argue, though, that a closer examination of the signifying practices employed by Glass, notwithstanding the subject matter of the operas and broader questions of cultural context, reveals that attempts to historicize Glass as a theatrical composer have up until now been only partially successful.

Rockwell has observed that the trilogy is "more a retroactive attempt [by Glass] to impose coherence on his own career than a true statement of his original intentions."[6] But this is only partially true. Artistically, linking the trilogy operas, *Einstein*, *Satyagraha*, and *Akhnaten*, is not difficult. Because of the slowly evolving, incremental transformation of his musical idiom, Glass has always had a tendency to carry musical ideas over from one composition to the next. Thus, there is coherence in his oeuvre, and it is there in abundance, so much so that he has been accused, to some extent justifiably, of recycling ideas ad nauseam.[7] It is not surprising, then, that thematic material from *Einstein* crops up also in *Satyagraha*. Nor is it surprising that the composer learned from his collaborators on *Einstein* and incorporated its ideas in the subsequent trilogy operas; he was, after all, working with several of the foremost theatrical talents of his time. Indeed, many aspects of Glass's approach in *Satyagraha* can be traced to his affiliation with Robert Wilson. But where that opera also diverges in certain significant respects from the *Einstein* mold, *Akhnaten* is a conscious attempt by the composer to bind the three pieces together by highlighting their commonalities. Thus, although *Einstein* is commonly characterized as sui generis among the works of the trilogy, it could be argued that *Satyagraha* is really the odd opera out, insofar as it is tied to its predecessor in only a very general way; further, Glass had a markedly different relationship to his subject matter in that opera. Does this imply that the entire idea of the trilogy is nothing but a shrewd marketing ploy? Not quite. The very nature of Glass's aesthetic, which places a strong emphasis on implicit levels of signification and steers clear of conventional "storytelling" narrative strategies, implies less of a need for integration than in the Wagnerian *Gesamtkunstwerk*, for example. It would be a mistake, however, to discuss *Akhnaten* as though it is an autonomous work—it is, more than either of its predecessors, very much a trilogy piece. Indeed, a definite profile can be identified in the trilogy as a whole that does not appear in Glass's other operas. The fact that it was put there in part retrospectively does not matter all that much.

How, then, does Glass go about putting together an operatic trilogy? It is clear from his comments in the autobiographical account of the making of the trilogy, *Music by Philip Glass* (henceforth *MPG*),[8] that he was thinking along Wilsonian lines. Robert Wilson was known in the 1970s for his visually striking, slowly unfolding portrayals of historical icons such as Sigmund Freud, Joseph Stalin, and Queen Victoria. Glass, too, was looking for a historical figure, one "of the same stature as Einstein and Gandhi"[9]—

not a protagonist in the conventional sense but more of a hollow figure-head, literally an icon (a term that implies semiological flatness and exteriority) around which a series of loosely related ideas, actions, and images could orbit freely. Robert Wilson had suggested Adolf Hitler as the figurehead of the first trilogy opera, but Glass thought this subject was "just too 'loaded.'"[10] Wilson, on the other hand, was not interested in Gandhi, whom Glass went on to make the subject of his second opera. Einstein eventually became "a compromise figure" for the two. But *Einstein* turned out to be more than just a straightforward homage to the scientist. In the opera, Einstein goes on trial, apparently for contributing to the body of knowledge that led to the invention of the atomic bomb. This subtext is implied even in the opera's title, which alludes to Nevil Shute's popular novel *On the Beach* (later turned into a classic science-fiction film), a stark portrayal of life in the wake of a global nuclear disaster.[11] That Einstein himself was an avowed pacifist and that he went to great lengths to prevent the deployment of the weapons his theories were partially responsible for creating is one of the central paradoxes addressed in the opera. This is not, of course, *all* that the opera is about. Some critics have gone so far as to claim that *Einstein* is not about anything, since one of its most powerful "messages" has to do with the very nature of signification itself and the Lyotardian "legitimation crisis" it has undergone in recent years.

Satyagraha, the opera Glass was contemplating prior to his first theatrical encounter with Wilson, represents a somewhat less complex scenario than his first major theatrical work. This opera is, as the composer himself is willing to concede, an idealization of the title character, a self-indulgent diversion into the imaginary by Glass and his collaborators.[12] Herein lies the key to the opera's extraordinary expressive force, though it is also a possible Achilles' heel from the standpoint of recent cultural theory. In the opera, important events in the life of Gandhi are depicted in a series of shimmering tableaux, but the genealogy of the idea of passive resistance itself, what Gandhi termed *satyagraha*, and its translation into musico-dramatic form is its most pervasive concern. Historical figures who influenced or were influenced by Gandhi's ideas are incorporated into the work as silent witnesses to the events—among them Leo Tolstoy, with whom Gandhi corresponded while formulating his first major treatise on civil disobedience, Rabindranath Tagore, the poet and political activist who was also a longtime confidant of Gandhi, and Martin Luther King Jr., who appropriated many of Gandhi's ideas and methods in the American civil-rights movement of the 1960s. These figures represent, from Gandhi's historical perspective, the past, present, and future of the satyagraha movement; thus, Tolstoy presides over the first act of the opera, Tagore the second, and King the third. The action of the opera proper comprises key events from Gandhi's formative years in South Africa (1893–1914), when he developed and refined the philosophy and methods of satyagraha as a means of resisting the discriminatory legislative measures taken by the South African government against the Indian community in that country. Although the action of the opera is concerned with actual historical events, the libretto is gleaned from the Hindu *Bhagavad-Gita* and is in the original Sanskrit. Gandhi, who was able to recite the *Bhagavad-Gita* verbatim, used it as an inspirational wellspring in the formulation of his political and spiritual ideas. The libretto of *Satyagraha* seeks to elucidate ideas in the Hindu text analogous to Gandhi's actions in his struggles on behalf of South Africa's Indian population—to trace the ideas behind the ideas, so to speak. Thus, myth and history are elaborately intertwined in *Satyagraha*, as they were later in *Akhnaten*. The protagonist of the former opera is seen to have constructed aspects of his character through identification with mythical figures, while the latter concerns itself with a historical figure who might have served as the model for one of the most pervasive myths in Western culture. In both operas, the relationship between myth and history is a pervasive subtext, as it is in *Einstein*, with its focus on a figure as mythological as any in the twentieth century.

All Too Human or Not Human Enough?

The common feature of the trilogy operas is what some critics have called their "posthumanist" orientation. (As with the term *postmodernism*, the prefix *post* here does not totally negate the concept it precedes; it merely throws it into a different epistemological light.) Evidence of a certain kind of humanism is not hard to perceive in the trilogy operas or in Glass's discourse concerning them. In *MPG*, the composer writes, "I saw that ideas (social, political, religious) could be central to the work. Though this may not have been seen as such by other people, for me it was a fundamental reorientation of my thinking about my relation to theatre. . . . The key is that we know Akhnaten as a man of ideas and, to me, the history of humanity is a history of ideas, of culture."[13]

The humanistic side of Glass probably comes out most forcefully in *Satyagraha*. But if we are to construe Glass's approach in this and the other trilogy operas as humanistic, why has it so often been described by hostile critics as "dehumanized" or "mechanical"? How does this version of humanism differ qualitatively from its historical namesake? Most important, perhaps, why should it? (In other words, what does the *post* in *posthumanism* mean?) Is Glass's approach all too human, or is it not human enough?

Is it possible for it to be both, as some critics seem to suggest? These questions defy succinct, unequivocal answers. For now, though, let it suffice to state that Glass's "humanity" often seems to emerge between the cracks, as it were, by means of the subjugation of many of the very qualities we are accustomed to regarding as most human.

If Glass shares anything with the classical humanist philosophers, it is a fundamentally secular outlook, even though two of the three trilogy operas are concerned with men who were widely regarded as spiritual leaders. Insofar as the trilogy operas are concerned with emancipation—and I claim this is a central concern in all three—Glass's philosophy is akin to that of the philosophers of the European Enlightenment. Both what is meant by the term and the means by which it is to be achieved bear little resemblance, however, to the Enlightenment credo as it has been passed down in philosophy and culture since the eighteenth century. In terms of contemporary thought, Glass's "humanism" can be identified with two "poles" in the recent debates over postmodernism. At one end of the continuum we have philosophers like Richard Rorty, who rejects shared standards of human decency based on metaphysical assumptions in favor of a solidarity based solely on historical contingencies; at the other, there are critics of postmodernism like Terry Eagleton, who while they recognize the shortcomings of the humanist paradigm, reject Rorty's relativism and other decentered postmodern subjectivities as politically ineffectual and ethically impoverished.[14] Glass's approach resembles certain aspects of both of these positions but is reducible to neither. His agenda is to all intents and purposes humanist (there does appear to be *some* supposition of a meritorious human "core" at the heart of the composer's philosophy—albeit an ever-elusive and radically non-personal one), but the musical and dramatic rhetoric he uses to convey his humanist "message" is very different from that which conventionally grounds humanist discourse. It would be an exaggeration to call Glass a feminist, but his position vis-à-vis Enlightenment humanism appears to be in some ways analogous to that of feminists, who have in the last two decades questioned many of the assumptions that reside at the core of the so-called humanist paradigm, sometimes substituting them with assumptions of their own but often preferring to leave the space formerly held by the hub of a centered, Cartesian subjectivity unoccupied.

Oedipus Unearthed

How, then, does the third trilogy opera fit in with the (post)humanist agendas of the first two? Glass chanced upon his third "man of ideas" while reading Immanuel Velikovsky's *Oedipus and Akhnaton: Myth and History*.[15] Velikovsky, a Russian-born Jew whose first area of expertise was psychoanalysis and who lived his later years in the United States, is best known for his controversial books *Worlds in Collision* (1950), *Ages in Chaos* (1952), and *Earth in Upheaval* (1955). In these works, Velikovsky applies his knowledge of diverse scholarly disciplines—including astrophysics, geology, biology, history, and psychoanalysis—to constructing alternative versions of events in ancient history. Velikovsky's writing was throughout his career highly speculative, but his willingness to go out on a limb in this way sometimes led him to insights that later proved extremely valuable to other, more cautious scholars.[16]

The main hypothesis of *Oedipus and Akhnaton* is that the central events of the Oedipus myth closely resemble the life of the fourteenth-century B.C.E. Egyptian pharaoh Akhnaten.[17] From this, Velikovsky infers that the various versions of the legends that have been passed down to us in the writings of Aeschylus, Sophocles, and Euripides are based upon the life of the eighteenth-dynasty pharaoh. Velikovsky's methods are at times suspect, his leaps of inference vertiginous, and his imagination unbounded, but the sheer weight and detail of the evidence he provides, combined with its elegant presentation, leave open the possibility that his arguments have some foundation in historical truth.

Velikovsky's hypothesis that the life of Akhnaten resembles the Oedipus myth to an uncanny degree, is, of course, a good deal easier to swallow than the assertion that Akhnaten and Oedipus were one and the same. The most telling evidence Velikovsky presents has to do with Akhnaten's relationship with his parents. Evidence of an incestuous marriage between the pharaoh and his mother is tenuous, to say the least, as is the claim that Akhnaten murdered his father, which Velikovsky quite wisely makes no attempts to substantiate, other than in a purely symbolic sense.[18] Akhnaten was, however, unusually close to his mother, and he was responsible for acts of sacrilege toward his deceased father that his subjects would almost certainly have considered on a par with murder. Other evidence is more convincing still—in particular, what appear to be a number of quite transparent references to Egypt in the Oedipus myth. The most obvious of these is the riddle addressed to Oedipus by a sphinx, which are found almost exclusively in Egypt. Furthermore, the name of the city in which Oedipus and his mother-wife, Jocasta, resided, Thebes, in addition to being the capital of Boeotia in Greece was also the considerably more populous capital of ancient Egypt and seat of the Egyptian pharaohs.[19]

Velikovsky brings numerous other parallels to light, some quite convincing, others less so. One of the most interesting of these is his rationale for the derivation of the name Oedipus (Greek: "swollen foot" or "swollen leg"), an appellation that has bemused many a twentieth-century scholar. Velikovsky proposes a link between the name of Oedipus and an unusual feature of the art of the Amarna period.[20] In the artifacts that have survived from this period, Akhnaten and the members of his family are depicted with noticeably enlarged lower limbs. Velikovsky surmises, as many others have before him, that the pharaoh (and therefore also the mythological Oedipus) was physically deformed.[21] Whether this was the case or whether the features in question were expressionistic or allegorical distortions remains a moot issue in the literature on the subject. I will return to this issue below since, regardless of its historical implications, it is an important—perhaps the most important—element of Glass's construction of the character of Akhnaten.

Velikovsky's writing has been widely maligned. This mattered little to Glass, however, who appears to have been able to identify with the controversy surrounding the Russian expatriate. "I was reading Velikovsky for the fun of it," he has commented. "I think that's a good way to read Velikovsky! I'm not a scientist, I don't care what Carl Sagan thinks about Velikovsky,[22] that doesn't matter to me at all. But I like Velikovsky because his mind was so lively; he asked so many questions, he turned over so many stones in looking for things."[23]

The resonance of the subject matter in its contemporary dramatic and cultural contexts appears, then, to have superseded any concern that the opera be factually watertight. In Velikovsky's account of Akhnaten, Glass found a subject compatible with the protagonists of the two earlier portrait operas, one both equal to the dramatic requirements of the genre and sufficiently engaging—both personally and intellectually—to hold his interest over the three years it took to select a production team, research, write, compose, and, finally, stage the opera. In *MPG*, the composer writes:

Historical validity hardly mattered to me at all. Practically from the moment I saw Velikovsky's title page, I knew that I had found the subject for my third opera, one that could stand up to the scale of music theater. I was happy to let others squabble over the possible or impossible historical connection between Oedipus and Akhnaten. Theatrically speaking, I knew it made perfect sense.[24]

Glass had hoped to collaborate with Velikovsky on the libretto, and he was in the process of setting up a meeting with him when he heard of his untimely demise in November 1979.[25] The original version of Glass's *Oedipus and Akhnaton* followed Velikovsky's hypothesis quite closely:

In the first version, the audience would have seen the two operas going on at the same time. Upstage and on a slightly higher level would be the Akhnaten story.

Downstage, closer to the audience, would be the Oedipus legend. In this way, their historical relationship could be reflected in their physical distancing from the viewer. As in Velikovsky's theory, the two plots would be similar, though I had arranged that the intermission for each story would occur at different times so the overall stage action would be continuous. I had already begun to work out the coordination of the two different musical elements, one for the Egyptian story and another for the Greek.[26]

The most pressing rationale for the (ostensible) dismissal of Oedipus from the libretto appears to have been clarity of presentation: the obvious difficulties involved in staging a double narrative and making this work in musical terms evidently outweighed the advantages of such an approach. "What happened is," comments Glass,

in the course of working on the libretto, I became increasingly interested in Akhnaten and less and less interested in Oedipus. There was, there actually exists somewhere, a treatment combining the two. In the end, I decided that what I was really interested in was Akhnaten, and I felt Oedipus was becoming kind of a burden to it dramatically. It became kind of an abstract idea and in the end I just dropped it.[27]

Abstract or not, Oedipus remains such a tangible presence in both the music and the libretto of *Akhnaten* that to place him side by side on the stage with his pharaonic doppelgänger would have been redundant in dramatic terms.

Early ("post-Oedipus") drafts of the libretto reflect this orientation most strongly; incestuous relations between Akhnaten and his mother, Queen Tye, as well as the ensuing power struggle between Tye and the pharaoh's "legitimate" wife, Nefertiti, are strongly to the fore. In addition, an incestuous tie between Akhnaten and one of his daughters, Bekhetaten, herself the incestuous offspring of the pharaoh's union with his mother, is strongly suggested. So central was Bekhetaten's role in these early drafts that her character had one of two spoken passages in what was otherwise to be a textless opera. (The other spoken text was assigned to Nefertiti. Akhnaten's hymn to the sun was, from the earliest drafts, to be translated into the language of the audience.)[28] Ironically, the final version of *Akhnaten* displays an almost-total reversal of this formulation, with Bekhetaten and her sisters singing pure vowel sounds in an opera that is heavy on text—albeit ones that are predominantly in archaic languages. So although Oedipus went underground in the final version of the libretto, he does emerge, as the composer himself seems willing to admit, at several key moments in the opera. Like a specter emerging from the Freudian id, the presence of the mythological figure is arguably made all the more compelling by the perceived act of suppression.

Archaeological Excavation

In composing "an Oedipus opera," Glass is engaging a musicodramatic tradition that, though it harks back both to the ancient Greek origins of the myth and to the origins of European opera, has enjoyed a new lease on life in the twentieth century, thanks to Sigmund Freud's influential psychoanalytical writings. Noteworthy precursors in music theater include Igor Stravinsky and Jean Cocteau's opera oratorio *Oedipus Rex* (1927) and minimalist precursor Carl Orff's *Oedipus der Tyrann* (1965).[29] Various aspects of Glass's approach in *Akhnaten*—for example, the use of a narrator to liaise between the actors and the audience—can be traced directly to Stravinsky and Cocteau's opera. There also appear to be a number of musical and dramatic allusions to *Oedipus Rex* in *Akhnaten*, which I will discuss below.

Velikovsky's *Oedipus and Akhnaton* is unquestionably Glass's ideational point of departure, but his research on the subject did not end there. From very early on in the project, Glass expanded his literary base, adopting a scholarly approach, familiar from his earlier theatrical endeavors. For the first time in his career, Glass called on a specialist to construct the libretto: historian Shalom Goldman. While both Glass and Goldman admit to taking certain liberties with their historical subject matter in order to make it function better in a twentieth-century musicotheatrical context, the extent of such interventions was minimal, and the alterations were executed carefully so as to preserve and convey to audiences something of the flavor of the original artifacts, or at least of the research team's impressions of them. This had a phenomenal impact on the principles of construction employed in the opera and on its semiotic modus operandi.

This underlying principle of minimal intervention has much in common with the "archaeological"[30] approach to historical texts advocated by historian Michel Foucault. Whereas the historian traditionally seeks out resemblances and connections between the fragments of his or her research data by using interpretive, or hermeneutic, procedures, the archaeologist is more inclined to minimize his or her involvement in the research process, leaving discontinuities and anomalies in sight, rather than seeking to incorporate them into an integrated, internally consistent whole. Archaeology, in Foucault's words, "does not treat discourse as *document*, as a sign of something else, as an element that ought to be transparent . . . ; it is concerned with discourse in its own volume, as a *monument*"[31]—not with turning monuments into documents by reconstructing missing narratives and meanings. Evidence of a similar sensibility is not hard to discern in Glass's discourse concerning *Akhnaten*. In the documentary on the making of the opera, while perusing the ruins of Akhnaten's holy city and looking not unlike a *real* archaeologist, Glass comments: "Rather than to try to complete the story, which is so often done, I would like to, as much as is possible, keep to what we know, and to believe it as incomplete. To tell the truth, it doesn't bother me that much that we don't know what happened to [Akhnaten]. I kind of like it, in fact."[32]

Both Glass and Foucault allow documents to speak for themselves, preferring not to impose on them their own interpretations, explanations, and predilections, although any representation of texts is invariably an interpretive and subjective act—something Foucault has been criticized for overlooking. The archaeological approach as Foucault applies it has more to do, however, with the play of identities, the donning of masks, than it does with the strategies of incorporation upon which interpretive practices have rested traditionally.

Foucault never entirely severed his attachment to the theoretical tenets of archaeology, but he did soften his approach somewhat in his later years, applying Friedrich Nietzsche's idea of genealogy. Like archaeology, genealogy as a method is premised on the willingness of the researcher to sift meticulously through vast quantities of artifacts.[33] Like hermeneutics, genealogy seeks connections between these artifacts, not with the ulterior motive of elucidating from them some hidden truth or essence but with the more immediate concern of showing how things are "fabricated in piecemeal fashion from alien forms."[34] These aims might seem closely related, but they are differentiated by the emphasis the former places on a perceived unity and that the latter places on surface-level disparities, anomalies, and discontinuities. Reducing my skimpy summary of Foucault's ideas further still, one might say that his approach is characterized by a fascination with surfaces.

In addition to Foucault's own efforts to bridge the gap between archaeology and hermeneutics, more recently attempts have been made by philosophers working within the hermeneutic paradigm. Paul Ricoeur is one such philosopher. Ricoeur's approach owes much to the Brechtian concept of distanciation (or alienation), paired by Ricoeur with the concept of appropriation. Both of these concepts suggest a greater distance between the interpreting subject and what used to be called the "aesthetic object" than traditional theories of interpretation allowed.[35] Like Foucault, Ricoeur has been criticized for placing too much emphasis on the "autonomous" aspects of texts, leading some theorists to "refine" his approach by combining or alternating it with more dialogically oriented models.[36]

Glass's approach in *Akhnaten* is archaeological in a looser sense than Foucault would probably have found acceptable. Linguistically, the opera is archaeology in the purest sense of the word—even more so than are

Foucault's historical studies. There is no newly composed linguistic material in *Akhnaten* at all, as all of the texts come from existing historical and contemporary sources. As in Stravinsky and Cocteau's *Oedipus Rex,* a narrator is employed; significantly, though, the narrator of *Akhnaten* is given only a superficial identity. The texts he recites—or, rather, translates, since the majority of his texts are simple translations of texts sung by other characters in other languages—are never his own. The libretto is composed solely of texts culled directly from found material, and, with the single exception of the hymn to the sun, those that are set to music are done so in the languages in which they were originally written: ancient Egyptian, Akkadian, and Hebrew. The same archaeological principle cannot, however, be said to apply to the music, though a different kind of archaeology can be perceived in Glass's widespread borrowing from the baroque, as well as from various other stylistic periods (including modernism). This form of archaeology is felt throughout the opera but is probably at its most sophisticated in the hymn to the sun.

The overall impression produced in *Akhnaten,* when words and music are combined, is of a different kind of *Gesamtkunstwerk*—one whose surface is anything but unified but one that nevertheless allows itself to be melded into an (imagined) unity of sorts by the audience. The elusive, all-encompassing unity of what Foucault terms "total histories" is withheld, however.[37] In *Akhnaten,* the visible, or in this case aural, presence of "the archive" is a constant reminder of its difference from the author's or our own interpretations of it. Foucault puts it like this: "The analysis of the archive . . . involves a privileged region: at once, close to us, and different from our present existence, it is the border of time that surrounds our presence, which overhangs it, and which indicates it in its otherness; it is that which outside ourselves, delimits us."[38]

Glass and Goldman refer to Akhnaten as "singing archaeology" on two occasions in *MPG,* and it is conceivable that they have in mind Foucault's methodology or something like it. The primary significance of the term for them seems to have been literal: They took archaeological artifacts and placed them on the stage, quite literally representing them. The result was "singing archaeology," but this pun would hardly resonate had there not been other ideas in circulation at the time that suggest a discursive formation around the word *archaeology* that has almost nothing to do with the activities of actual archaeologists. Real archaeology does not, after all, sing.[39]

When the performance artist and composer Meredith Monk describes her films *Quarry* and *Ellis Island* as archaeological, the former because it contains imagery that is evocative of photographs taken in Nazi concentration camps and the latter because various aspects of the work, most notably its location, allude to historical events, she is employing the nonliteral, Foucauldian sense of the term.[40] In both cases, we are concerned with, as Monk puts it, "digging up something that existed" and allowing it to resonate in a new, contemporary context without any conscious attempt to integrate the two aspects, to step in and elucidate any meanings that might inhere in the raw materials. A similar engagement with the past can be recognized in much of Michael Nyman's collaborative work with director Peter Greenaway. The archaeological attitude vis-à-vis historical material is an important index of the state of postmodern art in the late 1970s and early 1980s. It indicated above all else a growing awareness of the contingency of historical position, a new humility with respect to the past, but at the same time a certain trepidation when dealing with historically loaded subject matter, lest one should reembody (the Frankenstein's monster that is) history too fully.

The Search for Sources

How, then, did Glass and his collaborators go about choosing their "archive" material? Goldman conducted a seminar in which the collaborators were assigned archaeological readings, which were then debated as a group. The entire production team visited the various locations in Egypt relevant to the historical events portrayed in the opera, including the site of Karnak in Thebes (the location of the ancient Egyptian capital city) and the ruins of Akhnaten's holy city, Akhetaten. Glass himself seems to have been particularly affected by his visit to the Cairo Museum. Indeed, some aspects of the musicodramatic substance of the opera can be traced directly to artifacts the composer encountered in the museum; most noteworthy among these is the family scene, the mise-en-scène of which is based directly on one of the images Glass had seen there.

If the first book read by Glass in his research was Velikovsky's *Oedipus and Akhnaton*, the second is likely to have been Freud's *Moses and Monotheism*.[41] The influence of this second Jewish psychoanalyst on the final outcome of the opera was profound. Freud's main hypothesis is that the religious doctrine that Moses preached to the Israelites was the same as the one that Akhnaten and his followers attempted to establish in Egypt.[42] In Freud's view, the exodus from Egypt recounted in the Old Testament took place in the wake of Akhnaten's reforms and was the direct result of the violent counterreaction against these reforms.[43] Freud discovered a number of convincing corollaries between the faith of Akhnaten and early forms of Judaism, including, most significantly, the insistence on a universal god and the proscription of all worship of secondary deities. Included among the psychoanalyst's evidence that the god worshiped by Moses and the Israelites was Aten, the sun disk worshiped by Akhnaten, is the Jewish confession of faith, "Schema Jisroel Adonai Elohenu Adonai Echod" (Hear, o Israel: our god Aten [Adonai] is a sole god).[44] For Freud, Moses—whose name itself Freud held to be of Egyptian origin[45]—was a disciple and probably a close friend of Akhnaten's and sought to preserve the Atenist faith after Akhnaten's death by leading a group of refugees, comprising followers of the outlawed religious cult, over the border to Syria.[46] Eventually, however, the people of Israel grew tired of their uncompromising and fear-inspiring leader, as well as his equally wrathful and unbending god, onto whom Moses had grafted traits of his own personality. So when they eventually murdered their leader, as Freud claims they did, the Israelites were at the same time murdering their patriarchal god, a deed from which the Judeo-Christian tradition could never, in Freud's mind, recover fully.[47] For Freud, this symbolic act represents the historical birth of the Oedipus complex, at least in its Judeo-Christian form. Akhnaten and his Atenist faith, on the other hand, represent a time of pre-Oedipal innocence in the history of Western religion, a Garden of Eden to which there could be no return.[48]

Aside from the many covert and not-so-covert allusions to Oedipus in Glass's *Akhnaten*, the most obvious concrete link to Freud's ideas is found in the hymn to the sun, whose juxtaposition with Psalm 104 of the Old Testament (using the same musical accompaniment) is intended to imply a historical connection between the two texts. Glass has commented: "Freud wrote a book speculating that Moses may have been a priest of Akhnaten's. . . . That's one reason Act II of the opera ends with Akhnaten's 'Hymn to the Sun' followed by Psalm 104 from the Old Testament. They look suspiciously alike. There's reason to believe that the Old Testament psalms may actually be renderings of Egyptian hymns."[49]

It is true that Freud made a connection between Akhnaten's ideas and those of Moses; one that had been pointed out some years earlier by the distinguished North American Egyptologist James Henry Breasted.[50] Ideas that are specifically Freud's, however, are strongly in evidence in other aspects of the opera. Freud was, let it not be forgotten, Velikovsky's principal intellectual sparring partner in *Oedipus and Akhnaton*; indeed, it is very unlikely that Velikovsky would have written his book had Freud not first written *Moses and Monotheism*. What is more, Glass's conception of Akhnaten, although inspired by Velikovsky's book, seems in many respects closer to Freud's sympathetic vision of Akhnaten than Velikovsky's less-than-flattering characterization.

Freud was never, according to Velikovsky, aware of a connection between his antihero, Oedipus, and his hero, Akhnaten, a testimony either to the nearsightedness of the psychoanalyst or to the tenuousness of the connection. Velikovsky goes with the former view, claiming that Freud's unwillingness to recognize Akhnaten's identity with Oedipus was a symptom of his own Oedipus complex, manifested in his hostility toward his "father" religion, Judaism, and its physical embodiment in the fierce father figure of Moses—this at a time when the very existence of the Jewish people was beginning to be threatened.[51] That Akhnaten might have suffered from an acute case of the Oedipus complex was pointed out first by an associate of Freud's, Karl Abraham.[52] According to Velikovsky, Freud suppressed any awareness he might have had of such a connection when he chose to write about Akhnaten some two-and-a-half decades later.[53]

But let us play Freud's advocate and reverse this formulation and look for traits of Oedipalism in Velikovsky. Given that the psychoanalyst-turned-catastrophe-theorist had studied in Vienna under Freud's pupil Wilhelm Stekel and was for a time a junior member of Freud's group, contributing articles to *Imago* on a regular basis, it is not difficult to perceive traits of the father killer also in Velikovsky. Evidence of the emotional ambivalence (the love/hate relationship vis-à-vis the father) held by Freud to be a primary characteristic of the Oedipal condition can easily be perceived in Velikovsky's discourse regarding Freud.[54] On the one hand, he chastises Freud in the strongest possible terms for betraying his religion and his people, while on the other hand his own psychoanalytical work is staunchly Freudian, as evidenced in the following diagnosis of Akhnaten:

Were it possible for King Akhnaton to cross the time barrier and lie down on an analyst's couch, the analysis would at an early stage reveal autistic or narcissistic traits, a homosexual tendency, with sadism suppressed and feminine traits coming to the fore, and a strong unsuppressed Oedipus complex. The proper treatment for the historical Oedipus would not start by breaking down the Oedipus complex but by first demolishing the narcissistic component of the psychoneurosis.[55]

Velikovsky's putative Oedipalism notwithstanding, it might be significant that Freud's theory regarding the chronology of events in the life of Moses is implicitly discounted also in an earlier book, *Ages of Chaos: From the Exodus to King Akhnaton* (1952), in which Velikovsky put forward the idea—drawing on controversial evidence of volcanic eruptions in Sinai—that the Jewish exodus from Egypt had occurred some two thousand years prior to Akhnaten's reign, thus contradicting Freud's hypothesis that it occurred in the years immediately following it. Had he accepted Freud's chronology in *Oedipus and Akhnaton*, he would have done so at the cost of his own earlier theory. More significantly, perhaps, he would have had to discard, almost in its entirety, the Old Testament version of ancient history.

It is possible, therefore, that Velikovsky's closer relation to Judaism colored his perceptions of Freud. This, then, raises the interesting question of Glass's relationship to his subject matter. The composer was raised a Jew, but like Freud he rejected the religion in later years. (He became a practicing Tibetan Buddhist during his student years.) Both Freud's and Velikovsky's engagements with Akhnaten seem to reveal something about their relationship with the religion of their birth. Might the same be true of Glass? Might his choice of subject matter reveal something about his own religious or psychological orientations? Glass has never in his career engaged with Judaic subject matter in a direct way. Several of Glass's works could, however, be interpreted as engaging with the religion of his birth in an indirect fashion. *Einstein*, for example, is an opera about a self-professed secular Jew who did not, like Freud, accept the biblical idea of God, although he was, unlike Freud, a strong advocate of the Jewish community throughout his life. The famous scientist appears to have been something of a role model to Glass, who, as a child in Baltimore in the 1950s, admits to having been "swept up in the Einstein craze."[56] Whether this admiration has anything to do his religious background is, of course, open to debate. The second trilogy opera, *Satyagraha*, bears no obvious relation to Judaic subject matter. In the third, however, Glass could have been trying to establish a dialogue of sorts with his cultural inheritance, as both Freud and Velikovsky did before him, though with almost diametrically opposed results.

Glass's vision of the life and times of Akhnaten does not revolve solely around the Velikovsky/Freud axis, though knowledge of this axis certainly provides some useful insights into the cultural, religious, and psychological dimensions of the opera. From very early on in the project, however, Glass and his collaborators delved a good deal deeper into the literature on the subject than is customary in projects such as this. As we have seen already, archaeological opinion did matter to Glass, at least to the extent that it served his interests. The extent of its impact on the opera will become apparent below.

I should point out already at this early stage that I have no training in archaeology, so my comments on this aspect of the subject should be taken lightly. There is, however, and long has been, something about this particular juncture in Egyptian history that has prompted commentators on it to become more deeply involved with the subject than they might have expected or wanted to. Indeed, many of the issues that arise in discussions of Akhnaten—those of sexuality, religion, and warfare—seem to have a relevance that transcends the contingencies of any particular time or place. So if I do, from time to time, pass judgments on some hypothetical character I perceive to be the historical Akhnaten, I hope the reader will bear with me.

Despite the apparent universality of the issues surrounding Akhnaten, commentaries regarding him vary widely depending on where and when they were written, notwithstanding the political, religious, and possibly also the gender orientation of the writer. Glass appears to be no exception in this regard. In the mold of Foucault, though, the composer does not attempt to resolve all of the contradictions that invariably surface in discussions of Akhnaten. Contradictions that past commentators have regarded as irreconcilable are incorporated enthusiastically into Glass's multimedia portrait of the king. This is not the same thing as saying that Glass's vision is neutral or uncommitted—a blank pastiche; clearly it is not.

Before returning to the twentieth century and to the cultural climate that spawned Glass and this opera, let us briefly examine a few of the more central points of contention concerning our protagonist. Here are some statements commonly encountered in discussions of Akhnaten:

* He endorsed the exclusive worship of the sun and proscribed the worship of all secondary deities.
* He endorsed the worship of the sun disk, an abstract symbol that represented an underlying power or spirit (ka) that was held to be present in all things.

* He was the world's first monotheist.
* He was a cynical and intolerant atheist.

* He was the first family man in history.
* He was a sexual debaucher and pedophile.

* He was the world's first pacifist.
* He was inept as commander in chief of the military forces of the world's largest empire.

* He chose for religious or ideological reasons to be represented as androgynous.
* He was a hermaphrodite.
* "He" was a woman disguised as a man.

* He was a benevolent philanthropist, a lover of humanity and nature.
* He was a dictator.

* He was an idealist visionary.
* He was insane.

* He was Moses.
* He was a disciple of Moses.
* He was Oedipus.

* He was a protofeminist, choosing to co-rule his empire with his wife, Nefertiti.
* He co-ruled with his mother, Tye.
* He co-ruled with his brother, cousin, or homosexual lover, Smenkhare.

Glass has described his protagonist as a "complex character"[57] and a "very complicated person"[58]; if we understand by this that Akhnaten is a character made up of many diverse and even contradictory parts—a truly ambivalent figure—then Glass has furnished us with what I believe is a valuable clue to his interpretation of the subject. Further interpretive insights can be gained by means of a closer examination of the composer's background, which is the task of the following chapter.

CHAPTER TWO

Glass's Poetics of Postmodernism

This chapter addresses the genealogy of the ideas that led Philip Glass to compose in the way he did when he was working on *Akhnaten*. Here I will identify the various discursive practices that might have had a bearing on his approach, including its cultural, ideological, aesthetic, musical, and theatrical aspects. Later chapters take the music and drama of the opera itself as their more specific concern.

Early Days

Born in Baltimore on 31 January 1937, the grandchild of Lithuanian and Russian Orthodox Jewish immigrants, Glass started playing the violin at the age of six. At age eight, he changed to playing the flute, which he studied formally at the Peabody Conservatory of Music in Baltimore, where he also learned harmony. At the same time, he was receiving a less formal schooling by working part-time in his father's record shop, General Radio. As the name of the shop implies, Glass's musical upbringing was anything but sheltered: During his youth, he came into contact with the whole gamut of musical styles, from classical to popular to jazz. As for classical music, his father had a special liking for the works of Franz Schubert, whose E-flat Piano Trio is the first music the composer remembers hearing. Dmitri Shostakovich and Béla Bartók were also familiar names in his household. A precocious fifteen year old, Glass entered the University of Chicago, where he worked toward a bachelor's degree in mathematics and philosophy while also studying the piano. At nineteen, he transferred to the Juilliard School of Music, where he studied composition under Vincent Persichetti, William Bergsma, and, during the summer of 1960, Darius Milhaud. Here he met Steve Reich for the first time, an acquaintance he renewed upon his return from Paris several years later but that turned sour in the early 1970s, due to professional rivalry and possibly a personal quarrel between the two men. Glass graduated from Juilliard in 1962 with a master's degree and some seventy compositions under his belt, a number of which were published, at the insistence of his mentor, Persichetti. After graduating, he moved to Pittsburgh, where he worked for two years writing music for the Contemporary Music Project of the Pittsburgh public-school system.

Glass's first listed composition is a string trio, written when he was fifteen. This composition is dodecaphonic, as are a number of his subsequent works.[1] Glass quickly turned away from serialism, however, preferring to write in a modern tonal style influenced strongly by Aaron Copland, early-to mid-period Elliott Carter, and the music of his teachers at Juilliard.[2] Regarding his student music, Glass has commented:

I never bought the whole 12-tone bag of tricks, though I wrote some serial pieces so I could learn what it was all about. I was, at that point, basically just a very good student. As a young man I had no clear voice of my own, but I did feel that it was only a matter of time before one would emerge. . . . So I wrote music like my teachers', and was rewarded with scholarships and grants, and they were very nice to me. I was a good boy.[3]

Glass's departure for Paris in 1965 marked the end of his "good boy" days. Ostensibly training to be a good modernist, like Virgil Thomson and Elliott Carter before him, under the censorious eye of the renowned pedagoge Nadia Boulanger, he was fast becoming disillusioned with the direction in which his musical training seemed to be pointing him. He had witnessed firsthand the technocratic torpor surrounding Pierre Boulez's *Domaine musical* concerts. In stark contrast were his experiences of non-European music, in which he perceived a vibrancy and communicative directness that had long been missing from the music taught in conservatories and universities in Europe and America. Glass's first direct contact with Asian musical culture came when he worked as an assistant to the Indian musicians Ravi Shankar and Alla Rakha on the score of the Conrad Rooks film *Chappaqua*. Unlike fellow minimalists Terry Riley and La Monte Young, Glass never entered into a formal guru-student relationship with an Indian teacher, although he did take some private lessons on percussion with Rakha. Instead, he became increasingly aware through his acquaintance with various world-music traditions of the arbitrariness of the rules musical modernism had invented: "The whole tyranny of history and the historical imperative of contemporary music was demystified entirely. It didn't matter anymore. If you took one step outside of those institutions it simply didn't matter anymore. That's, of course, what [John] Cage was very good at. He was one of the people that I was reading at the time."[4]

Having thus abruptly discarded modernism in favor of post-Cagean experimentalism, Glass set about translating the precepts of cyclical form and additive rhythmic structure, which he had perceived in Indian music, into a musical language of his own. And yet, of the four major minimalists—Young, Riley, Reich, and Glass—Glass is arguably the most "Western."[5] This tendency might stem from his limitations as an ethnomusicologist, from some fundamental attachment to the sounds and syntax of Euro-American classical music, or from an awareness of the problematic issues surrounding questions of exoticism in music. He was undoubtedly influenced by composers such as Young and Riley, whose explorations in world music have always been more direct than his own, and their examples are likely to have contributed to his interest in working with Shankar. It would be a mistake, however, to attribute his sudden change in orientation solely to these figures, who were, after all, working on a different continent than Glass at the time of his "conversion" to minimalism. Given his interest in experimental theater, it seems highly likely that some of the impetus for Glass's stylistic self-transformation would have come from this direction. In theater as well as in music, although in the case of the latter this challenge was coming from a very small group of nonconformists, people were beginning to question the principles of temporal organization that had formerly grounded their art form. With everything that was going on in music, the theater, and more generally in culture, Glass must have had a growing sense that the time had come to jump the modernist ship.

Like so many composers of his generation, Glass was being pressured to write music that was premised on negations: the negation of repetitive and cyclical structures, the negation of modality, and the negation of rhythmic constancy. All of these elements, which are almost ubiquitous in non-Western, premodern, and popular styles but which were avoided strenuously in high-modern serialism, formed the foundations of the style later known as minimalism.[6] Itself often defined in terms of negations—nonlinear, nonnarrative, nondeveloping, nonteleological, postmodern—the essence of the new style was, for the reasons I have enumerated above, radically affirmative. And even if minimalism itself, as Glass readily admits, "turned out to be not very important,"[7] especially in its most reductive manifestations, it cleared a space in which new voices were heard, albeit voices that were yet to develop a language as sophisticated as those they were challenging.

Because of its explicit rejection of the precepts of modernism, minimalism in music is most often assigned to the category of postmodernism. One of the first music critics to discuss Glass and the other minimalists within the rubric of postmodern theory was Susan McClary. Other prominent critics who have included his music in this category include Fredric Jameson and Linda Hutcheon.[8] Others, however, such as K. Robert Schwarz and Robert Fink, see the more reductive forms of minimalism as occupying a space halfway between modernism and postmodernism.[9] The advantage of such a view is that it illustrates the continuity between the two categories; the disadvantage is that it tends to make light of the radical break with tradition that the minimalists perceived themselves to be making in their early works. Radicalism per se is, of course, easily associated with the avant-garde and thus with modernism. Moreover, notwithstanding all the talk of "regionalism" and "particularism" in certain strains of postmodern theory, there are those who argue that any level of commitment to a specific musical language, which the minimalists demonstrated quite clearly in their early works, is a form of modernist dogma.

The minimalists are probably guilty on both of the above counts. Consider Glass's controversial statements of the 1970s, the most notorious example being a 1976 interview with the composer Robert Ashley in which he described Paris under the influence of Pierre Boulez as "a wasteland, dominated by these maniacs, these creeps, who were trying to make everyone write this crazy creepy music."[10] In the early 1980s, a slightly more philosophical tone prevailed, although the message remained essentially unchanged: "The failure of modernism is clear. . . . Modern music had become truly decadent, stagnant, uncommunicative by the 1960's and 70's. Composers were writing for each other and the public didn't seem to care. People want to like new music, but how can they, when it's so ugly and intimidating, emotionally and intellectually."[11]

Lately, he has seemed more willing to give credit where it is due:

I think the experiments of the dodecaphonic and twelve tone school have been crucial in changing how we listen to music. Though I think that whole school didn't determine the future of music as it had thought. It didn't even develop useful techniques for other composers. But if you go to the movies now, the harmonic language is much denser. People think they're listening to triadic music and they aren't. They just don't know the name for it. It's actually much more complicated than they think because they're hearing differently. But in fact, we all do music in a much more complex way than we used to.[12]

This more conciliatory tone does not, however, mean that Glass has lost sight of the shortcomings of musical modernism: "The middle years of the twentieth century had basically almost finished off contemporary music for the public. It had been such a disaster that my generation simply couldn't, it was impossible not to see that it had been a complete devastation; in terms of audience, in terms of performance."[13]

Both iconoclasm and single-minded commitment to his own musical language also typify Steve Reich's discourse of the 1970s, as evidenced by his tersely written manifesto, *Writings about Music*. In this collection of writings, Reich rigorously lays out the premises of his own musical aesthetic, at the same time as he demolishes just about every other existing approach as anachronistic and irrelevant.[14]

The influence of modernism on the minimalists is not, of course, restricted solely to discourse concerning the music; it is felt strongly in certain aspects of the musical discourse itself. This is particularly true of Reich's music; his early tape pieces and the phase-shifting technique that developed out of them are quite obviously indebted to the rigorous principles of organization of the serialists as well as to Cage's nonintentionality. Strict process music is very definitely, as Michael Nyman was among the first to observe, the offspring of serialism.[15] Glass was never as rigorous in his application of systemic compositional procedures as Reich was, although his relatively stringent use of additive and subtractive procedures in the late 1960s and early 1970s combined with the music's unrelenting pulse do betray an obsession with technique not dissimilar to that of his counterpart.[16] Adding and subtracting notes or phrases incrementally, which was then the foundation of Glass's musical style,[17] does have a mechanical feel, but for Glass the decision of which note or phrase to add or take away always had an arbitrary and subjective aspect. Musical changes were never fully determined in advance, nor were they totally predictable. Although they have much in common, then, this small distinction between Reich and Glass is important, as it bears not only on the subsequent development of their respective musical styles but also on the attitude of the musical establishment toward them. Reich's relations with the modernist avant-garde have always been considerably warmer than Glass's.

The approach in these early minimalist works, particularly those of Reich, is now being seen by a growing number of critics as evidence of a fundamentally modernist attitude toward the handling of musical materials. *Village Voice* critic Kyle Gann, among others, has argued that minimalism and serialism should be viewed as two sides of the same coin and that this coin and others like it should be exchanged in favor of a new currency.[18] For Gann, the approaches of both the minimalists and the serialists are flawed by a fundamentally "objectivist mindset"—one whose distrust of subjectivity results in emotionally and expressively impoverished works of art. "The challenge," argues Gann, is to overcome our scientistic fascination with technique and in so doing "to rescue subjectivity from bad faith, to learn to rely once again on taste, feeling, inspiration, and the right brain."[19] Interestingly, many of the composers he cites as representing this new subjectivity were influenced strongly by early minimalism, collaborated closely with the minimalists, or else themselves belonged to the minimalist movement at one time or another; they include John Adams, Harold Budd, Ben Johnston, and Frederic Rzewski.[20]

Gann's arguments do seem to make sense, in an intuitive, right-side-of-the-brain kind of way, but they do, as Elaine Broad has pointed out, represent something of an oversimplification.[21] There is unquestionably some evidence of "objectivism" in the musical discourse of early minimalism. However, there are also a number of factors that seem to contradict Gann's theory of an overriding objectivist mindset. Among these factors are the minimalists' interest in non-European musics and their close relation to vernacular forms. In terms of reception and affect, as well, there are important differences between the music of the serialists, that of Cage and the other experimentalists, and that of the minimalists, and these mainly have to do with such nonanalytical concepts as sound, texture, and feel—categories more familiar to rock, jazz, and pop musicians than to their classical counterparts. In more "concrete" musical terms, the presence of a stable tonal center, a consistent rhythmic pulse, and an overall bright, energetic feel in early minimal music, even that of Reich, represented a marked departure from modernism as it was understood in the late 1960s. What the minimalists had in mind musically was clearly a far cry from what Reich, with characteristic eloquence, has called "the dark-brown Angst of Vienna."[22] Our retrospective point of view should not allow us to lose sight of the musical fact: Philip Glass and Pierre Boulez were worlds apart both in terms of the philosophy and the sound of their music in the mid-1960s.

What distinguished minimalism most markedly from serialism, however, as well as from its Romantic antecedents, was its temporal organization. "In early minimal music," writes Broad, "there is a distinct absence of the traditional notion of a piece of music as an object/artefact, perceived in linear continuity."[23] This notion was replaced by that of the musical event as a process; changes, although related to a larger whole (in minimal music that of a "given" rhythmic pulse and modal center), are in minimal music contingent largely on local, surface-level structural considerations. The Belgian composer and music critic Wim Mertens elaborates further: "The traditional work," he writes,

is teleological or end-orientated, because all musical events result in a directed end or synthesis. The composition appears as a musical product characterised by organic totality. . . . Repetition in the traditional work appears as a reference to what has gone before, so that one has to remember what was forgotten. . . . The music of the American composers can be described as non-narrative and a-teleological.[24]

Teleology implies that a certain purposefulness or directedness is felt as we move from one perceptually distinct musical event to another. The structuring of this purposefulness is where narrative comes in. Paul Ricoeur holds that the single most important aspect of narrative is the interreferentiality of temporal events—not according to real, linear time, although the intention might be to simulate real sequences of events in "realistically" or organically structured art forms, but according to whatever temporal schema happens to be selected or invented by the author or composer.[25] Ricoeur's idea of narrative—along with that of Roland Barthes, who links the narrating tendency with the Oedipus complex—form the foundations for my discussion of narrative in music.[26] Both of these theorists question the naturalness or inevitability of narrative structures, but both recognize the profound influence these structures have in many areas of human experience. In this respect, they are closely allied to the music I discuss.

The structuring of musical events in Western classical music is highly conventionalized, operating simultaneously on a number of interconnected planes. Musical narrative involves all or some of the following elements: the interplay of motific and thematic material; the unfolding of extended thematic/harmonic structures (involving exposition, development, and recapitulation in sonata form); and an elaborate system of harmonic hierarchy designed to imbue the music with various degrees of tension and release. When listening to music constructed in this way, the listener departs from and arrives at various musicotemporal locations, each of which is felt as being more or less stable than that which preceded it. Lack of stability engenders the need for stability; stability, conversely, engenders the need for instability, except when this stability is located at the end of a section or, more important, at the end of a work, where emphatic closure (total and final stability), is regarded as desirable and even necessary.

These processes inevitably carry a good deal of cultural baggage. In classical music, particularly that of the Romantic period, the primary rationale for the arrangement of musical events in terms of narrative was the so-called organic metaphor. Such a metaphor might seem abstract, but nested within these hidden "metanarratives" of the canon, as Jean-François Lyotard would call them, are elaborate networks of apparently incontestable (because unacknowledged) assumptions regarding our mode of being in the world and our perceptions of ourselves in relation to others. This still seems fairly abstract, but this abstract body of assumptions has profound implications in just about everything we do or experience; it reverberates through our whole existence when we listen to a piece of music.

A large and diverse body of criticism has emerged in recent years that has taken as its explicit concern the elucidation of these hidden subjective subtexts.[27] This interest in subjectivity and narrative has allowed musicologists in recent years to examine musical texts from standpoints of various critical paradigms, including gender theory, deconstruction, postcolonial theory, and in terms of ethnicity and locality. Whereas musicologists formerly talked about musical structures, forms, and styles, now they talk about the ways in which these structures, forms, and styles become meaningful to the people who make and listen to them. In short, musicology's primary concern is now the elucidation of relations. Musical narratology is one of the ways these relations have been brought into sight.

The idea of narrative is not simply the invention of critics with nothing better to do with their time but is integral to many artists', including Glass's, conception of their art form. "What sets the music apart," Glass has commented referring to his minimalist output,

is the fact that it's non-narrative, we don't hear it within the usual time frame of most musical experiences. As I look at most other music, I see that it takes ordinary time, day-to-day-time—what I call colloquial time—as a model for its own musical time. So you have story symphonies or story concertos—even the modernist tradition continues that to a certain extent. There's still almost a compulsion to deal with themes and treatment of themes. The themes become the focus of the listener's attention, and what happens to the theme happens to the listener via a certain psychological trick of identification. This happens in the great concertos of the nineteenth century, with the tortuous journey of the violin and so forth, with happy endings and sad endings.[28]

Rather, then, than be drawn into a maelstrom of tension and release, denial and fulfilment of desire (what Freud referred to as the "reality principle"), the minimalists chose to focus on the continuous "now"—the quality, structure, and sheer physical volume of the sound, what Barthes has termed "the grain of the voice."[29] The intention in bringing music back to its zero degree is to liberate the listener's consciousness from the constraints of historical forms and the "stories" embedded within those forms. This is, without any question, a utopian move,[30] one that, as Susan McClary has astutely observed in her discussion of the relationship between postmodernism and its modernist antecedents, can be identified easily as "an oedipal gesture, the announcement by the child of the fathers demise."[31] In later chapters, this interpretation will become one of the most pervasive leitmotivs of my discussion. *Akhnaten*, according to my interpretation, has a powerful subtext that addresses precisely the problematic relationship between postmodernism and its modern antecedents.

Minimalism in Music and the Plastic Arts

Despite the rhetoric of the exclusion and negativity surrounding the style, the focus on immediate, perceptually grounded experience, and the deadpan, descriptive terminology (e.g., the title of Glass's minimalist pieces: *Music in Fifths, Music with Changing Parts,* etc.), the minimalists were never able, or perhaps willing, to construct a totally impenetrable, self-referential style. As Eero Tarasti has observed, music that is reduced to its formal fundamentals *in presentia* frequently brings complex referential relationships into play *in absentia*.[32] Minimalism is not, therefore, a music devoid of "meaning." Rather, it is a music that, by eschewing the conventional semiotic carriers of meaning, opens the field to constellations of meaning previously unexplored or even suppressed.

Some of the more perceptive critics of minimalism in the plastic arts have observed the same phenomenon. Whittle a work of art down to its fundamentals, and what is left is an experiencing subject who is forced to confront his or her relationship with the object at hand, rather than attempting passively to identify with the internal world encoded within that object. For the art critic Kenneth Baker, minimalism is fundamentally an "art of circumstance."[33] As a result, observes Barbara Rose, the attempted "repudiation of content" is ultimately unconvincing in minimalist art.[34] "The simple denial of content can itself constitute the content of such a work," she points out.[35] Despite artists' efforts to "suppress or withdraw content" so as to make their works "as bland, neutral, and redundant as possible," "a certain poignant, if strangled expressiveness" invariably makes itself felt.[36] Michael Fried has observed that the encounter with what he calls "literalist art" is of its essence theatrical: the object is experienced "in a situation—one that, virtually by definition, includes the beholder."[37] Given this inherent, if veiled, theatricality, the eventual direction the minimalists took toward the theater, performance, and multimedia begins to look as though it had unfolded organically out of this earlier orientation, rather than constituting a radical change or compromise in the premises of the aesthetic.

These discussions of minimalism in the plastic arts throw interesting light on the parallel phenomenon of minimalism in music, but there are also significant differences between the two art forms. It is true that both forms of minimalism share an interest in highly reduced, so-called primary forms, are characterized by a cool, anonymous feel, and encourage immediate apprehension of the work of art as artifact, while at the same time shift attention away from the autonomous object, the *Ding an sich*, toward the negative space surrounding it as well as toward the eye of the beholder. But the differences between the two art forms, reflected directly in their very different reception histories, are also hard to overlook. Minimalist sculpture continues to baffle, to bemuse, or simply to bore the uninitiated, while minimalist music always had to it a familiar ring. Indeed, the intelligibility of this music to the music-listening "masses" seems to have been the most significant obstacle to its widespread acceptance by high-brow audiences. Anyone who dismisses the blank canvases of Robert Rauschenberg, Ad Reinhardt, or Frank Stella or the stark geometrical sculpture of Donald Judd, Carl Andre, or Robert Morris as simplistic without having the intellectual authority to back up the assertion risks being branded a philistine. In contrast, the guardians of good taste in music continue to dismiss its musical cousin as simple-minded hodgepodge without feeling the slightest need to explain themselves in anything approaching a coherent or civil manner.[38]

One recent attempt to justify the argument against minimal music has been made by the music theorist Jonathan W. Bernard.[39] As Bernard explores the genealogy of the minimalist movement in music and the plastic arts, one of the central enigmas for him is the belatedness of minimalism's canonization in the musical sphere.[40] Rather than looking for contextual reasons for the rejection of minimalism by the avant-garde, however, Bernard places the blame squarely on the language of minimal music itself. For Bernard, the minimalists, rather than developing their own language, unsuccessfully attempted to graft the precepts of a language developed specifically for the problems of the visual arts into a musical context. The fundamental incompatibility of the minimalist aesthetic with the medium of music is, for Bernard, the primary reason for its failure to achieve canonical status. Interestingly, Bernard focuses on the style's perceived failures rather than its successes, even though musical minimalism turned out to be extremely popular; much more so than its counterpart in the plastic arts. Depending on whether one looks at it from the position of the aesthetes or that of the public, the minimalist glass is either empty or full. In neglecting these very significant questions of affect and reception, Bernard reveals more about the limitations of his own interpretive framework than he does about the putative shortcomings of minimalist music, which is in danger of disappearing altogether from his discussion, detached as it is from the audiences that listen to it. It is no coincidence that minimal art entered the canon with relatively little resistance, while remaining the almost-exclusive cultural property of a small group of initiates, whereas minimal music largely failed to achieve canonical status yet spread far beyond the pale of the musical intelligentsia. Judging from the critical reception of musical minimalism, it was precisely its success with a broader public that made its incorporation into the canon an impossibility.

Back to Postmodernism

Notwithstanding his Lyotardian disaffection from musical narrative, Glass's ongoing fascination with technology might easily be perceived as modernist, although the mechanical feel and organization of much of his music seems not to underscore but rather to undermine one of the main tenets of modernism: the principle of organic unity as the primary organizational imperative in music. In this respect, Glass's orientation seems to have much in common with a large part of recent "French theory." Gilles Deleuze and Félix Guattari's "desiring machines" are perhaps the most obvious example of a self-consciously constructed subjectivity pitted against existing organicist models, although a similar orientation can be perceived in much of the writing of Lyotard and Foucault as well.[41] Glass's relationship with technology is, as it is in Lyotard's writing (but *not* in Deleuze's and Guattari's), extremely ambivalent: on one level, the music seems to critique the Enlightenment ideal of a totally transparent subjectivity; on another, it seems to evoke the Enlightenment view of man as the unrivaled master of his environment, with technology as the primary means of this mastery; and on another still, it seems to make the listener more aware of the dehumanizing and debilitating effects of technological advances on human subjectivity.

A similar ambivalence can be identified when viewing the music through the two opposing lenses of the Frankfurt School. The bright, diatonic surface textures and the propulsive rhythms of *Einstein*, *Koyaanisqatsi* (1982), and *The Photographer* (1982) make them among the most exuberant music Glass has written, suggesting a position akin to Walter Benjamin's, in which the liberating and democratizing effects of technology are celebrated. This impression is contradicted, however, by a more oppressive aspect that plays an important part in the dramatization of *Akhnaten*, for example (specifically, the music associated with the "old order"), but is present also in sections of earlier works such as *Einstein*. This side might easily be identified with skepticism like Theodor Adorno's. All of this suggests that Glass and other postmodern musicians have relationships with technology that are far more complex and ambivalent than some critics have made them out to be. Only by looking in detail at specific examples, therefore, can any reliable critical assertions be made.

Like a number of recent studies on postmodernism, a central premise of this study is a twofold division between early forms of postmodernism, which some critics have traced to the late 1950s but which most agree came to fruition in the mid-sixties, and the more eclectic, explicitly intertextual forms that emerged in the mid-seventies and have continued to inform artistic and cultural practices and tastes to this day. To these I will add a third category of emergent postmodernism, an anarchic and experimental precursor of postmodernism that could be seen as developing in the mid-1950s to mid-1960s. It includes such figures as John Cage, Morton

Feldman, Earle Brown, Christian Wolf, Cornelius Cardew, and movements such as Fluxus, Indeterminacy, the "West Coast school," and concept music. In addition, postmodernism in music was adumbrated in the music of a number of maverick composers who were strongly influenced by tonality, popular idioms, and African, Asian, and Native American musical practices: these include the likes of Lou Harrison, La Monte Young, Harry Partch, and Dane Rudhyar. The music of film composers such as Maurice Jarre and Bernard Herrmann might also be said to have anticipated certain aspects of postmodernism. While such music was influenced strongly by the modernist tradition, it typically placed a stronger emphasis on questions of reception and communication than was usual in high-modern musical practices, as exemplified by serialist practices. Significant precursors of postmodernism not included in the category of emergent postmodernism include such figures as Erik Satie, Carl Orff, (preserialist) Igor Stravinsky, Kurt Weill, Marcel Duchamp, Bertolt Brecht, Antonin Artaud, and various nonrealist, panartistic movements such as Dada, surrealism, and futurism.

Film music notwithstanding, a parallel form of emergent postmodernism is difficult to identify in the popular sphere, unlike its successor early postmodernism, whose ideational background might fruitfully be compared to the underground, punk, and new-wave movements of the 1970s. Postmodernism in popular culture in the 1980s and 1990s accommodates such diverse figures as Madonna, U2 (post–Zoo TV), Annie Lennox, Suzanne Vega, David Byrne, Björk, and the Pet Shop Boys among others. All of these artists in one way or another address issues in their music that are similar to those that have been discussed in recent critical theory. The very fact that representatives of "popular" as well as "high" culture are included in the category of postmodernism is, as we shall see, highly significant. A characteristic feature of much of what has been called postmodern involves the blurring of boundary lines between popular and high idioms as well as the problematization of the assumptions that formerly grounded that distinction.

The twofold distinction between 1960s critical or oppositional postmodernism and the more eclectic and conciliatory strains that surfaced in the 1970s and 1980s is made in the writing of Andreas Huyssen and Sally Banes.[42] Huyssen lists the following as the four most distinctive traits of 1960s, specifically North American, postmodernism:

1. An iconoclastic rupture with existing ideas, comparable to earlier avant-garde movements such as Dada and surrealism. The cultural background to 1960s postmodernism (the civil-rights movement, the antiwar movement and the counterculture), however, gives it a distinctly North American flavor.

2. An aversion to institutionalized art and its ideology of autonomy, as manifested both in the life/art dichotomy and in the unassailable (i.e., autonomous) position of an aesthetic intelligentsia whose purpose is to defend the distinction between good and bad taste ("high" and "low" art).
3. A (somewhat uncritical) fascination with technology. Media technology and cybernetics are seen as major emancipatory forces. This harks back to Marxist-influenced cultural criticism of the 1920s (Benjamin, Brecht, etc.).
4. Advocacy of popular art forms. Clement Greenberg's and Adorno's aesthetic elitism is effectively reversed, with popular forms taking precedence over high art.

Mapping these traits onto minimalism is not without its problems, but it does provide a more suitable cultural framework than models that force the movement into the domain of late modernism. What it leaves out, for example, is the ambivalence of much early postmodern art vis-à-vis technology. Huyssen's formulation appears, moreover, to view the highbrow/lowbrow distinction as more solid than many critics and artists would allow. Erosions and transgressions of the distinction both from above and below are arguably more characteristic of early postmodernism than simple advocation of popular forms by highbrow critics and artists, at least where minimalism is concerned.

Sally Banes's discussion of postmodern dance probably provides one of the soundest points of reference for discussions of postmodernism in music, centered as it is largely around the New York downtown movement and privileging the viewpoint of the artists themselves and their immediate cultural environment over other, more abstract considerations. Banes recognizes that even while 1960s postmodernism "aligned itself with that consummately modernist visual art, minimalist sculpture," characteristics of postmodernism such as "pastiche, irony, playfulness, historical reference, the use of vernacular materials, the continuity of cultures, an interest in process over product, breakdowns of boundaries between art forms and between art and life, and new relationships between artist and audience" were invariably present in works of art from that period, albeit in embryonic form.[43] Postmodern dance pieces were never, according to Banes, entirely abstract; they were never the "cool analyses of forms" their cousins in the visual arts are often made out to be "but urgent reconsiderations of the medium."[44]

Minimal music appears in this regard to be related more closely to postmodern dance than to minimal art, particularly, borrowing Banes's criteria, in its use of vernacular materials (triads, tonality, a steady rhythmic beat), its interest in process over product, and its relationship to world music. Pastiche, irony, and playfulness all entered the (post)minimalist vocabulary later, ushered in largely by musicians such as John Adams, Laurie Anderson, and John Zorn. Glass more than any other composer was responsible for reestablishing a dialogue with tradition in the wake of the post-Cagean rupture (not forgetting, of course, that many composers had never stopped composing music using traditional techniques). Glass was the first to take minimalism to the opera, and he was among the first to revert back to traditional forms as the basic building blocks for a musical language that nevertheless continued to problematize these forms.

A final theoretical model, one that this time foregrounds the continuity of the postmodernist movement, is provided by Hal Foster's "oppositional postmodernism." Foster's influential essay both summarizes the ideas of others and distills from them an overview of the subject that is among the most compact yet multifaceted to date. Some of the most important features of postmodernism listed by Foster include:

> a critique of Western representation(s) and modern "supreme fictions"; a desire to think in terms sensitive to difference (of others without opposition, of heterogeneity without hierarchy); a skepticism regarding autonomous spheres of culture or separate "fields" of experts; an imperative to go beyond formal filiations (of text to text) to trace social affiliations (the institutional "density" of the text in the world); in short a will to grasp the present nexus of culture and politics and to affirm a practice resistant both to academic modernism and political reaction.[45]

Foster's postmodernism of resistance is important because of the emphasis it places on political engagement. The postmodern musicians I am discussing, particularly Glass, do not conceive of what they do as politically neutral pastiche; there is always an urgent political subtext to their work, just as in the sphere of postmodern dance. Initially, this took the form of a mode of "deconstruction"; modernist discourse was deconstructed "not in order to seal it in its own image but in order to open it, to rewrite it; to open its closed systems to the 'heterogeneity of texts,' . . . to rewrite its universal techniques in terms of 'synthetic contradictions' . . . in short, to challenge its master narratives with the 'discourse of others.'"[46]

Notwithstanding the disillusionment of postmodernists with modernist isolationism, it is clear there could be no (uncritical) return to premodern modes of structuring discourse. Minimalism had to expand in order to remain a viable force, and the most obvious way to do this was to make more explicit the critiques that were implicit in the early style. Skepticism toward master narratives would continue, at least among some exponents of postmodernism, but this skepticism would use the very thing it was resisting to assert its critical stance.

For Glass, a distinct rupture occurred in his relation to his medium at about the time he began working on *Einstein*. This rupture coincides quite neatly with the categories we have been discussing. "All of my works," comments Glass, "which predate 1976 fall within the highly reductive style known as minimalism. I feel that minimalism can be traced to a fairly specific timeframe, from 1965 through 1975, and nearly all of my compositions during this period may be placed in this general category."[47]

Glass's minimal period (1967–1975) can be identified directly with oppositional forms of postmodernism and his postminimal period (1976–) with the more eclectic and relational strains of recent years, which nevertheless have retained a critical edge. The keystone of the latter orientation is a renewed if somewhat self-conscious interest in relationships. Theater and illustrative music became the vehicles for Glass's explorations in this new area. While there can be little doubt that his early minimal pieces stood in diametric opposition to many of the precepts of modernism, significantly the term *postmodernism* is reserved by the composer for those pieces that belong to what I have defined as relational postmodernism. Starting with his work in the theater, Glass "came to see the idea of art content tied in with our relationship to it, an idea providing the basis of a truly modern, or perhaps postmodern, aesthetic. Furthermore, it was an aesthetic that, in a very satisfying way, tied artists from all fields to other contemporary thought, be it philosophy, science or psychology."[48]

From Music Theater to Opera:
Negotiations with the "Grandfather of Tradition"

Only reluctantly did Glass first employ the term *opera* to describe his work in the theater. In fact, while working on *Einstein*, he explicitly rejected it, this particular work becoming identified with the genre only at the insistence of Robert Wilson and because it was performed in venues with strong operatic traditions.[49] The opening words of *MPG* reveal something of an aversion to the traditional precepts of the genre. Glass writes: "I have often said that I became an opera composer by accident. I never set out to become one, and even today I use the word 'opera' with reluctance."[50] Later he writes: "The operatic tradition seemed to me hopelessly dead, with no prospect for resurrection in the world of performance in which I worked. To me it seemed a far better idea to start somewhere else. As a description of Einstein, I preferred 'music theater' to 'opera.'"[51] By the time he began working on *Satyagraha*, however, "the subject of opera was becoming interesting," although allusions to "the great tradition of opera" were still, from his standpoint, "utterly beside the point and best avoided altogether."[52] In an interview given during the early stages of his work on *Akhnaten*, one is able to identify a clear gendered subtext in the composer's alienation from traditional precepts of the genre.

The tradition of theatre that I feel a part of is the one that begins with the Living Theater; the Open Theater, the Performance Group, the Mabou Mines, Richard Foreman, Bob Wilson, Meredith Monk. They are the *godparents* [note: male and female]⁵³ of modern American non-literary theatre. . . . Clearly, my idea of opera springs from the very recent past; one that, like a lot of American art, doesn't recognise a *grandfather* [male, patriarchal] of tradition.⁵⁴

Could it be that, like Catherine Clément, Glass simply did not care for the stories historical opera was telling and so decided, like the contemporaries he mentions, to replace the tyranny of the (patriarchal) word with his own brand of nonliterary theater; one that counters the symbol with the sign, dialogue with *jouissance*?⁵⁵ The grandfather metaphor is an interesting one, because it is one he uses in other circumstances as well; namely, in reference to the legacy of Anton Webern and Arnold Schoenberg: "I began by studying Webern and Schoenberg. You have to remember that in 1952/3 we thought that was contemporary music. . . . I think at some point I also began to realize that that was music my *grandfather* would have written."⁵⁶

Whether Glass's real grandfather, an Orthodox Jew from Eastern Europe, would have written music like Webern or Schoenberg is perhaps beside the point. Or is it? We have seen already that the question of Judaism is central to the subject matter of this opera, as Freud and Velikovsky both came to realize in their own discussions of Akhnaten. The idea of Glass doing battle or seeking reconciliation with his ancestors in this work does seem a little far-fetched, and I will resist the temptation to follow this particular line of inquiry further than is necessary in order to illuminate the critical issues at hand. But since this is an opera that explicitly addresses religious subject matter and boldly posits a controversial alternative genealogy to religious ideas, some personal level of engagement on the part of the composer seems not unlikely. More important than this, however, is the fact that the composer finds it necessary in both cases (when discussing opera and when discussing the genealogy of his music language) to distinguish his approach from that of an imaginary grandfather. He is careful not to refer to the nuclear family, which is evidently too close to home to be useful in a symbolic sense, but he finds it necessary to go beyond the pale of the family or of any blood relations in identifying the "parentage" of his art. Both postmodern music and music theater, it seems, are orphan arts. The presumably dead grandfather is, however, the interesting figure in this scenario; it is he who points most directly to the Oedipus complex.

With *Akhnaten*, certainly, came a new willingness in Glass to engage with historical forms—forms his grandfather would have recognized. His comments concerning the genre in *MPG* are quite telling in this respect. The most conspicuous allusions to tradition, however, are found in the music and drama of the opera itself. Glass himself observed that by the end of the trilogy, "clearly, I had become a composer of operas."⁵⁷

In all likelihood, the unknowing opera buff who chanced upon a performance of *Akhnaten* would recognize without any difficulty that the work is in some way related to Monteverdi's *Orfeo*, or Mozart's *Don Giovanni*, or Wagner's *Parsifal*, which probably could not be said of *Einstein*. The operatic world is, moreover, no stranger to ancient Egypt: Giuseppe Verdi's orientalist classic *Aïda* has, since its debut performance in Cairo in 1869, been a pillar of the opera canon. There are some superficial similarities between the two operas: Verdi sought the aid of an Egyptologist, Auguste Mariette, when working on the libretto of *Aïda*, as Glass did in collaborating with Shalom Goldman. Despite both composers' attention to the question of historical accuracy, both of these operas probably tell us more about the composer and the culture that produced them than they do about the realities of life in ancient Egypt. For reasons I will go into more fully below, the more stylized and symbolic approaches of pre-Romantic operas, like Handel's *Giulio Cesare* and Mozart's *Die Zauberflöte*, are far more valuable points of reference to the present discussion than more "realistic" operas like *Aïda* or Jules Massenet's *Thaïs*. There is good reason to believe that Mozart, for example, was not even trying to depict ancient Egypt in his opera but was more or less directly tackling ethical and philosophical questions pertinent to his own time using the symbolic tools of Freemasonry.[58] Glass's "nonrealist" approach is quite close, in this respect, to that of Mozart.

The difference between Mozart's and Verdi's operas to some extent illustrates the breadth of approaches encompassed by the category. If, however, one includes experimental music-theatre works like John Cage's *Europeras* under its umbrella, it is clear that the term ultimately reveals very little. Glass's first music-theater work, *Einstein*, has, like Cage's operas, frequently been described using terms such as *nonlinear* and *nonnarrative*. In *Einstein*, whatever content there is takes the form of an implied subtext rather than a clearly defined narrative, although the choice of a nonnarrative as opposed to a received historical form can arguably be interpreted as its own kind of narrative, the meaning of which inheres precisely in the act of negation. Even in Glass's earliest music-theater works, nonnarrativity never meant that the work had no story line at all; rather, it had a story line that was characterized by its nonspecific, ambiguous, and refractory nature. Speaking of *Einstein*, he has commented:

You don't have to tell whole stories. . . . People say, "Why aren't there any plots?" When I do an opera, there are three thousand plots in the audience. Besides, I give enough of a plot, but I don't do the whole story. . . . Of course, the risk you run is that people are unwilling to do that. They say, all these obvious negative remarks: "This is simplistic. This is simple minded. This isn't music."[59]

It is clear, however, that the essential character of this work is abstract, or pragmatic,[60] in comparison to the composer's subsequent works for the theater, in which a more explicitly defined narrative—albeit still a sketchy, allusive, or, to borrow the composer's own term, "poetic" one—can invariably be perceived.

Although loosely termed a nonnarrative opera by some critics, *Satyagraha* is distinguished from its predecessor by an increased emphasis on narrative elements; Glass had begun to realize that "subject or content in music theater could remain neither passive nor accidental, so what an opera was 'about' began to emerge . . . as a major issue."[61] Regarding this opera, he has commented: "[The music] has been narrative for the last twelve years [since 1975]! . . . In fact, an opera like *Satyagraha*, in a way, it tells a [story]. There are many, many ways of telling a story. So to say a piece tells a story does not tell us very much. It's according to how we do it. And also, it has a lot to do with the listener and where the listener is in relation to the story."[62]

The transition from the (relative) nonnarrative collage of *Einstein* to what I will term poetic (or estranged) narrative is only partially accomplished in *Satyagraha*, where nonnarrative elements—such as the, to most Western ears, arcane Sanskrit text of the opera, its quasi-mythological setting, and the historicocultural disjunction involved in combining characters as disparate as Tolstoy, Tagore, and King with texts from the *Bhagavad-Gita*—are at odds with more traditional, chronologically depicted events in the life of Gandhi. All in all, three or perhaps four temporal layers can be identified in *Satyagraha*: first, the chronological but episodically subdivided time of events in Gandhi's life in South Africa, which are nevertheless juxtaposed with the mythical time of the *Bhagavad-Gita* characters who enact these events; second, the historical time of each of the three observers who govern over the opera's scenes; third, the span of a single day from dawn to dusk during which the action of the opera unfolds. If the historical observers and other rhetorical devices employed by the composer serve to heighten the audience's awareness of the artifactual foundations of the opera, then we can add a fourth temporal category: that of the actual, lived time of the audience members. Like the wheels inside wheels of the chaconne variations and the macrolevel cadential arches that comprise the greater part of the opera's music, the theatrical construction of *Satyagraha* is cyclical and heavily stratified.[63] These principles of organization are carried over in *Akhnaten*, although there the contingencies of dramatic events seem to take precedence over formal considerations more often than in *Satyagraha*.

If *Einstein* was something of an enigma to critics in political terms, in *Satyagraha* the political force of the subject matter is clearly hard to ignore, despite Glass's claim that it was the personal charisma of Gandhi, the power of his personality rather than his "great moral and political consciousness," that originally attracted him to this subject.[64] The difference in approach between the first two trilogy operas was sufficient, however, for the composer to describe it as "a fundamental reorientation of my thinking about my relation to theater."[65] *Einstein* and *Satyagraha* are certainly very different operas; different enough to make some critics—and, implicitly, the composer himself—wonder whether they even belong to the same genre.[66] The third opera of the trilogy represents another stage in the gradual transformation of Glass's approach to music theater toward poetic narrative, although tellingly he still describes it as "not a 'story' opera but an episodic-symbolic portrait."[67] He says, "*Akhnaten* is really done, there's something that's very abstract about it in a certain way. There're kind of touching moments with the family and so forth, but basically there's nothing, one doesn't try to reveal motivation or anything like that in that opera."[68]

If a single factor has stood in the way of Glass's widespread acceptance in operatic circles, it is precisely his unwillingness (interpreted by some as his inability) to provide clear musical and dramatic signposts regarding the interior (i.e., emotional and experiential) worlds of his characters. He gives his characters voices, but only in very limited senses. And his spin on his subject matter (or that of his adopted narrating persona) is often difficult to pin down with certainty. It is understandable, then, that some critics, like Winton Dean, feel frustrated under such circumstances and end up giving up the interpretive ghost.[69]

But why did Glass find it necessary to change the rules? Why not go on giving audiences and critics what they want hear?[70] We have already looked at some of the reasons for the birth of minimalism, as a reaction to the asphyxiating constraints introduced and upheld by musical modernism. The roots of Glass's and his contemporaries' art go deeper than that, however, and it is to the world of theater that we must turn in order to elucidate further the specific set or sets of rules that were developed by Glass and other exponents of postmodern music theater in the 1970s and to better understand the broader significance of these rules.

The assault on classic modes of representation in Glass's music theater was three pronged, drawing on the ideas of Artaud and Brecht and on various non-European approaches to the theater, in particular the Kathakali tradition of the Kerala region in southern India. Since Artaud and Brecht were both strongly influenced by Asiatic theatrical practices and by many of the same features that drew Glass to the Kathakali, establishing the exact genealogy of these ideas is almost impossible. The search for origins becomes even more futile when we take into account the fact that many of these ideas were a part of the general artistic zeitgeist in New York's Off Off Broadway community in the early 1970s, when Glass was learning his trade. So it is almost impossible to ascertain which ideas were imported by Glass himself from non–North American sources and which he picked up from people working with and around him in New York. But it is not necessary to identify with any certainty the origins of specific ideas; a more general picture will adequately serve our purposes.

Glass's interest in the theater took root in his student days in Paris and was developed further in the early 1970s in his work as musical director for the experimental-theater group the Mabou Mines. At this time, he was married to the cofounder of this group, the leading postmodern director JoAnne Akalaitis. Glass and Akalaitis traveled widely in Europe and Asia in the 1960s and early 1970s, absorbing diverse theatrical influences, from Jean Genet's *The Screens* to the Kathakali. Upon their return to the United States, the group rehearsed in a disused mine near Glass's house in Nova Scotia; hence the name of the group. Productions by the Mabou Mines were, like those of Robert Wilson, characterized by their rich visual imagery, by their use of sophisticated staging techniques, and by their incorporation of techniques from popular culture. Plays by Brecht and Samuel Beckett became the mainstay of the Mabou Mines repertoire, in addition to original works by Akalaitis and Lee Breuer, the group's other leading director.[71]

A further influence on both Glass and Akalaitis was the Living Theater, a politically oriented performance group that in the 1960s sought to revolutionize Western theater by breaking down the barriers between performers and audience. Other groups and individuals Glass mentions as having had an influence on his approach to the theater include Joseph Chaikin's Open Theater, Richard Schechner's Performance Group, Meredith Monk, Richard Foreman, and Robert Wilson.[72] All of these were influenced in one way or another by the Living Theater and, either directly or indirectly, by the theoretical ideas of Artaud. In addition, Glass acknowledges the theatrical work of contemporaries such as Laurie Anderson, Julia Heyward, Stuart Sherman, and Vito Acconci, all of whom "blurred the boundaries between art and *performance* of art until the distinction finally disappeared and performance art emerged."[73] From these names, it is not hard to piece together a fairly cogent picture of the scene from which Glass the theater composer emerged.

Artaud's Positive(-ist) "Negativity"

In the performance art and theater of all of the above, the influence of earlier—specifically, antirealist—artistic movements, like Dada and surrealism, can be felt. The prominent French actor, director, playwright, and essayist Antonin Artaud, who emerged but was later expelled from the latter of these movements, is perhaps the strongest influence. In a series of influential essays and manifestos, Artaud rejected the traditional precepts of Western theater in favor of a new approach that he called the Theater of Cruelty.[74] This appellation is something of a misnomer, since Artaud's intention was never to inflict actual cruelty on actors or audiences, something avant-garde performance groups of the 1960s and 1970s on occasion failed to realize. Instead, he sought to disable the discursive thought patterns of audience members by directly assaulting their senses. This assault was the cornerstone of Artaud's theory.[75] This was to be a theater of mise-en-scène, in which each medium involved had its own sign language, one whose immediacy or iconicity suggested to Artaud the analogy of hieroglyphs; these were signs whose actual physical presence was in some ways as potent as, if not more potent than, the message they were trying to convey.[76] Artaud was strongly influenced by Balinese theater, in which he perceived a perfect balance between diverse theatrical media. Each of these media had its own syntax, its own sense, yet each was elaborately connected to a larger whole.[77] In comparison, Western theater appeared impoverished to Artaud, because of its overreliance on dialogue, whose essence was not, in his mind, theatrical but literary.[78]

Artaud was the first to envision a nonliterary, nonnarrative form of theater.[79] It was he, too, who first spoke of the elimination or death of the author, an idea that later became one of the foundation stones of poststructuralist literary and cultural theory, thanks to Roland Barthes and his followers.[80] And Artaud was among the first theorists to strongly resist the notion of masterpieces, preferring to think of theatrical performances as events, orchestrated by a director whose status was not that of a monolithic creator but rather a kind of alchemist who manipulated the materials at hand so as to bring about the best possible theatrical transformations.[81] Like Brecht, Artaud challenged existing performance practices, advocating inverting the performance space so that it was the audience rather than the performers who were the focus of attention and staging performances in unconventional locations, where the assumptions regarding what does and does not constitute theater do not apply. He also endorsed a stylized, opaque mode of performance in preference to the prevalent realist doctrines of theorists such as Constantin Stanislavsky.

One of the most incisive recent critiques of Artaud's theories is Jacques Derrida's essay "The Theatre of Cruelty and the Closure of Representation."[82] Derrida applauds Artaud for liberating the theater from its dependence on "the text" and its controlling "author-god." He perceives the

Theater of Cruelty as an affront to the logocentrism of classical, imitative forms of theater in which immediate, nonrepresentative communication is subordinated to the written word. Artaud's theater would, according to Derrida, "no longer operate as a repetition of a *present*, will no longer re-present a present that would exist elsewhere and prior to it, a present whose plenitude would be older than it, absent from it, and rightfully capable of doing without it: the being-present-to-itself of the absolute Logos, the living present of God."[83]

The Theater of Cruelty, for Derrida, represents an inversion of literary theatrical practices but one whose essence was affirmative, the restoration of "existence" and "flesh" in Artaud's theater contrasting starkly with conventional theater's "romantic negativity."[84] At the same time as he recognizes the desirability of a theater based on the principle of "pure presence as pure difference," however, Derrida also recognizes the impossibility of such a theater ever coming into existence. For Derrida, theater can never break free of its own fundamental theatricality; it can never shake free the shadows of its own repetition. Performance invariably ends up representing itself, if nothing else. Thus, Artaud's efforts to close off his theater from the symbolic domain were destined to fail, making the Theater of Cruelty a utopian if not a wholly superfluous enterprise. It is easy to understand Derrida's affinity with Artaud's aesthetic: both the Theater of Cruelty and deconstruction are characterized by their puritanical distrust of any form of representation; both construct utopian negative spaces where anything or nothing is possible; and both fail to draw adequate attention to the more "positive," civilizational aspects of the symbolic domain.

The current fascination with multimedia performance is easy to tie in to Artaud's aesthetic, as is the whole notion of performance art. In addition to the Living Theater, Richard Foreman's Ontological-Hysteric Theater is, of its essence, Artaudian. Similarly, many aspects of Robert Wilson's approach can be traced directly to the influence of Artaud—more, for example, than to Brecht. A common denominator of much of the new music theater, including that of Glass, can be attributed largely to Artaud: its strong ritualistic feel. If there is a spirituality to this orientation, its essence is either non-Western or pre-Christian (or pagan). Post-Artaudian, postmodern theater might easily be described as Jungian, given that its avoidance of conventional narrative elements results in a fundamental duality between inner and outer space and time, between the interiority of the Jungian self and the exteriority of total sensual saturation. The middle ground of mediated narrative, the gray area, although present in the most austere works of this type, often takes on a distinct phantasmagorical appearance. The images that occupy this gray area exert a twofold influence:

they pull one's attention inward toward a hypothetical but ever-elusive center of consciousness (the primordial Jungian self or the Freudian id); when no center is found, however, on which to ground one's perceptions, such images end up deflecting attention outward toward pure exteriority.[85] Hence Julia Kristeva's assertion that the new theater, specifically that of Robert Wilson, is one which "does not take (a) place," since the centrifugal and centripetal forces at work are constantly deflecting attention away from any specific temporal or spatial location.[86]

It is this side of postmodernism—its "spiritual" or "sublime" aspect— that has arguably caused the most controversy; John Rockwell equates the lush "visionary/mystical" quality of Robert Wilson's theater of images directly with the approach of Richard Wagner.[87] In this he is almost certainly correct; it is this aspect more than any other that resembles Wagner's *Gesamtkunstwerk* and that jars most disturbingly with Brecht's and Benjamin's conception of the epic theater. There are important differences, however, between postmodern and Wagnerian forms of spectacle: Wagner's unified work of art was the product of a fundamentally literary theatrical tradition. For Wagner, music was always at the service of poetry. Opera, for him, was an androgynous art form in which poetry (male) exerted total control over its passive bedfellow, music (female).[88] Each element in Wagner's operas is painstakingly defined in relation to each other element; hence, his elaborate system of leitmotivs, whose raison d'être was to remove any uncertainty in the mind of the audience as to what was happening in the music in discursive terms. This degree of specificity is quite intentionally absent in Wilson's music-theater pieces; in fact, his type of theater seems to actively resist any attempts at discursive specificity. The onus is very much on the audience to weave together the gaps left in the fabric of the performance and to make their own sense of the piece as they perceive it. Putting spectacle and ritual aside for a moment, this idea of theatre is just about as non-Wagnerian as you can get.

Wilson's operas do unquestionably allude to Wagner, however—just as their Artaudian bombardment of the senses brings to mind the power wielded in postindustrial society by the (predominantly corporation-controlled) media. This power can both satisfy and stultify the senses, both enable and disable. In Wilson's theater, the gray area—why not call it "the gray matter"—is missing, leaving a number of (nonexclusive) options: first, let your senses be disabled, let yourself go, as it were, trusting that you will not be taken anywhere you do not want to go; second, immerse yourself in the materiality of the event without losing control of your senses; third, contemplate the absence itself and the possible rationales for this absence; and fourth, remain totally or partially detached from the aesthetic experience. The very presence of these options or interpretive layers suggests an aesthetic very different to that which predominated at the end of the eighteenth century, at the same time as it reminds us of the legacy of that century and of the ever-present possibility of either consciously or unconsciously abdicating control over one's faculties and the consequences, good and bad, of such an abdication. If that sounds complicated, it is. The principles behind the new music theater might be simple, but what is going on in it in psychological terms is not at all easy to explain.

Nonliterary theater was first envisioned by Artaud, but it was fully realized in the performances of the directors, groups, and individual performers Glass mentions in *MPG*.[89] Regarding the sonorous implication of the aesthetic, Artaud's writings are peppered with terms such as *vibration, repetition*, and *incantations*, terms that could easily be applied to Glass's music. Obvious examples of incantational language can be found in all three trilogy operas. The sung sections of text in *Einstein* consist solely of numbers and solfège symbols, which, in addition to foregrounding musical structure, function as mnemonic aids for performers. The recited texts in that opera are, moreover, fragmentary and nonsensical—closer to prayer than to dialogue. *Satyagraha* is set in its entirety in a language unfamiliar to Western audiences: Sanskrit. Furthermore, its mythological subject matter does not connect in a one-to-one manner with the dramatic events enacted on the stage. *Akhnaten*'s text is written predominantly in archaic languages: ancient Egyptian, Akkadian, and biblical Hebrew. Here we have Artaudian hieroglyphs in a near-uncorrupted form. Moreover, a number of scenes, like those at the temple and during the attack and fall, contain lengthy passages of vocalese, and in the family scene discursive language is dispensed with altogether. In this opera, however, a number of compromises are made to facilitate the emergence of a more coherent narrative schema. These include the presence of a narrator who addresses the audience in their own language; further, one scene, the hymn to the sun, is sung in the dominant language of the audience. Glass's use of language in *Akhnaten* is, therefore, incantational, nonnarrative, and refractory, but that is certainly not *all* that it is.

Although Glass is well known for his use of "nonsensical" texts, he is certainly not the only postmodern musician to use language in this way. A similar effect is achieved in the ritualistic vocal styles of performance artists such as Meredith Monk, Diamanda Galas, and, a precursor of them all, Yoko Ono; in Laurie Anderson's mechanically treated vocals and in her otherwise crisp, rhythmically and intonationally detached manner of articulation; in the similar manner of articulation in the narrated text of Frederic

Rzewski's *Attica*; and in Steve Reich's use of tape loops in compositions such as *It's Gonna Rain* (1965) and *Come Out* (1966), where the linguistic utterance is, by mechanical means, gradually pried free of its semantic and sociolinguistic components, thus transforming it into more of a poetic or "musical" entity. In the sphere of popular music, a number of musicians, particularly those based in New York, have explored similar modes of expression; take, for example, the vocalese passages in Lou Reed's "Walk on the Wild Side" or Suzanne Vega's "Tom's Diner."[90]

Signs that divert attention toward their site or means of production, toward their materiality as acoustic events, function differently than those familiar to us from the tradition of naturalistic realism as it has been passed down to us in Romantic art. The Romantic sign seems to draw the listener in, playing on his or her empathic powers in order to simulate the emotional state of the protagonist in the mind of what structuralist theories of communication aptly term "the receiver" of the semiotic message. The structuralist aesthetic places a strong emphasis on authorial intention and what it views as objective significations. It favors meanings that appear to be transparently present in the work of art itself, as opposed to those that might resonate in a looser fashion with "subjective" experiences outside of it or those that might arise in the materiality of the performance situation itself. This latter type of sign, that which eschews empathic identification, is an integral part of Brecht's conceptual arsenal.[91]

Brecht and Alienation

Brecht defined his so-called Epic Theater in opposition to traditional dramatically oriented approaches to the theater and to the *Gesamtkunstwerk* of Wagner.[92] Rather than striving for artistic unity, Brecht's theater favored elements that were at odds with one another, montage taking precedence over the diachronic or linear unfolding of a plot and counterpoint between theatrical media taking precedence over harmony. He was deeply suspicious of unities and went to great lengths to foreground the irregularities and exceptions that inhered in apparently unified entities.[93] The Epic Theater was in his words "non-Aristotelian," meaning that it did not require cathartic involvement by the audience; its purpose was not, therefore, to mirror the lives of audience members, nor were audience members encouraged to identify directly with characters.[94] Instead, it sought to encourage a kind of communal individuality, engaging in signifying practices but at the same time urging the audience to keep one foot firmly planted in the experiential domain of the physical—the area of experience that most doggedly remains the dominion of the individual subject but that is nevertheless available to all. Brecht's ideas, which were resurrected and transformed in Roland Barthes's writing, revealed the extent to which natural and historically conditioned signs have become confused in the modern world and pulled the mat out from under representations that appear to mask that distinction.[95]

The Brechtian aesthetic takes Artaud's assumptions regarding the experiential primacy of the incantational and the imagistic one step further; at the center of the Brechtian view is the notion of the divided sign, a form of double coding that on the one hand posits the preaesthetic domain of the embodied voice but on the other hand allows representations to unfold. These representations are grounded strongly in direct physical experience and lean toward connotative rather than denotative modes of signification. Brechtian discourse superficially resembles Jean Baudrillard's empty play of signs—the now-infamous "simulacrum."[96] Brechtian significations are not inarticulate, however; in their most elegant forms they are extremely efficacious semiotic tools. Barthes's "grain of the voice" perhaps comes closest to the Brechtian view, although the French poststructuralist's idealistic privileging of the signifier over the signified, of *jouissance* over pleasure, has a dogmatic force rarely detected in Brecht's writing. Barthes was one of the strongest and most perceptive advocates of Brecht's aesthetic in France, but his own theoretical position drove him inexorably away from Brechtian double coding and implicit significations, toward "purer," apparently more immediate fields of signification—such as music, which for him was the ideal toward which all signifying practices should strive.[97] That music might be in the same way positional as language, in the same way open and susceptible to interruptions, although one of the central premises of Brecht's theories was evidently not accepted by Barthes. Brecht was deeply ambivalent when it came to music; he saw it as both an articulate and an extremely powerful medium. Music was, however, more than any other semiotic medium, capable of imparting to events the illusion of necessity.[98]

The poetic force of language, then, of "music" in language, holds the key to prying open the Saussurean dichotomy of signified and signifier and brings about the epistemological slippage that dislodges Romantic significations from their metaphysical foundations but which nonetheless allows them to be put forth—albeit in a more alienated, pellucid guise.

Not by chance does Glass characterize his own brand of opera as "a species of poetry" and, moreover, distinguish this conception of art from conventional, realistic-looking narrative.[99] The poetic conception espoused by Glass is very definitely Artaud's; in *The Theatre and Its Double*, Artaud writes of a "poetry in space" that "will be resolved in precisely the domain which does not belong strictly to words."[100] Artaud's "very difficult and complex poetry," far from being the exclusive property of spoken or aural language, permeates every layer of theatrical expression, including "music, dance, plastic arts, pantomime, mimicry, gesticulation, intonation, architecture, lighting, and scenery."[101] If Glass's "poetics" is Artaudian, however, the rhetorical operations by which these ostensibly denuded signs become semiotically garbed are post-Artaudian and (post-)Brechtian. That is, they are done with the knowledge of these precursors but taken to places they were unlikely and probably unwilling to have gone.

The idea of poetic aspects in language has been explored rigorously also by linguists such as Roman Jakobson.[102] It is Julia Kristeva's perspective, however, which incorporates both Artaud's intuitions and the rigor of structural linguistics, that is probably the most useful to the present discussion. Utilizing Freudian and Lacanian psychology, Kristeva interprets the move in literature and art toward poetic language and away from any coherent "message" as constituting a return to a more instinctual mode of communication—one that acknowledges rather than represses the continuing relation of the child to its mother. Because of this relation, however, poetic language is, for Kristeva, the semiotic "equivalent of incest."[103] Resisting the structuralists' proclivity for abstraction, Kristeva points out that

the dominance of semiotic constraint in poetic language cannot be solely interpreted, as formalist poetics would have it, as a preoccupation with the "sign," or with the "signifier" at the expense of the "message"; rather, it is more deeply indicative of the instinctual drives' activity relative to the first structurations (constitutive of the body as self) and identifications (with the mother).[104]

Artaud seems to recognize the affinity between inbreeding and poetic self-absorption when he writes: "I am my father, my mother, my son, and me."[105] And so does Glass: Those scenes in *Akhnaten* that deal explicitly with incest—either mother/son or father/daughter—are also those whose musical and theatrical language best encapsulates Artaud's notion of poetic expression. This includes the family scene in act 3, which is sung in vocalese throughout and in which a strong incestuous bond is suggested between Akhnaten and his daughters, and the temple scene in act 2, in which Akhnaten and his mother (Oedipus and Jocasta, according to Velikovsky) unite to purge their kingdom of the old religious order. It is only because of its relation to symbolic discourse, however, that we recognize poetic discourse for what it is in this opera. Indeed, understanding how these two semiotic modes, which Kristeva would call the symbolic and the semiotic, operate in relation to one another is the most important key to understanding both Glass's treatment of his subject matter and the premises of Glass's entire poetics of music theater at that time.

In order to shed further light on the relation between symbolic and poetic discourse in *Akhnaten*, we must return to Brecht. While Artaud foregrounded presentation at the expense of representation, Brecht envisaged a kind of representation that, without denying the symbolic, would be grounded more firmly than ever before in presentation. His approach relied heavily on what he called "alienation" or "distanciation effects"—the famous *Verfremdungeffekt*. As Brecht himself put it, alienation is a form of representation "which allows us to recognise its subject, but at the same time makes it seem unfamiliar."[106] His intention, then, was to effect a change in the way the people perceived works of art, using alienation to dislodge conditioned responses, resulting in the abrogation of what Benjamin called the "aura" of a work.[107] With the so-called fourth wall, which separates the "imaginary" world of the performers from the "real" world of the audience, demolished, the field would be open for the emergence of new theatrical experiences and for an enhanced awareness of the groundedness of these experiences in space, time, and the body.

All of this seems very abstract and theoretical. But Brecht, unlike Artaud, was nothing if not meticulous in enumerating the means by which his theatrical vision could be realized in actual performances. The following are some of the most distinctive features of the Epic Theater as envisioned by Brecht:

* Actors are encouraged to display their awareness of being observed by an audience, and, by the same token, they are permitted to react to events that occur outside of the aesthetic frame.

* Actors are encouraged to react to or comment on the actions of the characters they are portraying, resulting in a clearly perceptible split between actor and role. (This rift imparts to the spoken word the opaqueness of quotation, as opposed to the transparency of direct artistic expression.)

* Stage props and scenery can be recognized as what they are. Lighting apparatus is conspicuously visible. Stagehands are seen performing their duties.

* Nonparticipating observers are placed on the stage.

* Banners adorn the stage (which play no part in the diegesis), thus setting up a counterpoint between the actions portrayed and the interpretations offered in writing.

* The plot is interrupted regularly by clearly delineated musical numbers, whose purpose is not to heighten the emotional force of the action but rather to add to the artificiality of the experience.

* Differing interpretations of the same event are offered—often simultaneously and in different media (for example, music vs. dialogue vs. body language).

* Apparently insignificant events are foregrounded to an unusual degree.

Brecht, like Artaud, was profoundly influenced by his encounters with Asian theater. His alienation effects, for example, were inspired directly by the techniques of Chinese actors. Alienation was not, therefore, Brecht's invention and has probably been around as long as people have been doing art; it is found in many different cultures around the world in many different forms. In Europe, the idea was formulated in very similar terms by the Russian formalist school of linguistics. The formalists listed as markers of alienation, what they called "foregrounding," the use of conspicuous rhetorical figures, highly patterned syntax, and phonetic repetitions and parallelisms, all of which served to increase the opacity of representations, thus placing a stronger emphasis on their "poetic" aspects and bringing about a sense of distance in relation to semantic components.[108]

Up until now I have focused almost exclusively on the theatrical side of the music-theater dyad, for music played an important role in both Artaud's and Brecht's notions of theater, but neither were trained in music theory. Only Adorno really applied himself to the question of what musical alienation might sound like, although, unlike his Frankfurt school colleague Benjamin, he remained skeptical as to the emancipatory powers of alienated musical discourse, which he astutely identified with the music of Stravinsky.[109] Adorno's distrust of Stravinsky is easy to understand; he was put off, above all else, by this composer's disturbing propensity to see the products of his musical imagination as manifestations of a distilled objectivity. Adorno distrusted the truth claims underlying Stravinsky's aesthetic position; the notion that by eschewing the conventional markers of subjective expression and by honing in on technique and rhetoric, the listening subject would somehow gain access to an experiential realm seen as existing beyond subjectivity—i.e., the subjective domain post-Lacanian criticism refers to as "the real." For Adorno, the putative authenticity of this realm posed grave philosophical problems. He was willing to forgive Schoenberg his subjective indulgences, but found the form of deception he believed Stravinsky to be perpetrating in his music considerably harder to accept.

What, then, is alienation in specific musical terms? Taking the criteria of the Russian formalists as building blocks, alienated musical discourse would consist of conspicuous rhetorical figures (i.e., the structures would be clearly audible), its syntax would be stylized and opaque, and it would rely heavily upon the use of repeated material. This sounds strangely like a description of Glass's musical language. It is possible, then, that Brecht's influence, or the influence of ideas related to his, extends to Glass's musical discourse. And maybe Glass's alienation, if it is alienation, is closer to that of Brecht than Stravinsky. For Glass, let us not forget, "subject or content in music theater could remain neither passive nor accidental."[110] This represents almost the antithesis of Stravinsky's aesthetic view, as propounded in his *Poetics of Music*.[111] Does Adorno's critique of Stravinsky have any bearing, then, on the present discussion? If Glass's musical discourse is "alienated," is the composer rehearsing precisely the same dubious truth claims Adorno perceived his twentieth-century precursor Stravinsky to be making in his music? or is Glass's approach different? I will attempt to show that it is; that clear signposts are provided in Glass's musical discourse that undermine any impression that the music is striving to be more authentic than the music from which it distances itself. Glass's position is, as we shall see, not without its own problems, which Adorno would certainly have recognized. But they are different problems than those this critic identified in his discussions of Stravinsky's music. I will return to this question below (in chapters 4 and 7), since only by illuminating the discussion with specific musical examples can any worthwhile conclusions be drawn. There are other, more directly theatrical, ways, however, in which the influence of Brecht can be perceived in *Akhnaten*.

The most obvious of these has to do with Glass's preference for episodic form, in contrast to traditional, linear, dramatic approaches. This way of conceiving narrative, and the related aversion to episodic forms, goes all the way back to Aristotle: in his *Poetics*, the Greek philosopher wrote: "Among simple plots and actions the episodic are the worst. By 'episodic' plot I mean one in which there is no probability or necessity for the order in which the events follow one another."[112] Brecht took Aristotle's assumptions about the temporality of events and inverted them. For him, the idea that events were not completely determined in advance by the trajectory of the narrative was emancipatory. Moreover, this assumption brought his theater into closer line with vernacular art forms, in which episodic structural principles had long been the norm. For this reason, John Gay's *The Beggar's Opera* was held by Brecht and his collaborator Kurt Weill to be an apt model for the Epic Theater when they came to write their *Threepenny Opera*; this was a form of theater with the sophistication of the high art from which it appropriated freely but one that drew much of its vitality from popular culture. Moreover, this was an art form that made little effort to resemble events in the external world; it was what Artaud would have called a poetic art form.

Because of its use of episode structure, *The Threepenny Opera* is an obvious precursor of Glass's approach, as is the North American tradition of music theater represented by figures such as George Gershwin and Leonard Bernstein, composers highly trained in the classical idiom but determined to reach beyond the pale of concert audiences. The Tin Pan Alley tradition of songwriting, which was always closely related to the film and theater industries, is another significant precursor. Glass is not, of course, a songwriter in the classical meaning of the word, and *Akhnaten* is not made up of song numbers. It is, however, structured according to episodic principles that resemble those of song-based forms as well as of the classical ("art" music) song cycle. Like so much of what Glass does, this aspect of his writing straddles "high" and "low" categories, which might explain his preference for the term *music theater* for his earlier theatrical pieces. These precursors were unquestionably more a part of the North American collective consciousness when Glass was growing up than were the Central European founders of musical modernism that Glass and other minimalists spurned. Episodic form also ties in with certain aspects of contemporary popular culture and the technologies that allow the production and dispersion of this culture.

Glass's use of episodic structure in *Akhnaten* does not imply that the scenes of the opera are totally disconnected, nor that no sense of linear continuity is imparted as we proceed from one scene to the next. The unfolding of musical and dramatic transformations out of previous events in *Akhnaten* is usually quite sophisticated; changes emerge effortlessly from the material that preceded them, but still they have the capacity to surprise. Artaud would have termed these changes in *intensity*, a term favored also by Fredric Jameson in reference to specifically postmodern ways of construing time.[113]

Glass's taste for semiautonomous, tableauxlike musicodramatic images is closely related to another aspect of his aesthetic—namely, what I have called his archaeological approach. If the composer wanted to preserve something of the artifactual essence of the preexisting texts in performances of the opera, episodic form appears to be the ideal solution, since it is less likely to encroach upon the "concrete" material than might conventional narrative approaches. Indeed, the very use of *objets trouvées*—archaeological material—in *Akhnaten* can be construed as a kind of alienation effect, given that its primary purpose is to ground our perceptions of historical events in the present. This is what Brecht would have termed "historification," and it is an important part of Glass's ethos in this work, as evidence by the following statement:

I didn't like the idea of doing just a period piece. We're not pretending it's something that happened; it's something that happened three thousand five hundred years ago.

It's something that happened three thousand five hundred years ago, but we're seeing it through our twentieth-century eyes. And, in fact, there's nothing in the story that isn't contemporary, really; it's about power, and upholding old ideas, and trying to force new ideas into the world, and what happens to the people that do that.[114]

Aside from foregrounding the artifactual constitution of the material from which the opera is constructed, there are other, more obvious ways of bringing into sight the contemporary filter through which our perceptions of past events must invariably pass. One of the ways Glass did this was by setting the epilogue of *Akhnaten* in the present-day ruins of Akhnaten's holy city. In *MPG*, the composer writes: "I wanted to somehow underscore the fact that although we twentieth-century people were looking at an imaginary version of Egypt in 1400 BC, the very real ruins of that Egypt exist today. Therefore I decided to create an epilogue set in the present."[115] Just how successful this attempt at historification is will depend on how it is dramatized in individual productions. I will discuss some of the problems posed for directors by this post-Brechtian strategy in chapter 7.

The Kathakali

As I have mentioned, Glass, like both Artaud and Brecht before him, has been influenced profoundly by his encounters with Asian music theater. In his case, the influence can be traced to the Kathakali, a form of dance drama indigenous to the Kerala district of southwest India. According to the composer, his acquaintance with the Kathakali must in some way have "conditioned the way [he] think[s] about what [he does] in the theater."[116] The qualities he admires in this theatrical form are, tellingly, its ability to combine the sophisticated and the communicative and its connectedness both in terms of music-drama interpenetration and in terms of its relation to other aspects of Indian life.[117] Since many of the techniques and ideas from the Kathakali that are likely to have influenced Glass's approach are found also in the Chinese and Balinese forms of theater that influenced Artaud and Brecht, it is very difficult to pinpoint any more specific features than those the composer himself mentions. A closer inspection of the Kathakali does reveal a number of parallels between their practices and Glass's approach in *Akhnaten*, albeit ones that can be attributed equally well to influences closer to home.

Although essentially a nonliterary form of theater, the dramatic events enacted in the Kathakali draw on the mythology of Indian classics such as the *Mahabharata* and the *Ramayana*. Significantly, the original Sanskrit texts performed in the Kathakali are translated by a narrator—a clownlike figure who represents the alter ego of the hero—into the vernacular of the region. Leslie Lassetter has perceptively equated this technique with the use of a narrator in *Akhnaten*.[118] The only qualification I might add is that a parallel influence from Stravinsky and Cocteau's *Oedipus Rex*, which also features a narrator/translator, seems likely.

But in the Kathakali, as in *Akhnaten*, a significant part of the meaning is not conveyed by the narrator but by elements of what Artaud called the mise-en-scène. Especially sophisticated is the system of hand gestures, or *mudras*, employed by Kathakali actors. Sixty-four basic hand gestures can be permutated to connote as many as five hundred different words, thus allowing the actors to communicate complex dramatic messages in this medium alone. In addition, footwork and facial expressions play an important role in connoting dramatic nuances. Achim Freyer attempted in his Stuttgart production of *Akhnaten* to complement Glass's music with stylized gestures similar to those of the Kathakali. Although more abstract and less elaborate than Indian *mudras*, Freyer's gestures do provide a stimulating and stylistically appropriate counterpoint to Glass's music, just as the repetitive, mechanical choreography by Lucinda Childs for *Einstein* aptly complements Glass's music.

The music of the Kathakali has been described as "demoniacally vigorous."[119] This demonic nature is attributable largely to the constitution of the musical ensemble, which features a strong percussive contingent, comprising a gong, a triangle, cymbals, and two to four drums. Other instruments, include flutes, stringed instruments, and, occasionally, a harmonium. Kathakali performances also feature song numbers that are not unlike operatic arias. Rhythmic vitality, however, is the most distinctive musical element, something that must have appealed to Glass, whose own musical language is defined largely by its emphasis on rhythm. The use of percussion in the Kathakali might, therefore, have influenced Glass's use of percussion in Akhnaten.

It is not difficult to perceive an affinity between Glass's music theater and this, to most Western ears, strange and exotic form of music drama. Significantly, though, *Akhnaten* does not look or sound like Indian theater. As with the influence of Asian music on Glass's early minimal style, certain principles of organization might have inspired changes in the composer's approach; before reemerging in specific works of art, however, these influences passed through the filter of his own artistic sensibilities, which in large part were conditioned by his Euro-American musical heritage.

Glass's cross-cultural borrowings are, on the whole, philosophical and abstract by nature. In other words, one rarely gets the impression what one is listening to is not the composer's "property." This matters for fairly obvious, although often unrecognized, reasons: benefiting from the music of other individuals or cultures in some way that does not in turn benefit the source (for example, financially) is, particularly when the exchange reflects the current imbalance in global economic and technological power relations, an ethically questionable pastime that anthropologists and cultural theorists have justifiably been critical of for some time. Glass is not entirely innocent in this respect, but there is a self-consciousness in his borrowings from other cultures—an acknowledgment of his own complicity in the politics of dominance, as well as a willingness to address issues of cultural dominance in his works (for example, the Godfrey Reggio collaboration *Powaqqatsi* [1988])—that suffices to make his one of the least problematic cases of this kind of "appropriation" to have emerged in recent years. The subject matter of *Akhnaten* raises complex issues pertaining to representations of African and "Oriental" cultures in the West, which I will discuss in some detail in chapter 6. These issues are somewhat different, though, than those which arise in connection with straightforward cases of appropriation.

Glass draws together strands from many different theatrical and broader cultural traditions in his approach. The end result is one that is instantly recognizable, however. This is as true of *Akhnaten* as it is of any other of his works. In fact, this particular opera represents a coming together of influences for Glass, resulting in the genesis of a style that is truly the composer's own. The success of *Einstein* can arguably be attributed as much to Robert Wilson and the other collaborators on that project as to Glass, while *Satyagraha* is, with good reason, referred to by the composer himself as "a transitional work."[120] In *Akhnaten*, an operatic style crystallized that is quite distinctive—one that has informed all of Glass's subsequent works as well as those of many other composers.

CHAPTER THREE

The Musical Language of Akhnaten

Like the high jumper who glides effortlessly over the bar with inches to spare while executing a perfect Fosbury arch, or the potter who deftly fashions a vase from an amorphous lump of clay, Glass makes his craft look easier than it is. This is one of the reasons why his style has been so widely imitated but also why it has been so widely maligned; it sounds as if you could do it if you just sat down at the piano and strung together some modally inflected broken chords in strict metronomic time. And up to a point, you are justified in thinking that you could. The textures and feel of Glass's music are easily imitated. Other aspects of his compositional technique are more demanding, however, although even those can be imitated if you know what to listen for—which requires some fairly advanced musical training.

What makes these structures, these techniques, this style matter is the way in which they communicate meanings to audiences by relating the immediate to the remembered, the perceived to the preconfigured, the actual to the known, experiences to the experienced. In other words, what matters is how the techniques employed are construed relationally, with respect to performance-contextual, personal, cultural, and historical considerations. This is the same poetics of relations discussed in the previous chapter; and it is the key to understanding the extraordinary power *Akhnaten* has wielded over audiences around the world and the relevance and resonance it is felt by many to have.

There is not all that much that is "new" or "innovative" musically in this opera, taken as such. In fact, the self-reflexive, retrospective, and perhaps (auto)biographical nature of it seems to a large extent to dictate its stylistic orientation, which has more to do with reexamining past techniques, including those of the composer himself, than inventing new ones. The specific combinations of techniques found in this work are new, however, as are the meanings produced by these combinations. Not all of this will become apparent in this chapter, but this chapter will provide a point of reference of particular value to those with some musical training for the less technical discussions that follow. Readers not specifically interested in the music should feel free to skip over these pages if the material is not of interest or seems overly technical.

Additive Processes

In terms of musical technique, Glass has become most widely known for his use of additive processes. Inspired by the *talas* of Indian music and adumbrated in early minimalist works like Terry Riley's *In C* (1964), the use of additive and subtractive rhythmic cells in Glass's early minimalist output is extensive and applied rigorously. Instead of punctuating musical time with regularly or less regularly placed bar lines, Glass conceived of rhythm in more fluid terms, as emerging from the addition or subtraction of individual notes or cells to or from the notes or cells that preceded them. Rhythmic regularity would be present on the micro level, however, because of the strict regulation of rhythm on the level of individual notes. Like the binary languages used in computer programming, there were just two options available in the rhythmic language of Glass's early minimal style: o or 1, an eighth note or a rest, the former being considerably more copious than the latter. Thus, the music unfolded in an unrelenting, hyperactive stream of eighth notes. The computer analogy is a valid one also as regards performance practices. The performance marking of an early piece, *Strung Out* (1967), in which the violinist is instructed to play "mechanically," set the agenda for the whole next decade in Glass's music. This principle was adhered to more or less rigorously by Glass himself, by other performers, and by the Philip Glass Ensemble in performances of works up to and including *Einstein*. Performers quickly noticed that the addition of any interpretive flourishes, far from enhancing performances, in fact threatened to sabotage the primary modus operandi of the music. By approaching their musical material coolly and impersonally, performers better served the requirements of the piece, allowing listeners to home in on surface-level transformations, to focus on the particularities of the moment rather than to create expectations of and desires for future changes.

Additive rhythmic structures are present in two compositions of Glass's from 1967, *One + One* and *Strung Out*. The former is constructed from two rhythmic cells that the score designates should be alternated at the discretion of the performer (see example 1). Additive patterns emerge easily when rhythmic material is stripped to its fundamentals in this way and

Example 1. *One + One* (1967) (excerpt from the composer's example).

when the composer's instructions to combine the cells in "continuous, regular arithmetic progressions" are observed.

Additive structures are further illuminated musically by adding a second parameter, that of pitch, to that of rhythm. The introduction of pitch allows a steady pulse of eighth notes to continue uninterrupted, while at the same time providing listeners with further musical stimulation to compensate, as it were, for the absence of rests. In Glass's early minimal style, rhythm is still the dominant parameter, as evidenced by the strict pentatonicism of compositions such as *Two Pages* (1968) (see example 2). This example shows the influence pitch can have on rhythmic accent. Even when played evenly, the lowest and the highest notes of each cell become foregrounded rhythmically simply by virtue of their pitch. Rather than accenting the one or the three or consistently emphasizing the backbeat or whatever the bar structure dictates, this music is characterized by its strongly syncopated, pulsating feel. The example given is monophonic (it has a single melodic line). The introduction of additional (polyphonic) voices, however, can result in the emergence of complex, multilayered rhythmic textures.

Additive processes are used less extensively in *Akhnaten* than in earlier works. A typical feature of Glass's approach in this opera, however, is the combination of these earlier techniques of his own with stock procedures. Thus, the additive rhythms of the upper parts in the drumming pattern

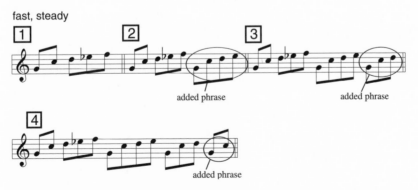

Example 2. *Two Pages* (1968) (first four patterns).

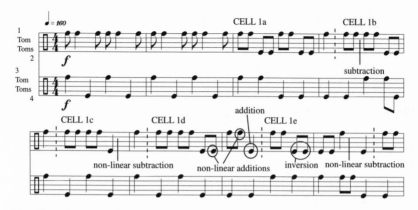

Example 3. Act I, scene I, funeral of Amenhotep III. The use of additive processes in combination with a stable rhythmic anchor.

from the funeral scene are contrasted with the conventional, four-square rhythms of the lower part (see example 3). The writing in the upper staff directly recalls the last composition of Glass's scored for percussive instruments, *One + One*, written a decade and a half earlier. Here, though, the tension between the two parts is what is important: The upper part tries to break free from the influence of the bar line but is eventually pulled back into compliance at the end of the cycle.

The following example (example 4), from the opening bars of the prelude, is more typical of the score. Here, the subtractive technique is used to instigate a simple change in meter. A basic polyrhythmic texture results (6/8 time in the top staff against 3/4 time in the bottom staff) that, although relatively straightforward at this point, is elaborated in interesting ways later in the scene, as we shall see in a moment.

Block Additive Processes

The term *block additive processes* is borrowed from Dan Warburton, who contrasts them with *linear additive processes*, which for him refer to the

Example 4. Act I, prelude.

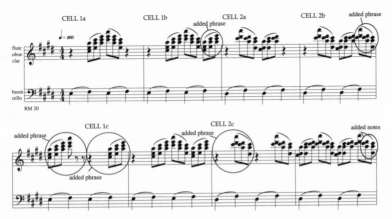

Example 5. Act I, scene I, funeral of Amenhotep III. Linear and block additive processes.

techniques discussed in the previous section.[1] By block additive processes Warburton means additions or subtractions that are made within a frame of fixed duration. This technique is closely related to traditional techniques of variation; a note or cell might be subtracted from a phrase, leaving a rest in its place; the same might happen again immediately afterward, or a note or cell might be added. More typical of Steve Reich's music, examples of this technique are found in Glass's music as well. Certain passages of *Strung Out*, for example, where a note located in the middle of a cell is replaced by a rest, could be categorized as examples of block subtractive processes. The first four bars of a sequence from the funeral scene look like a fairly clear example of block additive processes (see example 5). When the pattern overshoots the bar lines in bar five, however, it starts to look more like an example of the linear additive approach. Note, though, that harmonically and in relation to the bass line the pattern never actually deviates from the metrical designation of the time signature. The effect of the top part pulling away from the bar lines is very similar to that produced in the drum pattern from the same scene (see examples 3 and 5).

"Wheels Inside Wheels": *Polyrhythm and Cyclical Stratification*

One of most distinctive features of Glass's music in all three trilogy operas is the ubiquity of what might be termed textural polyrhythm. By *textural* I mean that changes in polyrhythmic texture, as well as being the focus of attention because of their structural qualities, also serve textural ends; that is, by adjusting the density and complexity of the polyrhythmic fabrics with which he is working, the composer is able to suggest changes in intensity comparable to, although qualitatively different from, the changes in dynamics and tempo familiar to us from Romantic music.

The technique was first introduced by Glass in one of his last minimalist works, the mammoth *Music in Twelve Parts* (1971–74). He describes the technique as follows:

> I have used rhythmic cycles (repeated fixed rhythmic patterns of specific lengths) to create extended structures in my music by superimposing two different rhythmic patterns of different lengths. Depending on the length of each pattern, they will eventually arrive back at the their starting points, making one complete cycle. This has been described by some writers as "wheels within wheels," a rather fanciful but not wholly inaccurate way of evoking the resulting effect.[2]

In the following example from the Train One section of *Einstein*, three cycles of the upper voice are equivalent in length to four cycles of the lower voice (see example 6). As can be seen, Glass developed his own abbreviated form of notation for this music: a simple multiplication sign indicates to performers the number of repeats required in each voice, while a double bar line shows the point of rhythmic convergence.

If *Akhnaten* is not as complex rhythmically as its trilogy predecessors, here the textural implications of the technique are certainly explored more fully. Example 4 shows how a simple polyrhythmic texture is introduced in the first macrocycle of the prelude. This is elaborated by means of rhythmic diminution (from a quarter note in cycle one to an eighth note in cycle two in the lower part) and increased independence of melodic lines (from homophony in cycles one to three to polyphony in cycle four). Changes in polyrhythmic texture are, in addition, underlined by and complemented in Glass's increasingly skillful use of the orchestra. In cycle three of the prelude, trumpets alternate antiphonically with horns and trombones (see example 7). Each of these groups bellows out an urgent string of eighth notes interspersed with a driving syncopated pattern. At the same time, strings and winds ascend and descend in mirrored oblique motion to these,

Example 6. *Einstein on the Beach*, Train One. Rhythmic cycles.

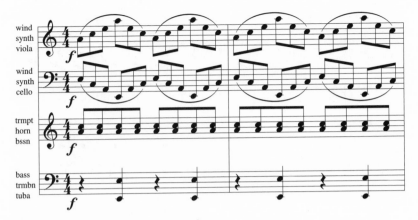

Example 7. Act I, prelude. Macrocycle three.

asserting their own pulsating groups of six eighth notes against the brass instruments' emphatic groups of four eighth notes.[3] Although quieter and more pensive than its immediate predecessor, cycle four of the prelude is more complex rhythmically (see example 8). Here, the binary-ternary combination of the earlier cycles is more pronounced contrapuntally, the mechanical upward push of the upper part contrasting starkly with the babbling undertow of the lower part. Thus, although this cycle is more subdued in terms of orchestration, the sense of a gradual heightening of activity, a growing excitement, continues unabated, relenting momentarily only with the entrance of the narrator in the fifth cycle.

Elsewhere in *Akhnaten*, polyrhythm is used to create instabilities that engender the need for musical change, in much the same way as common language tonality uses dissonance to create a sense of striving toward a goal. An example is the coronation scene, where the rhythmic disjunction produced by a three-part polyrhythm engenders a strong desire for rhythmic stability (see example 9). Here, we are presented with what is probably best described as a strict canon on the octave in the lower two voices, both

Example 8. Act I, prelude. Macrocycle four.

Example 9. Act 1, scene 2, the coronation of Akhnaten.

of whose binary meters contradict the ternary meter of the upper voice, and both of whose points of convergence with the upper voice come every four bars. Resolution comes only with the abrupt cessation of the pattern, however, since, being of the same length, the two lower voices can never converge.

As with most of the procedures we shall be discussing, there is a strong dramatic rationale for the use of this technique. The musical instability produced in these passages and in this scene in general reflects the instability caused by the transition of power from the recently buried king, Amenhotep III, to his son, Akhnaten. The higher, ternary voice, played by the higher wind instruments, is easily associated with the new religious order's desire for change; the lower, binary voices with the establishment's resistance to change. It is noteworthy that this unusual rhythmic solution does not stand on its own musically but coincides with a number of other signifiers of instability. Melodically, this passage is characterized by its extensive use of dissonant passing tones (b' and d"); harmonically, by the tonal ambiguity that characterizes much of the opera, between its two main key centers, E and A. It comes, moreover, right in the middle of a five-tiered increase in tempo: from 96 beats per minute (at rehearsal mark 42) to 132 (at rehearsal mark 44) to 144 (at rehearsal mark 46) to 176 (at rehearsal mark 50) and, finally, to 192 (at rehearsal mark 51).

Harmonic Cycles:
The Trilogy Motif, the Chaconne, and the Lament

Glass initially turned to repeated chord progressions as a means of expanding and illuminating the additive rhythmic processes that were the hallmark of his early style. Eventually, however, his renewed interest in harmonic and textural considerations led to the almost total abandonment of the tenets of his earlier language, mutable rhythmic units ceding in most places to units of fixed duration. The first combination of a harmonic progression with additive rhythmic structures in Glass's music was in the composition *Another Look at Harmony* (1975). The musical material developed in this composition was reincarnated as the core musical material of *Einstein*. The following example shows how harmonic cycles are modified in Trial One of *Einstein* by means of additive procedures applied at the level of short melodic/rhythmic cells (see example 10).

Both harmonic cycles and additive rhythms are used extensively in *Satyagraha* (see example 11) but identified explicitly with a historical form: the chaconne. Needless to say, Glass's combination of the chaconne with additive rhythmic structures is not found in seventeenth- and eighteenth-century examples of the form. In some sections of *Satyagraha*, the composer does revert to fixed bar lines, however, thus making the allusion

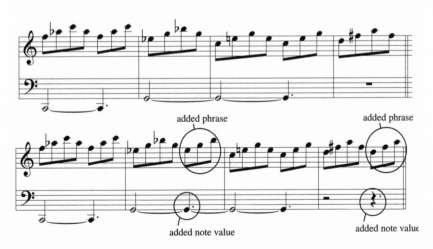

Example 10. *Einstein on the Beach*, Trial One. Additive rhythms applied on the level of cycles.

Example 11. *Satyagraha*, act 1, scene 1. Additive rhythms.

more obvious.[4] In *Akhnaten*, this tendency toward historical reference became stronger still.

In the chaconne, we find a quite distinctive musical form,[5] one that spread rapidly from its origins in the Spanish guitar and lute music of composers like Giovanni Foscarini to the keyboard variations of Girolamo Frescobaldi and Monteverdi. Later, it infiltrated the musical languages of virtually every noteworthy composer of the Baroque period. Eventually the form found its way to opera, where it was usually heard as an instrumental dance form—for example, in the music of the French composers Lully, Lalande, and Rameau. It played a particularly significant role in the court of Louis XVI, where it was heard at the conclusion of lengthy stage works performed in honor of the Sun King. Accompanying allegorical ballets in which the stars and planets all revolved around the sun, the chaconne, and its subtext connoting the platonic harmony of the spheres came to stand for the relationship between the king of France and his subjects. The cyclical structure of the chaconne, combined with the slow, stately rhythms that were favored in France at the time, made the dance the perfect vehicle for this function. This use of the chaconne resonates strongly in both of the scenes of *Akhnaten* where it is found, particularly in the hymn to the sun.

In Baroque music, the chaconne is recognizable by a number of structural traits, the most important of which is the bass ostinato or ground,

Example 12a. Act 1, scene 2, the coronation of Akhnaten. Trilogy theme.

which moves from the tonic to the dominant, in most cases within a fixed
four-bar frame. The ground serves as a constant against the shape-shifting
melodic and harmonic material it underpins, in a manner similar to other
variation forms, like the *romanesca, la folia, passamezzo,* and *bergamasca.*
The most common bass formula found in the chaconne is the descending
tetrachord, whose affective implications I shall turn to in a moment. This is
the formula Glass uses in *Satyagraha* and which he identifies as the paradigm example of the form in his discussions of that opera (see example 11).[6]

In *Akhnaten*, three (usually twice-repeated) variations of the chaconne
are heard in succession at various points in the opera (at the beginning of
the coronation scene and on three occasions in the hymn to the sun). The
first of these is not based on the descending tetrachord but on the so-called
trilogy theme (see example 12a). As the name implies, Glass identifies this
theme with all three trilogy operas and with their protagonists. It is heard
at the very beginning of *Einstein* and in all of the transitional passages in
that opera (see example 12b). Dubbed "knee plays" by Robert Wilson because of their flexible and transitional musicodramatic identity, these passages function in much the same way as the intermezzi (or interludes) of
Italian *opera seria.* In *Satyagraha*, the trilogy theme is heard at various dramatically significant junctures, most noticeably in act 1, scene 2 (Tolstoy
Farm [1904]; see example 12c), the scene in which the principles of the
Satyagraha lifestyle are first realized in the commune founded by Gandhi in

Example 12b. *Einstein on the Beach*, act 1, scene 1, knee play. Trilogy theme.

Example 12c. *Satyagraha*, act 3, scene 2, Tolstoy Farm. Trilogy theme.

South Africa, and in the final section of the final scene (act 3, New Castle March [1910]), a solo sung by the performer portraying Gandhi. The distinctive musical element of the theme is the descending melody a'–g'–c. At the beginning of *Einstein*, the motif is heard in precisely that form. In *Satyagraha*, it assumes the form of a harmonic variant that is at times only faintly recognizable as the same theme, casting doubt on whether the composer was actually thinking of the *Einstein* motif when writing *Satyagraha* or whether he simply found it convenient to associate the operas retrospectively when he decided to turn them into trilogy operas.[7] In *Akhnaten*, appearances of the theme are more leitmotivic and—not surprisingly, since Glass knew he was writing a trilogy opera at this time—more obvious, at times resembling *Einstein*'s melodic incarnation (e.g., act 3, epilogue, see example 12d), at others *Satyagraha*'s harmonic variant (e.g., act 1, scene 2, the coronation, and act 2, scene 3, the hymn to the sun; see example 12a).

The first articulation of the trilogy theme in *Akhnaten* is relatively hard to spot if you do not know where to look for it (see example 12a). Its first two notes are outlined in the arpeggio patterning of the upper voice. The final note is entirely absent from this voice, however. Its articulation in the strings is probably the clearest indication, then, that this is the *Einstein* theme, although the G-major and A-minor chords point more directly to its *Satyagraha* transformation. The melodic motif, which unlike its *Einstein* counterpart resolves to e in the final bar of the four-bar pattern, is heard only twice, after which it is merely implied in the harmony (A minor–G major first inversion–A minor first inversion–E dominant seventh). Otherwise, this pattern is a clearly identifiable manifestation of an ostinato formula known to Italian composers in the seventeenth century.

Example 12d. Act 3, epilogue. Trilogy theme.

Example 13. Act 1, scene 2, the coronation of Akhnaten. Chaconne pattern 2.

The bass formula a–b–c'–e' (1–2–3–5)—arrived at by inverting the descend-ing tetrachord, but jumping to the dominant instead of the subdominant in the final step, so as to preserve the harmonic integrity of the chord pro-gression—was found in both the chaconne and the passacaglia and could be related to its historical precursors on the strength of this information alone.[8] The second chaconne pattern (rehearsal marks 4 and 6; see example 13) consists of high winds (flutes, oboes, and clarinets) in contrary motion with low winds (a bass clarinet and bassoons). The motific foundation for both parts is the descending tetrachord. Upward and downward from each note of the tetrachord stream cascades of aeolian eighth notes. The third chaconne pattern (rehearsal marks 5 and 7; see example 14) comprises vio-las and cellos accompanying a descending trumpet line (c"–g'–e') that lags a constant eighth note behind the beat. The motif played by the trumpet is once again a transformation of the trilogy theme, this time found in Knee Plays Four and Five of *Einstein*.

Although based on historical practices, these passages have to them a distinct modern flavor, directly traceable to the music of antecedents like Bartók, Glass's teachers at Juilliard, Milhaud and Persichetti, and other in-fluential Americans, such as Copland. The "mirror" writing in the second pattern and the "echo" effect of the trumpet in the third pattern are both stock techniques in the modern repertory. Both of these techniques were also known to composers in the Baroque period, such as Monteverdi and

Example 14. Act 1, scene 2, the coronation of Akhnaten. Chaconne pattern 3.

Pietro Cavalli. The resulting ambiguity between old and new extends to broader considerations of form. While the surrounding musical context is unmistakably contemporary, structurally these passages function as ritornellos (or little returns). The origins of the ritornello go back to the formative period of opera as a genre. They were commonplace in late Renaissance madrigals and early Baroque operas such as Monteverdi's *Orfeo* (1607) and Emilio del Cavaliere's *La rappresentazione di anima e di corpo* (1600). The chaconne passages in both the coronation and the hymn to the sun are about as clear examples of the form as one is likely to find: In the coronation, the chaconne ritornello serves a conventional introductory function, while the structure of the hymn is divided into three sung sections, each of which is preceded by a chaconne ritornello (thus, the hymn can be said to be composed in "ritornello form").

Charles Jencks might refer to this harmonious combination of old and new as "double-coding," a distinctive feature of the postmodern ethos; Jann Pasler might term it "the emancipation of memory."[9] Such a combination, however, while constituting an emancipation of sorts, in a way goes beyond emancipation—in other words, what we are hearing is not only an emancipation *of* memory but a post-Cagean emancipation *from* memory, since the past is steadfastly grounded in the present in the combination of techniques employed by Glass and in the opaqueness, the "literalness," of his musical idiom.

Another feature of Glass's musical language that can be related to recent trends in postmodernism is his interest in representation. The passages discussed here represent on a number of elaborately intertwined levels. First, they represent simply by virtue of alluding to the past. Second, they represent within the dramatic context of the opera. The trumpet, for example, has a clear symbolic function in the opera, particularly in the hymn to the sun, where it serves as an obbligato, complementing and reinforcing the title character's solo voice. Given that this scene is essentially a one-on-one communication between Akhnaten and his god, written in the second person throughout, the obbligato easily becomes the personification of the sun god itself, its surrogate voice. Third, the passage is one of the clearest examples in the classical repertory of mimetic music; it belongs to the style of music known as *stile rappresentativo* (literally, representational style). The descending minor tetrachord was a universally recognized and powerful symbol of lament for Baroque musicians and audiences.[10] Indeed, Glass's use of this quite specific affective topos in *Akhnaten* is entirely appropriate, historically speaking. According to Ellan Rosand, the lament was understood by seventeenth-century audiences as "a soliloquy, a moment of particularly intense expression within the movement of a narrative structure" a moment that is set aside formally and dramatically, "as if in quotes."[11] Rosand explains the strong affective charge produced in the lament as follows: "Its strongly minor configuration, emphasising two of the most crucial degrees of the mode, invokes the full range of somber affects traditionally associated with the minor since the Renaissance; and, in its unremitting descent, its gravity, the pattern offers an analogue of obsession, perceptible as an expression of hopeless suffering."[12]

Other music critics, like Susan McClary and Joseph Kerman, have also drawn attention to the obsessional qualities of the lament. In the music of composers like Monteverdi and Purcell, this musical affect becomes a site of dysphorically marked excess, sandwiched between but distinct from the surrounding musical narrative, from the standpoint of which it is a deviation that musical rhetoric dictates *must* eventually be overcome.[13]

Glass appears to be well acquainted with this musical trope. In the chaconne passages in the coronation scene and the hymn to sun, the impression is of a period of time that has been partitioned off for the protagonist's tortured soul-searching—a moment of unsullied interiority or insight in the midst of the surrounding narrative turmoil. It is a moment when the suffering that is intrinsic to the human condition is magnified through repetition yet at the same time is transformed into something other than itself by the very act of enclosure, the very act of (partially noninvolved or alienated) perception.

How, then, does a musical form whose purpose is to evoke "endless suffering" fit in with the subject matter of the trilogy operas?[14] Glass is a practitioner of Tibetan Buddhism, and the idea that life is an endless round of suffering, what Buddhists refer to as samsara, is easily associated with the endless return of the chaconne combined with the negative affective charge of the lament. Glass himself concurs with a description of this music as "wheels inside wheels"; in addition to connoting the overall mechanical, clockwork feel of the music, the composer's Buddhist orientation combined with the subject matter of *Satyagraha* strongly suggests a discursive connection with the Buddhist and Hindu "wheel of life."

Glass goes further than this, however. So compelling to him is the association between the chaconne and Indian ideas that he tentatively posits an Asian origin to the musical form:

An interesting feature of this progression is that it is the same as one often heard in flamenco guitar music. This particular form of folk music was introduced into Spain by gypsies, who, it is believed, originated in India. There are very few harmonic practices shared by East and West since harmonic practice hardly ever turns up at all in Eastern music. This particular pattern is one of the few I know of that is common in the West and may have had its origin in the East.[15]

The genealogy Glass points to is speculative. His association of the chaconne with flamenco is historically accurate, but linking the form directly with Indian music requires something of a leap of faith. Whatever its origins, it represented for Glass, and perhaps for some listeners, a synthesis of what are conventionally regarded as European and Asian temporal modalities. Harmonic cadences tied together in even cyclical chains impart to the music a sense of stasis and rhythmic vitality that we recognize both from Western popular music and non-European musical styles. At the same time, they reminds us of a Western musical form whose effectiveness is premised not on its entanglement with large-scale narrative structures but on its ability to offer listeners a kind of sanctuary, a place apart from the influence of these structures. A utopia? Perhaps.

The chaconne and similar variation forms exerted an almost unparalleled influence over the public imagination in the 1980s. (Pachelbel's *Canon* has never had so good!) At around the same time as Glass began his work on *Akhnaten*, Michael Nyman was composing the soundtrack to the Peter Greenaway film *The Draughtsman's Contract* (1982), in which both the chaconne and the countertenor voice were used liberally. Another Nyman and Greenaway collaboration, *A Zed and Two Noughts* (1985), which came out a year after the premiere of *Akhnaten*, consists predominantly of chaconnelike repeated figures. While some of the popularity of this kind of music can be attributed to composers such as Glass and Nyman, other things were going on in the 1980s that might have influenced both of these composers' orientations. The most important of these was a growing interest in preclassical forms of Western music in general; Nyman, for example, regularly performs with and composes for groups interested in historical performance practices. He is one of many (post)minimalists who have taken an interest in such practices, such as Steve Reich and Louis Andriessen. Glass's interest in the chaconne can therefore be seen as reflecting a broader tendency.

Harmonic Ambiguity, Bitonality, and Dual Modality

Probably the most distinctive feature of the music of *Akhnaten* is its ambiguous tonality. Various aspects of Glass's style play a part in making the music ambiguous: First, Glass avoids or disregards the conventional markers of common language tonality. One of the most potent and stereotyped of these is the leading note, the raised seventh degree of the major or minor scale. There is some use of the leading note in *Akhnaten*, part of which is conventional, but typically it does not dictate the harmonic movement to the same degree as one might expect.

Second, Glass's voices move in mysterious (i.e., unconventional) ways. An obvious example is the widespread use of parallel movement. Parallel movement was common, of course, at the beginning of the twentieth century, due to the influence of Claude Debussy and the impressionists. Examples of parallel voice leading can also be found in the music of Stravinsky, Bartók, and many other twentieth-century composers, particularly in the first half of the twentieth century. The technique became less common as the century progressed, however, in large part because of the growing feeling among composers that they should somehow differentiate their music from popular idioms. (Parallel movement is extremely commonplace in popular music due to the pervasiveness of modal practices as well as the widespread use of the guitar, on which parallel voice leading is idiomatic. In the present cultural climate, therefore, parallel voice leading invariably carries popular connotations.) Movement in parallel fifths is typical of Glass's musical language, but so is movement in fourths and sixths, which are produced when he treats a chord like the second inversion major triad, whose usage is highly conventionalized, in an unconventional way. Glass's technique resembles the *fauxbourdon* (or false bass) practices of the fifteenth and sixteenth centuries. The term denotes the "false" tonal relations that arise when a first inversion chord moves to other similar chords in parallel motion. In such circumstances, the movement of the bass and other coloristic considerations take precedence over tonal function.

Third, Glass uses chords that are intrinsically ambiguous. Inversions are a case in point. The second inversion, or tonic six-four, is an important part of conventional tonal practice precisely because of its functional ambiguity. Even though it is marked in analytical practice as a first-degree or tonic chord, its tonal function is closer to that of the fifth degree, or dominant, because of its bass note, which is the fifth. Thus, it is construed primarily as a dominant with some superimposed coloristic properties of the tonic. The tonal ambiguity of this chord is exploited by Glass but in some quite unconventional ways: rather than serving simply as a cadence chord, as they do in common language tonality, six-fours are likely to turn up just about anywhere. Another example of unstable chords are chords to which tones have been added or subtracted. This practice of adding, subtracting, or simply omitting tones can be compared to additive rhythmic procedures, but here "arithmetical" processes are construed horizontally. Adding one new tone to a chord, say a second or sixth, produces interesting coloristic effects but does not challenge the tonality significantly. Add another harmonically related tone to this, say a perfect fifth or major third from the initial tone, and then subtract a tone from the initial chord, say its fifth, and the balance can easily tip in favor of a new chord function, with the chord tones of the initial chord sounding as added tones in their new functional context. Glass typically does this over extended periods of time. A single chord progression may doggedly assert itself for ten minutes or longer, as in the funeral scene, but all the time minute transformations are taking place in the pitch constitution of the individual chords. These changes and the ambiguities engendered by them, in combination with other coloristic, thematic, and rhythmic devices, produce sufficient musical interest to prevent the listener who is attentive to everything that is going on in the music from getting bored.

Fourth, in "classic" major/minor tonality, there is some degree of functional specificity to chords; the diminished triad, for example, is characteristically built on the subtonic, and the dominant (or flattened) seventh is characteristically built on the dominant. In Glass's musical language, any chord construct can, in principle, fall on any degree of the scale, which means that the chances of tonally ambiguous chord progressions arising and being sustained over extended periods of time are greater, since there is little indication in the pitch constitution of the individual chords of their place within the tonal hierarchy. Even when dissonant tones are included within a chord construct, rarely do they determine its behavior in the context of the music in the manner that tradition dictates. And this has a great deal to do with repetition. Instead of signaling the need for immediate release, dissonances are incorporated into the sonorous fabric of the progression. In other words, we are reconditioned to accept them.

Fifth, Glass often uses pedal notes or chords. The effect of these pedals varies greatly: They can reinforce the dominant tonality of the music; they can create a dissonant undercurrent to the dominant tonality (often undermining it completely, as in the final moments of the funeral scene); and they can produce subtle polytonal effects when sounded in the upper voices, especially in the case of chords. A pedal chord in the upper voices can be heard in the background or the foreground. It can be heard as a coloristic addition to the dominant tonality; if it becomes strong enough, however, it may usurp tonal prominence. When two different chords are sounded at the same time and these chords are distinguished from one another in register and timbre, as is the case in the hymn to the sun, one might refer to one of these chords as a pedal chord; depending on the relationship between the two chords and the dominant tonality of the passage, however, it might be more accurate to speak of bitonality.

Finally, the music of Akhnaten makes frequent references to the tonal center of A—usually A minor, although there is some fluctuation between major and minor modes, the dramatic implications of which I will discuss below. So powerful are the references that one might even say that the entire opera is in the key of A minor. Ambiguous chord progressions almost invariably arise when reference is made to the home key of the opera from the vantage point of another key.

DUAL MODALITY

Perhaps the simplest but also one of the most striking forms of ambiguity found in the opera is what is sometimes referred to as dual modality. It denotes a form of ambiguity in which the key center is the same in two parts but the modal characteristics of these parts are different. Although theoretically possible with all of the so-called church modes, the most common and immediately recognizable form of dual modality arises when the major and minor modes are superimposed. The result is a pungent minor-second dissonance between the third degrees of the two modes. This technique is found in the music of Copland, Bartók, and Milhaud, among others, all of whom influence strongly other aspects of Glass's style.

Pitch class theory may tell us that the two are merely different pitches in a slightly expanded diatonic subset, and the savvy twelve-tone analyst may claim that the technique is redundant, since composers have so systematically undermined the premises of common language tonality that we no longer hear things in terms of major and minor. From the standpoint of recent postmodern theory, however, which is specifically interested in relationships and is reluctant to view musical phenomena from the vantage point of a detached aesthetic "high ground," both of these arguments run into difficulties. For starters, major/minor tonality continues to exert a profound influence over the public imagination. If it did not, then the Romantic repertory would no longer occupy the privileged position it does. In popular culture, too, the major/minor binarism continues to be a force to be reckoned with, although it is definitely not the force it once was. For the postmodern musician, who has abandoned the search for an authentic language and who does not wish to view the world around him or her with ironic condescension, the appropriation of techniques from the past usually serves some specific representational or dramatic purpose. The use of this technique by Glass is a nonironic tipping of the cap in the direction of his "teachers" (in the case of Milhaud, ignore the quotation marks), which, given the rebellious zeal with which the minimalists shook off the influence of these teachers in the 1960s, easily takes on a conciliatory appearance. The musical context in which the technique is found is not, however, one his teachers would have recognized.

Major/minor "coincidences" can be found in both of the previous trilogy operas. In *Akhnaten*, however, their leitmotivic and specifically illustrative resonances are exploited more fully. Examples of dual modality can be found at various points in this opera, especially in those scenes and tonal centers that are closely associated with Akhnaten's adversaries. This has important implications for the narrative construction of the opera, which I will discuss in chapter 4.

In the following example from the prelude (example 15), the major/minor clash takes place in the key center of B-flat. The simultaneous presence of D-flat and D-natural in the fourth chord of the progression indicates to the listener that something is awry. The composer does not leave it to chance, however, that we will recognize this musical sign when we hear it; it is underlined in unequivocal terms in one of the strongest and most ominous themes in the opera. The theme begins on F, the fifth of the B-flat chord, jumps to its root and then onto its minor third, D-flat, dislodging at the same time the major modality of the chord onto its minor counterpart. Because this motif becomes associated directly with Akhnaten's transgression, his heresy, I will refer to it as the transgression motif; more on this below.

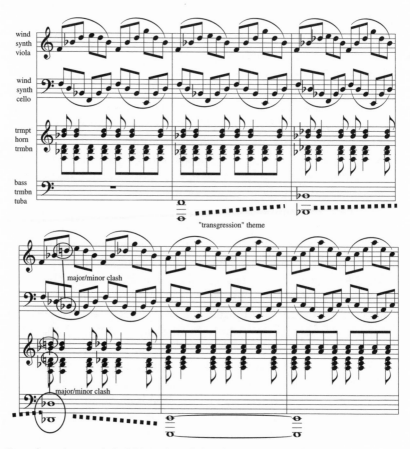

Example 15. Act 1, prelude. Major/minor clash and "transgression" theme.

Glass's first acquaintance with polytonality can be traced to his student days and his studies with Vincent Persichetti and Darius Milhaud. Along with Stravinsky, Milhaud was one of the earliest and most prominent exponents of polytonality in the twentieth century. The paradigm example of polytonality, Stravinsky's famous "*Petrushka* chord," in which C-major and F-sharp major triads are heard simultaneously, is one of jarring dissonance. Stravinsky's clashing tonalities—as well as those of other noteworthy polytonalists such as Bartók (in his *Bagatelles* for piano), Charles Ives (in his *Sixty-seventh Psalm*), and even Benjamin Britten *(Folk Songs of the British Isles, Vol. 1, No. 6)*—can be regarded as largely independent of and even totally oblivious to one another. In such music, which has earned itself the droll title "the school of wrong notes," the contradictory element invariably outweighs the complementary one. Perhaps the best evidence of this is Milhaud's second violin sonata, in certain passages of which the upper part comprises only sharps (the black notes of the piano) and the lower part only naturals (the white notes of the piano). The result is a strange kind of musical apartheid that can produce interesting musical effects but that in the long run is taxing on the ear and on many listeners' patience.

In the first theoretical exposition on the subject, "Polytonalité et atonalité" (1923), Milhaud concentrates predominantly on the technicalities of setting up two strongly dissonant tonalities at the same time.[16] The fact that he begins his exposition by discussing Bach's duets attests to the fundamentally contrapuntal assumptions of his approach. Other more recent discussions of polytonality, such as those of Persichetti and Leon Dallin, have invariably followed suit, focusing on the "wrong notes" aspect of the technique, what jazz musicians refer to as "playing out."[17] Even in supposedly homophonic music the essence of polytonality is contrapuntal; it is grounded in the ability of the listener to distinguish between two more or less perceptually distinct parts.

Milhaud's approach to polytonality provides some valuable clues to the mechanics of tonal ambiguity in Glass's music, but it is important to recognize the differences between the two techniques, the most significant of which is the degree of stability achieved for tonal centers in Glass's music as a result of repetition combined with the euphonious diatonic texture of the music. Repetition permits a high level of stability to be maintained in the music, as does the strong emphasis the composer places on pitches that remain sonorous in each of the key centers. Only rarely do the parts wander off on contradictory tonal crusades. Both of these factors contribute to the overall effect produced in the music, which tends to vacillate gently from one key center to another and back again rather than modulating endlessly. In these tonally ambiguous passages, modulations are in fact a kind of deceptive pseudomodulation. The music appears to change key, but just when the listener thinks he or she has arrived at a new tonal center, the music swings back to the initial key, whose own tonal foundation might be less than convincing. Glass puts it like this:

Of course I was [influenced by Milhaud], but I don't think it sounds very much like him. It's a very different approach to it. It's not so much about setting up two keys at the same time, which is what those composers did, but we're treating a situation where a piece can be viewed as being in more than one key at the same time. . . . An example is those kinds of optical illusions where you can look at a stair going one way or you can look at it going the other way but you really can't look both ways. So basically, you can hear it in one tonality with added tones or you can hear it in another tonality with added tones but the idea is not to hear them going on at the same time. But I did study with Milhaud. I like him very much, I like his music, but that's a much "notier" way of writing music.[18]

Examples of "classic" polytonality can be found in *Akhnaten*. Typically, though, the independence of Glass's parts is less pronounced than in early twentieth-century examples of the technique. Polytonality often arises when the music modulates away from the home key of the opera, A minor (e.g., the temple scene [act 2, scene 1], the attack and fall [act 3, scene 2], and the hymn to the sun [act 2, scene 4]). These modulations are seldom entirely convincing, however, since the music invariably makes reference back to the home key, even while it is in the process of establishing a new key center. In the temple scene, for example, a pedal chord of A (no third) remains in place while the rest of the music descends through a broken chord of A-flat major before eventually resolving back to A (see example 16).

This kind of polytonality is not, however, restricted to the opera's home key. The trumpet fanfare at the beginning of the scene called City/Dance (act 2, scene 3; see example 17) is made up predominantly of black notes, with some significant exceptions: middle C is sounded in the first two bars, and serves as a kind of pivot tone between A minor, the tonality of the scene

Example 16. Act 2, scene 1, the temple.

Example 17. Act 2, scene 3, City/Dance. Fanfare.

and arguably the entire opera, and A-flat major, the tonality of the passage; a "passing chord" of F minor is sounded in the lower part in the fourth bar, and F is again heard in the final chord of the progression (bar 6), facilitating the transition between the penultimate chord of the progression, a pungent E-flat second chord, and the initial chord of the dance proper, A minor. The tonal foundation of the passage is provided by the initially stated A-flat major (added second) chord. The root and fifth of this chord form a pedal that is held until the end of the passage. As the bass line sinks down through an extended version of the descending tetrachord motif—a pentachord that comes to rest on a menacing D-flat, a tritone away from A—a number of bitonal compound chords are produced: G-flat major/A-flat (no third)/E-flat minor, F minor/A-flat/E-flat (no third), and E-flat dominant seventh (no third)/A-flat (no third). Note that the added second of the initial A-flat chord, b-flat', turns this chord, which is held over all of the subsequent chords, into a kind of ambiguous A-flat/E-flat hybrid. Like the second inversion tonic, the added second chord is drawn toward both the tonic and the dominant tonal functions, so when the passage resolves onto A minor, it does so not from the standpoint of A-flat or E-flat but from a conglomeration of both of these chords. In fact, the linear motion suggested in the voice leading is so strong that it might take precedence over *any* tonal considerations, given that the tonality is more than a little ambiguous. The ear easily fixes on two melodic lines: the descending pentachord, a-flat to D-flat, which, in order to avoid an inelegant augmented second jump, slides up a major third onto f before eventually sinking down onto e, the bass note of the second inversion A-minor chord that comes next; and, even more significantly, a simple step-wise motion from c', the third of both A minor and A-flat major, down a major second to b-flat and up again. This voice leading is both simple and ingenious, and, like the tonal environment in which it is found, it is para-digmatically Glassian.

Hybrid chords are characteristic of the opera in general. Numerous pas-sages are written in a kind of elusive A/E hybrid tonality that frequently plays on the ambiguity of the added second chord. Significant examples of A/E hybrids occur in the coronation (act 1, scene 2), the temple (act 2, scene 1), and the family (act 3, scene 1) scenes. This example from the tem-ple scene illuminates two kinds of bitonality (see example 18): classic "wrong notes" bitonality, between the black-note chord A-flat minor and the surrounding white-note chords and the intrinsic ambiguity of the added second chord, which here includes not only the second, b and b', but also the flat seventh, g" (the third of E minor), making the ambiguity be-tween the tonic and the dominant tonal function even more pronounced.

In Akhnaten's hymn to the sun we see the same perfect fifth pedal in the upper voices, as in the first example from the temple scene (rehearsal mark 10; see example 19). What makes this passage interesting is that bar can be interpreted in two ways. From the perspective we have been discussing, it looks like a fairly obvious example of polytonality. The A (no third) of the upper part is separated in both register and timbre from the F-sharp (no third) of the lower part. In combination, however, the two chords form a euphonious F-sharp minor seventh chord, which would seem to under-mine this interpretation. Ingenious use of ambiguous chords in the re-mainder of the progression, however, strengthens the impression of two distinct tonal centers. (I will return to the question of ambiguous tonality in this passage below.)

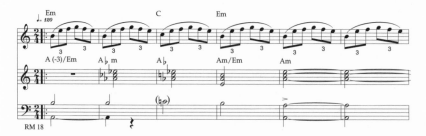

Example 18. Act 2, scene 1, the temple. "Classic" bitonality and use of ambiguous compound chords.

Example 19. Act 2, scene 3, hymn to the sun. First stanza.

Glass's use of polytonality, in combination with tonal ambiguity, is arguably at its most sophisticated in the first scene of the opera, the funeral of Amenhotep III. The opening twenty bars of the scene consist of a straightforward alternation of e to f-sharp and d-sharp to f-sharp ostinatos, the key movement in terms of voice leading being the half-tone descent from the fifth of A minor, e, to its tritone, d-sharp (see the cello/bassoon part in example 20). There is no indication at this stage, however, that the music is in that key, although some sense of A minor may be carried over from the prelude. The sense of E as the tonic in these opening bars is supported not only because it is heard first but also because of our musical conditioning: it is extremely rare in common language tonal practice, first, for a bass ostinato—or riff—such as this to begin on any degree of the scale other than the tonic and, second, for the initially stated chord to be in any position other than its root. The chord with which it alternates, a first inversion B major (initially with no root) might appear pallid by comparison were it not for the sense of release we are conditioned to hear when the initially stated major second (e to f-sharp) transforms itself

Example 20. Act 1, scene 1, funeral of Amenhotep III.

into a minor third (d-sharp to f-sharp), the latter being the more stable interval of the two. Thus, we are presented with something of a contradiction in tonal terms right from the outset. There is a strong sense that the music is circling around the tone E, but our harmonic conditioning seems to be telling us otherwise.

The ambiguity of the opening bars is exacerbated upon the entry of the male chorus and brass (rehearsal mark 4), when the initially stated e to f-sharp ostinato transforms itself into a root-position A chord (initially no third) (see the appropriate parts in example 20). Soon afterward, a pedal on c-sharp is added (rehearsal mark 6), and this becomes the major third of A major and the ninth of B major, or, according to a more obvious interpretation, the major third of both the perfect and the diminished, or lydian, A major chords.[19] The psychological impact of the original ostinato on e is sufficient, however, to remain ingrained in the memory of the listener, undermining to some extent the manifest tonality of the upper voices. Although heard only intermittently in the initial cycle, the ostinato movement from e to d-sharp (over a constant of f-sharp) is heard continuously in the second and the third (and final) cycles of the scene, turning the initial chord into an ambiguous six-four chord. The bass ostinato in E never entirely succeeds in ousting A major from its position of tonal dominance, but it does arguably constitute a second (polyphonic *and* polytonal) voice that is to some extent experientially distinct from the surrounding harmonic texture.

In tonal terms, this passage is extremely difficult to categorize. Assuming that the funeral is in E, the vacillation between the two chords (in jazz/rock chord terminology, E sus. 4 [no fifth] to B9) would be a fairly standard I–V progression. If the initial chord is not E but A major, however, we are looking at a modally inflected stepwise movement from the tonic to the supertonic (I–II), or, as Robert Fink has claimed, a harmonically static A-major to A-lydian linear movement. I tend to hear the music in three, none too distinct, phases: initially, the overriding impression is of an implied E to B (I–V) chord movement. This impression is gradually eclipsed, although certainly not refuted (the gravitational pull of E is felt throughout the scene), by the harmonically static A-major to A-lydian shift in the upper voices. Toward the end of the scene, however, the tonic to supertonic movement in A major gains the upper hand, weakened somewhat, however, by the influence of the implied pedal on E.

If this already seems complicated, the influence of a third polyphonic/polytonal line makes the tonality of the scene even more difficult to get a handle on. The entire tonal fabric of the scene is regularly shaken by the addition of three noxious D-sharp notes in the bass instruments (basses, bass clarinet, bassoons, and trombones), resolving to a fourth, F-sharp (the pedal note of the initial ostinato and the fifth of B), in the final bar of the four-bar pattern (rehearsal mark 7) (see the bottom line of example 20). Once again, the emphasis is on the diminished fifth, or tritone, the *diabolus in musica* of medieval music. This undermines particularly the initial chord of the two, although the resolution onto the second chord, B major, is not complete either, as the new line moves from the third in the first bar of this chord to its fifth in the second, turning it from a first inversion into a second-inversion chord that itself demands resolution. What is significant about this bitonal intrusion is not only the disruption it causes from the "horizontal" standpoint of chord functions but the impact it has on large-scale linear formations in the opera as a whole. In a manner reminiscent of block additive procedures, this pattern accumulates momentum as the scene progresses, and this momentum's influence extends into the next scene and arguably beyond. At rehearsal mark 18, the two-note pattern becomes the three-note D-sharp–F-sharp–F-sharp–G-sharp, thus guiding the listener toward the instrumental interlude (in A) that follows. When the pattern is reintroduced in the next section, initially it sticks doggedly to a single note, D-sharp (rehearsal mark 36). Shortly afterward, however, melodic movement is introduced gradually, at rehearsal mark 38 from D-sharp to F-sharp; and at rehearsal mark 39 once again from D-sharp to F-sharp to G-sharp, the leading note of A. Thus, the whole scene is effectively pushed toward the key signature of the next scene. At the beginning of that scene (the coronation of Akhnaten), the melodic line continues upward, initially according to the implied harmonic pattern of the final moments of the funeral, from the tonic, a, to the supertonic, b, and then, in first chaconne pattern of three, onward to c' and e'. As Fink correctly observes, the transition from one scene to the next is experienced as a substantial release of accumulated linear energy; the result of the upward linear motion in the bass line is an important part of this, as is the pent-up frustration caused by oscillating maniacally between A and B. The tonal ambiguity of the music also participates in creating this impression, however. Due to the prominence of the second-inversion tonic, the whole of the funeral can thus be regarded as a pseudomodulation to the dominant, which resolves back to the tonic at the beginning of the coronation.

Both the tonal ambiguity of the funeral and the "stacked" triads of the hymn to the sun directly recall Milhaud's early approach to polytonality. We have discussed already how the polytonal composers generally wanted to make the technique as audible as possible by sharply contrasting the two tonalities they were using. The genesis of the style, however, suggests a somewhat different approach. The first examples of polytonality in twentieth-century music arose as a direct result of the use of the extended ninth, eleven, and thirteenth chords that were the mainstay of the French impressionist school. In early examples of the technique, the stacked triads that these chords comprised were allowed to emerge and submerge from their original tonal context and in so doing to assert new tonal bases that called into question the tonality from which they emerged. The effect produced was of continual modulation: A new key center was suggested and, depending on its degree of sonority in relation to the original key center, it was allowed to usurp the position of the latter, at the same time rendering its constituent tones either unwelcome dissonances in the new tonal context or else subsuming them into the new key center as happy consonant coincidences. The technique is very similar to the harmonic ambiguity I will discuss in the next section. The prominence of nonsonorous independent lines in Milhaud's music differentiates it from Glass's technique, however.

As I have mentioned, the presence of ambiguity in much of *Akhnaten* can be attributed to the reluctance of opera's home key, A minor, to take a backseat, functionally speaking. Nowhere is this more apparent than in the family scene (act 3, scene 1). The eight-bar chord progression sung by Akhnaten's daughters at the beginning of this scene remains essentially unchanged throughout its course. It consists of a straightforward alternation of E-minor (predominantly in its second inversion) and A-minor chords, deviating briefly to a G-minor/major modally inflected cadence chord at the end. E minor seem to be the stronger candidate for tonic, given its position at the head of the progression and the presence of a fairly ineffectual quasi-pedal on E sounded by a solo bassoon. The bassoon part would, of course, turn the chord inversions on their head under ordinary circumstances, but its tessitural and textural separation from the female voices weakens its hold somewhat over the harmonies it underpins. It is moreover, silent for the greater part of each E-minor bar. The uninverted voicing of A minor in the choral voices compensates, then, for these factors, since it is intrinsically more stable than its counterpart, E minor, which is never, except in the final bar of the progression, heard in root position. G minor/major is a congenial choice as pivotal chord, its minor triad being the flatted seventh degree of A minor, arrived at by a simple parallel movement in all voices, and its major triad the third degree in E minor, transformed into the tonic by the simple addition of the root of that chord.

In functional terms, then, the gravitational pull of the following two tonal centers is felt (see also example 21):

chords	$e^6\,^6_4$	a	$e^6\,^6_4$	a	$e^6\,^6_4$	a	g^6	$G^6\,e^6$	$e^6\,^5_3$
E min.	i	iv	i	iv	i	i	iii	III i	i
A min.	v	i	v	i	v	i	♭vii	♭VII v	v

The ambiguity of this passage is heightened by a number of clashing overlaps between the soprano and alto voices. The altos' inverted E-minor triad is held from the first bar through to the first two beats of the second, resulting in two abrasive dissonances: b' and g' in the altos against a' and c" in the sopranos. In the second bar, A minor is transferred from the sopranos to the altos and is carried over the bar line to the first two beats of the third bar, resulting, once again, in friction with the chord tones of E minor, now in the sopranos. For one third of each bar, then, it is inaccurate to refer to

The Musical Language of Akhnaten / 81

Example 21. Act 3, scene 1, the family.

these chords as simple minor triads; they mingle to such a degree that they should rather be thought of as A-minor/E-minor compound chords.

One of the most intriguing examples of tonal ambiguity in the opera can be found in the hymn to the sun (see example 19, page 77). Extending the dual tonal perspective of the initial chord of the hymn to the rest of the progression, it is interesting to note that at no point are either of the two tonal centers, F-sharp minor seventh and A major, refuted in a convincing way. The crucial chord is the final chord in the pattern, E (in the initial pattern, no third). The presence of the expected major third in this chord would instantly deprive the progression of its ambiguity. If this pitch, the leading note of A major, G-sharp, was added, we would have a nice, conventional dominant fifth-degree chord, which would situate the progression unequivocally in the key of A major, the third chord in the cycle. But that does not appear to be Glass's intention. The third of this chord is withheld, and when it does make a fleeting appearance—as a passing note in the scalar ascent that marks the culmination of the cadence in its later manifestations— the pitch that is sounded is not G-sharp, with its strong gravitational pull toward the tonic (A major) but G-natural. The E-minor chord that results resolves just as convincingly onto F-sharp minor seventh as it does onto A major, thus retaining the ambiguity between the two tonal centers: the former is a conventional dominant to tonic movement, the latter a stepwise diatonic movement with a modal feel, but both are equally tenable hearings. So the question becomes, when and onto what chord does the cadence resolve: in the penultimate bar of the sequence, onto A major, or in the initial bar, onto F-sharp minor seventh? In fact, the E (no third) (or E minor) chord resolves simultaneously onto both of these chords in the initial bar, as well as resolving in the third chord of the sequence onto an uninverted A-major chord. Both this chord and the initial compound chord make direct reference back to the home key of the opera, A minor, whose presence is underlined in the three chaconne ritornellos that interrupt this progression during the course of the scene. The tonally ambiguous passage emerges out of the chaconne progression as a deceptive (or interrupted) cadence, a deception that is reenacted every time E minor resolves onto the initial chord of the pattern. As we have seen, however, the deception is twofold, since the F-sharp minor of the initial measure has been deprived of much of its tonal clout by its binary dissection into semiautonomous tonal entities.

I have attempted to schematize the unusual tonal effects produced in this pattern in the table below. I am aware of the shortcomings endemic to this kind of representation. It is, however, the best way I could think of illuminating the idea of contradictory gravitational pulls exerted by distinct tonal centers. Chords separated by slashes denote bitonal compound chords. The tonality that precedes the slash is the one that I perceive to be strongest. Bold type is used as a tentative indication of how the listener's perceptual attention might fluctuate between the two tonal poles.

chord progression	f♯ /A	f♯ /b	A	e
A major	**vi**/ I	**vi**/ II	I	v
F-sharp minor	i	i	III	♭**vii**

This progression is expanded and contracted throughout the hymn, usually as dictated by the text, often using procedures that resemble the additive processes found in Glass's earlier music. In the second stanza of the hymn a macrostructural pattern emerges that forms the foundation for the remainder of the scene; it comprises two contracted variants of the initial cadence followed by one that is expanded (rehearsal mark 21; see example 22).

Example 22. Act 2, scene 3, hymn to the sun. Macrocycle two, first stanza.

chord progression	f♯/A	e	f♯/A	
A maj./min.	vi/ I	v	vi/ I	v
F-sharp minor	i	♭vii	i	♭vii

chord progression	f♯A	a	b/ a (-3)	A	e
A maj./min.	vi/ I	i	ii / i	I	v
F-sharp minor	i	iii	iv / iii	III	♭vii

Despite its contraction and expansion, the harmonic ambiguity of the original progression is maintained in these variants. It is significant that the third chord of the final cadence in the above example is split into the bitonal compound chord B minor/A minor (no third); this bitonal division was also indicated strongly in the initial pattern we discussed in Akhnaten's melodic line, which traverses two of the chord tones of B minor, b' and d". Here, the chord movement is confirmed in the cello, which outlines a third-less B arpeggio against a viola part that comprises the first and fifth of A and the minor third of B. Most striking, however, is the major second dissonance that is heard in the upper voices between Akhnaten and his obbligato trumpet accompaniment. This, more than anything else, drives home the fact that we are dealing with two perceptually distinct tonal centers.

Robert Fink makes a convincing case that the first, penultimate, and final chords of the hymn progression are related thematically to the three-pitch trilogy motif (see examples 12a–d, pp. 63–64).[20] If he is correct, then the whole hymn can be heard as an impressive elaboration and reiteration of the opening bars of *Einstein*—a fitting moment of apotheosis for the trilogy as a whole. Add to that the fact that hymn progression is interspersed with chaconne ritornellos that closely resemble those found in *Satyagraha* and we have a coming together of musical resources that seems to justify talking of the trilogy operas as a coherent musical entity.

No matter how closely related the hymn is thematically to *Einstein*, it is certainly related to it in terms of compositional technique. The kind of ambiguous tonality found in the hymn is present in another of the core musical themes from *Einstein*. Glass analyzes this progression as follows:

key of F minor

f	D♭	B♭♭		
(I)	(VI)	(♭IV)		
		A	B	E
		(IV)	(V)	(I)

key of E major

"At first glance," he writes,

[this] appears to be a traditional cadential formula, the time-honoured closing phrase which, in a variety of forms, became highly developed in the Baroque period and lasted well into the present. However, there is an altered or pivotal chord in the middle that results in a closing chord a half-step below what one would normally expect. It is this lowered resolution of the cadence that motivates its repetition. In the final scene of Einstein, this goes on for over eight minutes. What sustains musical interest over that length of time is the additive process which, when applied to the cadence, produces a lengthy and dramatic rhythmic development.[21]

Milos Raickovich has shown that this is just one of many tonally ambiguous progressions in *Einstein*. In fact, tonal ambiguity appears to be one that opera's governing features.[22] In *Einstein*, however, tonal ambiguity is not made explicit using polytonal devices, as it is in *Akhnaten*.

The same can be said of *Satyagraha*. *Village Voice* critic Gregory Sandow describes the initial chord progression in the final act of *Satyagraha* thus: "[The third act] begins with more than a hundred repetitions of a single two-chord harmonic progression, F minor to E major, light brown to dark blue, which might better be called an oscillation because it has no root; either chord could be home base."[23] This is not an isolated example, however: In the final progression of the scene, a "three-chord oscillation" is also heard, this one between F major, G major, and A minor.[24] Sandow's reference to more than a hundred repetitions is, of course, slightly misleading, since, like most of Glass's music, the passage in question contains very little literal repetition. As in the *Einstein* passage analyzed by the composer, the chord progression from *Satyagraha* is the subject of myriad rhythmic, melodic, and textural alterations.

While it is useful to distinguish between classic polytonality and the kind of tonal ambiguity Glass seems to favor, from the standpoint of perception the two techniques are not all that different. Polytonality is an elaborate form of counterpoint; the way we hear tonally ambiguous music is similar. When listening to contrapuntal music, we are generally unable to concentrate on more than one line at a time; one line becomes the focus of our attention, and the other becomes a kind of background line, which is not to say that we are totally unaware of its movement: typically, attention flickers between the voice that is prominent or manifest at any given moment and that which is secondary or latent. One analogy that has been used to describe the cognitive processes involved in listening to contrapuntal music is the Gestalt-psychology idea of a visual pattern that is capable of ground-figure reversal. A similar perceptual process is involved with the kind of ambiguous tonality in which Glass has taken an interest. The tonal ground for one's perceptions is governed by the initial key center until an increasing amount of evidence supporting a second key center persuades the listener to shift perspective. Provided that the music neither continues modulating nor abandons the initial key center entirely, this key center remains a latent force until it reappears at the end of the cycle.

Glass's example of reversing stairs provides a valid analogy for the cognitive processes involved in listening to music constructed in this way. In optical illusions such as Sandro del Prete's *Winding Staircase up to Belvédère II* or M. C. Escher's *Relativity*, regardless of whether one begins looking from above or below, at some point one is forced to shift perspective in order to make sense of what one is seeing. But at the same time, the integrity of the picture as a whole is not forfeited. A similar shift of perspective is involved in the transition from one tonal center to another in harmonically ambiguous passages of music. And a similar sense of the uncanny results from the effortless way in which contradictory parts are combined to form a harmonious whole. There are no *wrong* notes, just an unfathomable strangeness.

Harmonic ambiguity was not, of course, invented by Glass. It has probably been around in one form or another since people first began to make music, and it is present in much of today's popular music as well as in many non-European styles. Glass's handling of harmonically ambiguous musical materials is distinctive, however. Ambiguity plays a significant role in Steve Reich's music as well, but it can be compared to Glass's approach only in the most general terms. Other artists such as Meredith Monk and Laurie Anderson admit to having been influenced by Glass, but both of these women transformed Glass's hallmark chord changes into something recognizably their own. An example of a tonally ambiguous passage similar to that which I have been discussing is analyzed by Susan McClary in her *Feminine Endings.*[25] Tonal ambiguity in Anderson's "O Superman" arises when A-flat major and C-minor triads are alternated over a pedal of middle C. A-flat, being the initially stated tonality and in conventional terms the "stronger" major chord, appears to have a valid claim to tonal precedence, except that it appears in its first inversion. As the music progresses, the ear tends to favor the more stable C-minor triad rather than the inverted major triad, which is ordinarily regarded as stronger. While there are fluctuations in the way the music is heard in favor of one or the other of the tonal centers, the ambivalence between the two is allowed to continue unresolved until the cessation of both. This handling of harmonic material is distinctly Glassian, although the musical end result sounds little like Glass, as a result of Anderson's distinctive approach in other musical parameters.

Large scale structures

A characteristic feature of *Akhnaten* is the palpability of its large-scale structures. The underlying presence of structures such as these in the previous two trilogy operas has been observed by a number of analysts and music critics. Milos Raickovich, in the final pages of his impressive analytical exposition of the first trilogy opera, notes that "it is possible to characterise *Einstein* by its main tonal-center, as an opera in C."[26] In a similar vein, Gregory Sandow refers to the final scene of *Satyagraha* as "a single plagal cadence, a gigantic 'Amen.'"[27] Finally, in a *Village Voice* review of *Akhnaten*, Leighton Kerner writes: "It begins and ends in A minor. Yards and yards of that tonality stretch over the score, and over the theater like a shroud."[28] For once agreeing with a critic, the composer concedes in *MPG* that this description is "both poetic and accurate."[29] In Glass's own words, he "began to think about musical material in a different way" when writing the final installment of the trilogy, "exploring key relationships in terms of the overall piece."[30] The overall piece can, in this particular case, be said to be in the key of A minor because of the frequent references that are made back to that key from other key centers. When I asked Glass if he thought of *Akhnaten* as an opera in A minor, he replied: "I think there must be some notion of that. . . . The feeling of A minor is almost always there somewhere."[31] A careful examination of the music, not only at the level of individual techniques but also at that of larger tonal blocks and the linear relations between these blocks, reveals this to be the case.

Cadencelike constructs similar to those found by Sandow in *Satyagraha* can be easily identified in *Akhnaten* as well. In fact, the whole opera could be regarded as a giant cadential arc encompassing within its trajectory a number of subsidiary cadences—"wheels within wheels" once again. The entire first act constitutes one such cadence, the dominant tonalities of each section outlining a recognizable authentic cadence (prelude, a–funeral, A/e–ritornello a–coronation, e [G]–window of appearances, a: thus, i–I/v–[i]–v [♭VII]–I). The second act vacillates, on the whole, between the dominant and the tonic, eventually resolving via the picardian tonic, A major (act 2, scene 4), to a thirdless *and* fifthless A: its governing tonal functions are i–v–i–I/i. The final act begins on the dominant, e minor (act 3, scene 1), and moves to the submediant, F minor/major (act 3, scene 2), before eventually falling back onto the tonic, A minor (act 3, scene 3), which, in turn, resolves once again to a simple unison on the pitch A— thus, the scene as a whole forms the cadence, v–vi/VI–i. A radically reduced tonal map of the opera might, therefore, look something like this:

Act 1: i–I/v–i–v [♭VII]–i
Act 2: i–v–i–I/i
Act 3: v–vi/VI–i

The presence of relationships such as this is scarcely likely to come as a surprise to post-Schenkerian analysts, who have been thinking of the symphonic repertory in this way for decades. In opera research, the idea of macrolevel key relations is considerably more controversial, however, although most opera specialists would agree that dramatic changes are reflected in some way in key relations. The hardest pill to swallow for opera researchers has been the claim that dramatic considerations should be viewed as somehow subordinate to autonomous "aesthetic" ones.[32] Opera lovers generally love opera because of all its histrionics, its often blatant sexuality, its semiotic promiscuity, its rarely-living-up-to-the-drama-it-is-portraying campiness, its groundedness in the human body, its connectedness with culture as a whole, its Artaudian ability to bombard the senses, and a whole host of other reasons—not because it is a poor imitation of symphonic music. In *Akhnaten*, as in most good operas, there is no danger that aesthetic considerations will entirely eclipse the "drama"; the tonal schema of the opera is elaborately and ingeniously intertwined with its theatrical subject matter. And although tonal relations analogous to those found in the symphonic repertory can be identified in much of Glass's music, the way in which these relations are articulated diverges in certain respects from most anything in the concert music repertory. The main difference might be that Schenkerian fundamental structures and, more importantly perhaps, the Schenkerian middleground are both, to some extent at least, perceptible in the surface structure of Glass's music. Schenkerian analysis argues that modulations are seldom convincing in tonal music; Glass *shows* us that they are not. Schenkerian analysis tells us that harmonic movement is motivated by distinct melodic lines; Glass *shows* us that this is the case. Schenkerian analysis tells us that everything is derived from the triad (preferably major); Glass *shows* us that it is—as Akhnaten's shift from A minor to A major in the hymn to the sun, the unrivaled moment of transcendence in the opera, more than adequately illustrates. In showing us all these things in such graphic detail, the composer in a sense demystifies the processes that go into putting together tonal music by exposing them for what they are but at the same time by taking a new kind of pleasure in them.

CHAPTER FOUR

Narrating from a Distance

Representations of the Old Order in the Prelude and the First Two Scenes

Layers of Meaning in the Prelude:
Alienation and Representation

That *Akhnaten* is Glass's first opera to open with a prelude, or in conventional operatic terms an overture, should come as no surprise, given the other numerous accommodations to the genre in this work. It was, however, almost an accident that a prelude was written at all. In the summer of 1982, the literary construction of the opera was well under way, and Glass was anxious to begin composing. The composer had intended to begin with the funeral scene, but Shalom Goldman, the historian working with him on the libretto, was having trouble tracking down an appropriate text, so Glass had to wait before setting the first scene to music: "To fill in the waiting time," he recounts, "which turned out to be two weeks, I wrote a prelude to the opera. Until then a prelude had not been planned but it turned out to be a striking beginning."[1]

It is true that the prelude sets the tone for much of the action that follows, and its import to the overall structure of the opera in musico-dramatic terms cannot be overstated. Traditionally the largest chunk of instrumental music in an opera, the overture plays an important role in channeling the attention and sensibilities of the audience toward what they are about to experience. Far from being an arbitrary appendage, a moment of instrumental self-indulgence on the part of the composer, or an elaborate form of Muzak played while people get comfortable in their seats, it is often a vital form of aesthetic conditioning. Somewhere in the passage between abstract music and less abstract musical and linguistic discourse, the distinction between life and art, the real and the imaginary, also becomes blurred. As audience members, we identify with the actions that unfold on the stage and the sounds that saturate our consciousnesses, usually without even realizing that we are doing so. This is why Richard Wagner's orchestra had to be hidden: The mechanics of musical performance and the flesh-and-blood corporeality of the musicians could not be allowed to get in the way of the spell being cast in the music. The agitated tremolo strings heard at the beginning of *The Flying Dutchman*[2] or the primordial undertow of *Das Rheingold*'s extended pedal on E-flat could not be compromised by the audience's amusement at the percussionist's poorly fitting toupee or their admiration for the octopuslike elasticity of the double-bass player's left hand. Any such distraction would instantly break the musical spell.

The spell cast by Glass in *Akhnaten* is of a different type. Glass's post-Brechtian compartmentalization of the opera's scenes into distinct "episodic-symbolic" blocks does much to deflect the kind of identification upon which Romantic and a good deal of modern opera has traditionally relied. The prelude and the musical discourse associated with it may work in a similar way. Operatic overtures are generally heard only once. The prelude music of *Akhnaten*, on the other hand, is heard three times: once as the prelude itself, once near the opera's golden-section point in the scene called City/Dance (act 2, scene 3), and once toward its end in the Ruins scene (act 3, scene 3). Thus, the same music is heard prior to the accession of Akhnaten, at the height of his reign, and immediately following his deposition. This reminder of our prediegetic involvement in the opera can be construed as a kind of large-scale foregrounding strategy. Rather than facilitating an effortless transition between life and art, the prelude's music seems to bring the transition itself into sharper focus, resulting in a twofold division into parallel perceptual universes, the real and the imaginary, the non-narrative and the narrative. This division is upheld throughout the opera and underlined in the opera's large-scale tonal plan: the prelude and each of its two reprises are in A minor, as are the chaconne ritornellos in the coronation and the hymn to the sun and a great deal of the opera's remaining music. The idea of the prelude as a frame or a gateway is, as we shall see shortly, pointed to explicitly in the text read by the scribe in its final cycle. From the standpoint of the opera's dramatic content, the gateway occupies a borderline position between such binary pairs as life and death and masculine and feminine. The post-Brechtian and post-Cagean dyad of life and art provides another way in which the gateway metaphor can be construed. Just as Brechtian theater would deliberately leave the lighting apparatus in sight as a means of weakening the fourth wall, so the three blocks of A-minor tonality in each scene of *Akhnaten*, initially understood as a portal to the interior world of the work, can equally well be understood as an exit sign deliberately left conspicuously in the listener's field of vision.

A lot, of course, depends on the details of the musical discourse itself. The music of the prelude is pieced together brick by brick before the listeners' ears; it is as if the master carpenter of the theater sat at the front of the stage, saw in hand, and continued to build scenery even after the show had begun, or if the actors were to finish putting on makeup on stage. Glass has never minded leaving the building blocks of his musical style conspicuously in sight, as with the first words of *Einstein*—1, 2, 3, 4, 1, 2, 3, 4, 5, 6, 1, 2, 3, 4, 5, 6, 7, 8—which explicitly draw attention to musical construction of that opera (see example 12b, p. 63). The construction of *Akhnaten* is rarely made that transparent, though the mechanics of musical process are foregrounded in the prelude and its reprises in an analogous way.

The first music of the opera is a group of evenly rising A minor arpeggios played by solo violas.[3] A low drone on the tonic is introduced that remains throughout the entire first cycle, moving only to an even lower B-flat in its second section. Against this backdrop, the cellos assert a steady quarter-note anchor, over which violas shoot incessantly upward. This constant cello pulse proves to be an essential point of reference, since the initially established binary meter is soon undermined by the subtraction of a single note from the four-note viola figuration. The resulting two-against-three polyrhythm provides the rhythmic fabric for the entire first cycle.

The prelude music consists of two chord changes, both of which emerge as a result of minimal musical change and are directly perceptible in terms of individual changed notes. The first requires the alteration of one note alone, the root of the new chord (f) for the fifth of the old (e); the second, to B-flat minor/major, is only slightly more marked.

In addition to these two sections, there are transitional passages between the cycles. One noteworthy feature of the transitions between the second, third, and fourth cycles is perhaps best described as a triadic countdown to the beginning of the opera proper. In the first passage, there is a single chord attack on A minor, in the second a double attack, and in the third an emphatic triple attack. For listeners familiar with the operatic repertoire, this procedure carries strong symbolic connotations, to which I will return to in a moment. In terms of musical rhetoric, however, it is a further example of the piece-by-piece assemblage of musical material that was initiated in the opening bars of the opera.

Other musical changes are explicitly pointed to using musicorhetorical means. The sections of the orchestra are introduced incrementally: woodwinds in the second cycle, brass in the third. Similarly, melodic movement accrues in the top note of the viola arppeggiation with each repetition of the A-minor to F-major chord sequence and with each cycle of the prelude. This gradual accretion of movement is mirrored loosely in the bass line, which in the third cycle starts to oscillates uneasily between chord tones and neighboring tones a diatonic step below them.

My point in describing these musical processes in this way is to demonstrate the frankness with which Glass puts his musical cards on the table right from the beginning of the opera. To draw attention to the simplicity of this music is to state the obvious; Glass has already done this. And to equate formal simplicity directly with simplicity of intent or affect is to subscribe to the formalist fallacy, which says that complex syntax equals complex semantics. If Glass had intended to dazzle the listener with technique right at the beginning of the opera, he could easily have done so; there are passages of *Akhnaten* that are quite impressive in terms of musical syntax. But that does not seem to be the way the music is meant to work. Instead, the listener is provided with an object lesson in the construction of musical meaning, from the foundations up. It as though a tourist wandering around the ruins of Akhetaten sees a few bricks, the floor plan of a building, a dried-up riverbed, and begins to let his or her imagination take control; bricks turn into walls, walls turn into halls, and halls turn into palaces. Before long, these places are teeming with life, vegetation, color, scent, and song. But the origins of all of this, the bricks and mortar, the nuts and bolts, are not forgotten. There is no sleight of hand; we know how it was done, how the meanings were put together. We participated in the process; we collaborated with the composer. The semiotic residue of this participation might fade, but it will not disappear. As the prelude progresses, the listener becomes more and more deeply enmeshed in various interwoven representational strata. But if the rhetorical strategy I have been describing is successful, the musical narrative that unfolds in this scene and in the opera as a whole is perceived from a distance.

Representation starts to become a more potent force at the beginning of the second cycle. As clarinets join violas in a repetitive and softly undulating arpeggio pattern, a visual analogy comes to mind: the gentle ripples of the River Nile dancing playfully under the rays of the hot afternoon sun. As I write these words, I sense the peremptory finger of formalist musicology wagging vigorously at me. I hear talk of program notes, of facile analogies, of naive referentialism, of a return to Romantic imprecision and hyperbole, of meaning defined in terms of what is absent from the musical text *itself* (the italics denote an impatient, derisive tone of voice; or then again, they might just denote italics). A cold shiver runs down my spine, and I rush to defend myself. This analogy is by no means contrived; it is both musico-dramatically and historically founded, though this is not to say that this is *all* that the music means nor that the music *necessarily* means precisely what I am saying it means. As I have shown already, an (anti)authorial voice of sorts is suggested strongly throughout the prelude and arguably throughout the opera, the explicit purpose of which is to deflect any ontologically grounded scraps of content listeners might think they are perceiving in the musical text.[4] The narrative that emerges in the prelude, and which remains until the final scene of the opera, does so from the hypothetical discursive space that post-Genettean narrative theory has often discussed, and with an opacity that is characteristic of so much recent art but with some of the intertextual depth we recognize from our encounters with more traditional forms.[5]

If, as Roland Barthes has suggested, the propensity to structure the world in which we live in terms of narrative first emerges at around the age of three, and at the same time infants "invent" other pervasive structures such as the sentence and the Oedipus, then it is here that Glass builds the foundation of his opera (originally, *Oedipus and Akhnaton*) and to here (the prelude music, and the key of A minor) that he returns whenever he finds it desirable to remind us where and whence our and our protagonist's musicodramatic journey has taken us.[6] This move reminds us not only of Akhnaten's (and our own?) Oedipus complex but also of the strong (salutary, if Julia Kristeva is to be believed)[7] *material* connection with the pre-Oedipal that he retains and that tends to resurface at moments of greatest insight—for Akhnaten, in the hymn to the sun—but also at moments of greatest anxiety.[8]

As for my aquatic metaphor, there are explicit references to the river in both of the later reprises of the prelude: In the first reprise, the scribe announces the founding of the royal city, Akhetaten, on the east bank of the Nile, while the second reprise refers to barks built by the new king, Tutankhamen, that "make the river shine." Most significant, however, is a strong implicit connection in the prelude itself. The first scene, the funeral of Amenhotep III, can actually be said to begin in the prelude, since a funereal text is recited by the scribe during its final cycle, which continues in the hiatus between the prelude and the initial scene. The river played an essential role in ancient Egyptian funeral proceedings, as it was customary to transport the body of the dead king in a ceremonial bark from Karnak on the east bank of the Nile to the Valley of the Kings on its west bank immediately prior to burial. More than this, the Nile became for the ancient Egyptians a symbol of the continuity of their civilization as well as the most important prerequisite for this continuity. Pharaohs came and went, and so did the ordinary peasant folk, but the Nile was always there to provide sustenance to those who abided in its vicinity. The Nile was, in addition, a symbol of the ancient Egyptian cyclical worldview. The river's source was thought to be in the underworld, whence it flowed down through the floodplains of Lower Egypt and out to sea before eventually returning to the land of the dead. The river, then, became the connecting principle between the living and the dead. In light of its import to the Egyptian people, it seems fitting that there is a scene devoted to its representation in each act of the opera. Allusions were made to the river in both the Stuttgart premiere of the opera, directed by Achim Freyer, and in the original Anglo-American production, directed by David Freeman, in which the collaborators on the libretto, costume and set designer Robert Israel, and lighting designer Richard Riddell were involved. In the Freyer production, Akhnaten is seen in the prelude unraveling himself from a Maypole-like construct at the center of the stage. As he gradually unfolds himself from the pole, the ribbon that is wrapped around his torso, blue at the center and pink/red at the periphery, ripples gently in sympathy with the accompanying music. Both the river metaphor and that of an umbilical cord come to mind, both of which are extremely perceptive interpretations of the subject matter that are strongly supported by the music. In the Freeman production, a scaled-down representation of the Nile actually traversed the stage.

At the moment we recognize the aquatic metaphor, we collide with another layer of meaning that has to do both with the history of opera and with the composer's relationship with his historical inheritance. The fact that Wagner liked aquatic imagery is common knowledge. There are countless examples of this in the Ring cycle, but also in the *The Flying Dutchman* and *Tristan und Isolde*.[9] However, the most elaborate representations of water are in the first tetralogy opera, *Das Rheingold*. Since the very act of writing a serial opera invites comparisons with Wagner, a connection with the Ring cycle might have been already established in many audience members' minds. For the listener who recognizes in Glass's opera what sounds suspiciously like a musical allusion to the overture (or *Vorspiel*, which is semantically closer to the word *prelude*) of *Das Rheingold*, this awareness would be foremost. The allusion in question is equivocal but easily recognizable: *Das Rheingold*'s extended pedal on E-flat is transformed in *Akhnaten* into a pedal on A; similarly, the low waves of string arpeggiation in *Das Rheingold* are transformed into more regular waves in Glass's opera. Undoubtedly the most striking isomorphism is in the third cycle, however, when Glass's undulating arpeggios are joined by a second group of arpeggios in contrary motion to these (see examples 23, p. 96; 7,

Example 23. *Das Rheingold*, Vorspiel. "Mirror" writing over a drone in the strings.

p. 59; and 15, p. 72). This technique directly recalls Wagner's musical depiction of the Rhine. The intertextuality extends further than this, however, to questions of key relations: E-flat and its enharmonic equivalent, D-sharp, play an important role in *Akhnaten*, as they are closely associated with Akhnaten's political and religious adversaries: the "old order," as Glass refers to them. We hear this most strongly in the funeral, where a pungently dissonant pedal on D-sharp effectively rips apart the tonal foundation of the scene. Might Glass have been thinking of Wagner here?[10]

In the third cycle of the prelude, the entire brass section joins mirrored waves of strings and winds in a resounding forte declamation of the might and glory, not to mention the stern militaristic authoritarianism of ancient Egypt. This is a fanfare not for the common man but for the *uncommon* man—a portentous musical representation of the power and influence of the pharaohs. The most significant musical event in the prelude takes place in this cycle over its most abrupt chord change, the exotic-sounding shift to the "lowered" second degree, B-flat. This shift is a conventional one, familiar both from classical music and from Hollywood film scores (ca. 1940–1970).[11] Its exotic effect derives largely from the fact that it is one of the few procedures in common language tonality where parallel movement in the voice leading is condoned. Thus, the functional orientation that ordinarily reigns supreme in tonal music is to some extent superseded by melodic/linear considerations. Some sense of functionality is retained, however, and from this standpoint the major chord built on the second degree of the Phrygian mode has a threatening feel, bearing down as it does on the minor tonic, which convention tells us is weaker than its major counterpart.

Glass takes full advantage of the dramatic implications of this procedure. The move to B major is perceived as a shift in perspective or, to be more precise, in point of view. This key center provides a convenient gateway to the various pitch centers that are associated with the old order—most noticeably that of E-flat (or D-sharp), in which it is the dominant. Being a tritone away from the home key, this key—and its close harmonic neighbor, A-flat, which is arrived at with even greater ease, being the altered seventh degree of A minor—has a special pungency, which is exploited already in the first scene of the opera (the funeral).

More striking than its association with *Das Rheingold* is E-flat major's association with Mozart's *Die Zauberflöte*, especially in light of the ancient Egypt subject matter of both operas. Mozart's opera begins and ends with triple cadences on E-flat major, and the music returns to that key at various dramatically significant junctures. Among the most powerful and dramatically significant moments in that opera, however, are the three emphatic chord strikes on the dominant of that key, B-flat major, in the middle of the overture (see example 24) and in the temple scene at the beginning of the second act. The threefold chord attack at the end of cycle four of the prelude is probably the most obvious allusion to Mozart's opera in *Akhnaten*, but a further association between the use of key centers in the two operas does not seem unlikely. Thus, the move to B-flat major in the prelude and Mozart's threefold accords on B-flat major (in the key of E-flat major) are easily associated with one another. We will return to the triple-chord attack shortly, but first let us look at the very different, even diametrically opposed, ways in which the same key center is encoded in the two operas. For Mozart, the key of E-flat major was marked as euphoric and represented spiritual apotheosis or enlightenment, whereas B-flat, the dominant of this key, was marked as dysphoric and represented the trials and tribulations through which the hero, Tamino, must pass in order to become enlightened. For Wagner, as well, the key of E-flat major represented some primordial source, some magical place of origin, which through its association with the Rhine was invested both with nationalist and universal significance. In Glass's opera, the significance of the musical material is inverted, with Mozart's and Wagner's euphoric music of enlightenment taking on a distinctly dysphoric appearance. Glass's music

Example 24. *Die Zauberflöte*, overture. Triple accord.

does modulate to B-flat, but the threefold accord in *Akhnaten* is not on E-flat or its dominant B but on A minor. It is easy to think of this harmonic reversal as a kind of musical deconstruction. This music invokes the rhetoric of enlightenment, as explicitly defined in the earlier works, but only to deprive it of its grounding in the metaphysical. The key of A minor has no "natural" or mimetic (imitative) subtext, organic or otherwise; it is self-consciously and meticulously constructed by the composer. Thus, "breaking through" to this key does not carry quite the same connotations as the move to E-flat carries in Mozart's opera; nor is the metaphor of "breaking through" particularly apposite in the case of *Akhnaten*, in which the move to the tonic is felt more as a peeling away of (to some extent coexisting) tonal layers than as a dialectic acted out between opposing tonal forces. Not even the move from the dysphorically marked B-flat to the tonic is experienced in this way, since, despite its uncomfortably feel, this key center does not implicate A minor in the same way as the conventional dominant-tonic move. In this respect, it is significant also that the main "other" (or away from home) key of the opera is E minor, not E major, which would impart a stronger sense of functionality and hence engender a greater need for release. With regard to the opera's key relations, then, the German opera critic Kurt Honalka's characterization of *Akhnaten* as a *"postmoderne Anti-Oper"* might be more appropriate than its writer realizes, since the assumptions that ground Glass's opera are in some ways the same as but in some ways very different from those found in two pillars of the opera repertory.[12]

Musical Point of View: First- and Third-Person Aspects of *Akhnaten's* "Transgression" Theme

The shift to B-flat has already lent the music an eerie feel, and this is confirmed in the next few bars when one of the opera's most disturbing themes makes a dramatic first appearance over the following chord progression: B-flat minor–B-flat major–B-flat minor–A minor. This theme emerges from the depths of the orchestra, with tuba, trombones, and double basses shaking the very foundations of the orderly musical scenario Glass has pieced together brick by brick in the opening two cycles. The theme begins on a low F (a significant pitch center in its own right, since it is the one to which the music reverts during the ousting of Akhnaten from the throne in the Attack and Fall scene [act 3, scene 2]), rises to B-flat (whose connotations are discussed above), and then moves onward to the minor third of the chord, d-flat, thus stubbornly contradicting the surrounding tonal context, which is now major (see example 15, p. 72). The major third has no alternative but to comply with the more powerful minor theme, resolving back to the minor mode. The victory of the minor mode is short-lived, however, since the theme drops abruptly to a low E as the underlying harmony for its part sinks down to A minor.

Glass understands this passage as follows:

Its most distinctive feature is the bass line, which ascends and then abruptly drops an octave. This first appears in the Prelude and gives it an ominous quality. Again we hear it in the City/Dance, this time accompanied in unison by the flutes. Finally, it forms the concluding phrases of Act III, scene 2 (Attack and Fall), in which Akhnaten's temple, and finally the pharaoh himself, are destroyed. For me, this music is synonymous with the downfall of Akhnaten. In the fourth measure [of the progression] there is a curious play between Bb Major and minor, this major/minor coincidence creating an uneasy harmonic ambiguity, which also occurs in its earlier appearances (in the Prelude, City/Dance, and destruction of the Temple). It is easy to see this as a musical metaphor for that part of Akhnaten's character that was so unusual and unsettling to the people of his time.[13]

The deeply troubling characteristic to which Glass refers is Akhnaten's sexual peculiarity; the composer explicitly spells out that this is the case in his numerous discussions of the pharaoh in *MPG*.[14] At this stage in the opera, the listener, as Glass suggests, senses only that something strange is afoot. As the opera proceeds, however, a number of musical and dramatic signposts are provided that, like the cumulative evidence in an Agatha Christie novel, eventually allow the listener to hear the events portrayed in the manner intended by the composer. It is possible, of course, that the listener who is familiar with archaeological literature and knowledgeable about twentieth-century music criticism will recognize the metaphor already at this early stage. Most Egyptologists who have dealt with the subject of Akhnaten have specifically drawn attention to the pharaoh's unusual sexual attributes. Moreover, the association of the sexes with the major/minor dyad is conventional; as Susan McClary has observed, everyone from the eighteenth-century theorist Georg Andreas Sorge to Arnold Schoenberg has made use of it.[15] So Glass is not inventing his own language, he is merely exploiting an existing convention. What is novel about Glass's association of the modes with the sexes, and what stops him from simply reinscribing dubious cultural stereotypes, is his use of the narrative strategy that literary theorists call point of view. In short, the voice that proclaims Akhnaten to be a sexual deviant (neither masculine nor feminine, although leaning toward the latter) is not Glass's own, nor is it Akhnaten's: It is the voice of Akhnaten's adversaries.

This theme becomes associated with Akhnaten's adversaries not only because of the opera's key relations, but also, and more directly, because of its register, which is the same as that of Aye, who is not only Akhnaten's father-in-law and adviser but also the staunchest and most powerful (musical and dramatic) opponent to his reforms. When this theme or variations of it are sung, as is the case later in the opera, it is usually Aye's bass that is most prominent. The theme would hardly have the resonance it does, however, if it did not closely correlate in some way with existing signifying practices. The power of this voice is that of the "fundamental bass." We can hear this in the way the theme bullies the higher voices into compliance. It is important to stress, however, that the power of this voice has nothing to do with its "natural" lowness. It is a matter of convention, not nature, that the lower voices in harmony control the higher voices to the extent that they do, and this convention has strong gendered implications.[16]

How, then, should we understand this musical discourse in semiotic terms? We have already established that the voice and the harmony represent the perspective or point of view of Akhnaten's adversaries, the old order. One factor does not fit in this formulation, however—the minor/major clash, which is associated explicitly with the sexual deviation of Akhnaten (which is encoded as feminine, being in the "weaker" minor mode)—unless we grant that music is a considerably more articulate and flexible communicative medium than most theorists have up until very recently been willing to allow.

The passage in question is easily explained if one understands the theme as being in the third person: That is, rather than saying "*I* have become an effeminate sexual deviant and will eventually pay for this transgression," it is in fact saying "*he* has become an effeminate sexual deviant and must be made to pay for this transgression." But the music says more than this. We have seen already that the B-flat harmony, associated with Aye and the other patriarchs by virtue of key relations, exotically marked voice leading, and historical allusion, is forced to comply with the minor modality stated in the theme. It is possible, then, that our third-person subject himself feels somehow "emasculated" as a result of the power wielded over him by the sexual deviant (thus the harmonic shift to the minor mode in bar 3 of the passage), decides to resist (by shifting to the major mode, despite the simultaneous movement of the stronger theme to the minor), and is then forced to comply (thus the shift back to the minor at the end of bar four). This implies the parallel presence of a first-person voice in the harmony. Indeed, it is clear that Aye perceives himself to be on the receiving end of the deviant's actions ("I—the harmony—have been forced into this submissive and therefore effeminate position"). So when the theme plunges down to a shuddering E with the change back to A minor, it is also saying, "He will (be made to) fall." It is inevitable, from the standpoint of Akhnaten's opponents, that he pay for his insurrection, as there is both cause (the sexually encoded deviation) and effect (the righting of this "wrong"). A second point of historical reference makes it clear that this is the case: namely, the cliché of the *tuba mirum*, the last trump in requiem masses (most notably in Louis-Hector Berlioz's *Grande messe des morts*).[17] In this way, the low E at the end of the transgression theme conjures up a quite specific historical association: It represents the crushing blow that will be dealt to Akhnaten by his adversaries in the penultimate scene.

My contention is that this is not the kind of musical discourse behind which Glass stands wholeheartedly. Quite the opposite: I believe there is plenty of evidence of this in this opera and more widely across his oeuvre. In fact, this whole passage has the feel of a quotation, and perhaps it is. It is worth mentioning in this respect that Akhnaten's theme is quite similar in terms of its pitch relations to the theme that marks the fall of Oedipus in *Oedipus Rex*. Both are derived from second-inversion minor triads, the former consisting of a rising B-flat minor arpeggio and the latter a falling B-minor arpeggio. Transposed up a half step (F-sharp–B–D), the Akhnaten theme can be recognized as partial retrograde of Stravinsky's descending F-sharp–D–B–F-sharp theme. Whether this is an intentional allusion or not is for the reader to decide, though a good deal of *Akhnaten* does seem to be related in some fairly tangible way to *Oedipus Rex*, in terms not only of themes and techniques but also of the overall weight of the piece.[18] Given this affinity of a general sort, it seems more than just a coincidence that exactly the same intervallic relationships are employed to represent exactly the same dramatic event in two operas dealing in one way or another with the plight of Oedipus.[19]

This brings us to another similarity between the two operas: the use of a narrator to translate the archaic texts enunciated by the singers into a form the audience will understand. The pensive fourth cycle prepares the way for the narrator's entrance. A babbling bassoon doubled with cellos provides a murky undercurrent over which high winds rise in mechanical straight lines (see example 8, p. 59). The upper part, which in relation to the lower part forms a striking four-against-six polyrhythm, is closely related motifically to the viola arpeggios of the first cycle. This motif is heard at a number of junctures in the opera, when the protagonist is faced either with death or extreme solitude. This music immediately follows the transgression theme, which represents for the composer and perhaps for the listener not only Akhnaten's transgression but the price he will pay for it—his destiny. Therefore, the rising arpeggios might represent whatever is left (or not) of the pharaoh or his ideas after his deposition or death. They are the zero degree of the opera's music.

Seeing Triple: Ternary Themes in Ancient Egypt, Opera History, and Buddhism

At the end of the fourth cycle, there are three emphatic double attacks on A minor. The allusion is all the more obvious because of the imagery associated with the music. The famous threefold accord in Mozart's *Die Zauberflöte* takes place as Sarastro and the priests are approaching the temple of Isis and Osiris; behind them stand two pyramids. Thus, the triple accord itself becomes associated directly with pyramids. The significance of the triadic imagery to the ancient Egyptians is common knowledge, particularly in those areas of Egyptian theology connected with sun worship. The reign of Akhnaten and Nefertiti was a renaissance of sorts not only for the sun cult, but also for the triangular and pyramidal imagery associated with it, making the pyramid symbolism in the music historically correct.[20]

A valuable clue to one of many conceivable dramatic implications of the triadic imagery in *Akhnaten* is provided by the photograph that adorns the sleeve of the CBS Masterworks recording of the opera, taken from Achim Freyer's Stuttgart production. The scene depicted is Akhnaten's and Nefertiti's duet (act 2, scene 2). In the photograph, the two protagonists sit face-to-face with their hands extended toward one another and their downstage palms interlocked. Each free hand, Akhnaten's left and Nefertiti's right, is extended upward toward the sun, and the space enclosed by their arms forms a truncated triangle. Here, the triangle represents a kind of holy trinity of the two rulers and the unifying principle represented by the sun god, the Aten. The ideology behind this image is androgynous, the sun disk becoming an abstract symbol of the couple's shared consciousness.[21] This is no mere invention of Glass's or Freyer's: It is a pervasive image in ancient Egyptian representations of the couple and one that was presumably sanctioned by Akhnaten himself.[22]

Perhaps as significant as the androgynous triangle of Akhnaten, Nefertiti, and their god is the Oedipal triangle of child, mother, and father, as found in both the myth itself and in Freud's psychoanalytical theories. This is a particularly salient subtext of the opera.[23] A second Oedipal triangle (we now have a triad of triangles) is the love triangle of Akhnaten, Tye, and Nefertiti. Triangles and triads abound in this opera, but the last of these is particularly important, since it is explicitly portrayed in the music and drama of several scenes, including the Window of Appearances scene (act 1, scene 3), the duet (act 2, scene 2), and the epilogue.

But the significance of triadic imagery goes beyond these specific dramatic and intertextual associations. As noted, the prelude music is heard three times in the opera, once in each act, and the hymn to the sun is interrupted by three chaconne ritornellos. In addition, trios play an important part in this opera, just as they do in *Die Zauberflöte*. There is an aspect of self-reflexivity in Glass's numerous and marked references to the number three in this the third and final installment of his operatic trilogy—one that could be interpreted as having post-Brechtian as well as narcissistic overtones. At the same time as it draws attention to some prediegetic and non-narrative level of (non)involvement on the part of the listener, to the construction of the work *as* construction, it is also pregnant with symbolic significance that encompasses much of the history of opera as a genre and perhaps a good deal more besides. The cynic might point out that this is a prime example of Glass's megalomania; and she or he might be right. In quoting historical texts in this way, Glass appears to be self-consciously drawing attention to the mammoth scale of the trilogy project and at the same time situating himself at the pinnacle of the pyramid of music history, the base of which includes "the two *great* opera composers" Mozart and Wagner.[24] But in leaving the signifying field open in the way that he does, in not pinning down his significations by spelling them out in so many words—"Here is a quotation from *Das Rheingold*: Listen carefully and admire my erudition!"—Glass actually shies away from the very thing that would guarantee him a place in the history books, as inheritor of the great tradition. Very few people have recognized these allusions—in contrast to John Adams's highbrow allusions, which are more widely recognized and usually indicated linguistically either in the title of the piece (e.g., *Harmonielehre*) or in the liner notes accompanying recordings, though this does not shake my conviction that Glass's allusions are there. Critics and audiences have (with good reason) recognized the affinity of his music with popular idioms (often taking issue with it on precisely those grounds), but the classical connection often seems have fallen on deaf ears. People evidently do not expect to find such things in Glass's music, which often appears antithetical in spirit to the music it is quoting. In other words, it is the perceived distance between Glass and the material to which he is alluding that throws people off. A prime example is an obvious allusion to the final movement of Sibelius's fifth symphony in the composition *Floe* (from the *Glassworks* recording [1982]), which critics and musicologists have universally missed but which to Glass's evident relief was eventually spotted by a young Finnish composer.[25] Most of the musical allusions in *Akhnaten* have likewise been missed or ignored. (See below, chapter 8.)

To return for a moment to the subject of triads and trilogies, Glass is otherwise something of a specialist in this area, as evidenced in his recent trilogy of Cocteau-inspired pieces and his trilogy of film collaborations with Godfrey Reggio (yes, that makes a trilogy of trilogies).[26] Could it be that there is some symbolic-numerological background to these games with threes, as was undoubtedly the case for Mozart? In Glass's case, it is unlikely that it has anything to do with Freemasonry, except indirectly by virtue of the connection with Mozart, but Buddhists of almost all denominations are likely to perceive a subtext of sorts in the composer's fascination with threes. The Buddhist "holy trinity" or *trikaya*—the threefold body of the Buddha, comprising the *dharmakaya* (the body of dharma, the Buddhist tradition), the *sambhogakaya* (the body of bliss), and the *nirmanakaya* (the body of transformation)—is one of the most central precepts across all the various schools of Mahayana teaching.[27] Moreover, the number three holds a special significance for Tibetan Buddhists, as it is closely connected to the ideas concerning death that lie at the heart of their religious practices.

After the triple accord, we are returned abruptly to the music of the opening cycle with some slight but important discrepancies: an occasional interpolation from the trombones, and the transgression theme is heard as if from afar, a faint echo of a stern prophecy of what will come to pass. A solemn voice then enunciates the first words of the opera:

> Open are the double doors of the horizon
> Unlocked are its bolts
> Clouds darken the sky
> The stars rain down
> The constellations stagger
> The bones of the hell hounds tremble
> The porters are silent
> When they see this king
> Dawning as a soul
> Open are the double doors of the horizon
> Unlocked are its bolts
> Men fall
> Their name is not
> Seize thou this king by his arm
> Take this king to the sky
> That he not die on earth
> Among men
> Open are the double doors of the horizon
> Unlocked are its bolts

The voice is that of the scribe, the deceased king's namesake, Amenhotep, son of Hapu, and the text is from the pyramid texts of the Old Kingdom. Part of the *Egyptian Book of the Dead*, this text is recited in funerary proceedings to ensure the passage of the dead pharaoh to the heavenly land of Ra. It is one of the many religious scriptures later discarded during the reign of Akhnaten and represents, therefore, the old order into which he is born. The metaphor of a dual doorway or gateway between relative and absolute planes of consciousness, between the living and the dead, and perhaps also between the sexes, is one known both in the East and the West. The use of this metaphor in the Buddhist scriptures is almost identical to the passage from the *Egyptian Book of the Dead* cited by Glass and his collaborators: "Opened are the gates of immortality, ye that have ears to hear, release thy faith. . . . Let your faith, your inner trust and confidence stream forth, remove your inner obstacles and open yourself to the truth."[28] William Blake expressed similar sentiments in his *Marriage of Heaven and Hell*: "If the doors of perception were cleansed every thing would appear to man as it is, infinite. For man has closed himself up, till he sees all things thro' narrow chinks of his cavern."

As when the young initiate Tamino knocks three times to gain entry to the Freemasons' temple in *Die Zauberflöte*, so the purpose of Glass's three tumultuous chords is to shake the hinges of his own doors: the "double doors" that separate the living from the dead. The doors open to allow Amenhotep III through to the underworld and to allow the young successor, Amenhotep IV, to embark upon his Oedipal quest; they also signal the audience as emphatically as possible that the story has begun.

Archaeology and Narration

But what of our guide? What are his special qualifications as mediator between these two planes; between past and the present; between the old order of Amenhotep III and the very different world of his son; and between those parallel universes of experience demarcated by sex and gender differences?

Identifying a counterpart to the seer of the Oedipus myth in the life and times of Akhnaten is, according to Velikovsky, no difficult task, given that Amenhotep, son of Hapu, was commonly attributed with the gift of foresight, was in Ptolemaic times regarded as the patron of the blind, and is known to have lived far beyond the ordinary life span of ancient Egyptians.[29] The ancient Egyptian scribe is, according to Velikovsky, none other than the famous seer of Greek mythology, Tiresias. But I have omitted one important trait that, for the writer of *Oedipus and Akhnaton* at least, clinches the argument: "A portrait of Hapu, has come down to us as a young person with long hair arranged not unlike the womenfolk of his time. If the seer was the prototype of Tiresias, this remarkable portrait, which made archaeologists wonder, may explain a curious detail in the legend of Tiresias."[30]

The curious detail to which Velikovsky refers is that of the miraculous transformation of Tiresias into a woman after striking two copulating snakes with his cane. The story, recounted also in Ovid's *Metamorphoses*, is one of the most pervasive of the antique world. After seven years as a women, Tiresias encountered the serpents again, struck them once more, and was this time transformed back into his original, male, form. He then found himself caught up in a dispute between Zeus and Hera. The cause of the dispute was Zeus's claim that women's pleasure in intercourse is considerably greater than that of men. Hera disagreed, so Tiresias, who had had experience both as a man and a woman, was called upon to settle the issue. To Hera's chagrin, Tiresias testified that women's pleasure is as much as ten times that enjoyed by men. Disgruntled at losing her wager, the goddess struck Tiresias blind, but as a compensation for his blindness he was granted a number of special skills by Zeus. These skills included the ability to know the future as well as exceptional longevity.

If the mythological Tiresias and Amenhotep are, as Velikovsky claims, one and the same, then this character is certainly singularly qualified to relate to us the events of Akhnaten's career. Having experienced the world as both man and woman and having himself paid a harsh price for flaunting the distinction between the sexes, he alone among mortals possesses the perspective and special insight required to mediate between Akhnaten and his opponents. And, perhaps more important, he alone has the longevity necessary to mediate between the ancient Egyptian past and the contemporary world. In the opera, he transcends time, appearing both as the scribe of the Amarna period and as a contemporary tour guide, he mediates between the living and the dead in the funeral passage, and he is intimately acquainted with the affairs of the Egyptian royals, as, indeed, was the historical Amenhotep.

As is the case with Oedipus, the presence of Tiresias in the opera is by no means explicit; knowledge of the connection between Tiresias and Amenhotep as postulated by Velikovsky is, nevertheless, an important key to understanding the nature of this character and his extraordinary abilities. There is no visible clue to his extraordinary transformation, except perhaps for his blindness or, as in T. S. Eliot's *The Waste Land* or Francis Poulenc's *Les mamelles de Tirésias*, physical traces of his seven years as a woman—Eliot's "wrinkled female dugs." Having two physically deformed, sexually ambiguous males in one opera may, however, cause some confusion, as well as be an unnecessary complication in a story already steeped in sociopolitical, religious, and psychosexual intrigue. In the debut performance in Stuttgart, the problem was solved with unabashed directness by casting Amenhotep, son of Hapu, as a woman. Glass himself seems somewhat taken aback by this casting, although it is noteworthy that he does not disapprove:

There were some . . . things I did not anticipate, though not all of them were off the mark, only a little unsuspected. The narrator was played by a large, deep-voiced woman who was also an excellent actress. Actually, Peter[31] and I had discussed that a year before, and I had agreed that it would be workable, though the Egyptian scribes were always male.[32]

It depends a great deal, of course, on the idiosyncrasies of individual productions whether Amenhotep, son of Hapu, is perceived as Tiresias or not. If he is perceived as the character from the Oedipus myth—and the evidence is compelling that he should be perceived in that way—then his first words in the opera and the surrounding music take on a whole new significance. When the narrator reads what sounds suspiciously like a damning prophecy ("Clouds darken the sky / The stars rain down / The constellations stagger / The bones of the hell hounds tremble") over the ominous transgression theme with its abrupt descent, the prophecy of Tiresias regarding the similar fate of Oedipus appears to be the intended point of reference.

Spoken narration has played an important role in twentieth-century music theater, the most conspicuous precursors of Glass's approach being Stravinsky's music-theater pieces *The Soldier's Tale* (1918), *Oedipus Rex* (1927), and *Perséphone* (1934). Glass's use of spoken narration in *Akhnaten* is almost certainly influenced by these works, particularly *Oedipus Rex*, with its combination of arcane Latin song texts and vernacular commentary. (*The Soldier's Tale* is a somewhat different case, since there is no sung text in that work.) It diverges, however, from all of the above in certain significant respects.

Carolyn Abbate has observed that "operatic narrators are assumed to be *reliable*, neither lying nor distorting the truth. Put another way: narrating is not seen as an *act* within *action*."[33] She then goes on to question this conception of the narrator, differentiating between monaural and reflexive modes of narration, which are simultaneously present in some of the more interesting works in the repertoire—when, for example, text and music assume contradictory narrative stances.[34] The narrator of Glass's opera, however, does not fit comfortably into Abbate's analytical framework: He seems to possess characteristics of both narrative modes, and yet he is not wholly commensurate with either. Amenhotep's narrative is clearly not one that Abbate would term monaural, as his adventures as a woman call into question the monolithic nature of his testimony; the nearest we could come to this category would be that of a *bi*aural narrative, although this is not an entirely satisfactory designation. Does he, on the other hand, draw attention to himself through the unreliability or partisanship of "his" story, thus differentiating "his" story from the metastory told by the composer? His is unquestionably a reflexive narrative, more so, probably, than in the repertory pieces Abbate discusses. The main shortcoming of categorizing Amenhotep in this way, however, is that his is not a unified story at all: It is gathered from many different strands and is merely carried by a unified voice (and I mean *voice* in the narrowest possible sense of the word here, since there is no subject, in the conventional sense, associated with this voice). Similarly, with regard to the relationship between spoken text and music, Amenhotep's discourse seems to slide in and out of Abbate's categories. At times, music and language form a compound monaural voice, the music merely inflecting the spoken text or vice versa; at other times, however, there is some element of contradiction or counterpoint between parallel musical and spoken lines.

Other typologies of narrators developed in semiotics and literary criticism are also only of limited use when it comes to explaining the role of the scribe in *Akhnaten*. Gérard Genette has distinguished on the one hand between extra- and intradiegetic narrators, narrators inside and outside of the story, and, on the other hand, between hetero- and homodiegetic narrators, narrators who are absent from or present in the portrayed events.[35] In strict semiotic terms, Amenhotep is an intradiegetic, heterodiegetic narrator; he is a historical character reflecting on (or simply reflecting) events that occur in the time in which he lives, but he has no direct role in those events (he does not converse with the other characters and is essentially invisible to them). Like extradiegetic narrators, however, Amenhotep is capable of entering the consciousness of his characters; more than that, he is capable of becoming the consciousness or the (linguistic) voice of the consciousness of the characters. In fact, so involved is he in the events portrayed that one could easily characterize him as homodiegetic, at the same time as he stands outside of the physical and musical body of the actual characters. Thus, his is not the conventional role of the omniscient outside observer. Amenhotep is incapable of seeing the world in a detached or objective manner; he is, like the extradiegetic narrator, capable of entering the consciousness of his characters and traveling across time and place, but once "inside" a character—and he invariably speaks from the subject position of a particular character—he is incapable of detaching himself from the specific point of view of that character until he moves on to another. Amenhotep does not, in other words, specialize in out of body experiences—he is panpersonal but not metapersonal.

Returning again to Abbate's terminology, Amenhotep's narrative is rendered unreliable and therefore reflexive by the sheer weight of the number of subject positions he adopts and by his conspicuous complicity with each of these positions. Amenhotep assumes many different and, indeed, contradictory stances during the course of the opera; he glides effortlessly from one persona to the next while speaking all the time in the same voice and, ostensibly at least, living inside the same character. He/she is a privileged witness to the intimate secrets of Akhnaten and Nefertiti, an indignant outside observer to the less healthy aspects of the royal family's personal life, an advocate of Aten, an advocate of Amon and the other gods of the pantheistic order, loyal to Akhnaten, and complicit in the plot to overthrow him. Like the Tiresias of the myth, he/she is not a god but is endowed with certain godly characteristics; like the man Amenhotep, he is divided in his loyalties between the uncompromising and, if current Egyptological opinion is to be believed, unattractive idealist who was his king and those who opposed the king, whose reality he knew all too well.

An epithet that was commonly associated with the Greek seer Tiresias usefully illuminates the role of his ancient Egyptian counterpart: Tiresias was also known as "he who delights in signs." In the early drafts of *Akhnaten*, there was to be no role for Velikovsky's sage, Amenhotep; there was, however, a role for the ancient Egyptian patron of interpretation, Thoth—scribe to Osiris, Lord of the underworld and the ancient Egyptian equivalent of the Greek god Hermes. In addition, Akhnaten's wife, Nefertiti, was to be granted the power of prophetic speech after the exile imposed on her at the end of Akhnaten's reign had ended.[36] Hers was to be one of two spoken texts in the opera—thus, she was originally to be a restricted kind of narrator. Nefertiti, having belonged both to Akhnaten's innermost clique and—like her father, Aye—to a rapidly growing list of religious and political dissidents, has much in common with Amenhotep, inasmuch as her loyalties were divided between her husband and his opponents. Perhaps in reverting to Velikovsky's choice, Glass found he is able to have the best of both worlds by combining Nefertiti's perspective with the panoramic, shape-shifting, multiple perspectives of the god of interpretation, Thoth. There is, moreover, a clear advantage to the character of Amenhotop over both the intra- and homodiegetic Nefertiti and the extra- and heterodiegetic Thoth, which may have something to do with the fortunate coincidence that the scribe shares Amenhotep III's name as well as Akhnaten's given name (Amenhotep IV). This is especially useful for Glass since Amenhotep, son of Hapu, adopts points of view compatible with both of these characters at different points in the opera, thus identifying himself with both sides of the Oedipal father-son matrix. In the sonorous and corporeal absence of Akhnaten's real father, Amenhotep in a way becomes the father figure of the opera, the surrogate voice of his namesake (a position arguably occupied by Aye as well). Indeed, given that he is granted the status of official translator, being the only verbally *and* linguistically articulate character in the opera (with the significant exception of Akhnaten himself in the hymn to the sun), he comes to occupy a privileged position in terms of his relationship with the audience, as only a god of interpretation can; thus, his word is not only the word of the father, it is also the Word of the Father, the only (linguistic) voice that can really be heard.

But if Amenhotep, son of Hapu, is an ancient Egyptian counterpart to the god of interpretation from whom the philosophical orientation known as hermeneutics received its name, then this is a god who either abdicates or is made to abdicate many of the powers with which he is ordinarily invested. A scribe, after all, whether he is a scribe to the pharaohs or to the lord of the underworld, is really nothing more than a glorified secretary. He does not constitute reality, he simply reflects it by writing it down. This makes the hermeneutics of Amenhotep a strange kind of antihermeneutics that is in fact closely related to Foucauldian archaeology. Like Foucault, the scribe of *Akhnaten* is not overtly interested in elucidating from the texts some univocal or monaural final truth, in forging from the texts at his disposal an integrated, internally consistent whole, but rather wants to show the audience how things are "fabricated in piecemeal fashion from alien forms,"[37] in this way allowing the audience itself—and perhaps the characters in the opera, who are not permitted to speak in language in a way that the audience will understand—to have the final word.

The Funeral of Amenhotep III (and of Modernism): Musical Representations of the Old Order

The scribe, who has remained on the stage after the cessation of the prelude music, continues his invocations unaccompanied:

> He flies who flies
> This king flies away from you
> Ye mortals
> He is not of the earth
> He is of the sky
> He flaps his wings like a zeret bird
> He goes to the sky
> He goes to the sky
> On the wind
> On the wind

A funeral procession appears downstage led by two drummers beating out a feverish rhythm derived from the motifs introduced by the brass in the belligerent third cycle of the prelude (see examples 3, p. 56, and 7, p. 59). Although never, to my knowledge, realized in an actual performance

Thank you for using the
3M SelfCheck™ System.

Bath Spa University

Title: Writings on Glass : essays,
interviews, criticism
ID: C0317788
Due: **11/12/2017,23:59**

Tota items: 1
20/11/2017 11:44

Thank you for using the
3M SelfCheck™ System.

of the opera, the appearance of these and other instruments on the stage, as stipulated in the libretto, has Brechtian implications that should not be overlooked, especially given the nature of the accompanying music. Here, as in the first reprise of the prelude music (the City/Dance scene [act 2, scene 3]), where instruments also appear on the stage, the music explicitly calls attention to the processes by which it is constructed. We have already seen how this works in the prelude. Like the beginning of the prelude, the opening bars of the funeral recollect the additive and subtractive rhythmic processes of Glass's early minimal style. The foregrounding of musical process in these passages serves as a counterpoint to the dramatic and narrative implications of other aspects of the musical discourse, such as the move to the dominant tonal function, that is implied but not confirmed in the bass riff that is now introduced.

The drums are joined by cellos doubled with bassoons, whose nervously shifting ostinato sets the mood for the storm ahead (see the cello/bassoon part of example 20, p. 78). This oscillating motif is related to the zigzagging top line of the viola arpeggiation in the prelude, which eventually spreads downward to the bass line, where it is heard in inverted form. Its transformation in this scene recalls the similar use of small melodic cells as the foundation for large-scale musical structures in *Pelléas et Mélisande*. Like Debussy, Glass possesses the ability to make a mountain out of a musical molehill. The ostinato continues for only sixteen bars, however, after which there is an abrupt transformation. In what is unquestionably the most striking change in the opera so far, male chorus—tenors close to the top of their range (e"), basses on a resonant a—and brass enter together in powerful open fifths. The ferocity of this music is perhaps best understood in relation to its opposite pole in the opera:

One of the most striking things I became aware of in our studies was the sharp contrast between the sophisticated and refined life of upper-class Egyptians, as shown in tomb paintings, and the militaristic and primitive manner in which Egypt treated its neighbors. . . . This cruel and barbaric side of Egyptian life made me speculate on what a royal Egyptian funeral may have sounded like. Musically speaking I was clearly on my own, since the only hints we have of how Egyptian music sounded comes from pictures of flutes, lyres and so forth found in tombs. To judge from the evidence, Egyptian music was soft, lyrical stuff. About funeral music, no mention is made at all. Thus the music I designed for the funeral of Amenhotep III in the opening scene of the opera does not resemble any funeral music I have ever heard before. The drumming that begins it, the flourishes for brass and wind and the emphatic entrance of the singing, give it a raw, primitive, quasi-military sound. In this music, coming as it does right after the prelude to Act I, my idea was to give an unmistakable and clear image of how, at least in part, "our" Egypt would be portrayed. By vividly portraying that world through the music, I hoped to set off the idealism of Akhnaten even more strongly. The blaring brass and pounding drums introduce the world into which Akhnaten was born.[38]

Glass is careful to stress that the Egypt that is portrayed in *Akhnaten* is "our" Egypt, an important move if any semblance of post-Brechtian awareness is to be conveyed in his discourse concerning the opera. But even so, his speculations regarding the instrumentation employed in ancient Egyptian funeral music are, if the archaeological literature is anything to go by, not all that far off the mark. Apparently, trumpets and drums did play an important role in ancient Egyptian musical culture, particularly in military and processional music. In point of fact, the presence of these instruments in military bands today can largely be attributed to the precedent of ancient Egyptian military culture.[39] The fact that they carry strong militaristic connotations is a fortunate coincidence in terms of the musico-dramatic construction of the opera, and one that is fully exploited in the portrayal of the pre- and post-Akhnaten pharaonic world.

The music of the funeral draws attention to the violence that is invariably the bottom line in establishing and maintaining imperial power. There is a second, more immediate rationale for the instrumentation of this scene, however, which is grounded in the belief system of the world into which Akhnaten is born. The image of ancient Egypt that has been passed down to us is one of a culture infatuated with death—one in which the lion's share of the material and human resources were directed toward ensuring the immortality of the dead pharaoh. The evidence that exists to this day attests to the lengths ancient Egyptians went in order to ensure the passage of their kings into the heavenly realm of Ra, from the mummification of their bodies to the construction of immense and costly edifices to the recitation in funeral ceremonies of lengthy scriptures intended to invoke the assistance of the deities of the underworld. It is easy to find a corollary of the burial practices of the ancient Egyptians in contemporary culture; indeed, some have attributed the need to stockpile ancient Egyptian artifacts, particularly mummies, in Western museums to a materialism identical to that of the pharaohs themselves. Jean Baudrillard has observed:

Rameses [II, whose mummy was recently "restored"] means nothing to us: only the mummy is of inestimable worth since it is what guarantees that accumulation means something. Our entire linear and accumulative culture would collapse if we could not stockpile the past in plain view. To this end the pharaohs must be brought out of their tombs and the mummies out of their silence. To this end they must be exhumed and given military honours.[40]

This "death anxiety," as Glass quite appropriately terms it,[41] whether ancient Egyptian or contemporary, forms the foundation of his depictions of the old Egyptian order and the pantheon of gods worshiped by the Egyptian people. "One aspect of this death thinking especially fascinated me," Glass has noted:

In reading the funeral texts . . . I learned that when the pharaoh dies and begins his journey to the heavenly kingdom of Ra, he is urged to employ certain strategies to ensure that the gods will *notice* what is happening. Of course, as son of Ra, he is entitled to a place beside his heavenly father, but what should happen, the texts seem to ask, if for some reason the gods do not notice the pharaoh's passing and are not prepared to assist him in finding his way to them and to welcome him? With that in mind, I strove to make my funeral music capable of drawing attention to itself in every way possible. If any of the gods in the heavenly land of Ra were dozing, I was determined that my music would wake them up.[42]

I have already discussed some parallels pursued by Glass between contemporary and ancient Egyptian musics, of which the above has to be one of the most shaky in historical terms. A good deal of what makes the music of this scene interesting, however, is its unmistakable contemporary flavor. In addition to its unconventional harmonic language, the powerful effect of the funeral music can be attributed largely to the scene's relentless tom-tom beat. While there are a number of precursors of such music in the classical world—for instance, in French opera of the late nineteenth and early twentieth centuries—the presence of percussive instruments, other than in ornamental or coloristic contexts, remains one of the most reliable litmus tests as to whether one is dealing with "high" or "low" cultural artifacts. Here the dichotomy is underscored, but in a sense it is turned against itself: What we are hearing is not popular or folk music but the ceremonial music of the Egyptian ruling patriarchy (the pinnacle of ancient Egyptian "high" culture). Glass's use of percussion does not, however, conceal its origins in contemporary popular culture, which is strange, because this is a harsh patriarchal regime that otherwise had little time or energy to "pander to the masses"—unless some kind of manipulation is going on. If so, there appears to be a sort of Adornian subtext to the vision created by Glass in this scene, of primal rhythms and stark, powerful sonorities stirring the passions of the simple ancient Egyptian peasant folk. But Adorno does not have the last word; neither does the ancient Egyptian patriarchy. There is a power in this music that mordernism never knew, although the long, dissonant tones sounded in the bass and the tritone-based melody sung by Aye later in the scene hint at some sense of agency from precisely this direction. But this is not the primary source of musical power in the scene; or if it is, then this power is quickly usurped by the crowd and turned to different ends. This is some of the ugliest, most frightening music in the opera, but it is also some of its most exuberant, without which the work as a whole would be decidedly lackluster. One senses some ambivalence about these two aspects in Glass's own descriptions of the scene. Compare, for example, the following passage to those cited earlier: "It was important to make the funeral as odd as it sounds. It's one of the first clues that this is gonna be an unusual work, when the funeral turns out to be a raucous, drum-rattling march. That gives us a clue that the whole order is going to be changed. So it's a prelude in a way."[43]

This appears to confirm that the prelude was not really a prelude, since it did not pull the listener into the story in the manner that tradition dictates. We are allowed to keep our distance. But in the funeral, we are wrenched headfirst into a kind of musical vortex that will continue unabated until the final scene of the act. This is extremely turbulent music, and turbulence engenders the desire for change, for stability. But Glass's turbulence is unlike any the operatic stage has known. Large blocks of sound pound loudly and relentlessly in an ever-tightening downward spiral, the tonal foundations of which shift restlessly. At the beginning of the funeral, it sounds as if we have moved from the tonic to the dominant of the opera's home key and that the music is vacillating between this key center, E, and its dominant, an altered B chord (a stereotypical I–V movement); but when the male chorus enters, it does so on A major, thus asserting the major tonic as a competing pitch center, making things a little more complicated in harmonic terms (see the discussion above, chapter 3). That Akhnaten and his father share the pitch center, A, with Amenhotep taking the major and Akhnaten the minor modality, is not surprising; Akhnaten is, after all, Amenhotep IV. More than this, the two characters prove ultimately to be inseparable, just as the deceased King Laius is a tangible if unacknowledged presence in the Oedipus myth from the moment of his death onward. Although nothing really appears to happen in the music harmonically or formally during what is an extremely long scene, or perhaps because nothing much seems to happen although the music is extremely unstable and ambiguous throughout, a growing sense of unease possesses the listener as the scene progresses (or does not progress). Sustained pedals on D-sharp (or E-flat, if we bring our operatic skeleton back out of its closet) poison the entire musicodramatic scenario with increasing frequency (see example 20, p. 78). If the prelude was a musical representation of the Nile, then the aural effect of this use of dissonance is like an octopus injecting its black ink into the clear blue water of the river. The interval formed between this tone and A is a tritone, the *diabolus in musica* given a new lease on life. This motif sets the sinister music of the old order apart from Akhnaten's spiritual idealism in no uncertain terms. Moreover, its corrupting influence leads one to believe that the modulation originally initiated, away from the relatively stable A minor of the prelude, was not a convincing modulation at all but rather an uncomfortable kind of pseudomodulation.

As the funeral continues, the impression is of growing unease. The text sung in the first cycle by the male choir, intended by its writers as an affirmation of life, takes on a decidedly sinister tone as a result of its setting.

Live life, thou shalt not die,	Ankh ankh, en mitak
Thou shalt exist for millions of millions of years	Yewk er heh en heh
For millions of millons of years	Ahau en heh

In both metaphorical and material senses, it is clear that the pharaohs succeeded in preserving themselves if not for millions of years then at least for thousands. If Baudrillard is to be believed, our own culture is intent on preserving them for millions and millions of years longer. The listener, however, is guided by the music toward Glass's and his protagonist Akhnaten's critique of this view that the reverse side of the pharaohs' ostensible affirmation of life was their denial of death—a schism that finds a ready counterpart in other binary constructs based on the distinction between self and other. Thus, the necessity of ensuring the pharaohs' immortality, when grafted onto the Egyptian empire, was used to justify any number of barbarous acts directed toward neighboring lands. The uncomfortable symmetrical division of the octave into tritones in this scene, not to mention the relentless polytonal vacillation between equally unsatisfactory key centers, could easily be viewed as a musical representation of the dualism inherent in these aspects of pharaonic culture.

After twenty vacillations of the two chords, including four threatening interpolations of the D-sharp tritone motif, there is a radical reduction of material (rehearsal mark 10). The nervous ostinato returns and, in the hiatus between cycles, in the wake of the funerary procession, the corpse of Amenhotep III enters, holding his decapitated head in his arms. The putrescent tritone motif returns followed shortly afterward by a return of the truculent drum rhythm (rehearsal mark 14).

We have been transported to the underworld, and the mutilation that Amenhotep displays is evidence of some terrible wrong that has been perpetrated against him or his memory, which for the ancient Egyptians were the same thing. It is also evidence of the identification of the deceased king with the lord of the underworld, Osiris, who was responsible for weighing the souls of the ancient Egyptian dead in order to establish who had and who had not earned "a place in the sun" in the afterlife (in the company of the sun god, Ra). The body of Osiris was also mutilated after his death and had to be reassembled by his sister/wife Isis before he could assume his position among the pantheon of underworld gods. Partly because of the Osiris myth, the physical integrity of the body, particularly of the head in relation to the torso, was held by the ancient Egyptians to be the most important prerequisite for life after death.[44] So the severance of Amenhotep's head from his body is the worst thing that could have happened to him from the standpoint of orthodox Egyptian religion. Only when the head has been returned to its rightful place on the hapless king's shoulders can life in the underworld be ensured. What, then, is this terrible wrong that Amenhotep III has been made to endure? If we follow Velikovsky, it has to be that he was killed by his son Amenhotep IV (Akhnaten). In real life, this almost certainly did not happen; but to the ancient Egyptians, the dead can be killed a second time in the afterlife by the profanation of their memory by living relatives.[45] Later in his reign, Akhnaten was to profane the memory of his father like no son had before. And in the mythical time of the underworld, past, present, and future converge, making it irrelevant whether a crime has already been committed or has yet to be committed, which is why Amenhotep already bears the scars of the injuries that his son will inflict on him in later scenes.

But here, once again, there are strong resonances for those familiar with the opera repertory. Decapitation plays an important role in another pillar of the operatic canon, Richard Strauss's *Salomé*. Like Jokanaan (John the Baptist) in Strauss's opera, Amenhotep III and his underworld double, Osiris, represent religious orthodoxy that is in some way challenged by a sacrilegious feminine or feminized other. In both cases, the decapitated head becomes to some extent associated with the phallus.[46] Salomé's decapitation of John the Baptist was a metaphorical act of castration, as is Akhnaten's decapitation of his father. But the isomorphism goes further than this. The association of traditional Egyptian religious practices with Judeo-Christian orthodoxy is made explicit in *Akhnaten* at the beginning of the temple scene (act 2, scene 1); thus, the decapitations of the two men may be perceived as closely linked also with respect to the specific orthodoxies to which the two composers were referring. Regarding the music, the "prophecy" motif in *Salomé*—g–c'–e' (the pitch relations are what matter, since the motif is transposed liberally)—a motif that whenever it makes an appearance in that opera points to its dramatic high point, the act of decapitation, is a transposed version of Akhnaten's transgression theme, which itself is a prophecy motif.

Rather than suggesting that this coincidence is a direct musical quotation, I would prefer to connect to two operas in a more general way. Much of the power of this scene derives from how it is more generally evocative of the dissonant textures of musical modernism. The construction of Akhnaten's transgression theme from the unstable second-inversion minor chord harks back to a popular "affect" in early modernist stage works such as *Salomé* and *Oedipus Rex*. The tritone is another unstable pitch relation, which is the very reason why it, too, plays an important role in modern operas, such as Alban Berg's *Wozzeck*, which abounds with tritones.[47] This, for Glass, is the old order: music his grandfather would have written—well, almost. It is at least intended to *evoke* the kind of music that his grandfather would have written.

The second cycle begins with an aggressive responsorial exchange between the male chorus and Aye, the first soloist of the opera, which soon changes into a more traditional soloist/accompaniment engagement. The rising motif (A–d-sharp–f-sharp–g-sharp) sung by Aye—who was personal adviser to Amenhotep III, is Akhnaten's father-in-law, and, following Akhnaten's inauguration as pharaoh, becomes his adviser—anticipates the changes that are about to take place in the pharaonic world; it is, of course, related to Akhnaten's transgression theme. However, the D-sharp diminished triad outlined by the motif and the leading note (of A minor/major) on which it culminates make it even more unnerving than when it was heard in its prelude guise. That he sings a variation of the theme that denotes Akhnaten's "destiny" in a stern bass voice and with added chromatic acerbity at this early stage in the opera goes some way beyond the conventional friction between father-in-law and son-in-law: It is strongly suggested already at this early stage that he views Akhnaten as a sexual deviant who will eventually have to be disposed of. Implicit, then, in Aye's rendering of the theme is a premonition of his complicity in the plot to overthrow his son-in-law. That he does not state this in so many words reveals something of his predicament as servant to the rebellious new pharaoh and as upholder of tradition. Aye was evidently something of a straggler between the old religious order and the cult of the sun disk. By all accounts, his character was more that of a shrewd opportunist—a friend to the new ideas when they were in vogue but quick to abandon them and return to orthodoxy when it served his interests. That he was ambitious there can be no doubt, since he rose to the position of pharaoh himself after the untimely death of Tutankhamen. Velikovsky claims, moreover, that Aye caused this death by initiating a feud between the two brothers and successors-to-the-throne after Akhnaten, Smenkhare and Tutankhamen, ending in the deposition of the former by the latter.[48] Thereafter, in Velikovsky's view, Aye encouraged the newly crowned child king Tutankhamen to risk his life in reckless military campaigns.[49] Having successfully disposed of both of the legitimate heirs to the throne, he then usurped the position of pharaoh through wedlock with Akhnaten's daughter (his own granddaughter), Ankhesenpaaten.[50] This, then, is the kind of man we are dealing with. His stern bass voice, his intimate exchanges with the male chorus, his aggressive declamatory singing style, and the forward-striving chromaticism of his melodic lines set him apart from the lyrical and ethereal voice of Akhnaten in no uncertain terms. His becomes, in a sense, the surrogate voice of Akhnaten's father, who, because he is dead, has no physical voice in the opera. Not since the statue of the commendatore came to life in the final act of *Don Giovanni* has the voice of a father-in-law (or potential father-in-law, in the case of *Don Giovanni*) so chilled the blood of a male hero.

While the dominant element of the prelude was water—to be specific, that of the Nile—in the first scene, two more elements are prominent. First, air or wind: the winds that blow in the turbulent pathways between sentient existence and the afterlife; or the winds of fortune and change that mark the end of one era and the dawning of the next. The text of the first cycle is a translation of the text recited by the scribe at the beginning of the scene: "He goes to the sky / He goes to the sky / On the wind / On the wind." But as the scene progresses, the dominant element of the opera is strongly evoked, in the text and arguably in the music, as the soul of the dead king traverses a fiery lake from one level of the underworld to the next.

The text of the second cycle, sung by Aye and the male chorus, is as follows:

Hail bringer of the boat of Ra	Ya inen makhent en Ra,
Strong are thy sails in the wind	rud akit em mehit
As thou sailest over the Lake of Fire	em khentik er she neserser
In the Underworld	em netcher khert

The second cycle finishes abruptly, leaving only the drums pounding out the primal rhythm established in the opening bars. Above the drumbeat, woodwind flourishes whirl and dance, coming to rest and then propelling themselves into motion once more, rising to their zenith, stopping dead, and then descending to their nadir—or rising and then rising again before eventually falling away—stabbing staccato spurts followed by longer labyrinthine licks (rehearsal marks 19–21; see example 5, p. 57). The breathy timbre of the high winds moving in similar motion to some extent connotes wind, at least inasmuch as they are all wind instruments. However, the darting, unpredictable movement of these lines probably finds a closer analogy in the flickering movement of fire. And given that the pitch center, A, becomes strongly associated with the sun god later in the opera, these passages seem to be an attempt by the composer to invoke a musical counterpart to the lines of the texts that refer to a fiery lake.

Be it the furnaces of hell or the edifying fire that is the agent, elemental forces are undoubtedly at work in ushering in the young successor to the throne. The mourning population of Thebes—including, for the first time in the opera, women, thus anticipating the central role they are to play in the religious revolution—now gather on the stage. The funeral procession moves upstage and further away from the audience. The drumming ceases temporarily, leaving only the whirling woodwinds and agitated ostinato.

Gradually, the musical forces gather once more for a final cycle, in praise of the departed king. In this cycle, there is an increasing sense of bustle and rhythmic disjunction. The E-centered ostinato motif takes on an almost overbearing urgency—similar to the sound of a police siren—when it is reinforced by the full power of the brass section and, later, is joined by high winds. In addition, there are four abrupt changes of meter, from 4/4 to 6/4 and back (rehearsal marks 31 and 32). After rhythmic stability has returned, the fire motif returns once again, and the mixed chorus sings wordlessly—absorbed, as it were, by the wind that is emanating from their mouths.[51] Aye's voice returns, at first in slight disjunction with the chorus but later merging until it is lost entirely. In this mass of sound, all individual identities are lost: All merge into one. The tritone motif returns but now stays locked firmly on D-sharp, not conceding an inch to the harmony it underpins (rehearsal mark 36). Eventually, after four chord changes, it begins to move, at first only to F-sharp, as it did immediately prior to the "fire" interlude, but in the last four patterns of the scene it rises in the final bar to a dangling G-sharp. This repeated bass line pushes the music forcefully onward to the next scene, which begins in the key of A minor. The fire motif, which is still spiraling in the background, is now joined by a shrill triplet diminution of the ostinato pattern. Strains of Wagner's "Ride of the Valkyries" are perceivable in this combination.

The course that has been set now feels irreversible. In the final bars, the text sung by the chorus reiterates a single word, *Ankh*, meaning life, a suitably universalist sentiment for the new religious order. The music then halts abruptly. The tension created is not released—it simply stops.

Refractions of Masculinity:
A New "Voice" Emerges out of the Old

The second scene begins with a short transition in which the musical material of the funeral is metamorphosed into one of the most important themes of the opera and, indeed, the entire trilogy. The music is a melodic and linear continuation of the bass line from the previous scene. Harmonically, the tonal forces exerted in the previous scene evaporate like clouds on a hot summer's day, leaving the home key of A minor to shine through unobscured. Two important themes are now introduced in counterpoint in the context of a single chaconne pattern; the higher of these (a–b–c'–e') is associated with Akhnaten's spiritual inclinations, the lower (a–g–C) is the so-called trilogy theme (see examples 12a–c, pp. 63–64). Glass explains the significance of the latter as follows:

This Trilogy theme, linked as it is to scenes in which essential aspects of Akhnaten's character are revealed, is strongly associated with Akhnaten himself. This is precisely how the Trilogy theme is used in *Satyagraha* and *Einstein* as well. In *Satyagraha*, it appears in the second scene when the young Gandhi embarks upon his life's work, and again in the final scene at the penultimate moment of his political victory. The Trilogy theme occurs in all five Knee Plays of *Einstein*, scenes that represent the more intimate portraits of Einstein.[52]

This music becomes associated directly with Akhnaten because at the very moment it is heard, Aye, the Amon high priest, the scribe, and the people of Thebes exit, leaving Akhnaten alone on the stage. Shortly afterward, he is joined by his aides, who prepare the young successor to the throne for the forthcoming coronation ceremony. If the motif heard in the prelude (and, in transposed form, in Aye's singing in the funeral) is identified with Akhnaten's anomalous sexuality as perceived by his opponents, as well as foreboding his tragic fate, the music we now hear represents a different perspective from which to view the character. This music or music related to it plays an important part in the opera from this moment on. In short, the music we now hear represents the interior world of the protagonist, as it does for those of the other trilogy operas. What, then, is the idea associating the same music with three very different men? These are, as Glass puts it, "people who changed the world through the power of ideas rather than through the force of arms."[53] Taken as it stands, this seems a little abstract and a little trite, as though Glass had invented the association after the fact. It is enough, for me at least, that these are three men whom the composer admired and deemed to be more worthwhile figures around which to construct operas than those who customarily frequent operatic stages. But why the same music, if these characters have very little in common, except that they are all people Philip Glass admires?

A closer look at Glass's discourse is quite revealing in this respect; he refers to the trilogy protagonists as people who changed the world "through the power of an inner vision" and not through the power of *their* inner *visions*.[54] Thus, the self conceived of by the composer is presumably viewed as radically inter- or even *non*personal, which brings us back to Glass's Buddhist orientation. The nonpersonal or nonindividual principle is identified in Buddhism with the most subtle plane of consciousness, the highest of the three Buddha bodies, *dharmakaya*. D. T. Suzuki has associated this concept with the notion of "personality," with the explicit intention of challenging or even inverting our conventional understanding of the word.[55] This conception of personality is a far cry from the Romantic cult of personality, an individual subjectivity that must somehow project itself against the backdrop of the surrounding world by the sheer exertion of its will in order to somehow become more "real" to itself. The Buddhist conception of personality is more quiescent, more receptive: "'Personality' in this original sense is more than 'individuality', because here no illusory indivisibility and uniqueness of a separate being is postulated, but only the idea that our momentary form of appearance is like a temporarily assumed mask, through which the voice of a higher reality sounds."[56]

This now sounds very metaphysical, New Agey, and otherwise hazy, but it need not be understood in that way. The idea that original and good ideas can often be realized best by momentarily releasing oneself from the shackles of the taken for granted, the preconceived, and the dogmatic has taken root in many different schools of psychology as well as in various creative spheres in recent years. This is the reason why people who are learning to draw are often instructed to copy an upside-down picture or to view the world through a mirror placed at an unusual angle. The idea is to encourage people to see what is actually in front of them rather than in terms of what they bring to what they see. Viewed from this standpoint, Glass's protagonists are not infallible supermen; they are, however, people who developed this faculty of questioning dogmas and thus were able to release their own innate creative potentials. They were people who had the knack of coming up with good ideas.

Particularly in this music, then, the characters of the trilogy are showing their true colors. But what musical colors does Glass select as indicative of the more meritorious, nonpersonal side of human nature? The form selected by Glass is the chaconne. Within the frame of three chaconne cadences, the first of which draws attention specifically to the trilogy theme and the remaining two of which are linked more closely to the specific attributes of Akhnaten, a descending tetrachord in A minor sinks downward time after time (see example 13, p. 65). The musical reference is to the lament, a topos intended in the early Baroque period to symbolize a seemingly endless round of suffering by the character associated with the music. It is a moment of interiority, of introspection, in which the hero or heroine responds to his or her unfortunate circumstances either with despair, resistance, or stoic resignation. For Akhnaten, the last of these options is suggested. Life is seen as an endless round of suffering, as suggested by the four-bar lament descent, but liberation from the wheel of becoming is possible. Like John Lennon, Akhnaten is "just sitting here watching the wheels go round and round," and like Lennon, he takes some solace in the very act of watching, which implies some sense of distance. This aspect is connoted in the final bar of the pattern when a (magic?) flute melodically articulates the final chord of the pattern, E major, setting out from the final note of Akhnaten's ascending theme in an upward-bound diatonic scale, thus striving toward transcendence. But it is also connoted in the composure of the musical discourse.

In the second of the chaconne patterns, scales fan out from each note of the tetrachord in opposite directions (see example 13). Music like this is richly evocative and, depending on the emphasis given to these matters in individual productions, a number of associations can be fostered. The first of these has to do with a ubiquitous image in the bas-reliefs produced during Akhnaten's reign: handed rays culminating in hands spread out from the sun disk (the Aten) like a fan, carrying the symbol of life (ankh) to the mouths of Akhnaten, Nefertiti, and their daughters. A second connotation has to do with Akhnaten's sexuality. This is the protagonist's first physical appearance in the opera, and under such circumstance his androgynous physical attributes are easily associated with the music we hear at this time, with its gently rising and descending contrapuntal lines. (More on this below, chapter 5.)

In the third of the chaconne patterns, a descending trumpet line is prominent (see example 14, p. 65). I shall discuss the symbolic significance of this pattern more fully in connection with the hymn to the sun. Suffice it for now to state that this line and the instrument on which it is played are closely associated with the sun god itself and with Akhnaten's relationship with his god.

A caveat is, however, in order. There is a literalness to this music that may once again be perceived as means of musical foregrounding or alienation. Both the diatonic descent through the tetrachord and the melodic lines that fan out from the notes of the tetrachord have to them a distinct scalar and therefore nonnarrative, even nonmusical quality to them. Thus, associations are suggested but have an opacity to them that is characteristic of so many of the representations in this opera.

The stoic tranquillity of Akhnaten's moment of self-communion does not last for long. The music of this section finishes with what I will term the "finality" motif (see example 25). This motif is heard at various junctures in the opera and, like the music that precedes it, imparts a plodding sense of stoicism and resignation. The resolution it provides is not complete,

Example 25. "Finality" motif.

Example 26. Act 1, scene 2, the coronation of Akhnaten. "Bell" motif.

however, until the very end of the opera, when it is inverted so that the tonic note a is finally heard in its root position (see example 12d, bottom part, p. 64). Even though a low pedal on A is heard as the music of this section finishes, the bassoon on which the motif itself is played resolves only to the dominant, e. And from here the music launches itself once again on a headlong flight into the imaginary.

Egyptologist Paul John Frandsen writes as follows on the relationship between the two dominant pitch centers in the opera: "If the 'Trilogy' theme represents the religious, revolutionary King Akhnaten, E minor must represent Akhnaten the human being."[57] Frandsen is correct, insofar as the key of A minor sees Akhnaten at his most poised and "grounded," while E minor is closely bound up with his relationships to and desires for others. He is even closer to the mark when he observes that "given the close relationship between E minor and A minor, we are tempted to interpret its effect in the scene as Akhnaten's achieving liberation from his parent,"[58] assuming that the parent in question is his recently interred father. It is precisely the scenes that are set in E minor, however—most notably the temple (act 2, scene 1) and family scenes (act 3, scene 1)—that show this character just about as far away from achieving liberation from his other parent, Queen Tye, as he could possibly be.

With e" as its note of departure, a new motif is now outlined on flute and celeste, anticipating an important motif that will be heard in the next scene (act 1, scene 3), played there on tubular bells: I will refer to this as the "bell" motif (rehearsal mark 13.3; see example 26). The musical material undergoes a gradual transformation now that will culminate eventually in the music of the cornonation ceremony proper. The musical textures of these passages are once again extremely restless. The tempo of the music increases in a series of stepwise increments, thus pushing the listener forward to the coming ceremony. Both the harmony and the rhythm of these passages are among the most ambiguous in the opera. Complex polyrhythmic effects are introduced, and the harmony struggles to build an identity for itself in the new key center of E minor (see example 9, p. 60). A phrygian feel, similar to that heard in the prelude, gradually starts to emerge, with E as a very shaky tonic and F major and G major the phrygian or "lowered" second and third degrees of the scale.

The Three Patriarchs and the Imaginary

The people of Thebes have once again gathered on the stage, led by the three upholders of the old order, the Amon high priest, Horemhab, and Aye. In terms of archetypes, these characters represent the ecclesiastical, the military, and the administrative patriarchs, respectively. In the years preceding Akhnaten's accession to the throne, the authority of the Amon high priests rivaled that of the pharaohs. Moreover, of all the three patriarchs—the ternary pillars holding the Egyptian empire firmly in place— this is the one who stood to lose most from the displacement of the traditional religious order by Atenism.

The commander of the military forces during Akhnaten's reign was a man named Horemhab. Like Aye, he was an ambitious man who is more likely to have been a shrewd pragmatist than a thinking man of any substance; also like Aye, he later manipulated his way to the exalted position of pharaoh, a position to which he also had no legitimate claim. It is unlikely that he was ever a sincere follower of Atenism, even when serving Akhnaten, as during his own reign as pharaoh he did everything in his power to stamp out all remaining traces of it: Temples were demolished, history books and laws were rewritten, and stern punishments were prescribed for those who did not follow the letter of the law.[59] Named by some "Horemhab the rebuilder," from the perspective of the Atenists he might more appropriately be termed Horemhab the demolition man, as there was not a temple to the sun god remaining in the kingdom after his term as pharaoh; Akhnaten's City of the Horizon, Akhetaten, was abandoned and leveled during Horemhab's reign.

The portrayal in the opera of the three patriarchs as collaborators appears to be accurate: During Aye's reign as pharaoh, he worked closely with Horemhab to restore the old order to its former position. Horemhab himself was on good terms with the priesthood of Amon and was, more than anyone else, responsible for carrying out the reinstatement of the pantheon of gods headed by Amon to its former elevated position in the years following the deposition of Akhnaten. Moreover, as close aides to the pharaoh, it is probable that the two men were intimately acquainted even earlier than this: Both came from military backgrounds, and their outlooks on life must have, as a result, been similar. More important, perhaps, their outlooks must have been markedly different from that of the young pharaoh to whom they were both obliged to pay obeisance, for the time being at least.

Glass's depiction of all three characters emphasizes the exotic and the phantasmagorical. This is true of the miragelike tonality associated with these characters. If Akhnaten's musical discourse and the home key of A in which it is usually found connote some pre-Oedipal sense of nondifferentiation, then both the declamatory singing style and the refractory harmonic language of the music associated with the patriarchs brings to mind the Lacanian mirror stage, in which the subject first constitutes itself as distinct from the surrounding world (and the mother) by observing itself in the mirror.[60] This very act results in a fundamental sense of alienation on the part of the subject, since the self is not construed as experienced but as seen—as an integrated, externalized image of oneself onto which subjective experiences are merely projected. This perceived wholeness, which in the theories of Lacan is associated with both the phallus and the symbolic domain—or as he terms it, The-Name-of-the-Father—is merely an empty facade, however; like a precariously constructed stack of cards, it is liable to cave in at any moment. Hence, there is a great deal of pent-up anxiety associated with the Lacanian "imaginary," for what is at stake is precisely what our culture has taught us to value most: our sense of wholeness, of individual uniqueness, and the power to determine our own destiny, irrespective of the ramifications such assertions may have on those around us.

Interpreting the patriarchs of the old order as messengers from the Lacanian imaginary seems consonant at least with the Stuttgart production of the opera, where the representatives of the old order appear in garish colors (predominantly red), are wearing masks, have painted faces, or else stand on stilts—in short they appear like grotesque circus clowns rather than real people. In contrast, Akhnaten's and Nefertiti's appearance is distinctly human: the favourite dictum of the religious revolution, "living in truth," at least as far this particular staging is concerned, is interpreted literally. This distinction between the imaginary world of the patriarchs and the real world of Akhnaten, Nefertiti, and their followers (which in the family scene [act 3, scene 1], is seen to be also not without its problems) is an important one to the overall musicodramatic conception of the opera:

The opera *Akhnaten* . . . aims at presenting a strikingly different picture of the "old" order as it appears in Act 1, Scene 1, and the years of Akhnaten's reign. The gods of ancient Egypt were effectively banished by Akhnaten. Their somewhat exotic treatment, both musically and visually, during scenes of the "old" order are meant to heighten this difference.[61]

At the beginning of the coronation ceremony, the three patriarchs of the old order enter once again in fifths with all of the phallic force of the similar entry of Aye and the male chorus in the previous scene. This contrasts sharply with the delicate contrapuntal entry of the three representatives of the new order in next scene. The first strophe of the coronation music is fairly static in musical terms, its declamatory style functioning to underline the ecclesiastical content of the first line of the text. Its chord progression is E minor–G major–B diminished six-four. In the second bar of the B diminished chord, the minor third (D) becomes a major third (D-sharp); the minor/major shift here is strongly evocative of Akhnaten's transgression theme, thus underlining that this is the musical discourse of Akhnaten's soon-to-be adversaries.

With the following section (which I will refer to as the A section) comes a new kind of tonal ambiguity, this time modal. In a new chord sequence, the move to G major from the introductory chord sequence is no longer followed by an E-minor tonic but continues its ascent through A-flat major, B-flat major, back to A-flat major, and then to G major, where it remains over four bars before slipping back to E minor with the simple addition of the bass note of this chord, E. (Later in the scene it remains on G, thus placing a stronger emphasis on this pitch center). Here, as elsewhere, Glass avoids the strong cadences of common-language tonal practice that would confirm that a modulation had occurred. The result is modal ambiguity. In addition, the influence of the opera's home key, A minor, continues, to some extent at least, to be felt in this passage, given that no entirely satisfactory conformation of any of the new tonal centers has been forthcoming and that the music resolves to A minor partially in the second chord progression of the coronation proper and, more fully, in the interlude during which Akhnaten receives his double crown.

While tonal ambiguity has been an important aspect of Glass's style since *Einstein*, this kind of pandiatonicism or panmodality is atypical of his mature style. It is quite apparent also from his own characterization of this scene that he has in mind an exotic effect, intended to convey the illusory worldview of the patriarchs rather than functioning as a musical language behind which he stands wholeheartedly. Modal harmony such as this is clearly not something that interests the composer, other than in specific theatrical contexts that require it:

I actually seem to prefer a stronger feeling of tonality than you get with modal harmony. In modal harmony, you don't really know where the key is very often. It can be in several places. . . . It's not that it can be in several places, but it can be in several places and you don't really care. I don't think that modal harmony makes a very strong statement musically, for me.[62]

Thus, not surprisingly perhaps, the composer selects a musical language in relation to which he already feels some sense of alienation in order to depict the musical and dramatic alienation of this scene. This alienation is specifically underlined in the use of conventional markers of the exotic (such as the phrygian I–♭II–♭III move), in the aggressive vocal style of the singers and other aspects of the arrangement, and in the most chimerical harmony of the opera so far.

The home tonality of A minor returns in the next section to remind one that it was never actually all that far away. This section (a–G–F–G–e/E–e) is also tonally ambiguous, although now there are only two competing key centers, A minor and E minor. Subsequent to the musical interlude in which the new pharaoh is crowned, a somewhat different transformation of the sequence is heard. The initial chord is no longer unequivocally cate-gorizable—it contains the pitch b', a chord tone of E minor but not of A minor. The result is a kind of A-minor/E-minor hybrid that is sufficiently unstable to shift the harmonic equilibrium from the former key to the lat-ter. It is weakened further as a result also of its first inversion voicing. Moreover, there is a growing gravitational pull toward the uninverted bass note of the E-minor chord, due to the fact that there is no longer any seri-ous challenge to its tonal hegemony. A descending ostinato line (c–B–A–G–E, a transposed version of the tetrachord motif from the cha-conne), which runs inexorably down toward E, adds considerable weight to this impression.

"(A) Power (That) Comes from Below"

It is noteworthy that the descending tetrachord motif heard in the bass ostinato is mirrored, as it was in the chaconne, with rising tetrachords in the vocal parts. The tetrachord motive a'–b'–c"–d" is heard at first in the tenors (rehearsal mark 57) and then, in the next repetition of the sequence, in the sopranos (rehearsal mark 58). Related motific material is found also in the alto and bass voices. Even more interesting than the reappearance of the motif itself is the fact that it appears concomitant with the return of the full mixed chorus (SATB). The message is as clear here as it was in the fu-neral scene: We are moving irrevocably away from the patriarchal hege-mony of the old order toward an order in which sex literally does not count. An alternative way of interpreting this shift in the two scenes is to surmise that the old order is one in which the patriarchy calls the shots and the ordinary people of Thebes and, indeed, of the entire Egyptian empire simply comply with their wishes. But that denies the pleasure of the chorus as they once again cross the threshold from the discursive ranting and rav-ing of their leaders to their own all-encompassing bliss, from mere pleasure toward what French criticism refers to as *jouissance*.[63] This seems to sug-gest a Foucauldian conception of power as force relations that circulate freely in the sociosymbolic sphere and that divorce themselves from the specific intentions of their progenitors, and in which resistance is not in a position of exteriority in relation to power but rather both "rulers" and "ruled" collaborate in constructing "polyphonic" and constantly changing

The three patriarchs, Aye, Horemhab, and the Amon high priest, crown Amenhotep IV (Akhnaten) (act 1, scene 2). United States premiere of *Akhnaten*, Houston Grand Opera. HGO photo by Jim Caldwell © 1984.

"force fields."[64] As the chorus once again loses itself in its own ecstasy, Foucault's adage, "power comes from below" and all the connotations it musters, both social and sexual, seems particularly apt.[65] Not since Mussorgsky's *Boris Godunov* has the diverse yet unified power of a "critical mass" been felt so strongly on the operatic stage.

But let us return to an earlier event that can be held largely responsible for the change of emphasis in the music described above. After two alternations of the two chord progressions discussed above, there is an abrupt return to a single A-minor chord. During the repetitions of this chord, the new pharaoh, Amenhotep IV, receives his crown. Even while the scribe is talking, there is a sudden change in tempo (from 192 to 96 beats per minute) and meter (from 3/4 to 4/4 time), the bell motif returns once again on flute and celeste—two instruments that are strongly associated with the new religious paradigm. Shortly afterward, the gradual buildup of musical material that was heard at the beginning of the scene is reinitiated. The meter changes from 4/4 time back to 3/4 time, and a quasi-accelerando unfolds, once more in a series of steps. But that is not all: Even though the rising arpeggios have shifted to 3/4 time, two bass notes separated by an octave stubbornly assert the tone E in contradictory 4/4 rhythmic patterns that cannot even agree with each other about which beat of the bar to begin on. These notes drag and pull at the forward-striving arpeggios, attempting to stop them in their tracks, but to no avail (see example 9, p. 60). It is easy to see this as a musical representation of the upholders of the old order dragging their heels, imploring the young pharaoh to respect tradition. As far as key relations are concerned, the move from A minor to E minor, from the "self" to the "other" key, from the real to the imaginary, marks also the journey of Akhnaten from his relatively sheltered private life to the more narcissistic ways of the pharaohs, as well as symbolizing the (imaginary) earthly inheritance that is now bestowed upon the new ruler.

While all of this is going on in the music, the scribe Amenhotep, son of Hapu, now adopting the voice of the Amon high priest, continues to recite the titulary list of the new pharaoh. Amenhotep IV receives his crown with all of the traditional honors:

> Live the Horus, Strong-Bull-Appearing-as-Justice;
> He of the Two Ladies, Establishing Laws
>   and causing the Two-Lands to be Pacified;
> Horus of Gold, Mighty-of-Arm-when-He-Smites-the-
>   Asiatics;
>
> King of Upper and Lower Egypt,
> Nefer Kheperu Ra Wa en Ra,
> Son of Neb-maet-Ra
> (Lord of the Truth like Ra)
> Son of Ra, Amenhotep (Amon is pleased)
> Hek Wase (Ruler of Thebes), Given Life.
>
> Mighty Bull, Lofty of Plumes;
> Favorite of the Two Goddesses,
> Great in Kingship in Karnak;
> Golden Hawk, wearer of Diadems in the Southern Heliopolis;
> King of Upper and Lower Egypt.

Thus, the fourth of the elements is introduced: earth. To the water of the prelude music and the air and fire of the funeral music is added Akhnaten's worldly inheritance, the land of Egypt, center of the most powerful empire of the ancient world. By a fortuitous coincidence, the crown the new pharaoh inherits is the double crown of Upper and Lower Egypt, the two regions of the country that were united in the epoch of the Old Kingdom. What could be more fitting? That an empire founded on dualism (the dualism of life and death mapped onto the dualism of ruler and ruled) should have a dual crown and be termed a dual land seems to fit Glass's depiction of the old order like a glove. A further dualism is the dualism of the Oedipal subject as he enters the mirror phase and for the first time distinguishes her- or himself as "other" to the harmonious, complete "self" seen in the mirror. At this stage of development, the mother is seen as separate from the self for the first time; thus, the "other" key of the opera, E minor, might easily be perceived as the "(M)other" key, given that the mother is the illusory object of desire that promises complete fulfillment for the emerging subject. And sure enough, this key center, E, is associated with Akhnaten's mother later on in the opera, as well as with the phantasmagorical world of the new pharaoh's adversaries.

As was the case with the fire motif in the funeral scene, the introduction of earth invokes a response from the full mixed chorus, from the women as well as the men of Thebes. It might be significant as well that the coronation music is heard now in three rather than two macrostructural blocks (AA BBB–AA BBB–AA BBB), thus reiterating the triadic motif of the opera. Now the subject of the opera is fully constituted, in all of his Oedipal glory. The only thing left is to furnish him with a voice.

CHAPTER FIVE

Higher Love

New Geometries of Power, Desire, and Exclusion in the Trio and Two "Duets" of Akhnaten, Nefertiti, and Tye

The Window of Appearances and the Real

The title of the third scene of act 1, "The Window of Appearances," denotes in the original Egyptian the windowed balcony of the palace in Thebes that was used for state appearances by the ancient Egyptian royals. Some of the most striking images of Akhnaten and his family that have survived the passing of time are depictions of these state appearances. But for Glass, who describes the phrase as "a lovely double-entendre," it has at least one other significance.[1] "The window of appearances" can imply that appearances *are* simply a window—that they are transparent and have no real substance; that all experience is somehow "framed"; and that we will never in life know complete immanence, complete symbolically unsullied actuality. One fairly traditional way of looking at this is as an adaptation of Plato's cave, according to which all that we experience in life is merely a reflection of some higher reality that, like our blind spot, remains perpetually outside of our field of vision.[2] Through this window, we may be able to catch glimpses of forms that somehow reflect this higher reality, but we will never be able to grasp the totality of the reality itself.

Some forms of postmodern theory place a slightly different emphasis on this formulation, arguing that to even entertain the notion of some other reality that is somehow prior to, and therefore more authentic than, the one in which we live is to indulge in idle speculation. We may feel nostalgia for a lost age in which we could back our arguments up with metaphysical certainties, or this "nostalgia" may be for a future age in which technological or

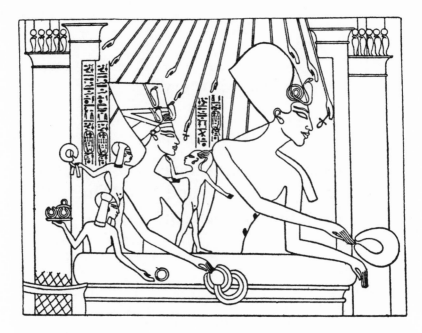

Akhnaten and Nefertiti at the palace balcony, or window of appearances, with their three eldest daughters bestowing gifts on their followers. Wallis Budge, *Tutankhamen: Amenism, Atenism, and Egyptian Monotheism* (New York: Dover, 1991 [1923]), p. 91.

human development or insight will provide the answers to many of the unanswered and possibly unanswerable questions of our age; but in any case, there can be no return to the status quo ante. Thus, the postmodernist could understand the window of appearances as denoting the symbolic domain in general, a limitless expanse of signifiers, the signifieds of which, in true Derridean (and Lacanian) style, signify something else, which in turn serve as the signifieds for another group of signifiers, and so on and so on, resulting, for some of the more skeptical theorists at least, in a total devaluation of meaning, a new meaninglessness, which Baudrillard refers to as a simulacrum. In such a scenario, there are only appearances; there is no hidden, final truth.

The main point of contention seems to be whether this bottom line that is not a bottom line implies a new kind of ethics based on respect for the individual, who should be free to pursue his or her own inner "truth," while hoping that it is unlikely, if not impossible, that one will end up harming others; or, does it simply imply a blank, "anything goes" relativity? The latter point of view, which has been associated with Richard Rorty and Jean Baudrillard, among others, and to which I do *not* subscribe, claims that there is a metaphysics lurking not too far behind the former of these assumptions, and they may or may not be correct.[3]

The title of the scene we are discussing, in addition to addressing these broader questions, might be seen simply as a way of drawing attention to the opacity of the representations before us. In light of the meticulous construction of representational strata in the prelude and the first two scenes, the composer might be forewarning us in the title of this scene that "everything is not what it appears to be, don't be completely duped by what you hear, don't be (completely) drawn in, be careful what meanings you invest this discourse with." And this is desirable because the return to the home key of the opera, A minor, is a return of (relative) transparency, which is easily and conventionally invested with meanings that post-Brechtian and postmodern notions of subjectivity have difficulty accepting. The return to A minor at this point in the opera clearly draws on these conventions: This is the site of Akhnaten's (re)constitution as a subject; our hero has overcome the various obstacles in his path and has finally achieved some level of subjective integration or wholeness (indeed, he appears to be *unusually* whole). But even, or particularly, here, it is important that we be urged to keep our distance from the events that are being played out on the stage and in the music, that we do not identify completely with the title character.

Lacanian concepts are once again useful here. For Lacan there is no subject, as such, prior to her or his entry into the symbolic sphere (during the mirror stage). This is not to say that the subject is nothing but language, but that some of the most fundamental aspects of human experience, which are conventionally held to be natural, under closer inspection are seen as emerging through processes analogous to those found in language.[4] If the musical diatribe of the old older took us on a roller-coaster ride into the Lacanian "imaginary," in this scene we are firmly entrenched in the domain of "the real." But how real is what Lacan calls "the real"? In short, it is as real as all other aspects of human experience, including the imaginary; no more so and no less so (i.e., there is an immanence, a reality, in them all). The real is a symptom above all else of the desire of the subject to achieve seamless integration with nature; it is the site where nature quite literally becomes real to the subject — as real, at least, as any other area of experience that is mediated by language. Two typically enigmatic phrases of Lacan's to some extent summarize and to some extent shed further light on (and yet to some extent obscure) what I have been saying: "The real is that which always returns to the same place" (thus, the key of A minor in *Akhnaten*); and "the real is the impossible" (thus, the opacity of the musical discourse).[5] A phrase of Alan Sheridan's further illuminates the position occupied by the real in the Oedipus complex: He describes it as "the umbil-ical cord of the symbolic,"[6] a particularly apt metaphor in this scene.

Not surprisingly, in this scene we see Amenhotep IV, who has now changed his name to Akhnaten (spirit of Aten), with his mother and his (other?) bride, Nefertiti. In accordance with the dictum of the new regime, "living in truth" (truth assertions are typical of the discourse of the real, as are references to nature). All pretenses are now stripped away: Akh-naten appears before his subjects as he really is, however shocking that might be to them. The two women who stand by him are both ardent fol-lowers of the new religious cult. Together, the three sing an exquisite trio in which they extol the manifold bounties of creation as manifestations of the power of the Aten. The text that is sung is unlike anything we have heard in the opera so far and, indeed, anything previously known to an-cient Egyptian culture:

AKHNATEN:

Oh, one creator of all things
Oh, one maker of all existence
Men came forth from his two eyes
The gods sprang into existence
    at the utterances of his mouth

AKHNATEN:

Tut wu-a yeri enti
Wa-a wa-u yeri wenenet
Perer en rem em yertif
Kheper netcheru tep ref

TYE & AKHNATEN:

He maketh the green herbs to make
    cattle live
And the staff of life for the use of man
He maketh the fish to live in the rivers,
The winged fowl in the sky

TYE & AKHNATEN:

Yeri semu se-ankh menmen
Khet en ankhu en henmenet
Yeri ankh-ti remu en yetru
Apdu genekh pet

AKHNATEN & NEFERTITI:

He giveth the breath of life to the egg
He maketh birds of all kinds to live
And likewise the reptiles that creep
    and fly
He causeth the rats to live in their holes

AKHNATEN & NEFERTITI:

Redi nefu en enti em suhet
Se-ankh apnentu yeri ankhti
    khenus
Djedfet puyu mitet yeri
Yeri kherti penu em babasen

TYE, AKHNATEN, NEFERTITI:

And the birds that are on every
    green thing
Hail to thee maker of all these things
Thou only one.

TYE, AKHNATEN, NEFERTITI:

Se-ankh puyu em khet nebet
Hrak yeri
Enen er a-u

Bells as a Symbol of the New Order

As the scene begins, the clouds of the various tonalities from the previ-ous scene evaporate once again to allow the A-minor rays of the sun to shine through unimpaired. After an eight-bar introduction, tubular bells chime out the euphoric bell motif, heard an octave lower than at the beginning of the coronation ceremony, where it was played on flute and celeste. At first, the motif spans two bars; then it is augmented over four bars (see example 27), after which the implied harmony of the motif forms the foundation of the music of the entire scene. It is accompanied initially by trombone fifths (A and e), a significant choice of instruments for reasons discussed below, after which a simple string accompaniment unfolds. As the scene proceeds, further orchestral color is gradually introduced.

Bells are a singularly rich musical instrument in both semiotic and acoustic terms. All three of Charles Sanders Peirce's semiotic categories—icon, index, and symbol—can be identified here with the bell: It represents religious insight and ceremony (i.e., it is a symbol); it points to and actually summons the congregation to the building in which religious ceremonies take place, the church or temple (i.e., it is an index); and, as it is used in religious ceremonies, it is itself what it represents (i.e., it is an icon).[7] Thus, a great deal of the force of this instrument can be attributed, aside from its acoustic properties, to its semiotic elasticity.

The bell has been a favorite instrument of what Glass refers to as the European "school" of "New Mystic" composers.[8] Glass has explicitly distanced himself from this group, although he has expressed respect for the Estonian composer Arvo Pärt, and has boasted that the Pärt once referred to *Akhnaten* as "the *only* modern opera."[9] Pärt's esteem for the opera should come as no surprise, considering the Estonian's preoccupation with religious subject matter and particularly with bells, not to mention the archaic countertenor voice, which Pärt himself has used in numerous compositions. Pärt's *tintinnabuli* style is inspired by the musical patterns that arise in bell-ringing practices, and bells are used as an instrument in their own right in a number of his compositions, including his poignant *Cantus in Memory of Benjamin Britten* (1977), in which a monotone bell chime forms the ground over which strands of descending string scales cascade. Other composers of a similarly devotional bent, including John Tavener

RM 4

Example 27. Act 1, scene 3, the window of appearances. Bell motif.

and Henryk Górecki, have either included bells in their respective instrumental arsenals or have written music that is either imitative or evocative of bell chimes.[10]

Another noteworthy example of the use of bell chimes in contemporary music is in Mike Oldfield's progressive-rock classic *Tubular Bells* (1972–1973). It is possible that there is some reciprocity of influence here, since Oldfield was quite strongly influenced by Glass's compositional style of the late 1960s to 1970s. Much of the musical texture of *Tubular Bells*, for example, betrays the influence of Glass's early minimal pieces. In addition, Oldfield has rearranged and recorded one of Glass's compositions: *North Star* (1977). The use of tubular bells in *Akhnaten* can easily be compared with their usage in Oldfield's composition. In *Tubular Bells*, the bells themselves are not heard until the very end of the lengthy first part, after each of the other instruments has been introduced, verbally and actually, by Oldfield himself. The effect of the delayed entry of the bells after their conspicuous absence is quite striking. In the same way, the tubular bells in *Akhnaten* appear only after all the other elements of the opera are in place. When they are finally heard, there is a distinct sense of the pieces of a puzzle falling into place, the distinctive percussive and at the same time sonorous sound of wood striking metal serving as an effective attention grabber.[11]

A final symbolic significance of the bell within the drama of the opera lies in the fact that it is an instrument that is cast in fire, the dominant element of the opera. Other metallic instruments appear to bear a similar relation to the sun god and its followers, including the brass instruments (the trumpet, the horn, and the trombone), the triangle (in the City/Dance scene [act 2, scene 3]), the flute, and the celeste. Thus, the combination of instruments at the beginning of this scene—bells, flute, and trombones—all of them cast in fire, has to be looked on as more than a coincidence. It should be noted that Mozart invested his instruments with similar significance in *Die Zauberflöte*—thus, the title of the opera itself and Papageno's magic glockenspiel (literally, "bell play"). The fact that this use of instruments coincides with the entry of the three principals, itself a clear Mozartian reference, underlines Glass's self-conscious relationship to his operatic antecedents.

The symbolic ramifications of the bell-ringing music do not end here. The bell theme includes every diatonic step of the aeolian pentachord a' to e". Given the rich sonorous qualities of the bell, what results is a cluster that, like the Atenist religious doctrine, seems to encompass just about everything. But it is the "just about" that gives cause for concern; the cluster does not, for example, include the sixth degree of the scale, F, nor does it include any of the intermediary or "altered" degrees of the scale, like E-flat (and its enharmonic equivalent D-sharp) or B-flat or A-flat. All of these pitch centers are strongly associated with the old order, and all of them are conspicuously absent here. Thus, although the sonorous and ideational spectrum appears particularly rich and resonant in these passages, this music is in fact characterized as much by what it excludes from its purview as by what it includes. One might even say it is defined by what it leaves out.

If a ceremonial context for this moment is to be envisaged, then the cheerful demeanor of the descending A-minor arpeggios is related more closely to the elated bell-ringing heard after weddings than to the solemn tolling that announces a death. This evocation might be deliberate, and it is certainly dramatically appropriate: The bells we are hearing announce not only the beginning of a new religious regime but the beginning of a tripartite marriage between Akhnaten, Nefertiti, and Tye—a "fatal triangle" if ever there was one.

Harmonically speaking, the music of this scene is fairly straightforward compared to what we have heard previously. Each verse comprises two cycles, the former of which is quite spartan in terms of its instrumentation, while the latter is more richly orchestrated. In terms of chord functions and meter, the sequence is as follows:

$$
\begin{array}{llllllll}
4/4\ a: & i & VII^6_5 & i & i\ VII^6_5 & i & & v^9 \\
3/4\ i & i & VII^6_5 & i & VII^6_5 & 4/4\ i & VII^6_5 & i \quad VII^6_5
\end{array}
$$

There is some overlap in the second bar of the sequence, with the trombone fifth (on A and e—the voice of the sun god?) carrying over to the first beat of the second bar. The resulting sonority, which is constructed in much the same way as the bitonality that forms the tonal foundation of the Hymn, can be regarded as a kind of cluster chord, which includes every note of the aeolian mode except C. Taken as a whole, the chord sequence does include every degree of the aeolian scale and shifts effortlessly between binary and ternary rhythms, the two primary rhythmic modes of the opera, by means of additive processes. Like the bell theme, this can be seen as a representation of the inclusive ideology of the new order. But, like the bell theme, this new inclusiveness has its limits: There is still a conspicuous absence of "black notes."

Transgressive Voices

It is Akhnaten himself who is the first to sing. The effect of withholding his voice until the final scene of the first act is quite startling. Glass describes his intentions in delaying Akhnaten's musical entrance in the following passage:

I heightened the effect of hearing that first note by Akhnaten by delaying his vocal entrance as long as possible. He is not heard in the prologue, of course, nor does he sing in the first-scene funeral music. We see him all through his coronation, including the preparations leading up to it, but still we do not hear his voice. Finally, some thirty-five minutes into Act I, in the third scene—named The Window of Appearances (a lovely double-entendre title taken from the Egyptian)—where he greets his subjects as the new pharaoh, we hear him for the first time as he is joined in duet by Nefertiti, a mezzo-soprano. This becomes a trio when his mother, Queen Tye, a soprano, joins them.[12]

This silent and peculiar-looking figure of the previous scenes is, then, suddenly given a voice, not only physically but in a broader sense that speaks to the power relations in the opera. He now has both the means and the inclination to give exterior form to his own distinctive interior voice, which we heard at the beginning of the coronation in the lament. Notably, the music out of which this scene is constructed is closely related thematically to the chaconne music from the previous scene.

With little of harmonic and rhythmic interest going on in the music, attention is shifted toward the voices and their particular qualities, as well as the interplay that takes place between them. Indeed, there is plenty of interest here. When Akhnaten finally opens his mouth and his ethereal countertenor voice is heard for the first time, it is undoubtedly one of the high points of the opera. Glass explains:

The attraction for me in using a countertenor for Akhnaten must . . . be obvious. The effect of hearing a high, beautiful voice coming from the lips of a full-grown man can at first be very startling. In one stroke, Akhnaten would be separated from everyone around him. It was a way of musically and dramatically indicating in the simplest possible way that here was a man unlike any who had come before.[13]

In the passage that follows, Glass makes it obvious that the intended musical referent in using the countertenor is the archaic castrato voice.

The figure of Akhnaten himself required special care. This was a man so unusual, even unique, as to be virtually unprecedented in Egyptian, and therefore human, history. . . . I thought a long while about how to present our title character. After all, you could use up the better part of Act I just indicating, in various ways, how extremely peculiar Akhnaten really was. There simply was no stage time for that. To demonstrate his strangeness with costuming could work, but that was risky because it left a crucial noninterpretative matter in the hands of people over whom, in future productions, I would have no control. More and more it seemed to me that the problem was best solved musically, and my solution was to make Akhnaten a countertenor. . . . Along the same musical lines were the famous castratri, men who had been castrated as boys so that they could retain the sweetness and strength of their boyish voices while adding the physical force of a mature male physique. This practice continued into this century, the last castrato of note being the Italian Alessandro Moreschi (admiring Italians called him "The Angel of Rome"), a soprano castrato who lived long enough to make a number of recordings that are the only surviving examples of castrato vocalism. (Moreschi died in 1922 at the age of sixty-four.) The last thirty or forty years have seen a renewed interest in music from earlier times, and this has brought about a resulting emergence of the modern countertenor who, through rigorous training of the falsetto part of his voice, can achieve impressive and beautiful vocal results.[14]

I quote this passage *in extenso* as evidence that the composer is referring explicitly to the castrato voice in his use of the countertenor and not employing the voice solely because of its unusual acoustical properties. The ability of the character of Akhnaten to partake of the pleasures of the higher register, to partake of *jouissance* as the male voice is rarely able to do, is, aside from its gendered reference, a quite obvious way of setting him apart from surroundings, of highlighting the transgressive aspects of his character. Glass's writing for the countertenor moves, on the whole, close to the top of this voice's compass: the high d"s and e"s in this scene, for example, are well within the compass of the female soprano—and the male castrated soprano. For most countertenors, the opera is sung in the "head" (or falsetto) voice throughout.

One of the most hotly debated points regarding high male voices and, similarly, low female voices, is the extent to which, as Freud put it in a now infamous phrase from his essay "The Dissolution of the Oedipus Complex," "anatomy is destiny"[15]—in other words, the extent to which voice compass is determined by nature or, conversely, the extent to which it is a sociosexual construction. Recent writing in gay and lesbian studies has offered some valuable new perspectives on this issue. Wayne Koestenbaum in particular has shed some important new light on the related questions of voice production and register.[16] The majority of voice manuals, Koestenbaum points out, divide the male voice into two voice types and the female into three, according to register, but others hold that there is only one register for all singers or that each individual note constitutes its own register. As important as the division between voice types is the threefold division between chest, throat, and head voices, which refers to the primary place of resonation for each voice type. More than simply designating a place of resonation, these terms carry strong positively and negatively charged associations. The chest voice has throughout history been regarded as the most "natural" of voice types, and the head voice, or falsetto, as its name implies, the least natural. Singers trained in bel-canto techniques are taught to gloss over the points of rupture between one place of production and the next in the hope that this will somehow make their singing sound more "natural"; ironically, however, the work that goes into perfecting such a technique guarantees that the end result will be anything but natural. Singers who take pleasure in these places of rupture, as well as those who otherwise adorn their vocal productions with unnecessary "artifice," such as trills and vibrato, risk rejection on precisely these grounds. Koestenbaum reverses traditional assumptions regarding the naturalness of voice types and places of production, taking distinct pleasure in the transgressive aspects of unconventional approaches to the voice, which he sees as "seismic shudders in the System-of-the-Line"—the line in question being the one that divides human beings neatly into masculine and feminine categories.[17] At the same time, however, he is skeptical that there can ever be complete liberation from the influence of the binary order as long as transgressions such as these are perceived and enjoyed *as transgressions*. By celebrating the "unnatural" in vocal production, which Koestenbaum sees as the musical equivalent of coming out, "do we," he pointedly asks, "inadvertently reaffirm the divided world?"[18]

For Koestenbaum, the main object of consideration is the falsetto voice (the voice of Akhnaten); for him, this is the model transgressive voice.[19] But recent writing in gender, gay, and lesbian studies has drawn attention also to the transgressive aspects of the castrato and contralto voices (the latter of which is Nefertiti's voice type). Joke Dame sees the male soprano voice, whether a castrato or an exceptionally high falsetto, as the ultimate transgressive voice, as it is easily confused with the female soprano.[20] Rather than regarding this voice simply as a symptom of androgyny, which she regards as a "strategy of annexation"—a means of appropriating the feminine in order to construct a larger, more complete masculine subjectivity (of which Akhnaten can justifiably be accused)—Dame stresses the ways in which the castrato challenges the binary gender order: the ways in which it goes beyond traditional notions of masculine and feminine to form its own distinctive construction of subjectivity, located specifically within the male body, albeit a somewhat altered one.[21] Michel Poizat makes a similar point, although his discussion comes from a slightly different intellectual tradition, which sees the immanent qualities of the voice as bringing to the surface some rarely experienced instinctual mode of being, which, to be sure, goes beyond the masculine and the feminine and a good deal more besides.[22] This tradition tends to place less of an emphasis on the voice as a sociosubjective construction and more on psychoanalytical questions.

The North American literature, on the other hand, tends to place more of an emphasis on the social construction of psychological categories. In an important and exhilarating article on gender coding in female voices, Elizabeth Wood has made a point similar to those of Koestenbaum and Dame.[23] Wood stresses the importance of register and place of production to what she calls "Sapphonic voices," which are female voices that in one way or another transgress the dominant gender order, usually by encompassing both the contralto register and areas of the higher soprano register.

Like Koestenbaum, Wood particularly prizes the areas of rupture in voice production as the low chest voice of the contralto transforms itself into a high falsetto. "This border-crossing voice I call Sapphonic," writes Wood,

is a transvestic enigma, belonging to neither male nor female as constructed—a synthesis, not a split. Having this voice entails risk, but not a necessary loss: it can be *both* butch and femme, *both* male and female. Its challenge is to the polarities of both gender and sexuality as these have been socially constructed as stable, unchangeable binary symmetry, for it suggests that both gender and sexuality are transferable. In acoustic effect, its combination of different registers refuses vocal categories and natural/unnatural polarities, and confounds simplistic messages about female desire (and relationships among female desire, class, age, sexual status, and identity) in music's texts and opera's roles conventionally assigned to specific female voice types. For listeners, the Sapphonic voice is a destabilizing agent of fantasy and desire. The woman with this voice, this capacity to traverse a range of sonic possibilities and overflow sonic boundaries, may vocalize inadmissible sexualities and a thrilling readiness to go beyond so-called natural limits, an erotics of risk and defiance, a desire for desire itself.[24]

I will return to the Sapphonic voice in my discussion below of Nefertiti, who is required to possess just such a voice. But for now what I am interested in is the thrill of transgression, which is shared by both Akhnaten's and Nefertiti's voice types as well as in their concatenation and which can be experienced by all listeners as pleasurable, regardless of their specific sexual orientation, if they drop their prejudices about the "naturalness" of voice types.

Both Koestenbaum's and Wood's ideas about transgressive voices bring to mind Georges Bataille's ideas concerning taboos and their transgression.[25] For Bataille, transgressions are not autonomous acts. Or to be more precise, the pleasure that is associated with transgressive acts is inextricably bound up with the taboos that are being transgressed. This reciprocity has profound implications in many spheres of human experience but most noticeably in those of sensuality and religion, which many theorists in France and elsewhere since Bataille have regarded as similarly inextricably intertwined. These two areas are closely interrelated also in *Akhnaten*. Akhnaten's and Nefertiti's transgressions are both sociosexual and religious. These characters achieve transcendence in terms of voice production and otherwise, but only by setting themselves off against another they perceive as somehow profane. The ecstasy they clearly experience, whether sexual or religious (and usually both), is, in part at least, the ecstasy of breaking taboos. This is not to imply that there is nothing at stake in these characters' musical discourse other than achieving the ecstasy of release—clearly there is much at stake both from the historical perspective and from that of the contemporary performance context of the opera, the pertinence of which goes beyond simple rule breaking. Clearly, it matters what rules are broken and for what reasons; it matters that Nefertiti's powerful low contralto and Akhnaten's high countertenor directly challenge the musical discourse of a harsh patriarchal regime.[26] More important than either of these considerations, however, may be the relationship between the two voices, to which I turn below.

Akhnaten Androgyne?

The male countertenor voice has always had to it a transgressive aura; and clearly this was important to Glass, who wanted to depict Akhnaten and his cohorts as religious and political revolutionaries. But this could have been done in many different ways. Why specifically cast Akhnaten as a countertenor? And why the obvious reference to the castrato singing tradition? Is it possible that the historical Akhnaten was a castrato? As I have already mentioned, there has been a good deal of speculation concerning Akhnaten's sexual makeup, due to depictions of the pharaoh in which he appears to be endowed with secondary physical characteristics usually associated with the female sex; these include enlarged thighs, hips, and buttocks, and something resembling a cleavage in the area of his chest. In one famous colossus found in Karnak which has confounded historians since it was discovered, he appears naked in his lower parts and is visibly lacking any signs of male genitalia.[27] Glass himself seems to take such representations at face value, although we have already established that historical accuracy was not his primary concern. He asserts in the film on the making of the opera, for example, that "the idea of all these roles [Einstein, Gandhi, and Akhnaten] is never to represent the person—this is a species of poetry, it's not documentation."[28] Thus, the question of whether the real Akhnaten's physique resembled its representations might not be all that important. To depict him in that way in the opera clearly makes for good drama, and it is, moreover, a highly appropriate allegory for his innovative religious and social ideas. Glass is not alone, however, in speculating whether the pharaoh might not have actually appeared as he was depicted.

The art of the Amarna period may be the first period of conscious naturalism in the history of art. One of Akhnaten's dictums was "living in truth," and presumably he chose to be portrayed as he really appeared, not in the formal, idealized style of the pharaohs who preceded him. If this is true, he certainly must have been an odd-looking character: swollen thighs, enlarged hips, breasts almost pendulous. At first glance he appears almost hermaphroditic. Medical analysis is not conclusive. Akhnaten's physical appearance could have been genetic in origin, or it may have been the result of disease. In any case he was male and capable of fathering children.[29]

Is it possible, then, that Akhnaten might actually have been a castrato? This seems unlikely, if the children he fathered are assumed to be his own.

These are, it should be stressed, consistently referred to in the writings of the period as "the daughter[s] of the King, of his loins."[30] Thus, if Akhnaten did suffer from a sexual disorder, it was certainly not serious enough to render him incapable of producing offspring. The archaeologist Cyril Aldred maintains, however, that Akhnaten and his daughters might have suffered from such a disorder, which he is bold enough to identify as Fröhlich's syndrome. According to Aldred's theory, the condition became more severe as the pharaoh aged, after which it began to affect his physical appearance.

It is not simply that Akhenaten had himself represented as effeminate or androgynous, he specified certain distortions that belong neither to normal men nor to normal women. In an exaggerated form these are the abnormalities that have enabled a number of pathologists independently to diagnose that the subject depicted in this way may have suffered from a disorder of the endocrine system, more specifically from a malfunctioning of the pituitary gland. Elliot Smith identified it in 1907 as Fröhlich's syndrome, a complaint in which male patients exhibit a corpulence similar to Akhnaten's. Adiposity may vary in degrees but there is a typical feminine distribution of fat in the regions of the breast, abdomen, pubis, thighs and buttocks. The lower limbs, however, are slender, and the legs, for instance, resemble "plus fours". . . . The diagnosis of Fröhlich's syndrome may only be made when the patient, having reached the age of puberty, fails to develop normally, *his voice stays shrill*, body hair does not appear and the sexual organs remain infantile. A later stage of the complaint is the plumping-out of breasts, abdomen, buttocks and thighs. An occasional concomitant is hydrocephalus, which, because it has arisen when the bones of the skull have hardened and closed, does not distort the cranium to the usual globular shape, but results in a bulging of the thinner parietal areas.[31]

This explanation would certainly seem to account for Akhnaten's peculiar physical characteristics, as well as shed some light on the cranial distortions discernible in portraits of the royal princesses. Moreover, it provides some "scientific" justification—as if needed—for Glass's decision to cast a countertenor in the title role. If the evidence cited by Aldred is to be believed, Akhnaten might well have been a "natural" male soprano in real life with a voice very similar to that of the castrati. Perhaps it is best to let speculation rest here, however, since this whole line of reasoning is weakened by the problem of categorically proving any assertions at all in this matter. But we should not let the paucity of the evidence upset us, as the enigma of Akhnaten's real sexual identity is less interesting than his gender construction in Glass's opera and the possible ramifications of this in the present-day world.

In this respect, a competing archaeological viewpoint, that of the Danish Egyptologist Paul John Frandsen, might offer some useful pointers.[32] Regarding Akhnaten's sexual constitution and its representation in ancient Egyptian art, Frandsen writes:

The atenist trio, Tye, Akhnaten, and Nefertiti. Akhnaten's hermaphroditic features were replicated in this production (act 3, epilogue). Houston Grand Opera. HGO photo by Jim Caldwell © 1984.

Although at present we are uncertain as to whether or not Akhnaten's mummy has, in fact, survived, and thus there is no possibility of testing the hypothesis of the androgyny syndrome, there is little probability that he should have been genetically "defective," as scholars in the 1930s believed. Nevertheless, the choice of the countertenor remains a congenial one. Scholars engaged in research on the Amarna period during recent years do now largely agree that the famous colossi of Akhnaten represents the king as god of creation, and hence androgynous, containing both the male and the female creative principle. The iconography of Akhnaten is the visual rendering of a theological dogma, and the musical rendering could hardly find a more apt expression than a voice that is neither male nor female, the countertenor.[33]

What we have, then, are two conflicting interpretations of the art of the Amarna period: One that views these works of art as realistic and accurate representations of the pharaoh and his family, and another that sees the same art as expressionistic portrayals that function in much the manner of devotional icons, representing in physical form the religious ideas that the depicted people extol. I am inclined toward the latter point of view. Regardless of whether Akhnaten and his children were deformed, the pharaoh nevertheless found it desirable to have them represented in this manner. Moreover, the evidence that Akhnaten's god—for whom the pharaoh was the self-appointed conduit—was androgynous is incontrovertible. The Aten is referred to in a number of texts written at the time as being the mother and father of all that exists. It is not unlikely, therefore, that the king would have wanted to be perceived as related in some fairly tangible way to his androgynous god.

The question of androgyny provides a springboard for many of the contemporary issues Glass might have been addressing in *Akhnaten*. Androgyny was one of the most hotly contested areas of debate in popular culture, feminism, and cultural theory in the late 1970s and early 1980s. David Bowie was one of the first pop artists to adopt a self-consciously androgynous persona, which in the 1980s he discarded in favor of an equally self-conscious heightened masculinity. Androgyny became de rigueur among many punk-rock and new-wave artists in the years that followed, when Bowie and somewhat similar performers such as Lou Reed and Iggy Pop had already moved on to other aestheticosexual categories. Everyone from Wayne County to Boy George to Annie Lennox to Suzanne Vega got in on the act. Jimmy Somerville's high falsetto voice shockingly broke gender barriers in the early eighties, as did Grace Jones's slinky urban contralto. Laurie Anderson provided an androgynous bridge between new-wave and downtown New York minimalism with apparent ease, revealing that the chasm that divided the two movements cannot have been very wide in the first place.[34] At the height of the movement—if it can even be called that— androgynies of one form or another permeated just about every stratum of popular music, from gay disco to heavy metal.[35] It should be noted, however, that many of the artists associated with androgyny in the early 1980s later discarded it, as Bowie had before them, in favor of a self-conscious gender construction focusing on the attributes of their own sex. Annie Lennox, Laurie Anderson, and Suzanne Vega are all examplar of this move. Androgynies were, by and large, ways of transgressing not only the dominant bipolar gender division but of resisting broader practices of cultural stereotyping. As such, they were at the hub of the counter- or even anticultural project of that particular time, which had a lot to do with postmodernism's skepticism about master narratives.

But the roots of androgyny go deeper than this. Androgynous assumptions lie at the heart of many of the world's religions, including Akhnaten's. Various forms of androgyny were also extremely pervasive in the Romantic period and came to the surface most strongly in the music of composers such as Wagner and Aleksandr Scriabin. Androgyny was appropriated also by feminists in the first half of the twentieth century, most notably in the writing of Virginia Woolf, and it exerted a powerful influence over several decades of feminist thought. The writing of Doris Lessing is particularly rich in androgynous imagery, especially the *Canopus in Argos: Archives* novels, two of which Lessing turned into librettos for Glass operas.[36] Androgyny was also appropriated by gay-rights activists like the poet Allen Ginsberg, another Glass collaborator and a fellow Buddhist. In the academic world, the work of literary critic Carolyn G. Heilbrun set a precedent for many future studies in that area, of which June Singer's is one of the better known examples.[37]

The concept of androgyny as transgression started to be discredited when it was realized that cultures that endorse androgynous worldviews do not always use them as a means of undermining constricting gender binarisms, as had been the case in feminist and postmodern forms of androgyny, but of reinforcing these binarisms. Wendy Doniger O'Flaherty's anthropological study *Women, Androgynes, and Other Mythical Beasts* (1980) shattered a number of the most pervasive illusions concerning androgynies.[38] A second challenge came from the French literature with its ideology of *différance* and the emphasis it placed on specifically "feminine" ways of writing: what came to be known as *écriture feminine*. The writings of Hélène Cixous and Julia Kristeva were particularly influential in this regard. Both Cixous and Kristeva placed a strong emphasis on the Lacanian imaginary, a kind of experiential sanctuary where the ordinary rules of language hold no sway, an area of pre-Oedipal nondifferentiation that, being strongly associated with the mother, is also strongly encoded in feminine terms. For both writers, this area of experience, with its emphasis on the instinctual and the immediate, serves as a source of empowerment and considerable pleasure, particularly for women, who do not have the same Oedipal imperative as men to break free from maternal influence.

Kristeva seems to have had her doubts, however, about just how far down the Oedipal path, or up the umbilical cord, women ought to go. In one of her most influential and controversial essays, she makes it clear that the imaginary, while providing a source of unity and strength for women, does not in itself provide a sufficiently sturdy springboard for instigating political change.[39] For such purposes, discursive strategies traditionally marked as masculine (i.e., symbolic and linear strategies) are, in her opinion, required. Kristeva is careful, however, not to impart to her gender categories any metaphysical significance; this move is sufficient, in her view, to distinguish her idea of feminism both from those that demand access to the symbolic order in order to effect change from the inside and those that assert the right to remain on its outside, occupying their own "feminine" space. It is tempting to view Kristeva's third strand of feminism as a species of androgyny, given that it combines discursive strategies that she herself acknowledges are encoded in masculine and feminine terms. But Kristeva pointedly asserts that this is not the case, that her notion of feminism is not what she calls bisexual,[40] which she understands to be a simple inversion of gender categories, the ontological status of which remains intact even after transgressive inversions.

One of the most perceptive Anglo-American specialists on Kristeva's writing, Toril Moi, has criticized Kristeva and other critics of androgyny on this count, claiming that the androgyny of Virginia Woolf, for example, does precisely what Kristeva's third strain of feminism claims to do: It disrupts the ontological status of existing categories by bending the boundary lines between the masculine and feminine to such an extent that they reach the semiotic equivalent of meltdown.[41] Incidentally, lest we are tempted to draw too rigid a line between androgynies and "antiandrogynies," the erosion more than the inversion of gender categories was the explicitly stated aim of Heilbrun's work.[42]

I am skeptical, in much the same way as Moi, as to the necessity of barricading oneself in on either side of the androgyny debate—considerably more skeptical than Jean-Jacques Nattiez, for example, who in *Wagner Androgyne* comes down with a vengeance against all forms of androgyny, even though he successfully identifies as many as three different types of androgyny in Wagner's discourse alone (a male-dominated one, a female-dominated one, and an asexual one).[43] Nattiez's book makes a valuable contribution to recent Wagner studies in other respects, but his implicit assumption that there are an unlimited number of androgynies out there makes it seem a little harsh of him to dismiss all forms of andogyny with a single swipe—even those of Woolf and other feminists—regardless of the political contingencies of individual cases.

Like critics of androgyny, I am suspicious of certain forms of androgyny and of the utopian and sometimes oppressive assumptions that lie behind them; but I am equally suspicious of the motives of some of the more vociferous critics of androgyny, many of whom, like Kristeva, have valid and cogently argued reasons for their objections,[44] but others of whom might simply be resisting one of the more potent forces of (predominantly positive) cultural change in recent years, particularly in popular culture, by means of a crafty rhetorical move whereby all forms of androgyny are lumped together as a single evil. This is, like the androgyny it critiques, a totalizing strategy, a way of erasing differences, of eradicating the nuances and the political force of complex arguments by a less-than-subtle process of overgeneralization by abstraction.

To return to the point after this long but necessary diversion, Akhnaten is, in my view at least, androgynous. I should add that Glass himself expressed some consternation when I used this term to describe the protagonist of his opera.[45] Like the term *minimalism*, which for two decades was the bane of all the composers to whom it was somewhat indiscriminately

The subtle body of Tantric Buddhism, with the male principle (Ida) on the right and the female (Pingala) on the left. Madhu Khanna, *Yantra: the Tantric Symbol of Cosmic Unity* (London: Thames and Hudson, 1979), p. 69.

applied, androgyny has become heavily laden with all kinds of semiotic baggage, a good deal of which the composer would probably prefer that audience members left at home when going to see the opera.

This is not to say that *Akhnaten* stands aloof somehow from the other androgynies of the 1970s and 1980s; this work did, in its own distinctive way, participate in the debates that were going on in the cultural sphere at the time. Moreover, the issue of androgyny is a recurring motif in a number of Glass's works for the stage: the role of Gandhi in *Satyagraha* was originally to be shared by two characters, one male, the other female[46]; *The Fall of the House of Usher* (1988) is concerned with the repercussions of an ill-fated love affair between male/female twins; and *The Voyage* (1992) has an androgynous subtext to do with exogamous "cross-pollination" between two pairs of male/female twins, one from earth, the other from another planet. None of these works, however, should be viewed as simple

A recent publicity photo of Philip Glass. Akhnaten, the composer has commented, is "very recognisably a part of all of us." Compare this photo to the icon facing (p. 148). Photo by Tom Caravaglia ©.

endorsements of a specific androgynous position; nor are they facile dismissals of all things androgynous, but, rather, they are carefully considered contemplations of the issues from various perspectives. Interestingly, Glass seems able to relate to *both* sides of the androgyny debate. In other words, Akhnaten, his chosen androgyne, is a complex character, with admirable and decidedly less admirable qualities, each of which comes to the surface at different points in the opera.

Androgyny is a controversial issue also outside of cultural studies. Sexual divergence or ambivalence of any sort, androgynous or otherwise, makes many people profoundly uncomfortable. When borderlines, sexual or otherwise, start to disintegrate or to merge, it undermines many of those "certainties" by which we define ourselves and our places in the world. It threatens what we think we are and what we work hard everyday to project ourselves as being. This is particularly true of received ideas of masculinity, which are brittle constructs at the best of times. It is noteworthy, therefore, that Glass seems to have little difficulty in accepting his protagonist's physiological abnormalities. Quite the contrary: There is a very different tone to the composer's discussions of Akhnaten than that in the discussions in the archaeological literature, which, as we shall see in the next chapter, tends to attribute Akhnaten's shortcomings as a ruler to his perceived physiological shortcomings. Glass's comments are not at all consistent with this point of view: When viewing statues of Akhnaten in the Cairo Museum, for example, he observes: "The profile is amazing, isn't it? I find that a very handsome profile. I don't know why the people who write about it talk about how misshapen he was. I don't find him misshapen at all."[47] Perhaps the most telling statement of all by the composer concerning not only the character but also the physique of Akhnaten is that "he's a very strange guy, he's a very weird guy, but he's also very recognizably a part of all of us."[48]

But Glass's attitude would not in all cases carry over to his audiences, particularly in the United States. When Christopher Robson, the courageous countertenor cast in the title role of the North American production of the opera, appeared before audiences in an appropriately padded-out body-suit, the tolerance of some audience members was apparently stretched to the breaking point:

Both the visual and vocal impression Christopher made as Akhnaten was decidedly startling, especially when Akhnaten sings for the first time at the end of Act I. A number of people in our audiences were quite upset by Christopher's appearance on the stage. One very famous musician, a man who had spent his life in the theater and might have been expected to be aware of the wonders achieved by make-up artists, expressed genuine sorrow that we had not been able to engage a less grotesque-looking singer for our title role! Near the end of the New York City Opera run, we received a letter denouncing us for (1) having found some poor hermaphrodite; (2) forcing him to display his deformities in public; and (3) making him sing my music![49]

Oedipal Entanglements

The first notes Akhnaten sings in the opera are taken from the rising chaconne motif from the beginning of the previous scene (a'–b'–c"–e": 1–2–3–5; see Akhnaten's part in example 28). The melody then moves diatonically down to the third, after which it jumps back up to the high e". During the final section of the stanza, Akhnaten simply resonates three times on the tonic (a'). Akhnaten's predominately rising melodic line could easily become associated with the rising of the sun—not to mention the metaphorical rising of the sun cult—as a result of the subject matter of the text. It could, in addition, quite easily take on phallic significance in light of

Example 28. Act 1, scene 3, the window of appearances. Fourth stanza.

the predominantly falling lines heard in the melodies sung by Nefertiti and
Tye in the verses that follow.

To heighten the impact of the singing, the orchestral accompaniment
for this first cycle is reduced radically. The arpeggio pattern heard prior to
Akhnaten's entry on the viola is transferred to flutes and, at the same time,
is shifted up an octave in register, resulting in a suitably ethereal texture for

the pharaoh's religious proclamations. Occasional interpolations are heard in low fifths on the trombones, but that is all. In the second cycle of Akhnaten's solo section, more instrumental color is added. The flute part is transferred to oboes and clarinets and drops an octave as a result: It is doubled an octave lower by violas. The "reedy" texture of the oboe/clarinet arpeggios is complemented by the transferral of the trombone fifths to bassoons. This imparts to the music an exotic, "ancient Egyptian" feel. Reed instruments were and are common in Egyptian musical practices.

Queen Tye enters at the beginning of the following cycle on a high e″, dropping to d″ on A minor, in anticipation of the G major seventh that follows (see Tye's and Akhnaten's parts in Example 28).[50] Thus, Tye assumes the strong fifth of both chords in contrast to her son, who moves from the root of the first chord to the third of the second. Tye's melodic movement is the exact mirror image of Akhnaten's (Tye descends by a major second while Akhnaten rises by the same interval), offset by a delay of a half note. It might be dramatically significant that Tye enters on the fifth and Akhnaten on the root. As I have suggested earlier, the fifth of A minor, E, represents the title character's sexually charged perceptions of others; in this way, a strong physical bond is suggested between the two. In the second line of the text, Tye leaps up to a high a″ and then descends through the tetrachord motif down to e″, thus underlining the opposition between this motif (a″–g″–f″–e″: 8–7–6–5) and Akhnaten's rising motif in the opening measures. Akhnaten joins his mother's feminine-marked descent through the final three notes of the tetrachord in lower thirds, as only he would be able (e″–d″–c″: 5–4–3). Here occurs one of the most interesting musicodramatic events of the entire opera: As Akhnaten remains on a steady c″ — the third of the A-minor chord, a chord tone that the composer himself has interpreted as gendered in connection with the transgression motif — Tye moves from the fifth of the chord (e″) in its first two beats to its root (a′) in the remaining two, thus surrounding him musically. It is not difficult to find an allegory for this in both psychological and sexual terms: Akhnaten is quite literally enclosed in the imaginary "feminine"; he has ascended the umbilical cord to his mother's womb. Thus, immediately following their respective initial statements of sexual identity, the son's sexual identity is blurred in his romantic descent with his mother, after which the act of Oedipal reintegration is enacted in music — at Tye's initiative, one might speculate, although it is clear that Akhnaten was more than just a consenting party, in light of his flirtatious scalar descent with his mother. In the measures that follow, mother and son are one, at first in perfect fifths (e′ against b′) in the tonal center connoting desire for the (M)other (during the E-minor cadence) and then in unison in the key center of "the real," A minor (both sing the note a'). The two sing three ecstatic wordless notes on the tonic before reiterating the entire cycle in reorchestrated and texted form. At the dramatic high point of the third scene, the ternary motif is once more, therefore, reiterated.

In the second cycle of this verse, there is a marked increase in musical texture, with all of the higher wind instruments playing undulating arpeggios in contrary motion to the cellos. Akhnaten's voice is reinforced now an octave below by violas and a solo horn: This procedure of doubling the countertenor voice with other solo instruments has its roots in Baroque compositional practices and was particularly common in writing for the castrato voice.[51] Here it is quite necessary, since Akhnaten's delicate countertenor could easily get lost in the midst of the orchestra and the considerably more powerful female voices with which it interweaves.[52] As the orchestration becomes denser, the horn is replaced by a more penetrating trumpet.[53] Once again, a symbolic significance can be identified: the trumpet, like the tubular bells heard at the beginning of the scene, is an instrument that is cast in fire. It is also the instrument conventionally wielded by the angel, the messenger of God.

In the next verse, Tye's powerful soprano is replaced by the lowest female voice, the contralto. The most surprising aspect of this casting is that Tye is the soprano and Nefertiti the contralto; ordinarily, one would expect the mother to have the lower voice and the romantic leading lady the higher. For example, the mother/wife in *Oedipus Rex*, Jocasta, is a mezzo-soprano. The same principle obtains apropos of low female voices for Herodias in *Salomé*, Hérodiade in Jules Massenet's opera of the same name, Mamma Lucia in *Cavalleria rusticana*, Geneviève in *Pelléas et Mélisande*, Arnalta in *L'incoronazione di Poppea*, Auntie, hostess of the Boar, in *Peter Grimes*, and a whole host of other maternal, matronly, or matriarchal mezzos and contraltos. Other conventional roles include queens (matriarchs of nations?), mother-earth figures, and female sidekicks. Such casting can be considered conventional.

There are, of course, numerous exceptions in the repertory to this tendency, all of which are justifiably considered extremely important by contraltos as well as in feminist and lesbian musicology. Travesti or other "cross-dressing" roles, like Bradamante in *Alcina*, do not fit comfortably into this category.[54] The most well known exception to the rule is Carmen, whose sultry mezzo-soprano totally eclipses Micaëla's wimpy soprano in Georges Bizet's opera. Ulrica the (black) fortune-telling contralto in Verdi's *Un ballo in maschera* is another role in which the low female voice is marked as "ethnic." Precisely because of their conspicuous "otherness," roles such as this often suggest a connection with the mystical and the sublime. Other sublime or godly contraltos include the goddess Erda in *Das Rheingold* and *Siegfried* and the title role in Britten's *The Rape of Lucretia*. Brahms's *Alto Rhapsody* and Edward Elgar's *The Dream of Gerontius* belong to this category as well. If Nefertiti belongs to either of these categories of low-voiced leading ladies, it is the latter. Hers is what Elizabeth Wood refers to as the Sapphonic voice: the dark, dusky, deeply sensual, dangerously or delightfully (depending on one's perspective) self-determined feminine voice, which confounds all expectations regarding the "natural" precedence of the high female voice. Such voices are seldom upstaged by sopranos or by anyone.

For Glass, there was another consideration, however, that had to do with the relationship between the three principals:

With Akhnaten cast as a countertenor, my three main leading voices were all high. I knew there would be frequent ensembles in the opera: duets and trios with Akhnaten; his mother, Queen Tye, sung by a soprano; and his wife, Nefertiti sung by a mezzo-soprano. (The score calls for a contralto, but true contraltos are rarely found.) By using the middle to upper range of the mezzo-soprano and countertenor voices with the lower and middle range of that of the soprano, voice crossing (where lower voices sing above higher voices, and vice versa) also could happen easily. In the final libretto, we stayed away from the Oedipus theme, since the text already seemed fully freighted with abundant social, religious and philosophical issues. However, a veiled reference to the ambiguous sexual relationship of the three principals does remain in this aspect of the vocal writing. Especially when they are heard together for the first time, in the final scene of Act I (The Window of Appearances), the voice crossings produce a purposely confusing effect, making it sometimes difficult for the listener to follow the separate parts.[55]

Nefertiti enters, as did Tye, on the fifth, thus underscoring, once again, the strong physical bond between the two (see Nefertiti's and Akhnaten's parts in example 28). The note on which she enters is not the higher fifth, however, but e', a perfect fourth lower than Akhnaten's opening note. The main difference between Tye's and Nefertiti's vocal parts, apart from voice compass, is the emphasis on counterpoint in the former compared to the predominantly homophonic orientation of the latter. This will not be the case in the duet (act 2, scene 2), but for now both Akhnaten and Nefertiti are to some extent under the spell of Tye's stronger soprano voice. Thus, although she enters on the fifth as Tye does, in the three measures that ensue Nefertiti fairly consistently shadows her husband's melodic line, singing a third below it. The fourth and fifth measures, however, see her striving toward melodic independence. Prior to this, Nefertiti follows Akhnaten's descent in seconds—enacted earlier as a romantic entanglement with his mother—but then takes two plunges of a perfect fourth on her own, first from a' to e' and then all the way down to b. Thus, like Tye, Nefertiti jumps from the root to the fifth over the A-minor chord preceding the cadence chord, but unlike Tye she does not enclose Akhnaten in so doing. In the cadence chord itself, E minor ninth, she descends to its fifth, b, after which she drops even lower to resonate with her husband on a, an octave lower than him. The octave separating the two is, in this particular case, also the difference between incest and nonincestuous sexual relations. The effect of this low a is as extraordinary as Akhnaten's high e"—Nefertiti has crossed into the realm of her husband both in terms of register and tonality, as indeed is the case with Akhnaten, who sings an octave higher than his wife. This places her well within the compasses of both the baritone and the bass. If Akhnaten's countertenor underlines in unmistakable terms what an extraordinary man the pharaoh was, then the same must surely be true of Nefertiti's beautifully seductive contralto. Combining the sexual and the capable, Nefertiti's is unquestionably the most sympathetic role in the opera. Unlike Akhnaten and Tye, who are guilty not only of forbidden incestuous love but also, as we shall shortly observe, acts of mindless brutality, Nefertiti does little to disenchant her audience during the course of the opera. If her voice has a melancholic tinge not found in the music of the other characters (particularly in the tart chromaticism of her duet with Akhnaten [act 2, scene 2]), it is perhaps not all that surprising: living with a man as strange as Akhnaten cannot have been easy.

In the fourth and final verse of the scene, all three principals—Tye, Akhnaten, and Nefertiti—at last sing together (as in example 28). Akhnaten, wooed first by his mother and then by his wife, remains in a state of ambivalence between the two. Caught between what he perceives as divine and earthly love, Akhnaten elects to partake of both. What is more, he evidently views this equilibrium between the internal and the external, between inbreeding and outbreeding, as further evidence of his own semidivine status. One who combines the masculine and the feminine; who traverses the path between the mundane and the eternal; who perceives the seeds of all diversity in his own mind and body; and one who confuses ordinary people with archetypes and angels and his own mother with the great cosmic mother, can just as easily confuse the face he sees in the mirror with the face of a god. The line that divides insight from madness, profundity from idiocy, and the sublime from the ridiculous, is a thin one indeed; and in stepping over it, Akhnaten's fate is, in a sense, already sealed.

In the Stuttgart premiere of the opera, directed by Achim Freyer, Akhnaten was appropriately equipped with a mirror in the spherical form of the sun disk. Since he is facing upstage, the audience can see that he is singing only by diverting their attention to his reflected image. Thus, the image of Oedipus becomes mapped onto that of Narcissus: both mythological characters who come to grief as a result of their attention to the interior and the general at the expense of the exterior and the contingent. In Oedipus's case, the malaise he suffers from is incestuous, in Narcissus's masturbatory, but both are ultimately symptoms of the same libidinal circularity. Lacan's period of primary narcissism, the mirror stage, is for him the stage in human development during which the Oedipus complex first emerges, when the subject first becomes aware of his or her separate ontological status.[56] Thereafter, the alienated post-Oedipal subject enters a refractory prison, much like Jean Genet's "hall of mirrors,"[57] in which he or she is entangled like a fly in a spider's web.[58] Paradoxically, however, the mirror, while constituting the fundamental cause of the Oedipal condition, offers the only possible means by which subjective reintegration can be effected. It is this paradox that is addressed in this scene.

The ambivalence between the voices of these three characters—and the sexual confusion of Akhnaten—were underlined visually in the German production by having all three face upstage, their backs turned toward the audience. When Akhnaten sings in the first verse, one can see that he is singing only because of the mirror he is holding, but when he is joined later by Tye, one can easily make the same mistake as the person who filmed the German premiere of the opera: When Tye's youthful soprano voice is heard for the first time, one instinctively directs one's attention toward the comely figure of Nefertiti (who is dressed in the same manner as Akhnaten and whose elegant arm gestures are the mirror image of her husband's) rather than Tye, from whom the voice actually emanates (and who is clothed in the same garish colors as the patriarchs, whose skin is painted, and whose angular gestures are also identical to those of the patriarchs).[59] It is a surprise to eventually realize that the femme fatale of the opera, the grotesque figure of Tye, not the beautiful Nefertiti, possesses the quintessentially wholesome soprano voice. This sense of surprise is reinscribed when Nefertiti's low contralto enters in the following verse. It is easy to assume that this voice is coming from the older, less attractive woman, but as it gradually becomes apparent that both the woman who is singing and her voice are in fact extremely attractive, one is forced to reexamine prejudices concerning voice types and the gender categories that go along with them.

The relational ambiguity between the three leading roles was interpreted in an entirely different, although equally ingenious, manner in David Freeman's English National Opera (ENO) production of the opera.[60] Here Tye and Nefertiti were similar in appearance—aside, that is, from the shaven head of the former, which is a feature shared by herself, her son, and his daughters, but not by Nefertiti. This similarity in the appearance of the two leading ladies is a result of the more "realistic" approach of this director compared to the German production. In general terms, Freeman's production placed a stronger emphasis on narrative and historical connectedness, while Freyer was more interested in psychological and sociopolitical allegory. Much of the beauty of the ENO production lies in its choreography. In the initial verse, Akhnaten circumambulates the stage, walking alternately forward and backward but always clockwise, in time with the music. In the second verse, he is joined by Tye, who precedes her son, walking backward with her face to him when he is walking forward, and turning forward away from him as he also turns away. In the third verse, Nefertiti replaces Tye but walks behind Akhnaten instead of leading him. The effect is much the same, however: The two alternate between facing each other and facing away from each other, between walking forward and backward. In the fourth and final verse, Akhnaten is caught between the two in much the same way as he is musically. When walking forward, he is face-to-face with Tye; when walking backward, he is face-to-face with Nefertiti. Thus, the choreography of this production beautifully complements the music, and together the two media eloquently illustrate the emotional ambivalence of the title character in this scene.

The singing ends with this unlikely ménage à trois resonating together on three final notes, the constituent notes of the A-minor chord that is the "keystone" of the entire opera—Akhnaten sings the root, Nefertiti the third, and Tye the fifth. With the manifesto of the new order announced to their subjects, the three royals depart to the accompaniment of a majestic and slightly portentous brass tutti arrangement of the music from the verses. Woodwinds and strings play the arpeggio pattern from the beginning of this scene in two opposing lines, while cymbal crashes add to the overall pomp of the situation. In the final cycle of the orchestral arrangement, the tubular bells are sounded once again. Now, however, they outline Queen Tye's descending motif (e"–d"–c": 5–4–3), followed immediately by Akhnaten's ascending motif (a'–b'–c"–e': 1–2–3–5). The theme in its entirety is androgynous, therefore, but the position of Tye's motif at its head reveals a certain degree of matriarchal dominance, which hints at the power Akhnaten's mother still exerts over him. This interpretation is confirmed in the very next scene.

The orchestral section ends abruptly with a return to the music of the opening measures of the scene. The harmony alternates between A minor and G major, while the bell motif returns in reduced form (e"–c"–d"–b'), initially over an oscillation of these two chords and then over a low A minor (no third) pedal chord. Finally, the other instruments are silenced, leaving only the bells. These fade away gradually until only their upper partials can be discerned. The bells continue to resonate long after the last time they are struck: a suitably auspicious ending to the first act.

Akhnaten at the Crossroads

The libretto stipulates that Akhnaten should be seen alone at this point, gazing at the funeral procession of his father as it floats on barks "across a mythical river to the Land of the Dead."[61] Ralph Lewis describes this highly significant part of the funeral ceremony:

The crossing of the Nile from east to west was a very solemn part of the funeral ritual. It corresponded to the apparent journey of Re (the sun) who rose in the east and sank beneath the horizon in the west. Thence Re was thought to journey in the nether world beneath the earth, rising again in the east. Part of the obsequies consisted of placing the deceased on a bier which, in turn, was placed on a funeral barque. This barque was then poled slowly across the Nile to the west bank. Accompanying were other boats on which were lamenting relatives and friends and the ritualistic mourners. On the west bank a solemn processional, led by the priests, wended its way into the hills to a tomb which had already been prepared for the deceased. Therefore, the west bank of the Nile opposite Thebes (now Luxor) became a virtual grand cemetery. The pharaohs built elaborate mortuary temples in this region, which were their tombs.[62]

This reappearance of the funeral cortege, although not enacted in all of the productions of the opera, underlines the symbolic significance of the river and, accordingly, the importance of water as a unifying factor in the musico-dramatic construction of the opera. I have shown earlier how the music of the prelude, which is repeated in slightly altered forms in the second and third acts, is strongly associated with the Nile. The arpeggio waves heard in the orchestral coda of this scene correspond closely with those in the prelude. Thus, the water music of the prelude, which connotes Akhnaten's pre-Oedipal attachment to his mother, is once again associated with water and, not surprisingly perhaps, with the death of his father, as well as foreboding his own death. Akhnaten is, in a very real sense, confronting his own destiny in this music. But it is the dead father, Amenhotep III, who is the overriding concern at this juncture. This swing toward the paternal axis of the Oedipus complex can be regarded as the natural consequence of the protagonist's actions earlier in the scene. Here we see what a confused man Akhnaten is; he has buried his father, in more ways than one, but refuses to let him rest in peace.

This train of thought carries over to the first scene of act 2. The second act covers years five to fifteen of Akhnaten's reign, the years in which he put into effect his most radical reforms. Having already changed his name from Amenhotep IV (spirit of Amon) to Akhnaten (spirit of Aten)—thus snubbing the local deity of Thebes and its priesthood, which had previously held sway over all other deities and churches—he went further still and rechanneled all state resources toward establishing the new religious order. These measures were greeted with staunch opposition from the Amon priesthood, and it is possible that a coup d'état was attempted at this time. Akhnaten's position was sufficiently strong, however, for him to withstand the opposition of traditionalists for the time being at least. But at this time the new pharaoh made an error of gargantuan proportions. With an iron hand, he outlawed the most powerful of all Egyptian religions, at the same time erasing all references to it in temples and tombs. This act of iconoclasm was without precedent in Egyptian history. While there is no evidence of physical violence—the priesthood of Amon remained a powerful critical force throughout Akhnaten's reign, even when dispossessed of their former material wealth and exalted status—there seem to have been few limits to the lengths to which Akhnaten was willing to go in order to establish Atenism as the sole state religion.

Perhaps the most potently symbolic act of the religious revolution was the chiseling out of Akhnaten's father's name from all the monuments on which it was found, including his tomb, because—or so it has been claimed—it contains within it the name of the outlawed god, Amon. This, of course, tallies with Velikovsky's theory of the identity of Oedipus and Akhnaten: in the eyes of the ancient Egyptians, the act of erasing the name of one's father from his tomb was equivalent to parricide. Velikovsky, citing the Freudian psychologist Karl Abraham,[63] claims that these acts of iconoclasm reveal something of the psychological condition of the young pharaoh responsible for putting them into effect:

It was generally thought and still is that the erasure of the name of the deity was the consequence of religious zeal and nothing else. But Abraham held that the name of Amon was hateful because it contained within it the name of his father, Amenhotep. "He had the name of Amon and the name of his father, Amenhotep, obliterated on all inscriptions and monuments." In this "purifying" action, as well as in the change of his own name from Amenhotep to Akhnaton, the hidden hatred of the son for his father came to light. "His strongest hatred was directed against his father whom he could not reach because he was no more among the living." By destroying his father's name, the king tried to erase the memory of his sire. By destroying a person's name his *ka*, or soul in afterlife, was also delivered to destruction.[64]

If Akhnaten's iconoclasm is easily related to Freudian theory, in post-Freudian theory an even clearer point of reference can be identified. In Lacan's psychoanalytical theories, The-Name-of-the-Father is the Law, which is synonymous with the entire symbolic domain. Lacan's father is not, of course, a real, living person but a figment of the Oedipal subject's imagination. And this is more than simply the archetypal father-figure-as-authority: What Lacan has in mind is specifically the *dead* father, or rather the shady representation of the dead father we carry around with us as a consequence of our entry into the symbolic sphere.[65] In obliterating all outward manifestations of The-Name-of-the-Father, Akhnaten is assuming control of the phallus and at the same time is on the first leg of a vertiginous flight of fantasy deep into the enclosed domain of the maternal imaginary. Because it is not recognized as a fantasy, however, Akhnaten's flight will, like Icarus's similar ill-fated solar-bound ascent, end up causing him considerable distress.

From the historical standpoint, Akhnaten and his mother might well have had good reason to despise Amenhotep III. It is clear that this pharaoh held his wife in extremely high esteem and that she wielded a great deal of influence over him. The Egyptologist Wallis Budge has gone so far as to speculate that Tye might have been Amenhotep's coruler, in practice if not in name.[66] In the art of the time, Tye appears almost equal in stature to her husband (in ancient Egyptian art, pharaohs' wives are ordinarily depicted as considerably smaller than pharaohs), she is seen to participate actively in religious and state affairs, and her name is inscribed side by side with that of her husband. According to Budge, "her power inside the palace and in the country generally was very great, and there is evidence that the king's orders, both private and public, were only issued after she had sanctioned them."[67]

Conflicting with all of this, however, are Amenhotep III's "diplomatic marriages" to both the sister and the daughter of the Mittanian king Tushratta, as well as his participation in one of the most widely acknowledged cases of father-daughter incest in Egyptian history, with his daughter Satamen.[68] It might, therefore, be more accurate to attribute the exalted position of Tye to her own extraordinary strength of character rather than to the progressive thinking of her husband. After Amenhotep III's death, Tye assumed full control of Egyptian affairs of state: She corresponded with foreign powers, she saw to it that her son was properly betrothed to a woman she approved (Nefertiti) prior to his installation as pharaoh, and by all accounts she ruled the country and the empire on her own while the young pharaoh, who was ten years old at the time, was schooled in the duties and manners of kings.[69] This, however, was a schooling with a difference. We know, for example, that Queen Tye was a zealous follower of the sun cult of Heliopolis and that she held her own god, the Aten, to be superior in every respect to Amon. We know that Amenhotep III had an artificial lake made on the estate of his wife in honor of the solar god and that the couple sailed across the lake on a royal barge named Aten-tehen (Aten sparkles) in a ceremony intended to mark the inauguration of Atenism at the Egyptian capital.[70] This, however, appears to be as far as Amenhotep III was willing to go. But four years after the death of Amenhotep III, with the education of Akhnaten by his mother nearing completion, an irreconcilable rift occurred between the monarchic and theocratic seats of power, culminating in a serious challenge to the monarchy from the powerful priesthood of Amon. This challenge was quickly quashed, but its reverberations troubled Akhnaten throughout his reign and eventually led to his downfall.

"The King's Mother and Great Royal Wife"

But what of the relationship between Akhnaten and his mother? We have seen already at the end of the first act that the two are depicted in the opera as being exceptionally close; so close, in fact, as to fuel suggestions of a romantic attachment between the two. Velikovsky's assertion that Akhnaten, like Oedipus, was engaged over an extended period of time in a sexual relationship with his own mother is likely the strongest one in the literature, and he has managed to convince a number of archaeologists.[71] The evidence is largely circumstantial and susceptible to conflicting interpretations, but it does appear to be difficult to dismiss altogether. The incest argument rests largely on the following evidence.

The appellation "The King's Mother and Great Royal Wife" was used commonly to refer to Tye some ten years after the death of Amenhotep III (subsequent, that is, to the removal of Amenhotep's name from his tomb—an act evidently sanctioned by Tye). In itself, this is scanty evidence: Those who are familiar with the nomenclature of the British royal family know that Queen Elizabeth II's mother is commonly referred to as the "Queen Mother" (not the Queen's Mother, as one might expect), an equally ambiguous title and one that appears to imply a quasi-incestuous relationship with her son-in-law, the Duke of Edinburgh. In this case, of course, nobody assumes such a relationship exists. Nomenclature in itself, then, is insufficient evidence, as it often has only a symbolic or conventional function. It is possible, for example, that Tye, who was one of the most respected and powerful of all Egyptian queens, retained her title of Great Royal Wife to add weight to her son's radical reforms. By adding her seal of approval to the changes initiated by Akhnaten, she was perhaps seeking to underline the continuity and stability of the royal lineage, despite the revolutionary changes that were being introduced in other areas of Egyptian life.[72]

Not only does Tye retain the title of Great Royal Wife—which rightly belongs to Nefertiti—but she is seen in a number of bas-reliefs carved at the time as occupying a position in keeping with such a title. She presides with her son and his wife over official ceremonies and religious rites, and in

Left, Nefertiti and her two eldest children; middle, Akhnaten; right, Tye and Bekhetaten. A banquet scene. Wallis Budge, *Tutankhamen: Amenism, Atenism, and Egyptian Monotheism* (New York: Dover, 1991 [1923]), p. 93.

one famous portrait of the two she is seen holding her son's hand affectionately as they proceed to a place of worship. This intimate, even erotic, display of affection between a king and his mother was unknown to the pharaonic world, where the image of the pharaoh as the paragon of manliness was fostered consciously. From the contemporary standpoint, of course, such portrayals appear perfectly natural, particularly for a boy in his early teens whose mother is his sole parent. Moreover, it appears commensurate with the king's favorite dictum, "living in truth" to depict familial relations as they really are rather than in their traditional idealized form. It is a different matter, of course, to establish the nature of the truth that is being depicted. We know that Tye continued to exercise considerable influence over her son not only in his youth but well into the latter part of his reign, when he was in his late twenties. Further, in one letter to Akhnaten from a foreign king, she is referred to as "the mistress of [his] house."[73]

The strongest piece of evidence, though, pertains to Tye's daughter, Bekhetaten, born over a decade after the death of Amenhotep III and referred to as the "king's daughter of his body, beloved by him, Beketaten."[74] That Tye is the mother there is little doubt: The only controversy that remains is in establishing the identity of the father. While the appellation cited appears to leave little doubt that it was Akhnaten, this remains a highly controversial issue and one that will probably never be resolved convincingly. Since Bekhetaten is listed among the daughters of Akhnaten in the libretto of *Akhnaten*, Glass is apparently once again following Velikovsky's theory in his treatment of the subject.[75]

Assuming that there was an incestuous bond between Akhnaten and his mother, should it be viewed as a simple case of child abuse? According to Velikovsky, it should not. He claims that the idea of a holy incestuous union was at the heart of the new religious order.[76] Inbreeding as such was nothing out of the ordinary for the ancient Egyptians: DNA testing of mummies, among other things, has shown that it was extremely common among pharaohs and their families. The most common forms of inbreeding, however, were between siblings and between fathers and their daughters. Mother-son incest was extremely rare and might even have been regarded as a crime. Velikovsky claims that the genealogies both of this idea and of the other central tenet of Atenism, the idea of an abstract solar godhead, can be traced to Persian religious thought.[77] In the latter of these assertions, at least, he is supported by a large part of the archaeological literature.[78] It is unlikely, however, that it will ever be proved in incontestable terms that an incestuous union took place between Akhnaten and his mother, although the evidence does seem compelling. But whether fact or fiction, the Oedipal aspects of the story add considerable psychological and intertextual resonance to Glass's opera.

To talk of Oedipus is not necessarily to talk of Freud, however; nor is it to invest the complex with the kind of metaphysical foundation to which anthropologists such as Bronislaw Malinowski and cultural theorists like Deleuze and Guattari have objected so vehemently.[79] But the Oedipus complex has, as the ancient Greek genealogy of the myth implies, been around for quite a while. And as Freud himself has suggested in his bold and highly controversial forays into the domain of cultural theory, it almost certainly did not find its first manifestation in Greek mythology.[80]

Freud's idea of a universal wish in infancy of the boy to annihilate his father and wed his mother came to full fruition in "The Ego and the Id."[81] He had been toying with this idea for many years previously, however, and an important part of his background work on the Oedipus theory involved scrutinizing examples of Oedipal behavior in the anthropological literature as well as seeking the historical origins of the Oedipus complex in the Judeo-Christian religious tradition. Thus, in "Totem and Taboo," Freud observes that the psychological condition of "savages"—particularly with regard to mother-son and sibling incest—"reveals a striking agreement with the mental life of neurotic patients."[82] In "Moses and Monotheism," he takes the cultural implications of the collective Oedipal complex the furthest. Here he identifies the Oedipal desire with the entire Jewish faith, tracing its historical origin back to the fear, instilled in the Jewish people by their spiritual leader, Moses, of the patriarchal God Jehovah.[83] The "unnameable crime" of incest is, according to Freud, transformed in Mediterranean forms of Christianity from the terror of the vengeful father figure encountered in Judaism to the "shadowy" suppressed guilt complex that came to be called original sin.[84] Freud did not make a connection between the other prominent characters of "Moses and Monotheism": Oedipus, the antihero, and Akhnaten, the hero. He did, however, posit Akhnaten as the progenitor of the Judeo-Christian religion, a religion that was fundamentally transformed by Akhnaten's heavy-handed disciple, Moses. Velikovsky reversed Freud's formulation, suggesting that it was not Moses but Akhnaten who, as the historical model for the mythological character, was responsible for the birth of the Oedipus complex. Interestingly, it is the very same action that connects both men with Oedipus. In Freud's discussion of Moses and in Velikovsky's discussions of Akhnaten, what identifies the two men with Oedipus is their intolerance toward other religions, manifested in their proscription of all "false idols." For Freud, this prohibition led to the killing of Moses by his people, after which emerged the collective-guilt complex he identified with original sin and that Lacan referred to as The-Name-of-the-Father. For Akhnaten, the proscription of the religion of his father was part of an already existing guilt (and Oedipus) complex.

The Rape of the (Father's) Temple

If Lacan's Name-of-the-Father offers an apt way of looking at Akhnaten's position vis-à-vis his dead father in this scene, what happens in the music is further illuminated from the standpoint of Julia Kristeva's conceptual framework.[85] Kristeva's distinction between the symbolic and the semiotic provides a useful means of accounting for the presence of competing discursive strategies in this scene. For Kristeva, the semiotic is closely associated with the poetic mode of discourse. In addition to poetry, this modality—which is strongly marked as feminine and, more specifically, as maternal—is associated also with madness and holiness. These are not essential categories, however; they have little to do with women's actual experiences of femininity and motherhood. Rather, like Lacan's similar categories, they are symbolic, and therefore phallic,[86] "reenactments" of early events in the constitution of the subject, with the semiotic corresponding to pre-Oedipal nondifferentiation and the symbolic to (post-)Oedipal processes of discrimination and alienation. The former accounts for the law-bound and positional aspects of discourse, the latter for transgressive breaches in the symbolic order. Because of the association of the semiotic with the pre-Oedipal, it is hardly surprising that the imaginary space in which semiotic disruptions occur is envisioned as an enclosed, womblike construction; this is referred to by Kristeva, after Plato, as the *chora*. The locus of the pre- or even antisymbolic, the *chora* is the site where the subject is both produced and annihilated. Like the death drive in Freud's "Beyond the Pleasure Principle," the *chora* is characterized by a preponderance of repetition or "pulsion." Unlike Freud, however, who invariably stressed the negative aspects of the death drive and who valued above all the ego-building imperative of the so-called reality principle, Kristeva is invariably more skeptical in her attitude toward the ego-centered discourse of the symbolic and more favorably disposed toward the semiotic. The symbolic, in her view, is a brittle construct of the imagination that is always in danger of caving in on itself; the semiotic is also an imaginary construct, but one that can be a source of considerable pleasure as well as a potent political force if its elemental energies are harnessed properly. The emphasis placed on the semiotic in the (exclusively male) writers Kristeva discusses is for the most part approved of, despite its imaginary nature, since the nondifferentiation it implies serves to weaken conventional gender categories.

Like Barthes, Kristeva has a tendency to idealize musical discourse and seems at times to place it in an autonomous space outside of the symbolic sphere.[87] A closer examination of her theoretical model, however, reveals a considerably more cautious position in this regard than characterizes Barthes's writing; Kristeva writes that even the "exclusivity" of nonverbal forms of discourse like music, which are almost invariably more semiotically weighted than language,

is relative, precisely because of the necessary dialectic between the two modalities of the signifying process, which is constitutive of the subject. Because the subject is *both* semiotic *and* symbolic, no signifying system he produces can be either 'exclusively' semiotic or 'exclusively' symbolic and is instead necessarily marked by an indebtedness to both.[88]

In recent years, there have been a number of attempts to translate Kristeva's conceptual framework into aural and even musical terms. Two of the most successful are, in the former category, Kaja Silverman's superbly erudite and insightful *The Acoustic Mirror: The Female Voice in Psychoanalysis and Cinema*, and, in the latter, an unusually perceptive and illuminating article by David Schwarz on the music of Steve Reich and John Adams.[89] Schwarz's work is extremely pertinent here since Reich has been closely associated with Glass, while Adams was strongly influenced by him. Another important early article on minimalism that intelligently uses French psychoanalytically orientated cultural theory (Kristeva and Deleuze, among others) long before it was an exportable commodity is Ivanka Stoianova's "Musique répétitive."[90] Written in 1977, Stoianova's article is, to my knowledge, the first discussion of minimalism to associate it explicitly with Kristeva's theoretical ideas, specifically that of the "subject in process," and with the instinctive and pulsional aspects of the Freudian pleasure principle. Wim Mertens made a similar association in his *American Minimal Music* and drew upon the theories of Deleuze, Derrida, and Lyotard, among others.[91] Mertens's Marcusean observation that "the breakdown of dialectics" in minimalist music is a utopian maneuver away from history that will ultimately turn against itself is quite astute. Unfortunately, he seems unable to perceive the more positive side of minimalism's disruptive "negativity,"[92] all the more so given that he himself was a prolific composer of minimalist music at the time he wrote his diagnosis. But to have understood the death drive in this way, he would have had to distance himself further from both Freud and Lacan and perhaps have turned in the direction of Kristeva and the feminist wing of post-Freudian theory. As it is, Mertens's conclusions regarding minimalism play conveniently into the hands of critics of the style, the least forgiving of whom condemn the whole movement as a primitivist regression with few or no redeeming qualities.[93]

David Schwarz's article can be regarded as a continuation of this research, although he does not appear to be familiar with the European writing on the subject. Schwarz uses terms of Silverman's such as "the acoustic mirror" (the aural equivalent of Lacan's mirror stage) and the "sonorous envelope" (the incoherent, pulsional "soundscapes" one might hear in the Kristevan *chora*) as analytical tools to account for different psychological modi operandi. In his view, John Adams's musical "quotes," which are very similar to Glass's practices,[94] function as acoustic mirrors that reenact the self-other split that marks our constitution as divided (post-)Oedipal subjects. In his discussion of Steve Reich's tape-loop pieces, *Come Out* and *It's Gonna Rain*, Schwarz shows how symbolic coherence gradually gives way to semiotic chaos as the two tape machines employed in these pieces slip slowly out of synchronization with one another. As the speaking subject aurally disintegrates, the effect is chilling to say the least; needless to say, this is the oppressive, destructive side of the *chora*.

To return to *Akhnaten*, we witnessed the "positive" side of the semiotic modality in the first and second scenes of the first act, in which the crowd takes their rulers' lofty and somewhat grotesque proclamations concerning the afterlife and transforms them into pulsating celebrations of their own lives. The power shift, which apparently reaches its conclusion in the Window of Appearances with the first state appearance of the Atenist triad, continues in the Temple scene. Here, though, we see the less attractive side of the semiotic modality. And it is noteworthy that the mixed chorus, the opera's voice of euphoric nondifferentiation, of grassroots power, is not present in this scene. With the notable exception of Tye, all of the voices we hear are male.

The assault on the temple is signaled by a distant bugle call on a', played on a solitary horn. A short orchestral introduction follows in which the two alternating chord progressions of the hymn to Amon are introduced; the first of which consists in an abrupt drop from A minor to A-flat major/A minor. The second chord is marked by a descending theme in the bass that works its way down through the chord tones of A-flat major, coming to rest on an ominous B-flat before resolving back to the tonic (e-flat–c–A-flat–E-flat–B-flat; see example 16, p. 74). In the treble clef, however, the root and fifth of A minor resolutely hold their positions, resulting in an abrasive type of bitonality that pits black notes against white notes, a style familiar to us from the music of Stravinsky and Milhaud. The pivotal tone c is the means by which some sense of tonal continuity is imparted, but otherwise the dissonance produced by combining three intervals of a minor second is quite disturbing. The tritone motif, strongly associated with the old order in the first two scenes of the opera, can be identified in the transition from A minor to the opening pitch of the fanfare, e-flat.

The second sequence (A minor–B diminished seventh–E major [i–ii–V]) is more conventional and brings to mind the musical language of Hollywood film scores. Traditional leading-note harmony (tonic-dominant), which has been conspicuously absent from much of the music so far, makes an appearance through the presence of G-sharp in the violas. The tension created by an insistent eighth-note rhythm (a gripping 264 eighth notes per minute) and two excited double appoggiaturas on the tonic (4-3 and 6-5) reinforces the impression that trouble is on its way. In a third pattern, the dominant tonal function of the previous pattern is confirmed, as is its resolution to the tonic, which is no longer drawn out with appoggiaturas. A bugle call is heard again in the distance (piano), like the flashes of lightning on a darkened horizon as a storm approaches from sea.

The Amon high priest enters with the other priests of Amon, the former simply reiterating the word *Amen* (implying a connection to the Judeo-Christian tradition) while the latter recite the liturgical text:

Oh Amon, creator of all things	Amen men khet nebet
All people say	Ya-u-nek em en djed
We adore you	Sen er ayu
In jubilation	Nek henu nek en
For resting among us	En wered ek imen

The music sung by the chorus is exclusively syllabic, whereas the high priest himself occasionally breaks into melismatic arcs over the troublesome bitonal chord A-flat major/A minor (a-flat–e-flat'–f'–e-flat'–c'), bringing to mind the chants of both Jewish and Christian church services, with their syllabic recitations followed by short melodic cadences, often culminating on the word *Amen*. The superimposition of the high priest's melisma over the dissonant chord suggests perhaps that his invocations are at the heart of the conflict; and it is precisely this aspect of his countenance that is called into question. This is the theocratic word, the core syllable that purports to be at the center of all language, the transcendental signifier; it is also, let us not forget, the Name-of-the-Father, *Amon*-hotep.

The priests' invocations are interrupted rudely by the sound of approaching trumpets, which grow in intensity until they can no longer be ignored. There is an abrupt transformation of musical material, with wind instruments entering in high arpeggios and three dissonant brass fanfares announcing the presence of Akhnaten. The fanfares, which pass through the "dominant" (E minor) and the seventh-degree major chord (A-flat major), are marked as announcing the arrival of the pharaoh by the third of A-flat major, which rises a half step from c-flat" to c-natural" (rehearsal mark 18), thus signaling Akhnaten's transgression, the effects of which are at their most visible in this scene.

In the highly rhythmically charged section that follows, Akhnaten makes his presence felt. Accompanied by the priests of his own church, he replaces the sentimental sighing of the priests of Amon with his own aggressive staccato vocalese. Through a bustling backdrop of shape-shifting arpeggios, the dissonant fanfare descent of the opening passages cuts a path once again, only now it is extended over three bars and is otherwise radically transformed. The tonality outlined by the fanfare now places a stronger emphasis on the pungent tritone-based chord (E-flat, no third) rather than the raised seventh-degree major chord, due to the omission of A-flat and a stronger emphasis on B-flat, which appeared earlier only as a passing tone (rehearsal mark 21: e-flat"–b-flat'–a'–e-flat'–b-flat–a–e-flat–B-flat–A–E-flat–B-flat₁). Spanning over three octaves and passing through the ranges of the entire brass section from trumpet to tuba, the effect of this bitonal passage, combining totally incompatible F major (no fifth) and E-flat tonalities, is quite striking. If Glass had wanted to depict Akhnaten as an iconoclast, he has certainly written the right music.

The bitonal fanfare is repeated three times (the triadic motif once again signaling change) before a second section is introduced that consists of three repetitions of the B-flat major–B-flat minor–A-minor sequence from the prelude. This is without question Akhnaten's music, and it is intended quite specifically to invoke his peculiarity (in more senses than one) in the eyes of his subjects—particularly those who are opposed to his radical reforms. Both sections are repeated twice, prior to the entry of the King's Mother and Great Royal Wife, Tye.

Tye enters on e-flat", the tritone of A minor, and the fearful symmetry of the tonality associates her more closely with the old order than the new. The tritone dissects the octave into equal halves with clinical precision. A similar symmetry can be heard in the brass fanfare, which, instead of descending, pushes its way up from a shuddering E-flat in the bass to a piercing trumpet blast on e-flat", some three octaves higher (rehearsal mark 28). This is an exact inversion of the theme heard concomitant with Akhnaten's earlier entry (at rehearsal mark 21).

Tye's role is, as Glass puts it, intended for "a high soprano with, hopefully, dramatic thrust"[95]; it is in this scene that we begin to realise what the composer means by "dramatic thrust." All of the voices in this scene— Akhnaten's "feminized" countertenor,[96] Tye's powerful soprano, and a large male choir—are strongly invested with phallic significance. The most obvious operatic antecedent of Tye's voice is the Queen of the Night: Tye sings in the same register as Mozart's famous femme fatale and fires out her staccato vocalese syllables with equal vigor. (Wilde's and Strauss's castrating madwoman, Salomé, is a less convincing point of reference, since Tye does, in both the Window of Appearances scene and the epilogue appear to have *some* redeeming qualities.) Jungian psychology would refer to both women as anima figures, those frightening phallic projections of the male unconscious who never fail both to enthrall and to terrify male onlookers. The feminist literature has been equally ambivalent in their assessments of such roles but for different reasons. The power these women wield is hard to deny; with female casualties littering the stages of opera houses around the world night in and night out, these "unsung voices" undeniably give what they get.[97] Unfortunately, though, it is at the cost of their humanity, suggesting perhaps that women and power somehow do not or should not go together. This is why the presence of Nefertiti is important in *Akhnaten*: She rises to a position of considerable power and influence but is not dehumanized, defeminized, or disposed of in an unpleasant way as a result. (Unlike another ancient Egyptian favorite of the operatic stage, Cleopatra, there is no asp waiting in the wings for Nefertiti; she appears simply to leave her husband when their marriage becomes "dysfunctional" in the final act.)[98]

The intensity of Akhnaten's and his mother's musical discourse grows to fever pitch as the scene proceeds. The "wrong-notes" bitonal theme is heard in its most striking form at the beginning of the following cycle, when both ascending and descending versions of it are sounded simultaneously (rehearsal mark 33; see example 29). Other symmetries include the

Example 29. Act 2, scene 1, the temple. Akhnaten and Tye's frightening symmetry.

chord movement itself. In the orchestral introduction, we heard two dia-metrically opposed chordal tendencies: one pushing upward from the tonic (to B-flat) and another pushing downward (to A-flat). Now this symmetry pushes outward farther still from the tonic: on the one hand down to G seventh and on the other up to C major.

That is not all. In the surface texture of the music, Tye's entry is marked by a resumption of the mirror-image wind arpeggios heard in earlier scenes. This is the dark, destructive side of the *chora*. In addition, an im-portant theme is introduced, the essence of which is defined both by its in-tervallic symmetry and its dissonance in relation to the tonic. This theme, which orbits on the whole a minor second away from the tonic (A-flat–G–A-flat–B-flat–A-flat–G–A-flat), is associated by Glass with violence and destruction, and it appears in both of the scenes where violent up-heaval is depicted (this scene and act 3, scene 2, the Attack and Fall).

The frightening symmetry of Akhnaten and his mother can be seen from a different perspective, however. The scene depicts not only the horror experienced by the priests as their temples are defiled but also the furious catharsis of those doing the defiling. To say that the excitement of the attackers borders on the orgasmic would not, I believe, misconstrue the composer's intentions. As Tye hits her high, wordless a"s in the latter part of this scene, exactly this sense of all-encompassing rapture is experienced—what French psychoanalytical theory calls *jouissance*. The wordless bliss of Akhnaten and his mother is contrasted with the Amon priests' reverence of "the Word"—in this case defined explicitly by the high priest as "Amen," which is also The-Name-of-the-Father. The Atenists dispute this claim, asserting that the nondifferentiating "It" is more powerful still than the word; the priest's earthly *plaisir* is, then, clearly no match for the all-encompassing beatitude of their assailants. The symbolic is engulfed and eventually annihilated by the semiotic.

Glass himself describes the events as follows: "The attack is complete, and the roof of the temple is pulled off as the light of 'the Aten' pours into what once was the 'holy of holies.' The attackers sing a vocalise, no words being necessary here."[99]

If the "holy of holies" is intended as a womblike sacred environment (and this is a commonly used metaphor for the innermost sanctum of a religious building in the Judeo-Christian, Buddhist, and many other religious traditions), and if the widely known metaphor of the body as the temple of the soul is applied, there is little difficulty in identifying the scenario Glass is invoking. What has taken place is without question the metaphorical rape of Akhnaten's father's religion. The violent entry into the temple, its destruction, and the light of the Aten pouring into the holy of holies require little elucidation: the last of these is a moment of climax itself, and there should be no problem in identifying this moment more explicitly with the union of Akhnaten in music with his mother. No words are necessary since, in the imaginary space they now occupy, all distinctions have fallen away: The temple and its assailants are one, as are Akhnaten and his mother.

The victory achieved by Akhnaten and his mother is, however, a hollow one. Instead of resolving to A minor, the music of this scene resolves to E minor. Early in the scene, the tonality had vacillated restlessly between A minor and E minor, due to the use of ambiguous compound chords. Here, too, the resolution is only partial, imaginary. There follows a sorrowful codetta (rehearsal mark 39), designed, no doubt, to suggest the king's remorse at his shameful acts. Mechanically rising arpeggios—redolent of the opening bars of the opera—are heard high up in the flute (a jerky jump

of an octave, interrupted by the fifth), underpinned by the ascending tetrachord motif (from the Window of Appearances and the chaconne ritornello), which we have come to associate with the more meritorious side of
Akhnaten's character. Transposed away from its original key, however, the
effect of this motif is somewhat different. Played in thirds on the violas, it
begins on the dominant and ends on the tonic (b'–c'–d'–e'). In taking the
dominant as its point of departure, the intervallic relations from this point
of reference—a minor second, a minor third, and, significantly, a tritone—
are all negatively marked. After ascending, the theme quickly drops away
to b-flat and then to d. It is as though Akhnaten is brooding on the noble
aspirations he has forfeited in his attempts to consolidate his worldly position. The "perfect symmetry" of his sacred marriage with his mother is another cause of concern and undoubtedly a related one. The libidinal circularity involved in this relationship, while enveloping Akhnaten in its
comforting embrace and providing a fertile, womblike environment for his
spiritual self-searching, is ultimately destructive for all the parties concerned. Tye is not the Divine Mother her son perceives her to be; she is an
ordinary woman. And the priests the pharaoh lashes out at are as much a
figment of his imagination as they are a real threat.

Akhnaten and Nefertiti

Scene 2 of the second act begins with a short orchestral transition that
continues to exploit the ambiguity between A minor and E minor. The
scene opens with the two tonalities in complete equilibrium: two bars of E
(no third) arpeggios in the strings alternating with two bars of A (no
third) in the winds (flute and oboe). Both chords are in root position. The
isolation motif, defined by the absence of the third in its rising arpeggios,
sets the mood for the opening phrases, the disillusionment of the previous
scene carrying over into the construction of this scene as well. This is a musical evocation of the pre-Oedipal imaginary—the zero degree of the
opera. The subject floats weightlessly between the two pitch centers—between the imaginary other (E minor), marked as feminine, and the self (A
minor) into which it is incorporated. After two repeats of tonally ambiguous vacillation, the isolation suggested by the thirdless arpeggios is gradually dissolved with the simple addition of a descending arpeggio after each
ascent, initially in the first bar of each chord (rehearsal mark 3) and then
throughout (rehearsal mark 4).

In the passage that follows, E minor seems to be confirmed as the tonic,
but certainty in this regard is denied as the prospective tonic appears only
in its most ambiguous guise, the second inversion (rehearsal mark 5). The

music that unfolds is interesting also in terms of its instrumentation. The solo trombone is an extraordinary choice for an arpeggio pattern such as this: Negotiating the string of sizable intervallic jumps Glass has prescribed without occasionally missing a note (the first pattern, for example, includes two jumps of a fourth) and, in addition, maintaining the steady flow demanded by the music without running out of breath (there are no rests in the entire twenty-bar passage) is no easy task. Either this is bad writing or the music is intended to sound clumsy and archaic. I suggest the latter. So there is an aspect of Egyptianism here, as well as an aspect of Freudianism—the discourse of the unconscious is archaic. But this is also the voice of the sun god, recalling the symbolic function of the brass instruments.

The sequence outlined by the trombone takes us from the unsatisfactory E minor six-four chord through C major seventh to C-sharp half-diminished seventh and finally back to tonic. From the standpoint of the pitch center A, of course, which is added later in the scene, the pitches C and C-sharp are the minor and major third, respectively. Thus, the motif denoting transgression constitutes the core musical material of this scene, here suggesting that gender roles simply do not matter to the two lovers, although they are everything in the eyes of their adversaries. The entire sequence can be regarded, then, as a tonic six-four to subdominant (minor/major) six movement: Conversely, assuming that the sense of A minor as root is strong enough to be retained at this stage—and there has been no convincing cadence to call it into question—then it can be interpreted as a dominant six-four to tonic (minor/major) six movement. E minor is unquestionably the stronger tonic of the two; occasional interpolations by the winds (flute and oboe: e'' and e''') and, in the final two bars of the sequence, by the bass instruments (cellos, basses, and tubas: E and E_I) confirm this. A strong relation to the home key of the opera is deliberately retained in this scene, however. Here it remains only a latent force, but it is nonetheless tangibly present.

This scene marks the coming of age of Akhnaten and traces his second initiation into the ways of love, but this time it is an initiation that is at the same time sacred and profane, instead of being heavily weighted toward the former in the way he perceived the incestuous relationship with his mother. Unfortunately, however, we have not seen the end of Akhnaten's libidinal circularity, although we will have to wait until the final act before it emerges once again.

Immediately after the orchestral transition, the text of the duet is recited twice, the first time accompanied by the ungainly trombone solo. The scribe Amenhotep, son of Hapu, translates the text, and in true postmodern style offers two apparently contradictory subject positions. This particular text, found on a royal sarcophagus initially thought to be that of Akhnaten himself, is one of the most controversial artifacts of the Amarna period. Glass observes that "[it] may well have been written by Nefertiti herself."[100] Its true authorship is, however, by no means certain.[101]

I breathe the sweet breath	Sesenet neftu nedjem
Which comes forth from thy mouth.	Per em rek
I behold thy beauty every day.	Peteri nefruk em menet
It is my desire	Ta-i nehet sedj emi
That I may be rejuvenated	Kheruk nedjem en mehit
With life through love	Renpu ha-i em ankh
Of thee.	en mertuk
Give me thy hands, holding thy spirit,	Di-ek eni aeik kher ka-ek
that I may receive it and may live by it.	Shesepi su ankhi yemef
Call thou upon my name unto eternity,	I ashek reni er heh
And it shall never fail.	Ben hehif em rek

The first reading presents the text as a hymn in praise of the sun god. It is read in the routine manner one would recite a prayer one has recited many hundreds of times without ever stopping to think about its meaning. Here Amenhotep assumes the role of priest.

The effect of the second reading is markedly different. The musical accompaniment is a lyrical string arrangement that is diametrically opposed in its effect to the stammering trombone accompaniment of the first reading. This music owes much of its appeal to its tantalizing chromatic bass line. Under the chord sequence discussed earlier, cellos and bassoon drop down to the depths of the orchestra twice before beginning a teasing chromatic climb from A-flat through A-natural to A-sharp and finally to b, the fifth of the tonic chord, E minor (see example 30). In agreement with the new musical environment, Amenhotep's inflection of the text is now totally transformed, and he reads it as though it is an intimate exchange between lovers. To confirm this impression, it is stipulated in the libretto that Akhnaten and Nefertiti both appear on the stage at precisely this point in time.[102] This might thus be the surrogate voice of Nefertiti, although the intimate interweaving of the two principals' voices suggests that whatever feeling is being expressed in the text is mutual. There is a beautiful ambiguity in the text as the author's desire for her lover becomes deliciously confused with her love for her god, and this aspect of the text is translated into musical terms by Glass in a quite direct way.

What, then, are the grounds for Glass's romantic treatment of the couple? We know that Akhnaten had himself, Nefertiti, and his daughters depicted in unusually intimate poses. One famous portrait depicts Akhnaten and Nefertiti in a passionate embrace with their lips touching. This honest depiction of domestic life can presumably be ascribed to Akhnaten's dictum of "living

Example 30. Act 2, scene 2, Akhnaten and Nefertiti. Introductory passage.

in truth." It appears that Nefertiti enjoyed the king's favor to an even greater degree than did her mother-in-law, Tye, in her marriage with Amenhotep III. The couple appears to have been virtually inseparable—apart from when Tye intervenes in their affairs. Hymns to the sun god frequently credit the queen with coauthorship, bearing the title "praise of Aton by king [A]khnaten and Nefernefruaten [Nefertiti]."[103] Moreover, the longer version of the famous hymn to the sun, thought to be written by Akhnaten himself, is dedicated to Nefertiti, whom, the text reveals, "he [Akhnaten] loves."[104] And small wonder: Adjectives seem barely to have sufficed to describe the queen's breathtaking beauty—her titulary list includes the attributes "Fair of Face, Mistress of Joy, Endowed with Favour, Great of Love."[105] The intimacy of the couple compounded with the egalitarian nature of their union, is, then, an essential aspect of Glass's characterization:

From the way Nefertiti appears in paintings, we know that Akhnaten thought very highly of her, elevating her to a place equal to his own, and this was highly unusual even in the royal families of Egypt. It is easy to imagine a romantic attachment between these two. If this is so, then Akhnaten and Nefertiti are among the earliest, if not *the* earliest romantic couple in recorded history, predating Anthony and Cleopatra by many hundreds of years.[106]

Of equal importance, however, was the symbolic value of Akhnaten's and Nefertiti's apparent marital bliss to the followers of their religious doctrine. With the conventional Egyptian gods supplanted by a faraway disk

Akhnaten, Nefertiti, and their two eldest children (in mirror image) worshiping the Aten. Wallis Budge, *Tutankhamen: Amenism, Atenism, and Egyptian Monotheism* (New York: Dover, 1991 [1923]), p. 67.

in the sky—which itself was not even a god in any conventional sense of the word but merely a manifestation of the spirit of God—the people of Egypt, as people of any time or place are wont to do, turned toward more tangible anthropomorphic icons. The royal family themselves were all too happy to assume the roles of "children of the sun"; of particular import was the "holy trinity" of Akhn-*aten*, Nefernefru-*aten* (Nefertiti), and the Aten itself. These represented the male, the female, and the unifying principals respectively—as noted, the Aten was commonly referred to as the "mother [and] father of what thou hast made."[107] According to the archaeologist Cyril Aldred, the image of the royal couple and their god as a kind of holy/mundane trinity might well have been cultivated deliberately by Akhnaten or his advisers:

One gains the impression that Akhenaten, in publicizing his domestic life as the family man with Nefertiti and one or more of their children, is consciously or otherwise creating a significant icon of a holy family as a focus of daily worship, particularly in the chapels attached to the private houses at Amarna. . . . One suspects that the erotic extravagance given to Nefertiti, both in her appearance and in the epithets lavished upon her, have the effect of elevating her into a love-goddess, a Venus figure like Hathor or Astarte. The door-jambs at the entrance to the tombs at Amarna, where they are complete, contain prayers, addressed to this trinity of powers, the Aten, the king and the queen.[108]

The depiction of the holy trinity of Aten in music is as subtle as it is in-genious. The truth is that the love duet of Akhnaten and Nefertiti is not a duet at all but a trio for countertenor, contralto, and trumpet—that is, for Akhn-aten, Nefernefru-aten, and the Aten itself. This use of the trumpet directly recalls eighteenth-century obbligato practices, the trumpet obbli-gato thus becoming the wordless other with whom the royal couple seek religiosexual union.

Dramatically, the holy-trinity theme was strongly to the fore both in the German premiere of opera and in the Anglo-American production. In Freyer's Stuttgart production, Akhnaten and Nefertiti were wheeled around the stage on royal thrones. Between the two, a snake was seen writhing on the stage: a symbol both of pharaonic power and of the mu-tual desire on which their relationship was founded. The couple were thus depicted as an ancient Egyptian counterpart to Adam and Eve, with the snake as the bisexual libido that unites them. As their thrones drew to-gether during the final cadences of the coda, the snake disappeared be-tween them. Akhnaten's and Nefertiti's downstage hands met to form the base of a triangle, while the other hands extended upward to form its sides. The fingers of the raised hands were splayed to represent the rays of the Aten. In Freeman's production of the opera, the trinity theme was invoked not by the choreography but by the placement of pyramids on the stage during the appropriate scenes.

The musical construction of the duet proper is, like the earlier trio (act I, scene 3), cyclical-strophic: The main musical interest comes from the in-teraction of the melodic lines as well as from various changes in rhythm and orchestration. Almost the entire scene is, like the trio, based on a single chord progression: the same sequence as was heard in the introductory passages on the trombone and then in the strings. Subtle changes in meter occur along with virtually every chord change. The initial cycles, in which the couple sing texted music, are, for example, as follows:

$$12/8: e^6_4 \qquad 4/4: \text{C maj. } 7 \qquad 12/8: \text{C\#half-dim.} 7 \qquad 4/4: e^6_4$$

Subsequent cycles—in which Akhnaten and Nefertiti sing vocalese—include the root note of A major/minor and are constructed from a slightly altered inverted version of the earlier rhythmic configuration. Here the presence of A minor as an alternative tonal center is more strongly suggested.

$$4/4: e^6_4 \qquad 12/8: \text{C maj. } 7 \qquad 4/4: \text{C\#half-dim.} 7 \qquad 6/8: \text{A}^6\, \text{a}^6 \qquad 12/8: e^6_4$$

These frequent changes in meter are accomplished by means of additive and subtractive rhythmic processes.

Like the earlier trio, the melodic construction of this scene has its roots in Renaissance and Baroque counterpoint. Glass's approach to counterpoint recalls the techniques of composers such as Monteverdi, Arcangelo Corelli, and Purcell. However, his liberal use of dissonance in this scene suggests the influence both of earlier (i.e., Carlo Gesualdo) and considerably more recent tonal practices (i.e., twelve-tone music). The voices linger on minor second and tritone dissonances for unexpectedly long periods of time before eventually converging in "perfect" sonorities in the cadences that mark the end of each cycle.

In the early stages of the duet, Nefertiti appears to take the initiative; her part is more in the nature of a "subject," while Akhnaten assumes the conventionally female role of "counter" or "second subject." This reversal of gender roles is evident in terms of voice compasses as well. Akhnaten's

Example 31. Act 2, scene 2, Akhnaten and Nefertiti.

Akhnaten and Nefertiti (act 2, scene 2). Houston Grand Opera. HGO photo by Jim Caldwell © 1984.

voice is predominantly higher than Nefertiti's, although in places the voices cross in the same way that Akhnaten's and Tye's voices did in the trio (act 1, scene 3, rehearsal mark 8.4; see example 31). This suggests not only some degree of gender balance between the two but also that Nefertiti appears to be replacing Tye in Akhnaten's affections. We discussed the erotic implications of this use of voices in connection with the earlier trio; in the duet, which is really a trio, the implications are the same. This, as Susan McClary writes so eloquently in reference to earlier musical practices, is "the erotic friction so beloved by seventeenth-century composers from Monteverdi through Corelli—trios in which two equal voices rub up against each other, pressing into dissonances that achingly resolve only into yet other knots, reaching satiety only at conclusions."[109]

The reciprocal nature of such exchanges has clear sociosexual implications; in music like this, it clearly makes no difference "who's on top"; each partner readily assumes and relinquishes control whenever it is fitting to do so.[110] This suggests an altogether different notion of power relations than that which pervaded in the earlier parts of the first two scenes of this opera and that which the Romantic tradition of indivi-*dualism* has passed down to us in its ideology and its music.

One can hardly blame Akhnaten for succumbing to Nefertiti's charms: Her melodic line combines a number of intriguing attributes. In the opening bar of the initial cycles, she enters on a' and rises to b', onto which she holds resolutely as Akhnaten joins her on a high e", and then descends diatonically to c" (see example 31). The agonizing minor second dissonance that results is held by her for an entire bar; finally, she drops down to another dissonant note, f-sharp, a tritone away from Akhnaten's c", before coming to rest on the fifth of C major seventh, g'. There then follows a crossing of voices similar to that between Akhnaten and Tye in the Window of Appearances (scene 1, scene 3), which was then strongly associated with the sexual foundation of those characters' relationship. Akhnaten rises from the root, a', to the third of A minor, c" (thus confirming that the chord is in fact A minor and not C major seventh), while Nefertiti descends from c" to f-sharp'. Preceding the cadence, as it does, it is not difficult to see that some sense of union—or perhaps intercourse would be a more apt expression—is enacted in this passage. After this brief interplay, they both settle onto the tonic, E minor, Nefertiti taking the root, e', and Akhnaten the fifth, b'. Liberated from the constraints of the binary order, the couple are thus able to arrive at a consensus that is not the result of the subordination of one party by the other. If anyone has made a concession here, it is Akhnaten, who is a major second away from his own preferred tonal base.

In the third repetition of the cycle (rehearsal mark 9; see example 31), the transcendental principal emerges with a tangible voice. The trumpet enters on a high g", supplying the missing third to the harmony of the lovers. It holds this note over the next bar, allowing Nefertiti's and Akhnaten's clashing counterpoint to distract the listener's attention. As Nefertiti rises, however, from f-sharp' to g', the trumpet descends in contrary motion from d" to c". This movement ties the latter in not only with Nefertiti's line, of which it is the mirror image, but also with Akhnaten's, which two bars earlier descends in a similar manner, from e' to d'. Over the next chord—A minor (the tonic of the opera)—the third voice joins Nefertiti's and Akhnaten's erotic voice crossing to form a kind of profane-divine ménage à trois. On the first notes of the exchange, it takes the fifth of this chord, e", thus completing the triad and bonding the two lovers together. As the lovers' voices cross, the Aten (the trumpet) joins Nefertiti on the octave, reinforcing her low f-sharp' with a high f-sharp". While Nefertiti descends to the root of E minor from this note, the Aten rises to its third, and Akhnaten drops to the fifth. In a very concrete way, then, the third voice becomes the unifying principle of the so-called duet; it combines motific elements from both voices and serves as the binding agent that transforms Nefertiti's and Akhnaten's counterpoint into harmony.

As in the previous scene, sexual transformation renders its participants not speechless but wordless. Nefertiti and Akhnaten's love enters a higher plane, on which mutual understanding occurs through pure intuition—words are no longer required. The two lovers cross the barrier, then, from mundane love to divine union, from the symbol to the sign, and from *plaisir* to *jouissance*. And so does the orchestra: the sparse string accompaniment of the opening cycles remains, apart from the changes in rhythm mentioned earlier, essentially unchanged. The addition of the entire wind section (flute, oboe, clarinet, bassoon) in total unison with the strings (rehearsal mark 10), suffices to metamorphose the meandering arpeggio pattern, with its supple syncopations, into a formidable musical force.

Nefertiti now resonates on the root note, e", while Akhnaten is perceivably transformed by the encounter. He begins on a low e', more within Nefertiti's tonal territory than his own. That is not all. He deviates temporarily into his spouse's chromatic domain when he stops off at f-sharp' on his way up to her high e". The love-smitten pharaoh then continues his diatonic ascent up through g' to a'—the root of the chord and this character's tonal center—where he hesitates a while before resuming his upward motion to b' and then jumps a perfect fourth to join Nefertiti on an ecstatic e".

After two cycles of this, the chromatic bass line from the beginning of the scene returns (rehearsal mark 11). Now, though, the theme assumes a darker persona than in its earlier transformation. The combination of bass clarinet, trombone, tuba, and basses in unison makes this undoubtedly one of the most somber themes of the opera, a surprising element in the middle of the love-duet. In the final section of the duet proper (rehearsal mark 12), the orchestral tutti becomes complete with the addition of the trumpets and horns. As in the trio, withholding the full power of the brass section until the last moment not only allows the music to grow organically toward its climax but also reinforces the association of these instruments with the power of the sun god. The cycle is heard four times with brass attacks; in the final two, the tragic theme returns, once again, in the bass.

There then follows an instrumental interlude in which the bass clarinet plays an eerie reduction of the chromatic theme. It is joined after two cycles by a high countermelody—played by the flute and piccolo—constructed from motific material culled from Akhnaten's and Nefertiti's melodic lines. The accompaniment is a gently bubbling clarinet set against a two-note cello ostinato, which oscillates the whole time between e and g. Apart from confirming the E-minor tonality of the scene, this engenders a two-against-three polyrhythm.

The dark mood of this section was exploited in much the same way in both of the major productions of the opera. At this particular point in the scene, Tye reappears. If the melancholic tinge in Nefertiti's voice and the threatening bass interpolations in this scene have bemused some members of the audience, the cause of this dysphoria now becomes quite apparent. In Freeman's production, Akhnaten crossed the stage and threw himself at his mother's feet. Tye lifted her son's face to hers and kissed him passionately on the lips. As the two parted, Tye turned away, beside herself with shame. Nefertiti watched on, powerless, as Akhnaten returned to her side, beseeching her forgiveness. In the Stuttgart production, the specterlike figure of Tye circumambulated the stage, her red gown hanging from her outstretched arms like wings.

The music is reduced to brooding cellos regularly punctuated by piercing high g"s on the flute (doubled an octave higher on piccolo) followed by low Es in the basses (doubled an octave lower on the synthesizer). There is a moment of silence (a one-bar tacet in all instruments). When the music resumes we and the two lovers have passed from the realm of the living to that of the dead. The libretto stipulates that Amenhotep III and his funeral procession is seen in the background, ascending on the wings of Ra to the heavens.[111] In the music, the return of Akhnaten's father is greeted by a chord sequence related to that of the funeral scene (E minor–D major first inversion–B diminished–E; the funeral music was based on the progression A six-four–B major), underpinned by a mutation of the bass ostinato from that scene (see example 32).

Akhnaten and Nefertiti come together musically in a series of canonical cadences resolving onto E minor; the text of the hymn speaks at this point of a physical and spiritual coming together of polarities; in both productions of the opera, this was enacted physically by the characters. In the German production, Akhnaten's and Nefertiti's hands met to form the symbol of the holy/mundane trinity. They sing,

Give me thy hands, holding thy spirit,	Di-ek eni awik kher ka-ek
that I may receive it and live by it.	Shesepi su ankhi yemef
Call thou upon my name unto eternity,	I ashek reni er heh
And it shall never fail.	Ben hehif em rek

In the music subsequent to the gap that marked Akhnaten's and Nefertiti's passage into the underworld, the separate identities of the two are now almost if not completely effaced. In the domain of the nonpersonal, fluidity and interpenetration replace (indivi)dualistic perception. Akhnaten's descending motif (c"–b'–a') is freely passed on to Nefertiti (d"–c"–b') and then down to a low bassoon (d-flat–c–b), signifying the nonpersonal principle in its dark, underworldly guise. Moreover, it appears that gender categories are, on this plane, almost totally interchangeable. Each cadence begins and ends on the octave: At the beginning of each, Akhnaten takes the higher note and Nefertiti the lower (b' and b, respectively), while at the

Example 32. Act 2, scene 2, Akhnaten and Nefertiti. Coda.

end these roles are inverted (Akhnaten sings e′ and Nefertiti e″; see example 32). First Akhnaten is on top; then it is Nefertiti's turn; then we loop back to the beginning of the pattern. The dissonance from the earlier verses has not dispersed, however: Here Nefertiti's b′ presses against Akhnaten's a′ over a span of two entire bars. This suggests some fundamental, irreducible tension between the two that has nothing to do with the sexes per se, nor is it necessarily the power of love. It is an altogether more intoxicating force: the power of desire.

Glass has referred to the hymn to the sun as "Akhnaten's finest moment."[112] I beg to differ. Akhnaten's and the opera's finest moments are here, in the Window of Appearance scene and the duet, as well as in their opposite pole in the opera, the funeral of Amenhotep III. Not by accident, these are, in the case of the former, Nefertiti's and Tye's finest moments and, in that of the latter, the crowd's. Many people, including the composer himself,[113] agree that these scenes are, in musical as well as dramatic terms, the most powerful in the opera. This is the music people hum to themselves or tap their feet to on their way home from the opera house or in their cars or homes. It is the music advertisers shamelessly plagiarize. It is also the locus of the most powerful political statements in the opera and arguably in the entire trilogy.

The choral passages at the end of the funeral tell us that power is plural and does not result from the simple imposition of the will of the rulers onto the ruled; in other words, it comes from below. The two trios, the Window of Appearances and the so-called duet, elaborate on this theme: They tell us that interpersonal power relations need not be based on rigid gender or other status-related categories and that power can flow freely from one party to another in accordance with the contingencies of the moment and the individual and collective needs of all involved parties. And by recognizing this in music, we are led toward a direct and highly intimate appreciation of these new kinds of pleasures; not a mere abstraction. Music can, indeed, as Plato realized when he spoke of the power of changing modes in music to instigate political upheaval, be a powerful, if not the most powerful, instrument for political change. And it wields this power not in spite of its pleasurable qualities but precisely because of them.

CHAPTER SIX

The Illusion of Autonomy
Apotheosis and Degeneration in Akhnaten's Hymn to the Sun and in the Family Scene

Utopia: Neurosis or a Room of One's Own?

Postmodern theory has, on the whole, been deeply suspicious of utopias. And with good reason. Theodor Adorno and Max Horkheimer's *Dialectic of Enlightenment* more than adequately showed the havoc utopias are capable of wreaking.[1] In the most frightening scenarios, even the most noble aspirations of a people can get twisted beyond recognition as they are projected onto some collective "other" that is seen as *essentially* the same as the self. (Others who are not willing or suitable to be incorporated into the [imaginary] collective self are, as they would be in computer-mediated forms of virtual reality, simply deleted.) Influenced largely by the writing of the Frankfurt School, by works of the imagination like George Orwell's *1984*, by Lyotard's distrust of master narratives and deconstruction's persistent and sometimes pedantic debunking of the symbolic emperor (in all of his various forms and attires), as well as by other important literary and critical texts of the twentieth century, many have come to view such conflations of the subject with an imaginary object as inseparable from, and even definitive of, the utopian condition. Thomas More's apparently harmless vision of a perfect world thus becomes a noxious subtext to countless acts of oppression. The evidence is damning: from Robespierre to Hitler to Stalin to recent events in Bosnia to the execution of two busloads of tourists in the Valley of the Kings (coincidentally, the site of Akhnaten's greatest "crime": the erasure of the name of his father from the tombs of his ancestors), utopias are almost certainly to blame.

But there are other utopias. A growing number of critics have found it necessary to distinguish qualitatively between the utopias of dictators and despots and those of the Martin Luther Kings, Mahatma Gandhis, Virginia Woolfs, and Mother Teresas of this world, implying a distinction between "good" and "bad" utopias. Such a distinction has, however, at least since the time of Nietzsche (and in some philosophical traditions long before that), been regarded rightly as a root cause of the problem rather than its solution. More useful than the simplistic dichotomy of utopian and anti-utopian are the distinctions made between different kinds of utopias by critics such as Fredric Jameson and Terry Eagleton.[2] Both of these critics and a good number of feminists, Marxists, and other candidly politically interested parties actively advocate the invention of new kinds of utopias. This does not, pace Eagleton, imply abandoning postmodernism and jumping back on the Enlightenment bandwagon (assuming that we left it in the first place), burning our copies of Lyotard's *The Postmodern Condition* as we go, and placing diligently underlined, heavily annotated copies of Habermas's various critiques of postmodernism in new positions of prominence in our real or virtual filing cabinets (if they are not already there). But by recognizing that change of any kind is contingent on the construction of utopias, on diversions into the imaginary, and on excursions into narrative terrain, we might be able to salvage some sense of continuity with the past and at the same time protect the present from its own puritanical propensities—which are, in any case, more firmly grounded in earlier thought patterns than we sometimes care to admit.

Linda Hutcheon, in her discussion of late modern and postmodern approaches to narrative, distinguishes between the repudiation of representations, which she holds to be a characteristically late-modern strategy, and the problematization of them, which she holds to be more typical of postmodernism.[3] The same point is made by Teresa de Lauretis, who sees "narrative and narrativity" as "mechanisms to be employed strategically and tactically in the effort to construct other forms of coherence."[4] The same can be said of utopias, which are often intertwined closely with questions of narrative. In post-Brechtian, postmodern modes of discourse, it is possible to represent utopias without requiring audiences to identify completely with a specific character or point of view in a story or with an outside observer such as a narrator—in other words, without implying that one must assume a fixed position on one side or the other of the utopian/ antiutopian fence. Utopians can appear to audiences with all of their (very human) strengths and weaknesses yet in some way estranged from the metaphysical foundations that formerly justified any given utopian position. Whether this is done using Bakhtinian strategies of intertextual "polyphony," by Brechtian means, or in some other way depends, of course, on the artistic sensibilities of the individual, the nature of the medium, and the specific questions at hand.

Akhnaten and his followers are utopians in the strictest sense of the word. The *Concise Oxford Dictionary* defines a utopian as "an ardent but unpractical reformer"—an apt description for our hero. His chosen place of residence in the later scenes also matches a dictionary definition: *Utopia* itself is defined as an "imaginary place with [a] perfect social and political system; [an] ideally perfect place or state of things." In the third scene of act 2 (the City/Dance), the Atenists create precisely such a place. Like Thomas More's Utopia, Akhnaten's is an island—metaphorically speaking, at least. It is surrounded on its east side by the River Nile and on its north, west, and south by a wall of cliffs, making it accessible only by water. Even today, the only practical way to reach El Amarna, the site of Akhnaten's ruined holy city, is by ferry, which partially explains why we hear Glass's "water music," a reprise of the prelude music, once again in this scene. It was absolutely necessary, of course, for the Atenists to build their city, Akhetaten, the "City of the Horizon," on "virgin soil." Only by transporting the entire royal family and its entourage, as well as the administrative and (radically thinned out) religious and military machinery of the Egyptian state, a good way downstream from the former capital of Thebes could Akhnaten and his followers ensure complete immunity—complete isolation—from the corrupting influence of tradition. Moreover, if Akhnaten was experiencing pangs of guilt from his clampdown on traditional religious practices, Thebes, with its massive temple of Amon standing in ruins and vast statues of his father staring down at him accusingly, cannot have offered much consolation. The fanfare, which heralds the founding of the new city, tellingly straddles the black-notes tonalities that represent the old order and Akhnaten's keys, A minor and E minor (see example 17, p. 75), which creates the aural impression that there is something not quite real about Akhnaten's city of the sun.

An Autobiographical Subtext?

The etymology of the word *utopia* opens up some interesting new connections: the Greek word *ou-topos* is translated literally as "not a place," or "no place," which implies either that the place has no foundation in reality, or that it claims jurisdiction over no specific place; it is an imaginary place of nothingness, where anything (or nothing) is possible. This bears a conspicuous resemblance to Julia Kristeva's conception of the *chora*, here associated with the prelude music, but also to her musings concerning avant-garde theatrical practices. The utopian idea of a theater that "does not take (a) place,"[5] identified by Kristeva with Glass collaborator Robert Wilson's theater of images and with various other exponents of nonnarrative theater, suggests the possibility of some degree of self-referentiality in the subject matter of *Akhnaten*. Perhaps there are similarities between Akhnaten's place that is not a place and Glass's nonnarrative music and theater that does not take (a) place.

This raises the complex but important question of the composer's and, more significantly, the audience's relationship to the subject matter of *Akhnaten* and the possible ramifications for contemporary readings of what is ostensibly a historical piece. Glass himself seems to encourage such readings, given his often stated post-Brechtian orientation and some quite specific remarks in the Michael Blackwood film on the making of *Akhnaten*. He comments, "There's nothing in the story that isn't contemporary really; it's about power, and upholding old ideas, and trying to force new ideas into the world and what happens to the people that do that."[6] Akhnaten can thus be seen not only as the physical manifestation of Glass's poetics of postmodern theater but also as a veiled commentary on this poetics and the changes it has undergone since the composer first forged a distinctive musical language in the mid-1960s. It is easy to relate Akhnaten's "new ideas" to Glass's musical ideas, the upholders of "old ideas" to the modernist establishment, and "what happens to the people that do that" to the vilification of Glass by the classical-music establishment. The music of the old order is on one level at least, strongly evocative of the musical "flavor" of high modernism. Further, Glass uses a combination of minimalist and postminimalist techniques with pre-Enlightenment (mainly Baroque and late Renaissance) musical practices to suggest notions of power and interpersonal relations that are based not on the heroic juxtaposition of the individual with the surrounding world but on a considerably more fluid, relational subjective orientation. The music discussed here, on one interpretive level at least, reads as a (re)evaluation of minimalism and postmodernism in general vis-à-vis its modernist (and earlier) musical antecedents—what Glass tellingly refers to as the "grandfather of tradition."[7] It may also be read as a (partial and heavily qualified) admission of guilt on Glass's part: an apologia for, or an explanation of, the break with tradition he and his postmodern collaborators deemed necessary in their earlier works.

This suggests some Oedipal "anxiety of influence" on Glass's part, in the sense in which the phrase is used by the literary critic Harold Bloom.[8] In breaking away from his musical antecedents with the force that he did, Glass was in fact waging war on the phallic imperative of the father; even while he was moving toward a "feminine" imaginary, which the quiescent, pulsional discourse of minimalism has been identified with by a number of critics,[9] he was on some level participating in a phallically marked quest against The-Name-of-the-Father. Bloom himself held quests such as this to be a necessary stage in the development of the (male) subject. Recent criticism has taken a somewhat different position, however. Lloyd Whitesell, for example, points out that this view is premised on an outmoded notion of masculinity that stresses competition and confrontation over cooperation and interdependence.[10] In its identification of Oedipal triangulation with the escapist discursive practices of postmodernism, as well as in its self-conscious reconciliation with tradition, *Akhnaten* could be experienced by the postmodern subject as a kind of therapy. Postmodern theory has had to look very carefully in recent years at its attitude toward signifying practices, at questions of narrative, as well as at its relationship with its modernist antecedents in order to avoid running headlong into expressive, philosophical, and political dead ends analogous to those it saw itself as revolting against in the first place.

All of this may surprise critics of Glass who have argued that his musical language is incapable of sustaining ideas as complex as these and who would probably dismiss the idea that a minimalist might be capable of criticizing himself. My interpretation does not, of course, rest solely on the premise of composerial intention; it has a strong intersubjective foundation that can be traced specifically to the music itself, which identifies the musical discourse of the old order specifically with Enlightenment, individualist, and modernist ideas and ideals and the new order with post-Enlightenment, nonindividualist, and postmodernist ones. What is *truly* interesting about this opera is not the distance suggested in its musical and dramatic discourse (and in the imagined composerial subject) vis-à-vis the former cluster of categories but that which is suggested vis-à-vis the latter. It is difficult to imagine Pierre Boulez or Milton Babbitt, for example, critiquing their own serialist practices in an analogous manner. Only by taking this particular nondramatic subtext into account can the far-reaching implications of the distancing strategies employed by Glass be fully appreciated.

A Place in the Sun

The enclave of the Atenists' holy city can be viewed as a womblike site of nurturing and exclusion—what Kristeva referred to as the *chora*. This refractory (imaginary) space is both prior to and part of the symbolic order. It is the space in which distinctions between mother and son, subject and object, become blurred and in which the utopian tendency to project the imagined self onto the outside world is born. For the Atenists, the extended self is demarcated by the walls of their city and by the strength of their denial of the world outside of those walls.[11] This delusional state is imparted once again in the music of the dance scene by tonal ambivalence between the two major key centers of the opera, A minor and E minor. A minor is heard only in its second inversion (with E as the root), and there is extensive use of ambiguous compound chords (most notably, F major seventh, which includes all of the constituent pitches of A minor, with the added pitch b', thus imparting a stronger sense of E as a competing tonal center). This use of tonality is a musical evocation of the blurring of boundary lines between self and other that characterizes the psychological orientation of this and the next scene, and it speaks to both the utopian and the Oedipal subtexts.

The destructive side of the *chora*, as represented by Akhnaten's transgression motif (a musical premonition of his death), is present, but here it is deprived of much of its phallic clout, transposed as it is away from the bass register. With Akhnaten nearing the height of his powers, the thought of his ultimate fall from grace evidently loses much of its imminence. The presence of the theme here, at the opposite pole in the opera from the prelude, is significant, however; like the incoherent noises a baby hears in utero, these reverberations are harbingers of a very different reality into which our protagonist will very soon be plunged.

The arrangement is light and vibrantly rhythmic, not in the way of the funeral music with its pounding drumbeat but like that of a bustling and ebullient street procession. The percussion instruments are all handheld and are supposed to be wielded by actors on the stage—a distinctly Brechtian maneuver that has not, to my knowledge, ever been so executed in an actual performance of the opera. The instruments are three in number, and one of them is a triangle. The presence of the triangle on the stage at this point is important, since it is associated both with the sun god, by virtue of the fact that it is produced in fire, and with the ternary theme of the opera, which has manifold discursive implications (for Oedipus, operatic history, the trilogy itself, and Buddhist philosophy). The other instruments are a tambourine, which is circular like the sun disk, and a wood block, which does not seem to have any obvious symbolic significance of its own (other than making up the number three). The City/Dance serves several key functions in the larger musicodramatic structure of the opera: It underlines the ternary theme that is otherwise so pervasive in the opera; it reinforces A minor as its tonal foundation, albeit in somewhat weakened form; and its infectious syncopations, lightning-fast arpeggios, and pulsating polyrhythms constitute a valuable point of contrast to the hymn, which is considerably slower and more relaxed. The dance comes to an abrupt halt at the end of the scene, thus heightening the contrast between the two scenes. With both the people of Akhetaten and the audience shaken and stirred into an appropriately receptive state of mind, the stage is set for Akhnaten's soliloquy.

"Ankh-em-maat"—*Living in Truth: Cynical Realism or Unrealistic Idealism?*

In the hymn to the sun, Glass pulls out all the stops in his attempts to represent Akhnaten's moment of epiphany. This is, after all, the theological high point of the opera. Here Akhnaten articulates the central tenets of the new religious doctrine, lauding the beauty and diversity of creation and at the same time illuminating his own (none too modest) role as intermediary between the sun god and the Egyptian people. Akhnaten's language in the hymn is, as in the Window of Appearances scene, that of the Lacanian real. And it is precisely the realist aspects of the Atenist religion that seem to have astonished archaeologists ever since the hymns to the sun were discovered at the end of the nineteenth century. In 1899, Flinders Petrie was awestruck by the parallels he perceived between Akhnaten's faith and the scientific worldview of his own time:

No one—Sun worshipper or philosopher—seems to have realized until within this century, the truth which was the basis of Akhnaton's worship, that the rays of the Sun are the means of the Sun's action, the source of all life, power and force in the universe. The abstraction of regarding the radiant energy as all-important was quite disregarded until recent views of the conservation of force, of heat as a mode of motion, and the identity of heat, light and electricity have made us familiar with the scientific conception which was the characteristic feature of Akhnaton's new worship. . . . Were it invented to satisfy our modern scientific conceptions [Akhnaten's religion] could not logically be improved upon at the present day.[12]

Similarly, the American Egyptologist James Henry Breasted, writing in 1909, finds the "fundamental idea" of Atenism to be, from the scientific standpoint of his time, "surprisingly true."[13]

Subsequent years saw a pendulum swing in Egyptological opinion, however, with numerous scholars taking issue with precisely those aspects of Akhnaten's religion that had so impressed their Romantic forebears. Thus, Atenism came to be seen as a cynical rationalism, an ontology altogether inadequate as a conduit for the higher spiritual aspirations of any people. Wallis Budge set the ball rolling when he commented in his discussion of versions of the hymn to the sun, "There is nothing spiritual in them, nothing to appeal to man's higher nature."[14]

Much of the recent writing on the subject has followed the example of Budge. Donald B. Redford, for instance, seems annoyed that Akhnaten chanced upon an atheistic worldview some thirty-three centuries before he was "supposed" to—before, that is, the unholy trinity of Nietzsche, Freud, and Marx appeared on the scene.[15] It is with nothing short of disgust that Redford observes that Atenism was not, as Romantic Egyptology had claimed, the world's first monotheism but "in the truest sense of the word, atheism."[16] Further, "if the king and his circle inspire me somewhat with contempt," he remarks, "it is apprehension I feel when I contemplate his 'religion.'"[17] This religion, as represented by the hymn to the sun, is, for this archaeologist, a "derivative," "almost 'positivist,' statement on the beauty of creation."[18] Strong words for a religion that was quashed more than three millennia ago.

The running call of the religious reformers, *ankh-em-maat* (living in truth or reality) can therefore be identified as one of the major stumbling blocks to the acceptance of Akhnaten's religious worldview in the accounts of archaeologists. There is either too much truth in Akhnaten's doctrine or not enough. The "unrealistic" side of Akhnaten is, revealingly, identified most strongly with the pharaoh's almost total neglect of military and colonial affairs, which resulted in the partial collapse of the Egyptian empire.[19] Passions run high in the literature on Akhnaten, suggesting that there are some pressing, ongoing concerns in these discussions of the supposedly distant past. Tensions tend to arise in the archaeological discourse because of the uncomfortable and self-contradictory position ancient Egypt occupies in the fantasies of "Western" historians concerning their own past. Much of the motivating force behind Romantic archaeological studies was the desire to trace, and where possible to appropriate (often literally, by shipping artifacts to European and North American museums), the origins of Western civilisation through the study of its ancient counterparts.[20]

Notwithstanding this tendency to view ancient Egyptian civilization as a source for Western ideas, the influence of a contradictory tendency is also strongly felt, which portrays ancient Egypt as a kind of anticivilization; the antithesis of everything Western. What is probably most interesting about this phenomenon is the fact that these seemingly irreconcilable positions are often simultaneously upheld by the same scholar: on the one hand, the desire to appropriate the strange and exotic other culture, and on the other, an unwillingness to fully acknowledge the influence of the culture from which one is appropriating. These apparently contradictory positions are both classic symptoms of the strain of thinking Edward Said has termed "Orientalist."[21]

As Said points out in his groundbreaking study of the phenomenon, notions of the East as the antithesis of Western civilization have frequently been the means by which European scholars have defined their own cultural identity: "European culture gained in strength by setting itself off against the Orient as a sort of surrogate or even underground self."[22]

If Said explores the psychology behind European fantasies concerning non-European cultures, another scholar, Martin Bernal, sheds important new light on the mechanisms by which connections with the non-European world are severed in order to construct the illusion of European ideational autonomy. In his highly controversial "deconstructive" account of antique civilization, Bernal claims that many of the ideas to which we traditionally and unquestioningly attribute Hellenic origin are in fact derivative of earlier ideas whose origins lie in Africa and Asia.[23] Connections to these ideas have either been knowingly or unconsciously severed in order to preserve a feeling of cultural superiority premised on the occidental/oriental dichotomy. As Bernal puts it:

For 18th- and 19th-century Romantics and racists it was simply intolerable for Greece, which was seen not merely as the epitome of Europe, but also as its pure childhood, to have been the result of the mixture of native Europeans and colonizing Africans and Semites. Therefore the ancient model has been overthrown and replaced by something more acceptable.[24]

Both Said and Bernal question the objectivity of Western accounts of the non-European world, the former concentrating on European misrepresentations of the Orient, the latter exposing the Hellenic model as a partially fictitious rewriting of history intended to expurgate the history books of undesirable connections with both Africa and Asia. Each of these writers in his own way unravels many of the premises upon which orientalist prejudice has traditionally been based. Both have been accused of overgeneralizing, but both have sent shock waves through their respective disciplines, causing even the most cautious of scholars to reexamine the premises that ground their ideas. The Said/Bernal axis offers some very useful tools for understanding certain aspects of Egyptology.

One aspect of the relationship with ancient Egyptian subject matter that is important in *Akhnaten*, and which has been equally important in earlier operatic representations of ancient Egypt, such as Verdi's *Aïda*, is the tendency to see Egyptian war faring and colonializing tendencies as metaphors for their Western counterparts.

Paul Robinson has argued against thinking of *Aïda* solely as an orientalist piece on the grounds that the "orientals" in it appear, from the standpoint of the music at least, to be black Ethiopians (predominantly the women). The white Egyptians, on the other hand, are, in terms of their music, the epitome of Western imperial strength.[25] Robinson makes a valid point. The grafting of the ancient Egyptian onto the occidental has been common practice in the Europe for many years; one detects aspects of this in much of the archaeological writing on ancient Egypt, in Mozart's "ancient Egyptian" stage pieces (*Die Zauberflöte* and *Thamos, König in*

Ägypten), and in the Masonic philosophy that inspired them. Moreover, the Romantic aesthetic as practiced by Verdi almost by definition calls for the identification of audiences with the characters, many of whom are ancient Egyptians. This is equally true of Massenet's *Thaïs* and *Cléopâtra* and many other operatic reconstructions of the ancient world. I disagree with Robinson, however, that the identification of audiences with ancient Egyptians somehow cancels out the orientalist argument. Egyptologists have lived with these contradictions for years, on the one hand elevating ancient Egyptian civilization to a position equal if not equivalent to their own cultures, and on the other hand dismissing it as barbaric.

This paradox is addressed in Edward Said's discussion of *Aïda*.[26] At the core of this discussion is Joseph Kerman's observation that this opera, far from exemplifying the Romantic aesthetic as manifested in Verdi's other repertory operas, in fact stands apart from the repertory in a number of significant ways. *Aïda* is distinguished, among other things, by the density and complexity of Verdi's musical language, the "noisiness" of the orchestra almost throughout the opera, and the extent to which the composer engages with the musical past. This approach has been accentuated in stagings of Verdi's opera from the premiere right up to the present day, which have consistently used its exotic subject matter as a pretext for putting on some of the most excessive and outlandish spectacles that have visited the operatic stage. This, in counterpoint to what Kerman calls "the glib simplicity of the libretto," imparts a sense of falseness that results in audiences becoming alienated from rather than identifying with the ancient Egyptian world portrayed on the stage and in the music. According to Said, Verdi thereby creates a vision of ancient Egypt in *Aïda* that, to be sure, utilizes all too familiar signifiers of the monumental and the imperial, but only to undermine any sympathies audiences might have with the otherwise acceptable (from the standpoint of imperialist thought) sentiments of the ancient Egyptian characters, and he employs a variety of musicorhetorical means to this end.

Both Robinson and Said make valid critical points. And even though these positions appear contradictory, I would contend that the reception of this opera in the West rests in no small measure on the assumptions that ground them both. Said's argument seems to acknowledge that the successful reception of *Aïda* depends largely on the ability of audience members to partake of familiar imperialist pleasures, albeit pleasures that, partially at least, appear to be parodying themselves in Verdi's opera. Sentiments undoubtedly fluctuate during the course of the opera between a subject position based on identification and one from the standpoint of which alienation is the more potent force. In other words it is possible for *Aïda* to be both an orientalist and a staunchly Western piece. The surrogate self Said speaks of in his writings on orientalism is a multifaceted and intriguing beast; he or she is both the antithesis of the imaginary Western self and a reflection of some of its most pervasive fantasies about itself; it is possible, therefore, for the Oriental other to be both reviled and exalted; indeed, one might even say that the two positions are mutually interdependent.

Ralph P. Locke recognizes this in his important article on Charles Camille Saint-Saëns's *Samson et Dalila*.[27] Like Robinson, Locke admits that there is often what he calls an "'endotic' subtext" in treatments of the Orient in European opera. However, he argues that "the very appropriation of the Other for the West's own purposes of self-criticism (or whatever) has probably contributed, however inadvertently, to the continued propagation of racial and ethnic stereotypes."[28] This raises some interesting ethical questions that pertain specifically to *Akhnaten*. One could, of course, counter Locke's argument by asking if relating the ancient history of geographical locations such as Egypt constitutes an appropriation of the culture of an actual, living "other," since ancient Egypt is every bit as "other" to contemporary Egyptians as it is to Europeans. The crucial question seems to be, therefore, whether there is anything in the music or the drama that marks the contemporary rather than the ancient culture as other and in this way stigmatizes it in the eyes or the ears of audiences. Is geographic location alone enough to establish such a link? The conflation of the contemporary and the ancient can, of course, be suggested in the music by using exotic scales or rhythms, for example, that evoke scales or rhythms that are still in use in the region in question or that in some way conjure up stereotyped images of that region for Western listeners. There is very little of that kind of representation in *Akhnaten*, although there are, admittedly, some moments when the music does seem to connote "ancient Egyptian-ness" in a relatively indirect way (in the use of reed and percussion instruments; in the use of the "lowered" second and third degrees of the scale; etc.).

But this does not imply that we should let Glass off the orientalist hook altogether; it is possible that *Akhnaten*, like other representations of the non-Euro-North American world in recent opera (Adams's *Nixon in China* and *The Death of Klinghoffer* and Reich's *The Cave* are obvious examples) in some way "reflects the unequal distribution of power among the nations of the world."[29] Simply by dint of the massive production and distribution machinery that backs them up, these composers are arguably complicit in some way in the orientalist/capitalist-imperialist project. Glass's "globalism" in this and other contexts is certainly susceptible to this kind of criticism. With Glass composing everything from a jingle for a specially designed Swatch watch to music for the opening ceremonies of two Olympic Games (Los Angeles in 1984 and Atlanta in 1996), it is easy to perceive a more problematic side in his more self-consciously "populist" projects (i.e., ones whose Adornian implications outweigh their Benjaminian ones). The question becomes how far we can push such arguments before the tendency to overgeneralize takes over and any representation at all of categories that are somehow marked as "other" begins to take on an oppressive appearance. And by identifying such categories as "other" are we not, on some interpretive level at least, reinscribing the very distinction we had hoped to undermine in the first place and at the same time essentializing the self?

Locke, I should add, is careful to avoid such pitfalls by painstakingly relating all of his assertions to specific musical and dramatic procedures in the works he discusses and in the surrounding cultural contexts. It is possible, however, to treat non-Euro-American subject matter in a manner that does not simply reinscribe orientalist prejudice but that actively challenges it. Admittedly, there have been very few representations of this kind in classical music, but to acknowledge them when they do occur would arguably strengthen rather than undermine the very important, indeed crucial, project of postcolonialist criticism.

Philip Brett's discussion of the influence of gamelan music on Benjamin Britten makes a valuable contribution in this respect.[30] For Britten, "oriental" music offered an idealized imaginary space (in the Lacanian sense) where the oppressive constraints of his own culture regarding gender did not apply. Arguably, the same is true not only of *Akhnaten* and Glass but of minimalism and postmodernism in general. This is not to deny the problematic nature of any such utopian projects (and the distorted visions of otherness they sometimes inadvertently propagate); it does, however, imply that discussions of "orientalist" phenomena should be examined on their own terms and those of the individuals and cultures that produce them rather than on the basis of any a priori model, however useful that model may be in other circumstances.

The more problematic side of identification with, rather than rejection of, the oriental is strongly evident in the archaeological literature on Akhnaten. A cursory examination of the literature reveals that ancient Egypt, as the dominant colonial power of its time, almost invariably becomes a privileged site for Western scholars' fantasies about themselves. Ancient Egypt, in the eyes of European scholars, was unable to match the Judeo-Christian tradition when it came to morality, and its capacity for abstract philosophical thought did not match that of the ancient Greece, but its war-faring prowess was arguably without parallel in the ancient world.

It is noteworthy, therefore, that the enthusiasm of Romantic intellectuals concerning Akhnaten was strongly tempered by the ethics of colonialism and its projection onto the largely empty canvas of the perceived ancient Egyptian "real." The Enlightenment project admires idealist dreamers, but only up to a point. If reformers like Akhnaten have no means of enforcing or are simply unwilling to enforce their "age of awareness" credo, admiration very soon turns to contempt. It is at this point that issues of gender filter into the tropes employed in archaeological discourse, and the sublimated masculine consciousness of Enlightenment rationality is invaded from below (i.e., from the body) by subversive alien elements, which are encoded in no uncertain terms as feminine. Thus, even the British Egyptologist Reverend James Baikie, who expresses great admiration for the ethical tenets of Akhnaten's religious thought, attributes Akhnaten's ineptness as a ruler largely to a subversive female influence: Akhnaten was "a boy bred in the half-lights and dimly seen facts of an Oriental harem, where practical knowledge of men and things are impossible."[31] He continues:

Much of the impracticability of the young king—and after all it was this which chiefly wrecked his work—may safely be traced to his early environment, which prevented him from that salutary contact with hard facts and hard men which is part of the necessary equipment of the man who is to be of any practical service to the world, and to the preponderating influence of a crowd of adoring women, always the surest ground for the growth of faith, who would assure the king of his infallibility, and of the triumph of his most impossible schemes.[32]

Hard men, hard facts, and the necessary equipment of men notwithstanding (or, on second thoughts, *with*standing), it is evident that we have hit a raw nerve in the body of Romantic Egyptological discourse. On this issue, we find more recent Egytological accounts to be in almost complete agreement. Wallis Budge writes:

[Akhnaten] . . . lacked a practical knowledge of men and things. . . . He never learnt the kingcraft of the Pharaohs, and he failed to see that only a warrior could hold what warriors had won for him. Instead of associating himself with men of action, he sat at the feet of Ay the priest, and occupied his mind with religious speculations; and so, helped by his adoring mother and kinswomen, he gradually became the courageous fanatic that tombs and monuments of Egypt show him to have been. His physical constitution and the circumstances of his surroundings made him what he was.[33]

This is a paradigmatic theme in the literature on Akhnaten: His fate was determined by the circumstances of his physiological constitution, or, to borrow from Freud once again, "anatomy is destiny."[34] Compare this comment by J. D. S. Pendlebury:

We may perhaps see in the prominence of [Akhnaten's] mother the beginning of the prominence of the feminine and the effeminate, which seems to be the clue to so much at Amarna, both in politics and art. He himself was certainly abnormal. There is no doubt that in the "monstrous regiment of women,"[35] under which he had been brought up, together with the undoubted feminine characteristics of his body, we can find the clue to much of his later policy.[36]

Thus, Akhnaten's perceived emasculation is regarded as the root cause of all of his other deficiencies. In short, his ineptness as a ruler is attributed largely to his sexuality, and this sexuality—both in terms of physiological sex (by virtue of the physical negation of his masculinity—i.e., his perceived castration[37]) and in terms of gender (by his close association with subversive female elements)—is perceived as feminine. Alan Gardiner writes, for example, of the "hideous portraits" of the pharaoh, so described because they are "the reverse of virile."[38] Gardiner describes sculptured reliefs of Akhnaten as showing him "lolling effeminately upon a cushioned chair."[39] With Akhnaten's sexual characteristics grafted onto those of his empire, Budge and more recent scholars automatically equate his unwillingness to pursue the expansionist military policies of his predecessors with his perceived sexual inadequacies. And when foreign powers threaten to invade Akhnaten's emasculated kingdom, national borders are confused with physical ones; the Egyptian nation is, like its ruler, transformed into a woman whose honor is in jeopardy. The only possible solution for an Egypt wallowing in what Baikie calls "supineness and apathy"[40]—or as Cyril Aldred puts it, "impotence and supineness"[41]—is, according to archaeological consensus, that of swift and emphatic phallic intervention: "What the age demanded was the presence of the Pharaoh as the all-powerful warlord at the head of his troops with his chariots and his archers, vanquishing the insolent and treacherous, and sustaining the morale of the loyal and resolute."[42]

The phallic imagery is the same in both Romantic and contemporary texts: On the one hand, we have hard men, hard facts, the essential equipment of men, and the pharaoh at the head of his troops, weapons unsheathed, while on the other hand, we have Akhnaten, a monarch who just does not seem to measure up. "Time and again," Donald Redford observes, "we glimpse [Akhnaten] lounging, completely limp, in a chair or on a stool. . . . Is this effete monarch, who could never hunt or do battle, a true descendent of the authors of Egypt's empire?"[43] Not surprisingly, the deposition of Akhnaten and the installment of a pharaoh of more traditional militaristic bent is greeted with ejaculatory exuberance. At the hands of General Horemhab, future pharaoh, and "smiter of the Asiatics," "some vigour was . . . injected into war-like operations."[44] Thus, with an appropriate discharge of seminal fluid, some semblance of order is restored temporarily to Egypt's unruly northern colonies. On the accession of Tutankhaten (who changed his name to Tutankh-*amen* after the quelling of the Atenist religious revolution), masculinity was once again restored to the Egyptian monarchy, even if it was in the unexpected physical form of a prepubescent ten-year-old:

The image of the "sportsman-king" was once again consciously cultivated by the young king. The "strong-man" Pharaoh was imbued with the spirit of imperialism, the sort the king of the gods Amun had put forward and nurtured. No monarch attempting to restore the status quo ante could afford to ignore it. And the adolescent Pharaoh was only too eager to step into this role. We see him, in a traditional motive, out hunting in his chariots, or charging in the same vehicle a horde of fleeing enemy. Is the military once again about to provide the ideal of masculine attainment?[45]

This is an apposite question and one that forms an essential subtext to Glass's and his collaborators' construction of *Akhnaten*. Akhnaten's sexuality, his religious outlook, and his reluctance to go to war are all elaborately interconnected in the interpretation we are discussing. Glass's treatment draws extensively on earlier interpretations of the Amarna period, such as those we have been reviewing, in some cases seeming to reinscribe archaeological interpretations of history, in other cases standing aloof from any openly interpretive stance, and in still others taking what Egyptologists have said and throwing it into a different light. The composer does seem willing to concede that Akhnaten "partook of the feminine"—that his reign represented a shift from an idealized "masculine" toward an idealized "feminine"—but in Glass's interpretation, Akhnaten's and his cohorts' "negatively" marked diversion to a "feminine" imaginary has many positive implications. Glass does, however—particularly in the temple and family scenes—identify this move as deeply problematic in psychological terms, at least from the (predominantly male) standpoint of Akhnaten, because of the skewed views of oneself and others that it propagates. Here in the hymn, though, Akhnaten is allowed to have his say, at least insofar as the musical discourse of the scene allows his voice to be heard.

Representing the Unpresentable

Akhnaten's hymn to the sun is the opera's moment of apotheosis.[46] It is the site where the protagonist achieves complete subjective fulfillment; where he quite literally becomes whole. This is signaled both in the music and the drama by a number of conventional and more original semiotic and rhetorical signposts. One of the more innovative of these is a sudden rhetorical shift toward an apparently more realist mode of (re)presentation. Gone is the narrator, who had previously translated all of the texts sung by the characters into the language of the audience. All post-Brechtian pretenses are now apparently dropped as Akhnaten communicates "directly" with his audience. Glass explains:

When Akhnaten sings his Hymn, I wanted it to affect the listener in a special way. The Hymn contains the kernels of Akhnaten's thought and appears as a highly personal statement. By the end of Act II the audience has been listening to more than one and one-half hours of singing which, though accompanied by explicit action requiring little explanation, they can hardly be expected to understand. Suddenly, with the Hymn, the words are intelligible. I wanted at that moment to create the effect of entering Akhnaten's mind, sharing his thoughts, and in this way making the moment highly intimate, a direct communication between Akhnaten and ourselves. It can be a very dramatic effect, achieved by the direct presentation of the text itself.[47]

In a sense, then, Akhnaten steps outside the frame, and in doing so he achieves transcendence. The universality of his religious doctrine is conveyed in the ease with which it can be decoded by audience members. Or is it? Edward Strickland has made a very pertinent point in this regard,[48] though it has also been made by Roland Barthes, Michel Poizat, and a number of other recent theorists: The high falsetto voice is not at all easily understood in orthodox linguistic terms—that is, in terms of the Saussurean binarism of signifier and signified. While the voice carries powerful connotative resonances, which are used to great effect in this and other scenes, it actively resists attempts to tie it down to any specific denotative agenda, which is one of the reasons why its presence was so powerful in the earlier scenes but also why it is destined to disappoint in the function it is intended to serve in this scene. Like our hero's ostensible incorporation of the feminine—as evidenced in his epicene physiological constitution and its auditory representation in the falsetto voice—as well as in the conspicuous absence of Nefertiti and Tye in this scene, his attempt to achieve transcendence by incorporating both the symbol and the sign, the semiotic and the symbolic, is perceptibly *false*. How could it be otherwise? The unpresentable can only be re-presented; it cannot be articulated in its own terms. Indeed, there is a definite campiness to many of the musical and dramatic strategies that are employed in this scene, some of which are clearly intentional on the composer's part, but others of which might not be. Not that it matters. Akhnaten's failure is decidedly not the opera's, as the composer himself seems to realize when at the end of the scene he passes his hero's musical message on to a mixed choir, who in a sense give up the (lost) cause of communicating directly with the audience in their return to an archaic language, biblical Hebrew. This is the "real" source of transcendental power in the opera, the voice that gets the heart beating faster, that brings the goose pimples out. It is in this collective "voice" and in the mingling voices of the three principals in the Window of Appearances scene and the duet that we experience the grace, power, and eloquence of a "truly" non-personal subjectivity.

But Glass has other means at his disposal for signifying sublimation. The very structure of the hymn, as well as its structural position vis-à-vis the rest of the opera, self-consciously plays on conventions in classical music of representing what Immanuel Kant called "the sublime." And it is precisely the self-consciousness of this relation to tradition, more evident here than anywhere else in the opera, that imparts to the representations an opacity that contradicts the move toward realism and away from post-Brechtian and "archaeological" (as defined by Foucault) strategies and that prevents total identification with Akhnaten and his religious worldview. The music of the hymn is archaeological not because it deals with real archaeological artifacts from ancient Egypt but because it treats the entire history of Western classical music as an archaeological site, digging up signifiers from the musical past and, by the very act of representation, uprooting them from the semantic field that formerly nourished them.[49]

In this sense, the music of Philip Glass and other postmodernists *is*, as Susan McClary puts it, a kind of "deconstruction."[50] One way of listening to this music is with a kind of skeptical credulity, a strategum related both to Foucault's attitude vis-à-vis the document and to the approaches of various exponents of deconstruction.[51] This implies a certain happy-go-lucky attitude with regard to the discourse with which one is engaging—a willingness to go along for the ride, as it were (though this is lacking from some of the more extreme examples of deconstruction)—but at the same time a readiness to step off at any juncture and enter the negative space surrounding the aesthetic object, a space that has its own pulsional pleasures that can adequately sustain the listening subject until he or she is ready to return to the symbolic domain. Whether this negative space is experienced as a "new" or "countersublime" (a sublime that goes beyond the sublime), or simply as a void will depend largely on the orientation of the listening subject. Lyotard interprets minimalism in the plastic arts thus, as a movement that posits the elusive "now" as the new sublime.[52] It is possible that Glass is representing this subjective orientation, as manifested in his early minimalist works, in the hymn, and is in this way distancing himself from what used to be the central philosophical tenet of his art. But in distancing himself from a sublime he now recognizes as imaginary or constructed, does he imply yet another level of sublimity, one that goes beyond the sublime that goes beyond the sublime? Or has he at last succeeded in breaking free from this chain of Oedipal precursors by keeping his distance from any form of sublimity, by "dropping out" of the avant-garde?[53] In refusing to play ball with the avant-garde, in "turning populist" and declining from writing "authentic" music (since sublimity is the primary marker of authenticity in avant-garde artifacts), is Glass recognizing the contradictions and anxieties inherent in avant-gardism, or is he, as his critics claim, simply selling out? *Akhnaten* is a pivotal work for Glass in this respect; it is here that the composer's second break with the avant-garde (this time one of his own creation) is indicated, which is probably why critics have had such a hard time getting a handle on this opera. Glass remains controversial not because he broke with tradition in the first place, a maneuver most exponents of avant-gardism can understand, but because works like *Akhnaten* problematize the very act of breaking with tradition upon which the whole concept of avant-gardism hinges.

In order to better understand Glass's articulation of these matters in the hymn, it is helpful to look closely at the ways in which the music appropriates—and by the very act of appropriation rewrites—the musical past. The structure of the hymn is, like so much of the opera, governed by the number three: It is divided into three sections, each of which is preceded by a chaconne ritornello in A minor, the same ritornello that was heard at the beginning of the coronation scene (act 1, scene 2). The bass ostinato of this chaconne pattern is a lament (a descending tetrachord), a form used in Baroque music to represent an apparently inescapable treadmill of suffering. Liberation from the wheel of suffering is suggested, however, in the three sections of the hymn proper. These sections can be described as loose forms of variation in which a constant harmonic formula is subtly transformed either as dictated by the text or by using formal musical procedures that resemble additive and subtractive processes. Here, as elsewhere in the opera, the composer gives the distinct impression of quoting himself, which speaks to the self-referential agenda.

The new chord progression emerges out of the A-minor lament as a deceptive or interrupted cadence. Thus, it is the raised sixth degree, F-sharp, that is its tonal point of departure. In the top voices of the F-sharp minor chord, however, we hear an A chord. (Timbral and tessitural separation ensures that we hear the two chords as distinct.) The chord then resolves onto A major by the simple subtraction of the bass note of F-sharp minor, although a second-degree chord is briefly suggested in the melody in-between these two chords. The sequence then moves to E (initially third-less, but later with a minor third), which is both the (altered) dominant of A minor and the "lowered" seventh degree of F-sharp minor (and also a chord that connotes both modal church music and oriental/archaic "otherness"), before swinging back to the beginning of the pattern. Thus, the sequence begins with a bitonal compound chord and retains its interpretive ambiguity from beginning to end.

In terms of the larger tonal constructions of the hymn and the opera, the resolution to A major is the crucial moment. The move from minor to major modality is one of the most pervasive clichés in tonal music; it signals the moment both of integration for the musical subject and of musical, and often spiritual, "homecoming." In sonata form, it is only when the theme is heard in the major mode at the end of the piece, in the recapitulation, often after having been heard in some less satisfactory form in the minor, that closure is fully realized. In opera, the move from minor to major carries strong religious connotations. Verdi frequently used it in prayers as a means of connoting religious "consummation" for the character singing. This is the case in Violetta's aria "Ah fors' é lui," in *La Traviata*, where F minor resolves to F major at its conclusion.[54] A similar technique is found also in operas such as *Un ballo in maschera*, *La forza del destino*, and *Aïda*. In an earlier "ancient Egyptian" work for the stage as well, *Thamos, König in Ägypten*, the moment of spiritual ascension for the protagonist is signaled when a tormented D minor gives way to a triumphant D major toward the end of the piece. Thus, the move from suffering to the transfigured self that is traced in the shift from the A-minor tonality of the lament to the resplendent A major of the verses of the hymn draws heavily on an existing convention.

A historical precedent can be identified also for the move to F-sharp minor, the chord that interrupts the lament. Modulation to the sixth degree of the scale (usually the major chord built on the minor-sixth degree) is a conventional means of signifying liberation from the forward pushing narrative impulse in classical music.[55] Examples of flat-six excursions can be found in the music of Schubert, Beethoven, and many other Romantic composers, the paradigm example being the final movement of Beethoven's Ninth. Modulations to this tonal area often give the impression of a subjective "place apart," where the ever-present pull toward the home key is temporarily suspended. The listener is allowed to entertain flights of musical fantasy in this utopian subjective space before being once again pulled down into the vortex of musical narrative. Being a stable major sonority, the chord built on the minor submediant can sustain these kinds of tonal diversions for extended periods of time, with different affective results depending on the individual orientation of the composer and the musical context. However, the root note of these minor-sixth modulations invariably proves to be their undoing; Schenkerian theory tells us that in Romantic harmonic practice the lowered sixth degree must eventually give way to the fifth.

What is significant about this procedure from the standpoint of the present discussion is its ability to impart in music some notion of communion with nature, the (extended) self, God, or some other transcendental force. For Romantic listeners, the association was often with specific religious material but could also be with the more abstract numinous plane of "the sublime." In Beethoven's music, this connection was made explicit through the use hymnlike musical material.

The deceptive cadence that signals the move to the sublime in the hymn to the sun is built not on the minor-sixth degree of the scale but on the somewhat more stable (in terms of root movement) major-sixth degree. The pivotal tone, shared by both the tonic and submediant (in this case, A), is the same in the minor chord built on the major-sixth degree of the scale as it is in the major chord build on the minor sixth. The root and fifth, however, are built on more sturdy tonal terrain in the former, thus lessening the need for tonal repudiation. In Glass's F-sharp minor chord, there is not one pivotal tone but three: A, C-sharp, and the "lowered" seventh, E. In fact, the whole A-major chord is found in enfolded form in F-sharp minor seventh, making its repudiation something of a redundancy. The traditional juxtaposition between utopia and dystopia is thus undermined, utopia being a place in our imagination that is always within reach rather than being attainable only at the culmination of some heroic quest. In fact, the whole idea of a heroic quest away from the self in order to achieve sublimation is rendered somewhat hollow by this procedure. The message is underlined in the cyclical structure of the hymn; rather than a momentary glimpse of fulfillment, we are offered alternating waves of suffering and fulfillment; three times we pass from the suffering of the lament to the sublimation of the hymn, and countless more times we swing between Akhnaten's imaginary vision of fulfillment, signaled by the F-sharp minor seventh chord, and "actual" fulfillment, signaled by the A-major chord itself, which was there even when we were only dreaming of it.

Significantly, this is the first music in the opera that effortlessly combines rather than juxtaposes black-note and white-note sonorities, the former being associated predominantly with the old order, the latter with the Atenist reformers. The pitch F-sharp, it should be noted, was associated explicitly with the old order and with Akhnaten's father in the funeral of Amenhotep III (act 1, scene 1), as was the major inflection of the home key. Being "Akhnaten's finest moment,"[56] this might also be the moment when he is the most willing to recognize the status and achievements of his forebears, including his father. It might, in other words, be the moment in the opera when the gravitational pull of the Oedipus complex is at its weakest. It might, on the other hand, be nothing of the sort. The association of A major both with Akhnaten's father and with the Aten strongly suggests that Akhnaten's androgynous sun god might, like the pharaoh himself, be more man than woman. In order to achieve spiritual transformation, Akhnaten must, as convention dictates, pass into the masculine-marked major mode. Akhnaten's spiritual aspirations might therefore be as much a symptom of his Oedipus complex as a sign of his recovery from it, inasmuch as they express desire for the father transferred to the sun disk. While this abstract symbol of the new religion is the "Mother/Father of all creation," it is referred to exclusively by the masculine personal pronoun in this version of the hymn. Ambivalence toward the father—attraction to as well as repulsion from him—was, it should be stressed, an important part of the Oedipus complex as formulated by Freud.[57] It is possible, therefore, that we are seeing and hearing the "negative" side of the protagonist's Oedipus complex in this scene, with desire for the (androgynous) father temporarily displacing desire for the mother.

All of the music of this scene is strongly gender inflected. The chaconne lament, which introduces each of the verses, is associated with both the nonpersonal and the bisexual characteristics of the protagonist: It includes the nonpersonal trilogy theme (which is associated directly with both Einstein and Gandhi) and mirrored thematic material that easily becomes associated with the two sexes as constructed, both of whose characteristics we see personified in the extraordinary physique of Akhnaten. The affective connotations of the lament also imply that this aspect of Akhnaten's psychophysiological constitution contributes largely to his own personal suffering and to the suffering he perceives in the world around him: The binary order as reflected in and represented by Akhnaten can ultimately offer little consolation to the divided subject, unless it somehow becomes estranged through the very act of contemplation, thus implying some "higher" mode of consciousness that transcends gender and all other divisions. (Precisely this assumption grounds Akhnaten's "spirituality.")

A caveat is in order, however: the chaconne variation is, as I have mentioned earlier, the very same form that Louis XIV used in operas and ballets to connote the platonic harmony of the spheres—with the Sun King himself at the center of the divine order. This historical point of reference may be sufficient to undermine Akhnaten's putative androgyny; all the while that it is governed over by the Sun King, who is male (enough, at least, to father children), the divine balance of opposites, as expounded by the pharaoh from his transcendental place apart, is destined to be perceived more as the product of a male than of a female consciousness.

This aspect of the opera was emphasized in different ways in both of the major productions of the opera in the 1980s. Even though this is Akhnaten's solo, in the Stuttgart production, in which the physical abnormalities of the pharaoh were not depicted, Nefertiti was present throughout. At the beginning of the scene, when the chaconne is heard for the first time, the couple was seen in profile on their thrones, their hand gestures tracing an intricate series of mirror images as they played out the role of the divine royal couple, or *hierosgamos*, personifying the unity of the opposing divine masculine and feminine principles. In Freeman's production, Akhnaten stood alone, center-stage, dressed from the waist down, in contrast to the earlier appearance of the lament, in which he was totally naked. His physical abnormalities were still clearly visible. In this production, Nefertiti was absent, presumably because her feminine principle was incorporated somehow in Akhnaten's physiology. Both of these interpretations can be supported by the music and the libretto; one features a man and a woman, and the other a paradoxical man-woman being (predominantly male). The shortcomings of Akhnaten regarding his dual sexuality seem to me to be an essential part of the story, the ramifications of which we shall witness in the very next scene. It would be nice, of course, to hear another duet with Nefertiti, especially since this is supposed to be the opera's moment of apotheosis, in which all of the opposing elements come together and are somehow transformed. But it might be just as well that Nefertiti is not aurally present in this scene, in light of what we will shortly witness.

An alternative and quite radical interpretation, which no director has to my knowledge pursued, would place the pharaoh Smenkhkare opposite Akhnaten in this scene and have both men sing the hymn, either as a duet or in unison. Smenkhkare was Akhnaten's coregent during the final years of his reign, and certain prominent specialists on the period have claimed that the two men were lovers.[58] Because of this, some homosexual groups have touted Akhnaten as the first openly homosexual man in history—an achievement that, if true, would be as significant as any other of his purported innovations. Smenkhkare was included in early drafts of *Akhnaten* but was later discarded.[59] Were he reincorporated into the story in future productions, his presence would certainly add a whole new dimension to the protagonist's bisexuality, that might even be beneficial to the opera as a whole. It would also explain the bittersweet tone in the duet with Nefertiti, which we earlier attributed to the influence of Akhnaten's mother.

Akhnaten singing is characterized by a declamatory style akin, once again, to that of liturgical chant. At the same time as it highlights the importance of the text, this also draws attention to the theological nature of its content. The trajectory of his melodies is predominantly rising, beginning on either the root or the fifth of A major and culminating on its major third, c-sharp". Each stanza of the hymn is tripartite in its construction, being made up of three cadences, the last of which is invariably the most conclusive and usually the longest. There is some melodic and harmonic variation in the constitution of individual phrases and some repetition, but this general structural pattern governs the construction of the entire hymn.

The text of the first two stanzas (the first verse) is as follows:

> Thou dost appear beautiful
> On the horizon of heaven
> Oh, living Aten
> He who was the first to live
>
> When thou hast risen on the Eastern Horizon
> Thou hast filled every land with thy beauty
> Thou art fair, great, dazzling,
> High above every land
> Thy rays encompass the land
> To the very end of all thou hast made

The first two lines of the text are accompanied by two rounds of the paradigmatic version of the progression (see example 19, p. 77). The words *beautiful* and *heaven* coincide with Akhnaten's first arrivals at the major third of A, thus strongly supporting the interpretation that the change of mode from minor to major in this scene denotes the protagonist's spiritual breakthrough.

The next two lines are accompanied by a prolonged version of the cadence, achieved by inserting two new chords, A minor and B minor, prior to the penultimate and final chords of the sequence, A major and E (minor) (see example 19). This results in a progression that passes through both modes of the opera's home key. Thus, the shift from minor to major that signals spiritual transformation, both in the relationship between the chaconne ritornellos and the verses of the hymn and between the hymn as a whole and the rest of the opera, is reenacted on the micro level. Melodically, this transformation of the pattern diverges from the initial two in setting out from the low fifth (e') rather than from the root of A major; in remaining on this note during the second bar and thus avoiding the troublesome B-minor chord; and in passing through both the minor and major thirds of A. The first appearances of this extended version of the hymn chord progression, incorporating both A minor and A major, coincides with the first mention of the Aten by name. As if summoned from the heavens by the utterance of its name, the voice of the sun disk is heard at the culmination of this pattern and in a fourth instrumental cadence in the guise of a short trumpet response to Akhnaten's invocations. The melody it plays here is identical to Akhnaten's melody of the previous pattern, apart from its initial note, which is an octave higher (e").

The extended Alberti bass pattern from the final two cadences of the previous four-cycle stanza forms the ground for all four cadences of the next stanza. The first two phrases are melodically similar to their counterparts in the previous stanza, though the melody is sustained over an extended version of the harmonic pattern. Here we find one of the most obvious cases of word painting in the hymn: the sustained c-sharp" coinciding with the word *horizon* in the phrase "when thou hast risen on the Eastern Horizon" and the diatonic ascent prior to it with the reference in the text to the rising sun (see example 33).

A point of considerable interest here is the trumpet, which seems to have been pursuing Akhnaten ever since his first mention of the Aten by name. To say that the voices of the two interweave as if they were partners in a duet is no exaggeration, and the composer himself uses this unconventional term (for a combination of vocal and instrumental parts) to describe their interplay in this scene.[60] Indeed, the relationship between the two bears more than a passing resemblance to that between Akhnaten and Nefertiti in the duet (act 2, scene 2), which was actually a trio between the two lovers and the obbligato trumpet. The same tension we encountered in the earlier scene is present here: In the duet it was between the notes A and B; here, it is between Akhnaten's c-sharp" and the trumpet's (or Aten's) b'. This pungent dissonance is held over a period of two entire bars (see example 33).

In the next pattern (rehearsal mark 15), the duet becomes a trio with the addition of a second trumpet. Hereafter, Akhnaten's voice and the trumpets merge, so much so that it is at times difficult to distinguish one from the other.[61] Here, once again, Akhnaten steps over the threshold of ego-consciousness and enters the polymorphous realm of the nonpersonal. His melody moves from the low e'—which was strongly identified earlier in the opera as the domain of Nefertiti—up a minor sixth to c", on to d", and finally down to c-sharp". Thus, his voice passes through both minor and major thirds. As the Aten traces its trajectory across the sky—"fair, great, dazzling, high above every land"—so Akhnaten passes through to a plane where the boundaries between self and others, between the masculine and the feminine, blurs. As we reach the culmination of the cadence, the pharaoh's c-sharp" is held while two streaming descents in thirds by the trumpets iterate its modal opposite, c" (see example 34). Here we witness the intimacy of the relationship between Akhnaten and his god: The mutual attraction of musical incompatibles functions as a metaphor for the quasi-sexual tension between the pharaoh and his ultimate other. The resulting bimodality is not only reminiscent of the duet but also identical to that heard in the transgression theme in the prelude and elsewhere in the opera; this suggests that Akhnaten's spirituality is founded on transgression (encoded in feminine terms) and is thus bound up inextricably with the binary order.

Example 33. Act 2, scene 3, hymn to the sun. Word painting in the first verse.

In the final two patterns of the verse (rehearsal mark 16), the text speaks of the Aten's "rays," which "encompass the land / To the very end" of all creation. As the verse comes to its conclusion, four diatonic descents are heard in succession on the trumpets. These are related to the lament motif, although the tetrachord here descends from e″, the "other" tonality of the opera, instead of from Akhnaten's and the opera's home tonality of A. Given the brilliant tone quality of these instruments, the simile of rays of sunlight streaming down toward the raised arms of the king—a pervasive image in the art of the Amarna period—is strongly evoked.

In the transition between the first and second verses, we are once again returned to the chaconne ritornello (rehearsal marks 17–20). The ritornello is almost identical to its earlier appearance, except for the addition of a horn in the first two cadences, presumably intended to suggest the ever more imminent presence of the sun god. The motif played by this instrument (A–B–c–e) is the same as was heard in the first appearance of the ritornello prior to Akhnaten's coronation (act 1, scene 2), which was transformed into a kind of cantus firmus when sung by Akhnaten in the trio (act 1, scene 3). In the second cadence, the simple octave leaps played by the

Example 34. Act 2, scene 3, hymn to the sun. Word painting and trumpet response.

The handed rays of aten giving life ("ankh") to Akhnaten. Wallis Budge, *Tutankhamen: Amenism, Atenism, and Egyptian Monotheism* (New York: Dover, 1991 [1923]), p. 99.

oboe at the beginning of the scene are filled in diatonically, making their descending streams the mirror images of the rising bassoon lines. The syncopated horn and converging string lines of the final pattern are identical to their earlier appearances. Instead of the finality motif, however, we now hear a cascade of descending trumpets at the culmination of the ritornello. As the rays of the Aten pour down on the sunstruck king, an ethereal flute ascends to the firmament, imploring the listener to follow its trajectory toward the second verse.

The text of the first and second stanzas of the second section of the hymn is as follows:

> All the beasts are satisfied with their pasture
> Trees and plants are verdant
> Birds fly from their nests, wings spread
> Flocks skip with their feet
> All that fly and alight
> Live when thou hast arisen
>
> How manifold is that which thou hast made
> Thou sole God
> There is no other like thee
> Thou didst create the earth

> According to thy will,
> Being alone, everything on earth
> Which walks and flies on high

At this point in the scene, Glass introduces one of the most pronounced polyrhythms of the opera, evidently to connote the idea of a Nile Valley or a planet teeming with life, a musical anima mundi (see example 22, p. 84). Harmonically, one of the most elaborate transformations of the tonally ambiguous progression now unfolds. The first two phrases consist in simple alternations of the compound chord F-sharp minor/A major and the unthirded E chord (with a "lowered," or dominant, seventh in the final bar); the third is a more typical extended form of the progression that resolves to A major in the penultimate bar (see example 22). In the third phrase of the pattern, grazing animals, vegetation, and birds are all drawn together under the watchful solar eye of their creator: All things "live when thou [the Aten] hast arisen," the direct reference to the sun god occurring on a high c-sharp". The cadence comes to its close with a vigorous zigzagging of lines in the strings, culminating in a light ascending scale on the flute.

The second stanza of the second verse is harmonically identical to the first, with the two shorter cadences followed by a longer cadence that includes the uninverted tonic, A major. Here, again, there is evidence of word painting in Akhnaten's melody: the word *high* in the lines "everything on earth / Which walks and flies on high" is the highest pitch in the melody of this particular cadence, c-sharp".

The texts of the final two stanzas of the verse are as follows:

> Thy rays nourish the fields
> When thou dost rise
> They live and thrive for thee
> Thou makest the seasons to nourish
> All thou hast made
> The winter to cool
> The heat that they may taste thee
>
> There is no other that know thee
> Save thy son, Akhnaten
> For thou hast made him skilled
> In thy plans and thy might
> Thou dost raise him up for thy son
> Who comes forth from thyself

Harmonically, the final three stanzas of the section (the second is repeated) are almost identical to the first two, the most noteworthy change being that the A-minor chord in the third phrase of the progression is beefed up somewhat by the addition of a bass note of F (played by the double basses), thus transforming it into a stronger major sonority. The gradual buildup in orchestration that has unfolded during the course of the hymn continues as well; the wind tutti implemented at its beginning is now supplemented by the remaining brass instruments, the trombone and the tuba.

Aside from orchestration, a good deal of the interest of this subsection arises as a result of the composer's meticulous attention to music-text relations. Here we continue to find extensive and blatant use of word painting, a common technique in Renaissance and Baroque music. In the lines "thy rays nourish the field / When thou dost rise" and "Thou dost raise him up for thy son," we hear two jumps of a perfect fifth (from e' to b' and from f-sharp' to c-sharp"), concomitant with the words *rise* and *up*, respectively. The words *live* and *thrive* in the phrase "They live and thrive for thee" are held for nearly a bar, the longest note durations heard during the first chord of the pattern (the compound, F-sharp major/A minor). The word *Akhnaten* in the phrase "There is no other that knows thee / Save thy son, Akhnaten" is highlighted by means of a minor third jump (from b' to d") followed by a diatonic descent back to the initial note. This little ego trip by the opera's protagonist reveals a narcissistic proclivity not altogether congruent with the other tenets of his credo. Whatever his reasons, it was important for the king to emphasize his own role as mediator between the Aten and his people. Whether his deeper motives were altruistic, selfish, or even fanatical (as Cyril Aldred has claimed) we shall perhaps never know for sure.[62]

Akhnaten's close relationship with his god is exemplified in the final phrases of the hymn (in the abridged version set by Glass). The penultimate phrase, "Thou dost raise him up for thy son," ends on the pitch c", while the final phrase, "Who comes forth from thyself," ends on c-sharp" (see example 35). Akhnaten is the minor and Aten the major third, but both belong to the same triad. The words of the final phrase of the hymn therefore confirm that the move from the minor to the major modality represents the spiritual transformation of the protagonist.

For the third and final time, we are returned to the music of the chaconne. The arrangement is the densest so far: strings are present throughout, as is the syncopated descending trumpet, which plays a transformation of the trilogy motif. The horn is also present in each of the chaconne patterns. It plays the ascending theme, which is closely associated with Akhnaten himself and with the sun god and which was the melodic core motif in the Window of Appearances, the scene that signaled the birth of the new religious order. The use of brass instruments here points specifically to the religious consummation of the protagonist, which is signaled also in the wind instruments. In the second pattern, streams of descending

Example 35. Act 2, scene 3, hymn to the sun. Akhnaten meets his maker.

scales are introduced in the clarinets, setting out from and arriving at the notes of the descending tetrachord. In the third pattern, the descending scales of the clarinet are replaced by ascending scales played by bassoons, once again setting out from and arriving at the notes of the descending tetrachord.

In the fourth and final chaconne variation, we hear the complete form of the pattern, with ascending and descending scales in contrary motion to each other. This is the connubial, where all of the musical forces of the new religious order converge. The Sun King's androgynous utopia is now a reality. This final transformation of the chaconne is a threshold to what follows. Like the weighty threefold chord attacks in Mozart's *Die Zauberflöte*, this third ritornello opens the doorway to a new vista of consciousness. Once again, the "double doors of the horizon" (act I, prelude) are ajar, and as we peer through the gap we catch a privileged transtemporal view of the influence of Akhnaten's ideas.

An angelic choir (SATB) now sings verses from Psalm 104 of the Old Testament in the original Hebrew, both the subject matter and wording of which are remarkably similar to Akhnaten's hymn. It is stipulated in the libretto that Akhnaten should leave the stage deserted at this point, while the disembodied choir takes up the singing from the wings,[63] a technique that recalls a similar moment in Massenet's *Thaïs*. In David Freeman's production of the opera, Akhnaten left the stage, quite appropriately, by climbing up a ladder leading to a skylight that was on a plane with the upper circle of the theater—known in theatrical terminology as "the gods." Eventually, Akhnaten disappeared into the dazzling white light that emerged from the opening, all traces of ego consciousness dissolving in the all-equalizing fire of the sun god. Although Glass's instructions were not followed to the letter in Achim Freyer's Stuttgart production, the overall effect is quite similar. In that version, Akhnaten quite literally became the sun god, visually speaking. He was first encircled by the choir, forming a mandalalike construct, with Akhnaten occupying the central position (the fiery drop at the hub of the mandala, known by the Sanskrit term *bindu*) in which all opposites—the masculine and feminine creative principles—converge. Strands of reflective material—the rays of the Aten—emanated from around Akhnaten's collar, linking the pharaoh at the center of the circle to the choir that was evenly spaced around its circumference. The "son of the sun" gradually raised himself to a standing position, and the people of Israel prostrated themselves before him. Powerful lights were focused on Akhnaten, whose luminescent presence became increasingly difficult to differentiate from the sun disk itself. As the chorus sang its three final wordless syllables, the pharaoh's mouth fell open, his lips forming the circumference of a perfect circle—son and sun; son and self; worshiper and worshiped, subject and object became one and the same.[64]

The text of the choral section is as follows:

Oh Lord, how manifold are Thy works	Ma rab-bu ma-a-se-kha-ha-shem
In wisdom hast Thou made them all	Ku-lam be-khokh-ma a-sita
The earth is full of Thy riches	Ma-le-a ha-a-rets kin-ya-ne-kha

Akhnaten's moment of apotheosis (hymn to the sun, act 2, scene 4). Houston Grand Opera. HGO photo by Jim Caldwell © 1984.

Who coverest Thyself with light
    as with a garment
Who stretchest out the Heavens
    like a curtain
	O-te or ka-sal-ma
	No-te sha-ma-yim ka-yi-ri-a

Thou makest darkness and it is night Wherein all the beasts of the forest do creep forth	Ta-shet kho-shekh vi-hi lay-la Bo tir-mos kol khay-to ya-a
Oh Lord, how manifold are Thy works In wisdom hast Thou made them all The earth is full of Thy riches	Ma rab-bu ma-a-se-kha ha-shem Ku-lam be-khokh-ma a-sita Ma-le-a ha-a-rets kin-ya-ne-kha

The harmonies voiced by the choir are essentially the same as those in the hymn to Aten, thus underlining the continuity between Akhnaten's ideas and those of the Judeo-Christian tradition. The music is the same and so are the ideas. Glass intent is quite clear:

I raise a very controversial point, that the Old Testament derived from earlier sources, principally Egyptian. This is a controversial idea and not a particularly popular one, but one that's hard to deny when you compare the texts of the Hymn to Aten and Psalm 104. It's very hard not to see that one came from the other. I was drawing attention to the continuity between the world of Akhnaten and the Judeo-Christian world.[65]

The controversy to which Glass alludes stretches back to the first quarter of the twentieth century. Breasted was among the first modern Egyptologists to recognize the correlation between Atenism and Western religious thought. He even positioned the hymn and the psalm side by side on the page in order to illustrate as directly as possible the correspondences between the two texts.[66] So while the idea of a link between Atenism and the Judeo-Christian tradition is controversial, it has also been a part of the received wisdom on Akhnaten for some time. Even Aldred, who is one of the staunchest contemporary critics of Akhnaten, is forced to concede on the final page of his exhaustive study on the pharaoh that his ideas "continued to haunt the minds of others, and eventually prevailed as the ordinances for the conduct of Man *vis-à-vis* God in the decalogue that was part of another 'teaching.'"[67]

Why, then, the powerful anxiety of influence when it comes to Akhnaten? Why the desperate and incredibly funny attempts by Egyptologists to cast the pharaoh as everything from a homosexual to a hermaphrodite to a pedophile to an effeminate "mummy's boy" to a dictator? In other words, why deploy just about every category that is negatively marked in contemporary culture? Freud was among the first scholars to face strong opposition because of his advocacy of Akhnaten; in the 1930s, representatives of the psychoanalyst's own Jewish faith strongly urged him not to publish *Moses and Monotheism*. More recently, the Egyptian scholar Ahmed Osman has claimed that Akhnaten *was* Moses. According to Osman, orientalist/ Africanist prejudice is one of the primary reasons for Western scholars' reluctance to acknowledge Akhnaten's status as the founding father of Western religious thought.[68] It also, for Osman, explains why the post–World War II research has been so intent on destroying the positive image of Akhnaten and his religion that was propagated in earlier years.[69] Skeptics might, of course, argue that Osman's claims are driven by their own nationalistic agenda. Nonetheless, it is difficult to explain the strength and the persistence of the attacks on Akhnaten and his religion in recent years without recourse to some such explanatory theory.

As for Glass, his words echo those of Bernal insofar as he identifies the Hellenic model as the main obstacle to the acceptance of Akhnaten in the West: "We always talk about Greece as the cradle of our civilization, when actually it was Egypt. The Greeks themselves turned to Egypt, Herodotus and so forth. They would visit and learn from it."[70] This is one light in which we might view the final moments of the hymn to the sun: as an attempt on Glass's part to rectify a number of pervasive misconceptions concerning Akhnaten, misconceptions that have arisen largely because of the tendency of historians to use their knowledge of the past as a tool for reshaping the present. To otherwise accept the vision of Akhnaten given to us in the archaeological literature *as is* is to accept many of the blatantly imperialistic, misogynistic, and homophobic assumptions that go along with it.

Glass provides us with his own vision of Akhnaten. And despite the distancing strategies he employs extensively in this work, he undoubtedly has his own ideologically colored agenda. This agenda might have its own shortcomings, but they are likely to be very different than those in the recent archaeological writing; insofar as this opera actively challenges the assumptions that ground those readings, it is hard not to see it as a timely and valuable intervention in this hotly contested area of debate. Cyril Aldred has spoken disapprovingly of recent works of the imagination concerning this pharaoh: "From being one whom his people did their best to forget," he writes, "he has become, thirty centuries later, the celebrated subject of novels, operas and other works of the imagination."[71] The opera to which Aldred refers can only be *Akhnaten*,[72] and the disapproval he expresses seems to stem from his awareness of the divergence between his own interpretation of the subject and Glass's. This must be frustrating for him, because archaeological studies tend to reach only a limited number of people, whereas Glass's opera and other artistic treatments of the subject have captured the imagination of many hundreds of thousands, if not millions. Could it be that here, too, the chorus will have the final word?

The hymn to the sun ends with three blissful pre-Oedipal *ahs* sung by the mixed chorus, accompanied by the "finality" motive, which connotes spiritual attainment and stoicism. There are three weighty chord attacks and the "double doors of the horizon" slam firmly shut.

The Fantasy of the Maternal Voice

If the use of archaeological strategies in the hymn, the self-conscious pillaging of tropes of the sublime, prompted the listener to maintain a certain distance in relation to the title character, we now find out why. In the first scene of act 3, we see Akhnaten with his six daughters and Nefertiti, who disappears toward the end of the scene with four of her daughters, leaving her husband and the two eldest daughters alone in the palace. Glass describes the dramatic intent of the scene as follows: "One interpretation of it, and the one that I've chosen, is that the more he became involved in his ideas and ideals, and involved in his family life, he simply lost interest in the affairs of state, and that lack of interest led to his downfall."[73] The music and the "drama" within the music elaborate on this theme.

The music that opens the scene is the same heard after the quasi-sexual assault on the temple by Akhnaten and his mother (act 2, scene 1). The symbolism of bursting into the temple, of letting the clear white light of the Aten "pour into what was once the holy of holies," requires little interpretation.[74] We also saw that the catharsis experienced by Akhnaten and his mother in their acts of mindless brutality, the wordless union of their frenzied staccato voices, the pure nondifferentiating bliss or *jouissance* experienced by them, was paralleled by, if not equivalent to, the pleasure of their "sacred" incestuous union—in other words, it was the phallically marked ecstasy of breaking taboos. Here, the family scene begins with the same incessantly rising thirdless arpeggios on E and the same despondent motif—a rising diminished-fifth tetrachord, played here on oboes in thirds, the higher voice moving from the fifth to the tonic (b–c–d–e') three times, after which it finds its way to a gloomy, modal-sounding melodic cadence.

The return of this music suggests that we have come full circle and that the protagonist is experiencing the same sense of isolation and shame that he experienced in the earlier scene. Isolation we can perhaps understand; the king has withdrawn not only into the utopia of his holy city but also into the comfortable insularity of family life. But why shame? Tye is no longer present, and Akhnaten appears to have successfully purged himself of his mother complex through his two "baptisms in fire" in the duets with Nefertiti and with his god, in the hymn to the sun. Is it possible that he is suffering a relapse of his earlier Oedipal affliction? The relentless arpeggios on A suggest an insularity, a libidinal circularity, an incestuous longing for the (imaginary) self that appears to give grounds to such a supposition.

Glass and his collaborators make no explicit references to incestuous relations between Akhnaten and his daughters, but others do. Akhnaten's is one of the most controversial cases of father-daughter incest in Egyptian history and one that will probably never be satisfactorily resolved—unlike that of his father, Amenhotep III, who almost certainly imposed connubial "duties" on his daughters. The evidence is far from conclusive, but some scholars believe that Akhnaten was a pedophile who fathered children with at least two of his own daughters. This is a highly controversial issue, the origins of which lie primarily in the nomenclature of the royal princesses. Akhnaten's daughters' daughters in certain cases inherited their mother's name, to which the suffix "minor" was simply added: thus, Ankhesenpaaten's daughter became Ankhesenpaaten-minor and Meretaten's Meretaten-minor.[75] Appended to these names, however, was a titulary list that in these cases included the title "daughter of the king." Whether this title was simply inherited from the mother or whether it was an accurate description is open to contention. Nomenclature alone, however, does not explain how Meretaten came to be called "the mistress of your house" in a letter sent to Akhnaten from the king of Babylon,[76] although it could be argued that understanding *mistress* to mean "lover" is just a case of overzealous interpretation. We know that Nefertiti disappeared (perhaps leaving her husband) toward the end of Akhnaten's reign. It is possible, then, that Meretaten simply assumed responsibility for the royal household in loco parentis, without taking on her mother's connubial duties as well.

The question of incest is a particularly sensitive one in this case, as Akhnaten comes across in every other respect as the model father. Romantic-period archaeological writing went so far as to claim that he was the first loving father in history—the first who openly expressed his emotional attachment to his family. He is commonly shown surrounded by his children, embracing them, playing with them, and kissing them. More recent studies—which, it is only fair to say, are bent on destroying the image of Akhnaten as the paragon of the benign, humanitarian ruler—interpret the same evidence very differently. Because of the fragmentary nature of this evidence, I reserve judgment on the question; however, an incestuous basis to relations between Akhnaten and his daughters is strongly suggested in the music and drama of this scene, particularly in its final section.

The protagonist's blurred perceptions regarding himself in relation to others are conveyed in the music sung at the beginning of the scene by Akhnaten's daughters (rehearsal mark 2). The overlapping of soprano and alto parts and of A-minor and E-minor chords produces the effect of complete harmonic disorientation. Waves of A minor, the tonality associated predominantly with the self as constructed and with the Lacanian "real" (in the prelude, the Window of Appearances scene, and the hymn to the sun), wash up against and into waves of E minor, the tonality associated with desire, delusion, "otherness," and the Lacanian imaginary (in the coronation, temple, and the duet). A brief cadence on G minor resolving to G major in the penultimate bar of the eight-bar sequence is reminiscent both of the chord sequence from the trio (act 1, scene 3) and of the move from the minor to the major modality in Akhnaten's hymn, but, located on the lowered third of E minor (the "lowered" seventh degree of A major) as it is, the effect is somewhat different. Indeed, the chord movement from an ambiguous or hybrid E/A sonority to G major/minor was associated explicitly with the old order in the coronation scene (act 1, scene 2); more specifically, it was the musical element that marked the old order as exotic and somehow strange. The same effect is produced here. After the G minor/major (pseudo)cadence, the music loops back to the beginning of the sequence. Altos alternate with sopranos in beginning the sequence, but otherwise the singing remains the same throughout the initial section. In the third and fourth repeats of the pattern (rehearsal mark 4), the motif suggesting isolation, remorse, and perhaps incestuous desire is reintroduced on the low oboes. The oboe motif is retained in the next two patterns (rehearsal marks 6 and 7; see example 21, p. 82), which are distinguished also by a return of the thirdless arpeggios on E in the upper voices.

What Glass is illustrating in this scene is clearly a predominance of otherness, encoded by the opera's protagonist in feminine terms: a gender imbalance weighted toward the interior, the cyclical, the static, and the (imagined) pre-Oedipal—qualities we have been explicitly encouraged to value since the beginning of the opera since they represent the antithesis of the destructive masculine forces of the old order. There is, however, nothing intrinsically *wrong* with the exterior, the linear, the forward striving, and the post-Oedipal; these categories and the mode of being they suggest can, as much recent feminism has shown, be extremely useful. Perhaps, then, the pendulum in the psychological equilibrium of our protagonist has swung too far in the (M)other direction. The problem is not so much a predominance of the feminine (which never was a "problem" in this opera) as a predominance of the "feminine": namely, Akhnaten's perceptions of the mystical other that he associates so closely with his god. Akhnaten can hardly be admonished for wishing to spend time with his wife and daughters, but his total immersion in otherness results in a skewed view of the world around him and an unconscious suppression of even the positive aspects of masculine qualities. By this I do not mean his reluctance to go to war, hunt, and so forth—a common source of criticism in the literature on the subject—but the complete insularity of the scenario that now unfolds. Akhnaten appears to be totally out of touch with both national and international affairs; rather than traveling around the country rallying support for his revolutionary ideas, he remains shut away in the palace at Akhetaten with his family; rarely is he depicted outside of the private chambers of the royal palace and rarely is he seen in the company of outsiders; friends and allies write repeatedly from abroad beseeching his assistance, and he does not even reply. The situation is exacerbated by an uncanny twist of fate: Akhnaten and Nefertiti beget six children and not one of them is a son. Aside from its obvious symbolic significance (i.e., the perceived emasculation of the king mapped onto his kingdom), this means that there is no male heir to the throne.

It is in this context that we hear the vocalese of Akhnaten's daughters. What we are hearing is the unmistakable sound of Akhnaten's self-constructed domestic bliss. Not by chance has Glass made this scene a vocalese: The intention is that we and the opera's protagonist be returned quite literally to the womb. Under the lulling spell of his six angelic daughters, Akhnaten is in a metaphorical if not physical sense back in his mother's embrace, not, as before, intoxicated by the totalizing and cleansing desire of *jouissance* but in the state of suspended animation that goes beyond it.[77] This "more than *jouissance*" is, interestingly, located by Lacan in the Freudian concept of repetition.[78] Of course, repetition is something you

Akhnaten, Nefertiti, and their six daughters (the family, act 3, scene 1). Houston Grand Opera. HGO photo by Jim Caldwell © 1984.

find quite a lot of in Glass's music, but seldom as it is heard now. Once again, I do not perceive the Freudian concept of repetition, associated by him with the death drive, as a solely negative force. The driving, pulsional qualities of what Kristeva calls the semiotic have both negative and positive aspects. It is the pulsional power of the semiotic that, together with linear strategies, propelled the music forward to the high point of the first act, the Window of Appearances scene. This was the power wielded by the chorus to carry an idea through to its conclusion; to keep on keeping on; to see to it that the religious revolution became a reality. It was the relentless, emphatic force of getting things done; the cogs of the reproductive machinery of the "new order" whirring inexorably, telling us that change *will* come; a time-bomb ticking in the lofty and musty halls of the temple of Amon. In the Window of Appearances scene, the duet, and the hymn, it was the secret place we need for psychical or spiritual regeneration; the place where the royal couple became rejuvenated through their mutual desire for each other and for their god; the comforting interior site where each of us can become whole again in a world that is constantly tearing us apart. In the chaconne lament, it was the site where the protagonist could step off the treadmill for a few moments and watch with stoic detachment as the wheels turn.

Here, though, we see the reverse side of this modality: the death drive in its near-Freudian form, the dysphoric or negative aspect of the semiotic.

As the incessant and unchanging waves of E minor (the "other" key of the opera) wash over him, then, we witness Akhnaten languishing in the luxurious domain of "woman"; the absolute realm of the (mystified) other; and, most importantly, the realm of the gods, as "the place of the Other is," in the words of Jacqueline Rose, "also the place of God."[79]

We find an interesting parallel here in Buddhist thought, where the "realm of the gods" and "the place of God" are two entirely different things. Buddhists are reluctant to speak of God at all, other than in negations and paradoxes, because the absolute cannot possibly be described in terms of the relative. For Buddhists, the realm of the gods is merely the highest of the six realms of the "wheel of life." Far from being a conducive abode for spiritual development, it is a realm in which stagnation, complacency, self-indulgence, egotism, and pride are rife. It is a realm of aesthetic pleasure, of dance and music; but this one-sided devotion to pleasure invariably leads to erroneous perceptions of oneself and others and thus of reality. Those who inhabit this realm do so as a result of past meritorious deeds (of accumulated positive karma), but once here they are wont to become desensitized to the sufferings of other, less fortunate life-forms. Buddhists speak of "the misery of the gods,"[80] not because they are unhappy as such but because their coveted bliss is self-constructed and transitory: What at first appears to be a realm of infinite joy turns out to be the source of infinite suffering as godlike life-forms condemn themselves to numerous nonpropitious future births as a result of the selfishness of their actions.[81] The following description of the godlike plane of consciousness could easily be applied to Akhnaten and his family as we see them now:

Aiming at the ever more peaceful, the ever more subtle, the ever more real, they are not safeguarded by the critical awareness of the constructedness of all states, their emptiness and relativity. They remain within realms of dead calm for extremely long periods of time, untroubled by any concern, secure in their sense of having achieved final ultimacy, of having become one with the absolute. They are most subtly locked by pride and delusion into the ultimate self-constructed world of alienation and self-preoccupation imaginable. Buddhists consider these heavens and the life forms of the gods to be the most dangerous pitfall for meditators, because they are so close to what the philosophically uneducated expect the absolute to be: an infinite objectivity, an infinite subjectivity, nothingness, and an infinite indefinability. Only an understanding of voidness, the relativity of all things and states, provides the critical defence against succumbing to the apparent calm and transcendentality of these heavens.[82]

As Akhnaten has deluded himself into believing that he inhabits the realm of the absolute, the music we hear is quite appropriately "absolute" music: It is the wordless, indefinable, exclusively objective or exclusively subjective (but either way essentially noncommunicative), semantically vacuous voices of angels. It is, or purports to be, pure, undefiled syntax,

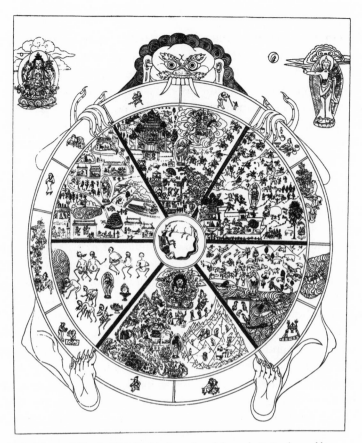

The Tibetan "Wheel of Life," with the realm of the gods (*top*) mirrored by that of hell (*bottom*). The other realms are those of human beings (*top left*), animals (*bottom left*), titans (*top right*), and pretas (*bottom right*). L. Austine Waddell, *Tibetan Buddhism* (New York: Dover, 1972 [1895]), opposite p. 108.

what Lawrence Kramer aptly calls the "Yellowstone Park" of absolute music.[83] In all of the scenes of the opera so far, we have witnessed a continuum between what Kristeva would term the spheres of the symbolic and the semiotic. A scene that begins with a recited text in our native tongue might become a setting of an ancient Egyptian text with at least some specified dramatic content; eventually it might transform itself into a mass of sheer undifferentiated, nonscripted, nonspecific energy. Thus, the two interpenetrate: They bleed into one another, they infuse each other with life. But now we find ourselves deep in the innermost sanctum, the holy of holies of absolute music, and just as earlier in the opera when we found ourselves barricaded within the holy of holies of those who revere the Word—the stone-faced priests of Amon who are the reverse of Akhnaten's and his mother's wordless "cult of ecstasy"—there appears to be no exit, no escape. The voices of Akhnaten's daughters are thus transformed into the voice of his mother, reverberating through the walls of her womb. At first he is comfortable and satisfied—his every need is catered to: his hunger satisfied, his thirst quenched, his anxieties find no footing; he is completely autonomous, completely self-sufficient, completely at one; there is no other reality, there is no other; this is all. But this pre-Oedipal sense of all-encompassing perfection—of the absolute other that is beyond desire, beyond *jouissance*—gradually gives way to a growing sense of unease. Is he really experiencing the real? Is he really, as his own dictum puts it, "living in truth"? Is he really seeing things as they are, or merely as he wants?

It is in this state of delusion, of decadence, of suspended animation that we find Akhnaten and his family at the beginning of act 3.[84] In the Stuttgart production of the opera, the royal palace assumed the guise of a circle in which Akhnaten and his six daughters—each of whom wielded an angelic lyre—were enclosed. The obvious referent is the Aten: The family has become the archetypal family of the sun god. A slightly less obvious referent is a womb. The latter appears to be a most appropriate metaphor for Akhnaten's state of mind at this stage in the opera, as well as for the music we are hearing. Nefertiti, who always represented the "healthier," outward-oriented aspect of Akhnaten's desires, is located on the periphery; she is barely visible, and her feet straddle the circumference of the circle. Historically, this is probably an accurate representation: Toward the end of Akhnaten's reign, the royal couple drifted apart. The consensus of opinion seems to be that Nefertiti left her husband. According to Velikovsky, this was because of her rivalry with Tye.[85] Whatever the reasons, Nefertiti's departure signals a final stage in the isolation—both personal and political—pursued by the king since the founding of Akhetaten.

After six cycles of singing, there are two sudden interjections by the trumpets and horns (rehearsal mark 8): Paradoxically, the instruments that in earlier scenes represented Akhnaten's connection with the divine are now appropriated by those who wish him ill. The E-flat tonality announced by them was, as we have seen, associated with the old order in the first act, as was the interval of a tritone—the devil's interval—between this tonality and the home key of the opera. The ominous effect produced by the shift in key is underlined in the second horn attack by a low tuba playing a dissonant D-flat, dropping down to B_I before eventually resolving, via the leading note, E-flat, onto the root of the family's tonic, E. This passage stands in stark contrast to the family's monotonous monologue; the major triad built on the raised seventh degree (the leading note) of the scale is rarely used by Glass, and when it is, its purpose is invariably to undermine or threaten the tonic. The dramatic implications of this musical procedure require little explication.

We are returned to the palace music. There are two duet cycles between Akhnaten and Nefertiti (rehearsal marks 9 and 11), alternating with two cycles for the entire family ensemble (rehearsal marks 10 and 12). In the four remaining cycles of the section, the octet of singers remains, although the musical material they sing is now radically reduced in all of its parts. The gloomy oboe theme returns, only doubled now in both of its parts with horns. The relentless A-minor arpeggios heard at the beginning of the scene in the flutes return after two cycles in the clarinets (an octave lower), where they remain until the end of the section (rehearsal mark 14). Akhnaten and Nefertiti are evidently still playing the role of the divine couple, as revealed by the mirror-image ascending and descending scales that accompany their singing. This music is obviously intended to suggest a "divine balance" or connubial between the opposing masculine and feminine forces. It is evocative, of course, of the "mirrored" lines in the chaconne (act 1, scene 2, and act 2, scene 4), but the move from A minor to E minor, from the key that represents the self (and the real) to that which represents the imaginary other (perceived as the "extended" or transfigured self), does not appear to have been a wholly successful one. Thus, the descending scales of the first half of the pattern (perhaps associated either with Nefertiti or the feminine in Akhnaten) remain in perfect balance, as do the first two ascents (perhaps associated with Akhnaten as male or masculine principle), but after this the equilibrium begins to disintegrate, leaving the disembodied subject to meander aimlessly about in the stratosphere, apparently searching for a tonal footing but finding none (rehearsal marks 9 and 10). Even when the lines resort to contrary motion (rehearsal marks 12–16), as they did in the chaconne, the center cannot hold, and the disoriented subject wanders off once again at a tangent.

The family's self-indulgent reveries are interrupted by another somber E-flat major call to arms, this time played by the entire brass section. The first two attacks resolve to the family's key of E minor, but the third resounding chord finally succeeds in dislodging the tonic. There is a shift to F minor, exploiting the ambiguity of the seventh degree chord—E-flat major being both the raised seventh degree of E minor and the "lowered" seventh degree of F minor. Unlike the major chord built on the "raised" sixth degree, which was so important in the hymn, the lowered sixth-degree chord (in the home key of A minor) must resolve to the tonic. Convention tells us that Akhnaten's sublime beyond the sublime must now fall; and it is only a matter of time before this happens. The abrupt shift in key is accompanied by a marked acceleration in tempo (100 half notes per minute compared to the 132 quarter notes in the family music), over which the scribe reads extracts from the so-called Amarna letters—the diplomatic correspondence between Egypt and its colonies found toward the end of the last century, buried in the ruins at Akhetaten.

It is extremely significant, of course, that Akhnaten's and his family's ecstatic, wordless music is interrupted by the revered Word of the old order. It is not music that provides the ultimate contrast to Akhnaten's "more than *jouissance*" but language. And since it is the namesake of Amenhotep III, Amenhotep, son of Hapu, who speaks, the disruption is explicitly associated with the now resurrected Name-of-the-Father. This stark contrast reveals the breadth and depth of the chasm that has opened between the symbolic and the semiotic, between inbreeding and outbreeding, between the particular and the whole, and between the clearly defined and delimited and the infinitely ambiguous. And it appears to be as much Akhnaten's withdrawal into his private pre-Oedipal utopia as his adversaries' phallic aggression that is to blame.

The chameleonic figure of Amenhotep, son of Hapu, whose prophecy of the pharaoh's ultimate fall from grace has haunted Akhnaten throughout the opera, now addresses the crowd that has gathered outside the royal palace, his clear intent being to incite the people of Egypt to overthrow their king. This cannot have been a difficult task as the Egyptian empire's disintegration, which began during the reign of Amenhotep III and accelerated during the seventeen-year span of Akhnaten's reign due to his total neglect of foreign affairs, is now almost complete. Only Nubia in the south remains under Egyptian rule; all of the traditional strongholds in Asia Minor have fallen into the hands of rival powers.

The music of this part of the scene can be divided into three sections, the first and last of which are centered around the tonality of F minor (Akhnaten's utopia turned sour) and are characterized by a nervously oscillating line in the upper horn part and violas (c'–b–c'–b–c'–b–c'–b–a-flat), set off against a motifically related theme in the cellos and trombones (e-flat–d–e-flat–d–d–d-flat–B–C). The middle subsection alternates between the submediant of the new key, D-flat, and its tonic, F minor. When transferred to the new tonal environment, the motif of the previous subsection sets out from the root of the chord rather than from its dominant. Played now on the bassoon, it is also transformed melodically, rising above as well as moving below its initial note. In its newly acquired form, it can be recognized as the "catharsis" (or phallically marked *jouissance*) motif from the temple scene (act 2, scene 1). This motif is associated by Glass with violence and destruction but is actually more evocative of the excitement accompanying violent acts. The key of its early appearance was A-flat major; now, however, it is transposed up a perfect fourth to D-flat (d-flat–C–d-flat–C–d-flat–C–d-natural–d-flat). The tonic onto which this chord resolves, F minor, is the relative minor of A-flat major, a prominent tonality in the earlier violent scene. Thus, with respect to its tonality, its motific material, and its dramatic content, there are explicit links between the two scenes: Both are scenarios of decadent isolationism, of stagnant insularity, followed by the violent intrusion of excluded others. This music shows us just how easy it is to get drawn into the intoxicating aesthetic of violence: In both cases, we are given grounds to wish for the fulfillment of the violent act, and part of us, if the music works as it should, collaborates with Akhnaten's adversaries in toppling the king's phantasmagorical ivory tower.

Another unmistakable signal of Akhnaten's impending doom is the return of the transgression theme, which signifies not only the pharaoh's unusual sexuality as perceived by his adversaries but also his awaiting destiny. In its third iteration, the motif is transposed away the submediant, D-flat, to the tonic, F minor. Even though its exact intervallic structure is not preserved in this new tonal context, the meaning of the motif is quite apparent. Akhnaten's sexually marked transgression, his flaunting of the most pervasive (in psychological terms) divide known to humanity, is now seen through the censorious eyes of his opponents and becomes a symbol of everything else they despise. In linear terms, the move from euphorically marked major to dysphorically marked minor mirrors the text, which here concerns the former virility of the Egyptian pharaohs ("As long as ships were upon the sea the strong arm of the king . . ."), but then sinks into despair at the losses incurred as a result of Akhnaten's unwillingness to assert his ("masculine") military might ("For if no troops come in this year, the whole territory of my lord, the king, will perish"). After three cadences of Akhnaten's life-span motif, we are returned to the initial pattern of this section. The last of the Amarna letters finishes with a bitter complaint at the inability of its writer to muster a response from Akhnaten: "For twenty years we have been sending to our lord, the king of Egypt, but there has not come to us a word—no, not one."

There are three piercing clarion calls, and we are returned to the royal palace, where Akhnaten is seen alone with his two eldest daughters. If the casting list of the booklet accompanying the CD recording is to be believed, one of them is Bekhetaten and the other Meretaten—these are the first names on the list, and so one assumes that they are the soloists.[86] This conjecture is supported by the fact that in the first drafts of the opera, Bekhetaten had a speaking part.[87] If one of the two soloists *is* her, some interesting questions are raised. Meretaten's close relationship with the king has already been discussed; Bekhetaten, on the other hand, is not ordinarily

Akhnaten, accompanied by Nefertiti and two of his
daughters, making offerings to the sun god. Wallis
Budge, *Tutankhamen: Amenism, Atenism, and Egyptian
Monotheism* (New York: Dover, 1991 [1923]), p. 88.

regarded as Akhnaten's daughter at all. Akhnaten was without question on
intimate terms with both princesses (just how intimate is open to debate),
but as far as conventional accounts of the family are concerned, Bekhetaten
is Akhnaten's baby sister (or half sister), not his daughter. Velikovsky, however, believes she is both.[88]

The main problem archaeologists have faced in their discussions of
Bekhetaten comes from the assumption that she is Amenhotep III's daughter; this is chronologically impossible, however, since Akhnaten's father
died long before the birth of Bekhetaten. Yet the princess is still referred to
as the king's daughter. Archaeologists have attempted to solve this riddle in
numerous ways, the most ingenious but least credible of which is Budge's
claim that there were two Bekhetatens: one Akhnaten's and Nefertiti's
daughter and the other Tye's and Amenhotep III's.[89] As far as their representation in the opera is concerned, there is little doubt that Glass is following Velikovsky's formulation of the princess's bloodline. This section is

easily associated with the earlier trio of Akhnaten, Nefertiti, and Tye (act 2, scene 1), though the pharaoh is now accompanied by the daughters of those women. The very fact that Akhnaten is left alone with his two eldest daughters is, moreover, an overt allusion to the Oedipus myth, the protagonist of which sought solace in the company of his two eldest daughters, Ismene and Antigone. Thus, the reference is not just a historical one; Glass is once again following Velikovsky's theory.[90]

For the Egyptian people to witness this latest (un)holy trinity is the final straw; it is *this* scenario, not the reading of the Amarna letters, that immediately precedes Akhnaten's violent deposition. The implication seems to be that it is not so much the pharaoh's neglect of foreign affairs that inspires contempt as what we are witnessing in this section; or maybe they are to be viewed as symptoms of the same condition. Glass writes that the three "continue to sing, appearing more withdrawn and isolated from the events outside,"[91] but one senses that there is more to this scenario than we are being told. The deliberately insipid music I have described above appears to confirms this impression. Meretaten's presence here can be easily accounted for; hers is the second most commonly acknowledged case of incest in Akhnaten's family circle. Not so with Bekhetaten. Were Glass to have included Ankhesenpaaten in the final section of this scene, there would have been little doubt that he was referring solely to father-daughter incest. But instead the composer chooses Bekhetaten, with the apparent purpose of referring to the only "concrete evidence" of the pharaoh's union with his mother. Instances of incest between father and daughter and between brother and sister were commonplace in ancient Egyptian royal circles: examples of the former include the pharaohs Tao II, Ahmose I, Amenhotep I, Thutmose I, II, III, and IV, and Amenhotep II; and of the latter, Rameses II, and Akhnaten's father, Amenhotep III. Incest between mother and son, on the other hand, was totally alien to ancient Egyptian and virtually every other culture. Were such a relationship to be openly displayed to his people by an already unpopular pharaoh, the consequences would, in all probability, have been disastrous. Velikovsky describes his own version of the course of events as follows:

After his complete rupture with the priests of Amon, Akhnaton apparently did not wish to keep his relation to his mother a secret. He boasted of "living in truth," and this phrase is an appellation attached to his proper name. After a period of indecision and concealment he made up his mind to bring his relation into the open and to compel the Egyptians to regard this union as holy and admirable. Thus he openly led his mother-wife and their daughter to their shades in the temple of Akhet-Aton, had this procession cut in wall bas-reliefs, and had it written of Beketaten, their child, that she was "the king's daughter of his body." However, this innovation in religion and morals — incest between son and mother — was alien to the

Egyptians, whose gods, religious customs, and ethics even then went back to grey antiquity; and when under Akhnaton it came into the open, the eruption of discontent was not long in coming.[92]

In the final section of the scene, we have before us, on the one hand, a daughter of Akhnaten who is also his wife and, on the other hand, one who is also his sister; his mother-wife Tye is not physically present, nor is his sister-wife Nefertiti.[93] The real objection for the people of Egypt can, however, as Velikovsky's passage indicates, be located in the higher of the two voices, that of Bekhetaten, as it refers explicitly to the forbidden union of Akhnaten and Tye. With the exit of Nefertiti at this point, Akhnaten's only, albeit tenuous, link to the external—in both sexual and social terms (as she is the daughter of Aye, who now joins the ranks of Akhnaten's adversaries)—is irredeemably severed.

As regards the musical representation of all of this, the delicately balanced scalar lines of the chaconne, which were already losing their grip on reality in the previous section, are now totally out of control. The disoriented subject (cellos, bass clarinet, and synthesizer) jumps up an octave at the beginning of the pattern and then spirals out of control on an ever-widening gyre for its remainder. In the next, it falls, begins an ascent, and then falls again before meandering its way up to the dizzy heights of the ether. This reckless roller-coaster ride continues unabated as first the dysphoric oboe motif and then the thirdless arpeggios on E return.

In the first pattern of the section (rehearsal mark 29), Akhnaten enters alone in two ungainly jumps, from e' to c". This awkward opening demonstrates just how seriously delusional the title character really is. To move directly from the root of the other key of the opera to the "ecstatic" major third of the self key is just not on. Not surprisingly, he reaches only the minor third and thus does not achieve union with his god. In the remainder of the pattern, he appears to accept his ineffectualness in the home key and thus avoids its stronger tones. The now familiar minor-major shift takes place not in this key but over the pivotal chord G minor-major, from which it resolves onto the stronger sonority of the section, E (b-flat–b-natural, over the chord progression G minor–G major–E). Thus, Akhnaten's delusion causes him to seek union not with his god (or surrogate father) but with (the fantasy of) his mother, whom he also mistakes for his androgynous god—not for the first time in the opera. That she has the outer appearance of his two eldest daughters does not seem to matter; in the realm of the (imagined) absolute, everything is ultimately the same as everything else.

In regard to motif, one of the most noteworthy events occurs when the lower soprano, "daughter two" (possibly Meretaten), takes over Akhnaten's melodic line. More specifically, she takes over the part that refers explicitly to Akhnaten's sexuality, the minor-major shift (rehearsal mark 32.5). Could this be a tacit reference to sexual relations between the two? Daughter one's (Bekhetaten's?) melodic line explicitly avoids any such excursions, suggesting perhaps that there was no sexual basis to their relationship. This voice is instead characterized by its exceptionally high tessitura, which could easily be described as shrill; tellingly, the only other character who has reached such heights (g" and a") is Tye (in the temple scene, act 2, scene 1). If this is Bekhetaten, then she is linked explicitly to the voice range of her mother. Meretaten's lower soprano is, on the other hand, well within the range of Nefertiti's contralto. It is Bekhetaten's high soprano, however, that is the hardest voice to ignore and that points explicitly to the Oedipus complex in Akhnaten and that must, therefore, have been the most abrasive to the ears of his subjects.

At this point, Akhnaten's fate is sealed. The pharaoh even seems to recognize this himself, as in the final cycle of the scene (rehearsal mark 36) his melodic line recalls the prophecy of the scribe; this is the only occasion on which the protagonist himself sings the tragic transgression motif (e'–[g']–a'–c"–a'–e'). In this his final hour, we can surmise only that Akhnaten is fully aware of how his people perceive him and of the destiny that awaits. There are three final calls to arms in the brass, underpinned by a restless chromatic line in the cellos, and then there is a brief moment of silence—the pregnant calm that precedes a storm.

CHAPTER SEVEN

Repudiation and Resurrection
The Final Three Scenes

A Prophecy Fulfilled

With the Amon high priest, General Horemhab and his military forces, and Aye—the ecclesiastical, military, and administrative patriarchs—reunited, the stage is set for the scourging of the new order grown old. Akhnaten, in lieu of the two charismatic women we saw him with in the Window of Appearances scene (act 1, scene 2), has only the two daughters of these women and himself: a trinity that, far from commanding the respect of the Egyptian people, fills them with contempt. And it is one whose manifesto is clearly no match, in its popular appeal, to that of the three patriarchs.

With regard to its text and vocal arrangements the Attack and Fall scene can be divided into three sections. In the first of these, the three patriarchs continue where the scribe has left off, inciting the crowd to overthrow Akhnaten by singing extracts from the Amarna letters, telling of the loss of Egypt's colonies in Asia Minor. In the second section, the people of Thebes respond, acknowledging that there is a threat to Egyptian national security and at the same time explicitly calling Akhnaten's masculinity into question. The third section begins with an antiphonal subsection that consists of the three patriarchs' pleas for swift phallic retaliation ("The mighty arm of the king / Will seize Nahrima and Kapasi") alternating with the people of Thebes' assent to these pleas and ends with a homophonic subsection in which the patriarchs and the people are in complete agreement. During this final section, the crowd breaks into the palace and carries out the violent deposition of their monarch.

Musically, the scene is constructed from a quasi-strophic configuration of four sections, followed by an instrumental coda in which a fifth section is introduced. Its overall structure can be schematized as AB AB CD CD AB CD CD : coda DE.

An eight-bar introduction by the brass instruments introduces the chord movement of the opening section: F minor to D-flat major (i–VI). The A section proper lunges immediately into a ferocious assault that continues unabated until the end of the scene. In this scene, there is none of the gradual organic growth of Akhnaten's and his family's music. The closest comparison is with the funeral of Amenhotop III (act 1, scene 1). All instruments are marked forte from the initial bar, the only dynamic marking in the entire scene. The entire orchestra is present from the beginning of the scene to its end, with the single noteworthy exception of the percussion section, whose entry I will discuss below. Although the brisk tempo of 175 quarter notes per minute and, more important, the relentless torrent of eighth notes played by virtually all the instruments remain until the final coda, the music of the scene is characterized also by its sporadic changes in meter, many of which coincide with raucous scalar nosedives. These kamikaze descents (there are some ascents, but they are in the minority), many of which are chromatically constructed, are clearly transformations of the meandering scalar lines of the previous scene, which, in turn, are related to the "divine" balance of opposing forces in the chaconne. What we are now hearing, then, is libido out of control, out of balance, lashing out at its despised other.

The three patriarchs are a united force right from their violent entry in the very first bar. Their singing is, as before, made all the more oppressive by the predominantly fifth-oriented harmonies of their parts. It is syllabic throughout, usually keeping to quarter-notes, and is predominantly diatonic. This diatonicism is interrupted, however, by each of the scalar lines, the more chromatic of which are coordinated with the most emotionally loaded lines of the text: the line "nu-kur tu a-na ya-shi" (there is hostility to me), for example, coincides with the melodic line e–d-sharp–C-sharp–C natural–A-sharp–B sung by Aye (rehearsal mark 6; see example 36).

The A section comprises three iterations of the chord change F minor to D-flat major; a relatively static and "conventional" tonic to submediant formula. The tension of the music is tangibly heightened in section B (rehearsal mark 5), however, in which the submediant, D-flat major is replaced by the raised seventh-degree chord, E major. The presence of a major chord constructed on the leading note, which appears, moreover, in its root position, constitutes a significant threat to the integrity of the tonic, one that demands release. In terms of the longterm linear structure of the opera, this chord also pulls toward the home key, since, unlike the minor fifth-degree chord of previous scenes, this chord includes the leading

Example 36. Act 3, scene 2, Attack and Fall.

note of A minor, G-sharp. This harmonic procedure, therefore, both in terms of the surface and deep structure of the opera, underlines the urgency of the situation as presented by the three patriarchs: The king must be deposed.

The response to the invocations of the three men is not long in coming. As the full mixed chorus—SATB (the people of Thebes)—enter, they do so at first on A minor (rehearsal mark 11) but in the next pattern on F major, thus dislodging the earlier minor chord onto its major counterpart (rehearsal mark 12). This chord is heard in conjunction with its related minor, the home key of the opera, making section C a kind of retrograde of the A section of the prelude, which consisted also of A minor alternating with F major. This passage is, like so much of the opera, tonally ambiguous: One assumes at the beginning of the section that F major is the tonic, as the music we have heard so far in the scene has been in the key of its modal opposite, F minor. This assumption is undermined, however, in section D, when the F-major chord functions as a disguised (because of the intermediary A minor) secondary dominant to B-flat major/minor, which in turn yields to A minor.

The harmony of the D section (rehearsal mark 13) is, of course, easily identified as the same as that heard in the second section of the prelude that has resurfaced in various guises during the course of the opera; it includes Akhnaten's transgression motif, which could easily be regarded as the opera's motif, since it is a microcosm of the most significant events in the opera. Now it is sung by the entire chorus (male and female voices), backed up by the full power of the orchestra. The sudden appearance of the chorus combined with the abrupt shift from the minor to the major mode in the key of F is unquestionably one of the opera's most striking moments of "revelation" because the Akhnaten that the patriarchs have been describing is at this precise moment revealed to the people of Thebes. It is a moment of quasi-religious (and perhaps religious, from Atenism to Amenism) conversion. Now the people see their king in an altogether different light. Their new vision is contrasted, however, with the blindness they perceive in Akhnaten. The text of this section is as follows:

But to me there is hostility.	
Although a man sees the facts	Ip-sha-ti e-nu-ma a-mel a-mir-i
Yet the two eyes of the king, my	u-la-mar i-na sha-ri be-li-ya
lord, do not see	ki nu-kur-tu
For hostility is firm against me.	a-na mukh-khi-ya shak-na-ti

As with the solace sought by Akhnaten in the company of his two eldest daughters, the metaphorical blinding of Akhnaten finds a counterpart in the actual blinding of Oedipus. The luckless hero of the Greek myth blinded himself with a golden brooch taken from the garment of his mother, Jocasta, upon realizing that he had committed the double crime of parricide and incest. Velikovsky does not seek a metaphorical reading of the myth, as many others have done, but instead—calling attention to the above and other texts (one of which is the text read by the scribe prior to the next scene)—claims that Akhnaten became physically blind in the final years of his reign.[1] There is good reason to believe, however, that Glass pursues a somewhat different interpretation. The text selected by the composer and his collaborators explicitly links the king's two eyes, which "do not see," and the assertion that "a man sees the facts." Thus, Akhnaten's ineffectual organs of vision are implicitly associated by the people of Thebes with his testicles. A similar interpretation of the Oedipus myth (blinding equals castration or emasculation) is so ubiquitous as not to warrant further comment:[2] What is truly fascinating is the possibility suggested here that such an association might have been made by contemporaries of Akhnaten while the king was still alive. What is *most* interesting about this whole issue, however, is Glass's musicodramatic treatment of it. This text coincides exactly with Akhnaten's gender marked transgression motif, which strays into the "feminized" minor mode (D-flat, the minor third of B-flat major), despite its "masculine" (major) accompaniment, and comes to grief (drops to a low E) precisely because of this insurrection. This motif, according to Glass, "is easy to see . . . as a metaphor for that part of Akhnaten's character that was so unusual and unsettling to the people of his time" and is also "synonymous with the downfall of Akhnaten."[3] With this realization, then, the fate of the pharaoh is sealed. As if to underline the condemnation of the Theban people, the entire sequence (both C and D sections) is repeated; thus the thrice-repeated motif is repeated twice.

The final two occurrences of the triadic transgression theme coincided with significant dramatic events in both major productions of the opera. In the Stuttgart premiere, the first appearance of the mixed choir during this section was at the point at which the sun, which lit the stage in the early part of the scene, set, leaving it in semidarkness. The Anglo-American productions, on the other hand, perceptively chose the three-times-three manifestation of the life-span motif that occurs at the very end of the scene to dispose of Akhnaten. His fate is that of Oedipus: He was surrounded by the circle of wrestlers that had been circumambulating the stage during the entire opera, whereupon he was coerced into committing the act of self-mutilation that is an allegory for his castration. He can be seen in this attitude—with fingers delving into his eye sockets—on the cover of the British edition of *MPG*.[4]

The scene culminates in the defilement of the temple of the Aten, the ransacking of the royal palace, and the bringing to justice of the heretic who lives there. Immediately after the resolution of the first series of transgression themes—concomitant with the same "transcendental" F-major chord on which the chorus entered—the only section of the orchestra not heard so far in the scene finds a voice (rehearsal mark 15). When the bass drum and cymbal enter (and, later, a snare drum), they do so in an uncompromising fashion. Their syncopations are so pronounced that not once does a rhythmic accent chance onto one of the "strong" beats of the bar: During both the 12/8 meter of the initial bar of each chord and the turbulent bar of 6/4 time that follows (usually accompanied by the scalar descent), the rhythmic emphasis remains resolutely first on the backbeat and then on the offbeat.

As we return to the key of F minor, the people of Thebes and their new leaders engage in a series of two-bar responsorial exchanges, the first bar consisting in the extended and predominantly diatonic calls of the people of Thebes and the second in the chromatically venomous and rhythmically charged (mostly eighth notes) responses of the Amon high priest, Horemhab, and Aye. One can feel the patriarchs of the rejuvenated old order propelling the people of Thebes to carry the violent deeds through to their ultimate conclusion. As we return to the music of the prelude and its transgression motif, the people of Thebes are in complete accord with the patriarchs. When they join forces to sing the motif that marks the end of Akhnaten's reign, they do so in complete homophonic assent—altos, basses, Aye, and Horemhab all sing the motif in its uncorrupted form, while the sopranos, tenors, and the Amon high priest (i.e., the higher voices of each choral section) resonate on the fifth of the B-flat major/minor chord, F (rehearsal marks 26–27 and 30–31).

When the third, now instrumental, series of transgression motifs is heard at the beginning of the coda (rehearsal mark 32), it is a celebration of victory. Water, the dominant element of the prelude, has succeeded in extinguishing the fire of the sun god and the fire of the son of the sun god.

For the third iteration of the thrice-repeated life-span motif, the orchestral arrangement is almost identical to third cycle of the prelude. The meter has changed to 4/4 time, and undulating aquatic arpeggios are heard in contrary motion in the winds, synthesizer, and strings. Insistent syncopated brass attacks herald the victory of the righteous assailants over the heretics.

As if stamping out the last smoldering embers of a fire, three final alternations of the raised seventh-degree major chord and the tonic are heard, only now transposed to the opera's home key (A-flat major to A minor/major). The second of these attempts to modulate to the opera's other or (imaginary) "feminine" key, E minor, but in vain (rehearsal mark 34). The minor fifth-degree chord (to call this chord the dominant would be misleading in both dramatic and musical senses) is quickly displaced by the tonic. The debunked, disenfranchised and disembodied other is seen no more in the opera proper—in the ancient time frame, that is. The third and final raised seventh-degree cadence resolves to A minor, and things are as they were before the religious revolution. In this section, the catharsis or *jouissance* motif is heard in three octaves in the bass, trombones, and tuba (A-flat–G–A-flat–B-flat–A-flat–G–F–E) but with little of the luster of its earlier manifestations. There are three emphatic chord attacks, accompanied by the same persistently rising arpeggios as were heard at the beginning of the opera, set against a low drone on the tonic. There are two low attacks stated in the trombones, tuba, and percussion: "the double doors of the horizon" slam fast once again, and so ends Akhnaten's life. The arpeggios continue their ascent undeterred.

Aquatic Transformations

The scribe appears, as the composer puts it, "out of the chaos to announce the end of Akhnaten's reign."[5] The text he reads, which was found in the tomb of Tutankhamen, has been aptly described by Savitri Devi as a "prayer of hate"[6] and by Reverend Baikie as "little more than a savage howl of joy at the downfall of Akhenaten and all his works."[7]

> The sun of him who knew thee not
> Has set, O Amon.
> But, as for him who knows thee,
> He shines.
> The temple of him who assailed
> Thee is in darkness,
> While the whole earth is in
> Sunlight.
> Who so puts thee in his heart,
> O Amon,
> Lo, his sun hath risen.

The new pharaoh is whisked away from the former City of the Horizon and back to the traditional seat of pharaonic power in Thebes, where he can be kept under the watchful eye of both the military and ecclesiastical authorities. A suitably macho image is constructed for the adolescent Tutankhamen by his aides in order to distinguish him as sharply as possible from his predecessor. Military campaigns are mounted that attempt to win back the territories in Asia Minor that were lost as a result of Amenhotep III's self-absorption and his son's pacifistically tinged foreign policy. Akhnaten's name is deemed unutterable by the new ruler and is replaced by the title "the criminal of Akhetaten." As was the case with Akhnaten's defilement of his own father's name earlier in the opera, this is more than just a change of name, as to defile a pharaoh's name was, to the ancient Egyptians, tantamount to destroying his soul.

The new pharaoh, Tutankhamen, dies young, however, presumably in battle, and is replaced by Aye, who wheedles his way to the throne by marrying his own granddaughter and the wife of his immediate predecessor, Ankhesenamen (formerly Ankhesenpaaten), but lives to enjoy his coveted position for only a few short years.[8] Upon the death of her first husband, Akhnaten's daughter, the only legitimate successor to the throne, writes a touching letter to the king of the Hittites asking for a prince to be sent in haste for her to marry so that she might continue the royal lineage and at the same time prevent her adversaries, those responsible for disposing of her father, from seizing power: A prince is finally sent but is murdered en route to Egypt.[9] Upon the death of her husband-grandfather, Ankhesenamen mysteriously disappears, allowing "smiter of the Asiatics" Horemhab to usurp the throne with no monarchical obstruction. Horemhab reigns for a quarter of a century and during this time sees to it that all traces of the Atenist heresy are erased from his kingdom. The vehemence of Horemhab's actions surpasses Akhnaten's acts of iconoclasm by a considerable margin: He demolishes or defiles not only all edifices and ideas connected in any way with Akhnaten but also many of those of Tutankhamen and Aye.[10]

Two new texts, presumably taken from the tombs of Tutankhamen and Aye, accompany the first cycle of the prelude reprise—a low-key arrangement for strings and synthesizer. They describe the rebuilding and refurbishing of the Amon temples following the downfall of Akhnaten, and allude to a ceremony on the River Nile to celebrate the victory of the Amonists: ("His majesty [Life! Prosperity! Health!] has built their barques upon the river of new cedar from the terraces. They make the river shine").

Immediately after this text, we are thrown into the powerful and pulsating third cycle of the prelude; this is a musical representation of the zeal with which the restorers of the old order set about their reconstructive task. That water is the element employed by them in their battle against Atenism should come as no surprise. Akhnaten explicitly rejected the "god of the overflowing Nile," Osiris, and all of his underworld companions in favor of the abstract power of the sun disk. This weakness in the Atenist philosophy—its solar bias compounded with its apparent rejection of the other central element of Egyptian life, water—was exploited ruthlessly by its adversaries and must have been instrumental in quenching the fire of the sun god.

Thus, we are transported upon the sparkling waves of the Nile into the underworld and across the bounds of mortality and time. At the beginning of the opera (in the prelude), we were transported back 3,500 years in time to the pharaonic world immediately prior to Akhnaten's accession; during the second act (City/Dance) the same music served as the medium in which Akhnaten was cleansed and reborn (i.e., baptized) prior to his spiritual apogee, the hymn to the sun. Now we are transported to, or reborn in, contemporary Egypt. When we emerge from the depths of the river, we do so in a now-familiar fashion: There are two emphatic chord attacks followed by a third double attack. The double doors of the horizon swing open, and we are standing in the midst of the ruined city of Akhetaten (known today as Tell el Amarna). Tourists are seen perusing the recently excavated buildings.

Amenhotep, the transpersonal, transsexual, multivalent, time traveler, shaman, prophet, translator, scribe, observer/actor who has been our faithful guide to the action of the opera so far, now appears as a twentieth-century tour guide for the tourists visiting the ruined city. The texts read by him are from *Frommer's Guide to Egypt* and *Fodor's Egypt*. The accompanying music, a somber string arrangement, corresponds to the fifth cycle of the prelude. Ostensibly a Brechtian strategy, the return to the present day at the end of the opera in fact adds a second diegetic stratum to its "rock formation": that of the "mythologized" contemporary. The text read by the scribe may be archaeological in the Foucauldian sense, but the tourists must be re-presented; real tourists cannot magically materialize on the stage for each performance of the opera—unless of course a video installment or some similar means of presentation is utilized. In order to fully realize the post-Brechtian potential of this moment, then—to properly ground the opera in the nondiegetic present—a strategy such as this might be called for. At the end of the scene, a triple chord attack on A minor once again fails to bring complete closure to the music. Once again, the arpeggios keep on rising even after the last attack. Akhnaten obstinately refuses to lie down and play dead!

If the opera ended at this point, the requirements of large-scale narrative structure as it has come to be defined from the seventeenth to the beginning of the twentieth century would otherwise be adequately fulfilled. Of course, the history of twentieth-century "art music" is also the history of challenging or repudiating that kind of narrative structure or of constructing alternative forms of narrative that work according to different principles. What is new about *Akhnaten* and characteristic of postmodernism more generally in the 1980s and to a lesser extent the 1990s is the way that it engages with and problematizes both the narrative *and* the non- or antinarrative. This makes *Akhnaten* a contemporary and an extremely relevant piece: its use of narrative as a means of getting its message across, and its distrust of the strategies, common in narrative forms, that make events seem as if they are bound by some unconscious but nonetheless widely recognized law to happen. Glass uses post-Brechtian strategies of alienation and Foucauldian archaeological strategies as ways of introducing a musical equivalent to point of view into his musical language. The imagined "I" that has traditionally been associated so closely with the voice of the composer in narrative music (we talk about listening to Beethoven or Mozart, not to their music) is by means of these distancing strategies dislodged from its former exalted position.[11] But does Glass succeed in killing off the metaphysical Romantic author or composer altogether? Does he even want to? I believe that he does not, that some vestigial authorial presence is nonetheless perceived by most listeners in Glass's meticulously constructed subjective scenarios. And it sounds, moreover, as though this trace was left there on purpose. But does this matter, when the opera we are discussing otherwise addresses important issues? As listening subjects, we are free to listen to *Akhnaten* with the same skeptical credulity the composer articulates in his relation to his musical antecedents (and also, as I have shown, to his own musical past); that is, we can keep our distance from the composer and his view of who Akhnaten is, what postmodernism is, and whatever else he is trying to tell us in the opera. The question becomes—in pretending that there is no subject there, in making out that we have broken free from what Barthes calls the (narrative) Oedipus, by couching what we do in terms of "the real"—are we being entirely honest with ourselves? In liberally furnishing his opera with rhetorical disclaimers stating that "this is a narrative" (a musical equivalent of René Magritte's "This is not a pipe," meaning "this is not authentic or real"), is the composer not, on some level and by the very act of negation, reverting to the language of the Lacanian real and in so doing positing a sublime beyond the sublime beyond the sublime? On the other hand, it is hard to think of an alternative—accept a kind of unselfconscious naïveté or populism that remains somehow aloof from or oblivious to this whole dialectic (which does not trouble any but a small number of people anyway)? These are slippery and circular arguments, and any discussion of subjectivity is almost predestined to self-destruct in this way, given that it is about what individual people experience and feel. These are, however, some of the fundamental issues the opera raises.

Oedipus Cured or Gone Underground?

Despite the emphatic closure of the final scene, the opera has yet to finish. Having returned to the home key with crushing brutality and thus fulfilled the chiseled-in-stone obligations of narrative structure, the (triple-) subject does not drop down and die, nor does it simply acquiesce and disappear but, in a sense, ends up having the last word, or, at the very least, the last sound. The "puppet pharaoh" Tutankhamen and his masters, Aye, Horemhab, and the Amon High Priest, go out with a bang in the bombastic recapitulation of the prelude, but they do go out. The epilogue is intended to break the intimidating symmetry we are left with at the end of the third scene by reminding us of earlier events. The patriarchs of the old order have not succeeded in erasing the memories of Akhnaten, Tye, and Nefertiti and thus destroying their spirits—on the contrary, it is them who we are most likely to remember. This was the message at the end of the hymn: The ideas of Akhnaten and his cohorts live on in the impact they had on subsequent ideas. The purpose of the epilogue is to make sure that this message is not forgotten.

The final scene of the opera is a synthesis of earlier musical material, so much so that the composer's discussion of this music in his book suffices to a large extent as an introduction to the thematic material of the entire work.[12] The music of the epilogue comprises four cycles, each of which is made up of three sections, which are further divided into three near-identical subsections. In addition, there is a short introduction and what the composer terms a "final resolution" at the end.[13] The overall form of the epilogue, which could be described as a three-section variation, can be schematized as ABC A'B'C' A"B"C" A'''B'''C'''.

Section A is related closely to the trilogy theme as it was heard in the chaconne ritornellos (act 1, scene 2, and act 2, scene 4) and, in slightly different form, in the Window of Appearances (act 1, scene 3). Section B is the much-repeated transgression progression, initially stated in the prelude and thus present in both of its reprises, as well as in the penultimate scene of the opera (act 3, scene 2). The third section is centered around the catharsis or phallic *jouissance* motif (from the temple, act 2, scene 1, and the

Attack and Fall, act 3, scene 2). Regarding its appearance in the epilogue, Glass notes that it has "taken on a lyrical, almost distant, quality, as if death and the passage of centuries . . . have softened the violence of those moments, making them almost beautiful."[14] Harmonically, the music of this section gravitates toward the most precarious (in relation the home key) sonorities in the opera, A-flat and E-flat.

During the course of the initial cycle, the ghosts of the Atenist trinity—Akhnaten, Tye, and Nefertiti—appear on the now empty stage. They wander about the ruins and "seem," at first, "not to know that they and their city all are dead and now a part of the past."[15] At the beginning of the second cycle, they begin to sing, significantly, in vocalese—this was always their domain and one to which the adversarial masculine trinity could never rise. Those who have suggested that the problematic story lines of the operatic repertoire are undermined by the predominantly feminine pleasures of the higher register would be absolutely correct in this particular case: Women are seldom allowed to win the symbolic war of words, but they do have almost exclusive access to a greater power, employed in this, the final vocal statement of this opera. Unfortunately, though, these vocal passages are not written with the deftness and sparkle of Glass's earlier writing for these characters. The scintillatingly sexy counterpoint of the trio (act 1, scene 3) and the duet (act 2, scene 2) has given way to a prosaic kind of homophony, which is more reminiscent of the dysphorically marked family scene (act 3, scene 1) than of these characters' finest moments. Let us assume, however, that, despite this shortcoming, the final scene is an unspoken (if not unsung) victory for the three Atenists.

As if to confirm the victory, a duet of horn and trombone states the three central motifs of the opera, beginning with the rising chaconne motif (a–b–c'–e') in counterpoint with the trilogy motif $(A–G–C_I)$—the music that is "strongly associated with Akhnaten himself"[16] but that is also strongly associated with Einstein and Gandhi in the two earlier trilogy operas. It is thus a symbol of the nonpersonal. As the instrumental cycle comes to its conclusion, there are four double attacks on the dominant chord (three on E minor and one on E major) by the entire orchestra (rehearsal mark 59.5), thus locating this final victory or resolution in the discourse of the reformers. This is followed by a marked deceleration of tempo during which the plodding "finality" motif is heard, accompanied by three emphatic chord attacks. A final statement of the trilogy motif becomes, according to Glass, "the key that turns the lock, setting the ending firmly in A minor, the 'relative minor' of C major, the key in which *Einstein* began."[17] The lock in question is, in tonal terms, the second inversion voicing of the finality motif, now heard in root position, and, as a result, it is considerably more final than in its earlier appearances. With the lock successfully picked, "the double doors of the horizon" swing open to the accompaniment of a double chord attack. This is followed by a much-elaborated flourish of the flute line from the chaconne sections of the hymn, reinforced now by the entire wind section, which in turn yields to three final resolute chords, the last of which consists solely of the note A—significantly, it is articulated in three separate octaves (A, a, a').

The final image of the opera is of the funeral cortege of Akhnaten's father, Amenhotep III, ascending to the heavenly land of Ra. The three protagonists are now fully aware that they are no longer alive, and thus are ready to follow in the wake of the procession. The vehicle for this final act of reconciliation is the Heliopolitan sun god, Ra, on whom the Atenist doctrine was based and who was appropriated by the Amenists as an aspect of their own deity in order to elevate the local Theban god to the status of supreme God above all others—thus, Amen became Amen-Ra. In the early days of the sun cult, the appellation Ra was a synonym for the Aten, but later, when Akhnaten wished to differentiate his own faith as sharply as possible from tradition (i.e., when he was in the full throes of his Oedipal affliction), it was explicitly rejected. Toward the end of his reign, however, it appears that Akhnaten grew more tolerant of traditional religious practices and allowed the appellation Ra to be used once again. Evidence of this is the name of his youngest daughter, Sotopen-re, in contrast to the Aten-derived names of the elder daughters. Thus, in the final moments of the opera, the name of the Aten is no more, but Ra, the unifying principle common to both his "mother" and "father" religions, is the catalyst that finally allows Akhnaten to overcome his Oedipus complex.

This can be seen as a metaphor for the juncture in Glass's career when *Akhnaten* was written. The third installment of the trilogy can be understood on one interpretive level as an announcement of the composer's retirement from the (Oedipal) avant-garde and the beginning of a reconciliation of sorts with musical tradition. (Whether this reconciliation itself has Oedipal overtones is another matter.) No longer languishing in the comforting and compelling interiority of minimalism, future works saw a more direct engagement with the music he was trained to write. Occupying an uncomfortable middle ground between his experimental background and his more populist inclinations, however, Glass seemed to flounder for a while in the late 1980s (with a few noteworthy exceptions, such as the beautifully meditative and soulful solo-piano collection). In the face of what others might have considered a creative block, however, he continued to write, as always, as if there was no tomorrow, attracting a good deal of criticism in the process. But the process was always Glass's strong point.

Perhaps this relentlessness in the face of adversity, this compulsion to re-
peat oneself (in the "positive" Kristevan or Kierkegaardian sense of the
word) and to take pleasure in doing so, was the driving force that kept him
going until something better came along. In his recent compositions, Glass
is sounding once again like an important figure in the contemporary music
scene; no longer at the vanguard of musical innovation but someone who
almost invariably has something relevant and engaging to say in his music.

CHAPTER EIGHT

Some Thoughts on
the Reception of Akhnaten

I look for those things that unconsciously we aren't allowed to do, and it's very, very difficult to do that because it's like trying to catch yourself thinking. Our normal way of thinking is the hardest thing to see. If we can only discover our own patterns of thinking, then we can maybe think in a new way. So a lot of my musical thinking has to do with this way of think-ing.[1] (Philip Glass)

It would be negligent of me to conclude my discussion of *Akhnaten* with-out paying more specific attention to the very important question of re-ception, particularly since it is, in a variety of ways, something of a phe-nomenon in this regard. *Akhnaten* is a contemporary-music phenomenon first and foremost because it drew audiences in droves to opera houses around the world at a time when very few composers were writing operas at all and when the operatic repertory was not exactly capturing the pub-lic's imagination—except, of course, in certain musical, social (predomi-nantly upper and upper-middle-class socialites), and sociosexual groups (gay men, for example). In the wake of the success of the Three Tenors, the rise to superstar status of opera divas such as Cecilia Bartoli, and the wide-spread televising and videotaping of opera productions since the mid-1980s, it is easy to be blasé about Glass's achievements. Rumors of opera's death, which circulated for the greater part of this century, seem now to have been greatly exaggerated, which makes it hard to see Glass's operatic trilogy in the perspective that it was seen from the mid-1970s to the mid-1980s. But his greatest achievement is not a small one: He brought young people back to opera houses, places they were brought up either to be scared of or angered by.[2] More than this, he told them they belonged there. Now you might denigrate these people all you like; call them yuppies, up-wardly mobile punks from the suburbs, or whatever, but these were people who had an intellectually and emotionally driven thirst for music theater that could be quenched neither by opera as it was then defined nor by more overtly commercial endeavors such as the genre of the Broadway/West End musical.

Many young people in the United Kingdom, and I can talk about only this region with any depth of knowledge since it is where I grew up, felt and to a certain extent still feel a deeply ingrained distrust of opera.[3] The reasons for this distrust are closely bound up with questions of class (probably the most significant of these categories), age, gender, and locality. In Britain, unlike North America, we had no Gershwins or Bernsteins to blur the boundary lines between popular and high art. Andrew Lloyd Webber, like Glass, became massively popular in the 1970s but did little actively to challenge anything. The one "great" British opera composer of the twentieth century, Benjamin Britten, wrote accessible and imaginative music, and was an important icon to the gay community and others, but for many socially committed young people growing up in the 1960s and 1970s in the United Kingdom, his credibility was undermined by his close associations with the monarchy and the upper classes.

All of this might, in part, explain the massive popularity of Philip Glass in the United Kingdom in the 1980s to the present day, as well as that of his "protégé" Michael Nyman, who is unquestionably the most popular English composer of classical music in living memory and arguably longer. Both Glass and Nyman greatly admired the ideological and philosophical precepts of 1960s experimentalism, both were strongly influenced by Cage, and both grappled with the problem of how to take the "message" of avant-garde experimentalism to a larger audience. As they grow older, however, both of these men have to some extent been tormented by the paradox of the category "angry young man": On some level, both of these men still yearn to be accepted by the tradition from which they struggled so hard to break free in their youths. While I remain convinced that engagement is a better alternative than repudiation—and this is one of the reasons that I like *Akhnaten* so much—it seems at times that both of these men are a little *too* keen to be accepted by their peers. Breaking free from the influence of one's ancestors is, on some level at least, an Oedipal maneuver, however justified, but reconciliation can be so too. (Let us not forget that there are two axes to the Oedipus complex as formulated by Freud: the negative and the positive.) Glass maintains a post-Brechtian distance from the music of his ancestors in much of his music—most effectively in *Akhnaten*—but is that distance always enough? Might it not be better, as Glass himself put it in *MPG*, to do as he did in *Einstein* and simply start somewhere else?[4] *Akhnaten* walks a very thin line between ancestor worship and iconoclasm, and precisely because of its self-reflexive ambiguity largely manages to avoid many of the pitfalls of such material. It is both a powerful critique of earlier practices and a testimony to the nurturing and replenishing qualities (which conventionally carry feminine connotations) of a healthy rapport with the past. But it could not be any of this effectively if it was not also a complex and compelling work of art.

Glass's relationship to his operatic precursors invariably comes up in discussions of this opera. For John Rockwell, Glass's trilogy is a modern-day Ring cycle. *Akhnaten* is the final installment of this cycle and a testimony to how far the composer has come in terms of compositional technique since writing *Einstein*. While at other times extremely perceptive, Rockwell fails to pay adequate attention to the critical implications of equating Glass's trilogy with the operas of Wagner. Rockwell was, on the whole, extremely impressed by the Stuttgart premiere of *Akhnaten*: "Most of this score," he wrote, "is simply wondrous in its refinement and imagination. The arpeggios are not simple triads, but strange, spikey chords that sound extremely difficult to play in the rapid, purling patterns Mr. Glass demands."[5] The composer did, according to Rockwell, "run out of ideas toward the end," where the music sounded "a little more ordinary" than in the rest of the opera.[6] But otherwise he finds little to fault in the opera or in Achim Freyer's staging, whose "painterly" approach Rockwell characterizes as that of a "theatre of genius."[7]

Rockwell is not alone in his criticism of the final act of *Akhnaten*. "In both *Akhnaten* and *Satyagraha*," writes Patrick J. Smith,

Glass has shown, like Puccini before him, a third-act weakness. His decision to recapitulate the opening music in shortened form at the end of the opera is understandable in schematic terms (the wheel of life coming full circle). But the music has little sense of completion or fulfillment; rather, it is only an overlong deliquescence and petering-out. At this moment the confinement inherent in the repetitive form becomes claustrophobic.[8]

While I to some extent agree with Smith's comments regarding *Akhnaten*, I feel compelled to take issue with his comments on the final act of *Satyagraha*, which I find to be one of the most mesmerizing in twentieth-century opera. Gandhi's soliloquy at the end of that opera encapsulates much of what is remarkable about Glass's style: the soaring high tenor of the protagonist, the gently shifting textures, and very fact that the music eschews closure (the aria in question is, after all, about reincarnation), which is its own kind of pleasure and one that deliberately and pointedly questions many Western assumptions about temporality.[9]

I agree with both Rockwell and Smith, however, that the final act of *Akhnaten* lacks the sparkle of the first two. Perhaps this has something to do with the nature of the subject matter as well as with the way the opera is put together dramatically. The family scene (act 3, scene 1) is intended to suggest the confinement of minimalism taken to its furthest extremes. In this it succeeds, although critics have failed to perceive that the composer might well be parodying himself in this music. The Attack and Fall scene (act 3, scene 2) goes on longer than it probably should; the recapitulation of the prelude (the ruins: act 3, scene 3) makes an important dramatic point, as does the epilogue (act 3, scene 4), although the musical treatment of the latter is a little prosaic, which is a shame, because the opera really needs something to pick itself up after the long downhill run after the hymn to the sun. There is, on the other hand, plenty of powerful writing in the early parts of *Akhnaten* to compensate for this deficiency, as Smith himself acknowledges when he describes the Stuttgart premiere of the opera as "an absorbing dramatic entity of beauty and power"[10] and "a work of operatic maturity" that holds "the promise of a distinguished operatic future."[11] With *Akhnaten*, writes Smith, "Glass emerges as the most significant American composer since Virgil Thomson."[12] He writes in another review, this time of the New York City Opera production, "Glass's score continues to impress one with his mastery of the repetitive style," manifested in the composer's "growing mastery of instrumental and coloristic handling of instruments and [his] control of the ethos of the piece."[13] Affectively, the music is characterized for Smith by its "sadness and a sort of elegiac plaintiveness, . . . at its most yearning in the love duet, at its most rapt in the Hymn to the Sun."[14] Like Rockwell, Smith acknowledges the increasingly close relationship between Glass and his operatic antecedents: "It is this plethora of reference," he writes astutely "that gives Glass's music such resonance."[15]

Daniel Warburton makes much the same point when he notes that "Glass seems now to be using his material in a narrative, even leitmotivic sense."[16] Although Warburton is critical of Glass's use of percussion in *Akhnaten*, which sounded at times "alarmingly like a circus-band" and brought to mind the "stock-signifiers of film music," he pays more attention in his review to what makes this opera "an accomplished and thought-provoking work."[17] For Warburton, it is the "simply beautiful writing" of scenes like the hymn to the sun, which is "probably the most expressive music Glass has written to date," that stands out.[18] The word setting in the hymn is described by Warburton as "musically as alive and natural as Debussy's in *Pelléas*."[19] Tim Page pays probably more attention to the harmonic rather than the melodic genealogy of the hymn when he writes: "Akhnaten's 13 minute 'Hymn' in the second act is probably the most chromatic music Glass has written since his student days and has something of the spirit of the spare, chant-like late compositions of Stravinsky."[20]

The German critics Horst Koegler and Kurt Honalka both come close to making some profound observations concerning the relationship of *Akhnaten* to its operatic antecedents in their reviews of the Stuttgart premiere. "Time and again," writes Koegler, "one is struck by the similarities of his melodic structures with Monteverdi, Gabrieli and Bach, with Berlioz and Wagner, even Orff. But taken out of their developing continuity, they sound like shadows of the shadows of the original models."[21] In other words, Koegler finds the opera a kind of "Window of Appearances," where nothing is really real—a Plato's cave in which the only reality is the shadows on the wall. "There exists an acute danger," he surmises, that Glass himself, in distancing himself from musical tradition in this way, assumes a sort of Akhnaton role among contemporary composers."[22] Koegler seems to have put his finger on what *Akhnaten* is all about, but far from appreciating the sentiments behind Glass's distancing strategies, he is baffled by them. Thus, at the same time as he recognizes that "the critical message of the work" is "a warning against the self-destructive power of progressive ideas if they are perverted to serve the cult of a self-instituted godlike figure," he does not hold "hieratic stiffness and distance" to be the best means of getting this message across.[23] It seems that Glass has gone too far in problematizing not only the content of his protagonist's Enlightenment agenda but also the musical rhetoric in which "progressive ideas" are conventionally couched. Koegler's criticism represents, therefore, an Adornian rather than a Brechtian or Benjaminian position; he remains oblivious to the subversive and emancipatory powers of any but the most palpably denotative of discursive means. In order to be subversive, the music and the drama must tell us in clear denotative terms, "I am being subversive."

The same tendency characterizes Honalka's writing. He identifies *Akhnaten* as a "postmoderne Anti-Oper" but having identified this potent ideologically tinged subtext fails to follow through and identify just what makes this opera an "antiopera."[24] Thus, at the same time as these critics argue that *Akhnaten* means nothing, that it is just a bunch of disembodied signifiers thrown together in an arbitrary mishmash, they deconstruct their own arguments by pointing to the very thing that makes the opera so meaningful. Patrick J. Smith has made an important observation in this regard: "The contemptuously dismissive attitude of certain critics to the work only accentuates its novelty and its innate quality."[25] It is very hard to get upset about something that means nothing; usually that "nothing" is something deeply disturbing that one does not want to confront or have to defend in public. On the other hand, it could be that these critics have a point, albeit in a more limited sense than they intended: namely, that *Akhnaten* and works of art like it are on some interpretive level not articulate enough; that in order to really get their messages across, postmodern artists such as Glass will have to revert with greater frequency to what Kristeva calls the symbolic. Glass seems to acknowledge and actually address this problem in *Akhnaten*—more so than in his earlier works at least.

One can, however, remain skeptical as to whether such criticism is motivated by a genuine desire to problematize past practices or by the more conservative impulse to preserve intact the monuments of a past that is seen as somehow more glorious and authentic than the present. Underlying these assertions seems also to be the naive assumption that *Kultur* is solely a civilizing force, an idealistic retreat that cannot be turned to unwholesome ends. In this case, it is not Glass or his opera that "assumes a sort of Akhnaton role" but musical tradition; we are, after all, told in no uncertain terms in the family scene of the opera that the refuge of absolute music and of Culture detached from culture, is an illusory one. Only in Walt Disney films can Pinocchio (that is, autonomous art) become a real boy once his strings have been severed. In the real world, he's just firewood—unless, of course, we invent a fairy godmother (a surrogate puppeteer) who remains perched out of sight above the wooden boy, deftly orchestrating his every move so as to make him appear as real as is possible.

Village Voice critic Gregory Sandow states most emphatically that *Akhnaten* is a work that engages with the musical past; at the same time, he recognizes the blinkeredness of fellow critics in not addressing this engagement. "How could Glass critics," Sandow writes, "miss the growing dissonance of his music, or the juxtaposed major and minor thirds, sometimes alternating, sometimes superimposed, that functioned both as a recurrent motif knitting separate parts of the piece together and as a melodic and harmonic metaphor for the large-scale structural alternation of A minor and A major?"[26]

Who could, indeed, miss such things? The answer, as Sandow's exasperation is no doubt intended to convey, is nearly every hostile critic who reviewed the opera. Not only did they miss the things Sandow mentions, they missed a lot else or deliberately oversimplified what they did not miss. Not willing to acknowledge that *Akhnaten* is a thoughtful critique of a musical tradition that for them transcends *true* criticism, and therefore (intentionally, one must presume) missing what are obvious points of musical reference in the opera, most hostile critics categorize it as a blind and philistine negation of all past practices.

So while for "friendly" critics like Robert T. Jones, *Akhnaten* "invokes a mystic, meditative, dreamlike atmosphere shaken by storms of extreme and sustained musical violence"[27]—an extremely apt description of this opera—for others, like Winton Dean, "the most impressive aspect of Glass's opera . . . is its resounding success with the public."[28] Loathe to give the composer credit, even those critics who concede that *Akhnaten* was a massive hit with the public are reluctant to draw the fairly obvious conclusion that this success might rub off on the genre as a whole. The British critic Andrew Clements writes, for example:

Akhnaten should really be regarded as part of the company's bid to fill its coffers rather than a significant contribution to the presentation of contemporary opera. A good deal has been made of Glass's attracting a 'cross-over' public into the opera house, as if those who come to soak up the blameless musical neutrality of Akhnaten will get a taste for the place and hurry along to the next production of Wagner or Verdi. It's a self-deception: the audience for progressive rock to which many of Glass's adherents reputedly belong is intelligent, sophisticated, and knows what it likes. To suggest that it is ignorant of what traditional opera has to offer is a mistake, and there is no likelihood of its being cowed intellectually into thinking that grand opera is an art form to which it should in future aspire.[29]

Clement's observations, and those of other critics like him, are clearly wrong.[30] Glass's success and that of other contemporary composers—John Adams, Michael Nyman, Louis Andriessen, Meredith Monk, and Gavin Bryars, among others—has clearly had an impact on box-office receipts for more traditional forms of music. To claim otherwise is to deceive oneself. Opera would hardly be regarded as a relevant and contemporary art form if there were not people writing exciting new works for the operatic stage as well as people doing imaginative new interpretations of historical pieces. People know these days that when they step over the threshold of the opera house they do not need to leave the better part of themselves outside; a magical transformation does not occur that forces them to accept values they are accustomed to thinking of as those of oppressors. Directors such as Peter Sellars and Achim Freyer might not always live up to their creative potentials; they might not always succeed in making repertory pieces work in contemporary contexts; and their efforts might at times seem ill conceived, but at least they try. More important, their boldly imaginative interpretations of contemporary works (Sellars's superb production of *Nixon in China* and Freyer's brilliant vision of *Akhnaten* are two of the most striking examples) remind us of what is best about opera and that opera can truly be about the world we live in today.

But traditionalists remain angry at this influx of new blood into opera houses, and so it becomes important for them to distinguish themselves in some way from the undiscriminating masses. It is no longer enough simply to attend performances of opera (anyone can do that); the *way* you attend becomes the overriding concern. Thus it is important that critics such as Robert Anderson and Kurt Honalka fall asleep when attending performances of operas like *Akhnaten*; or if they do not that they say in their reviews that they did.[31] One of the most entertaining experiences you can have when you go to performances of a work by Philip Glass or Michael Nyman is to sit among the critics and watch these frustrated late-middle-aged men compete to see who can look the most bored and irreverent. The question becomes not so much what they write in their reviews but who can make their inertia the most conspicuous when everyone else in the audience is clapping and who can create the most fuss about leaving when everyone else is comfortably seated. These people literally fall over themselves, and often over other members of the audience, in their attempts to express their contempt for this music.

I am going to give very little airplay to the most scathing reviews of *Akhnaten* as they are simply not interesting enough to warrant attention. In a much-cited review, Donal Henehan wrote that the score of *Akhnaten* "stand[s] to music as the sentence 'See Spot run' stands to literature."[32] Paul Griffiths, the renowned specialist on the modernist avant-garde, describes the opera as "regressive and childlike" and as "a child's drawing, but 10' square and executed with evident painstaking care."[33] As if to prove his point, he carefully selects a couple of the simplest musical phrases in *Akhnaten* and proceeds to simplify them further by detaching them from their musical and dramatic contexts. The scenes of the opera are reduced to a schematic diagram whose sole parameters are tempo (Griffiths misses many significant tempo changes) and the voice types of the singers.[34] Not very compelling stuff.

For Griffiths as for other critics of Glass, the key issue seems to have been putative unintelligibility.[35] These critics represent *Akhnaten* as being a totally impenetrable, refractory object—an enigmatic sphinx—that deflects any attempts by listeners to gain purchase on the drama of the piece. Many critics draw attention to the heretic linguistic texts as a significant obstacle to the reception of the opera. And this criticism might in some measure be valid, although let us not forget that the hymn to the sun is sung in the language of the country in which it is performed and that most of the other sung texts are translated by a narrator. On the other hand, it is an impoverished sign theory that privileges the most literal, denotative signifiers over other, more subtle forms of signification and, more important, since we are discussing music, that privileges linguistic over musical signifiers. In concentrating on the linguistic texts, critics such as Henehan and Griffiths fail to listen adequately to the music, which as we have seen is teeming with signifiers (which they either ignore or fail to recognize). And yet there is also a sense in which these critics appear to have understood the opera all too well but simply did not like what they heard. What other justification can there be for the intensity of their reactions?

But lest we be tempted to let the Ayes, Horemhabs, and Amon high priests of the present-day musical world have the last word, let us proceed. One of the most impressive aspects of Glass's opera is truly its resounding success with the public. Let us not mince our words: It is astounding that a contemporary opera, especially one that its critics describe as "unintelligible," should engender such widespread public interest. Obviously Glass's opera is saying something to these people, and something they evidently want to hear. People do not stand in line for, do not watch performance after performance of, something that they find incomprehensible. If they did, twentieth-century opera would have been doing a lot better than it was, in terms of box-office receipts, long before Glass came along. *Akhnaten* was a repertory piece both for Stuttgart's State Opera and the ENO, and both productions played to invariably full houses. North American performances in Houston and New York drew similar crowds, although judging from the "friendly" and "more neutral" criticism,[36] the opera was not so well received as it was in Europe, due largely, it appears, to deficiencies in the staging and a somewhat sloppy interpretation of the score. More recently, it has been performed successfully in other countries, including Sweden and Brazil.

But the critics are not the only factor that is likely to influence present and future perceptions of Glass and *Akhnaten* in a negative way. The mass media may well play a more significant, if less direct, role still in the character assassination of Glass. So ruthlessly has Glass's musical language been exploited by advertisers, television producers, and the composers for movies that at times I find myself (against my better judgment) wishing that he had not been *quite* so successful. This is not because I want to belong to a small clique of initiates who claim to genuinely understand this music but because of the influence this appropriation has had on my perceptions of original body of work. It seems that one can hardly turn on the television now without being bombarded by Glassian arpeggio figurations; or made to listen to a countertenor, backed up by bell chimes and low violas, singing the melody from the Window of Appearances scene backward; or coaxed to take out a mortgage on a house by a British building society to the accompaniment of *Einstein*ian intoned numbers recited in strict arithmetic patterns.

It does not take me long, however, to get over these negatively charged initial responses. What better evidence could there be of Glass's influence on the musical thinking of his time? And yet, many people in the Western world, if asked who Philip Glass is, are likely to respond that they do not know; and those who do know might hesitate before categorizing him as a "famous composer" in the same sense as the (deceased) greats of the classical music canon or other popular icons whom everybody knows. It is almost a certainty, however, that the majority of these people, unless they are ascetics of some kind, have at some time or other come into contact either with Glass's music or with music that is strongly derivative of it. The "copies" do not, of course, mean the same thing as the "original": Music is one of the most context-bound forms of discourse and cannot simply be grafted into new dramatic or cultural contexts without its meaning changing significantly. Glassian musical phrases do not mean exactly the same thing in an advertisement for the Honda Acura as they do in the middle of *Akhnaten* or *Satyagraha*, and rarely is the copy as interesting as the original either in formal musical terms or with regard to deeper musical, dramatic, or philosophical questions.[37]

Despite the possible negative effect of all this exposure on perceptions of Glass's music, I remain convinced that his influence on contemporary culture has been predominantly a salutary one. Indeed, it is precisely because he has become so popular, often tackling urgent social concerns in his works without compromising his artistic integrity, that Glass's music matters. It matters that a fairly large percentage of the population feels connected to rather than alienated from a distinguished musical tradition that, for the most part, has been a unifying force in Europe, the United States, and, more recently, the rest of the world; it matters if this tradition is to remain a vital force. Western classical music is no different from any of the other learned muscial traditions around the world in this respect. Glass's music has unquestionably played a part in bringing about a climate in the West in which there is a greater understanding of and respect for classical music than at any earlier juncture in the twentieth century. Paradoxically, in distancing himself from the past in the way that he has done in his music, and thus bringing upon himself the wrath of traditionalists, he has arguably brought the past closer to contemporary audiences than it has been for many years. Glass and other musicians like him have been able to do this because one of the central "messages" imparted to audiences in their music is that it is possible to learn from the past without having to live in it.

Accused sometimes of living in his own musical past, of not renewing his distinctive musical palette with sufficient abandon, Glass has demonstrated in recent years a new ambitiousness as well as a desire to take on novel artistic challenges. *The Voyage* is as ambitious an undertaking as any of the trilogy pieces, and the music of this opera is as complex and richly evocative as anything the composer has written. The quality of writing as well as the sheer scale of the Cocteau trilogy, probably Glass's most significant achievement of the 1990s, bear direct comparison to the project we have been discussing here, the portrait opera trilogy. The soon-to-be-published autobiographical account of the making of these works will be of great interest to all music enthusiasts interested in this composer's recent music. In addition to these colossal undertakings of Glass's, this decade has been peppered with numerous other large-scale works, such as a second Doris Lessing collaboration, *The Marriage Between Zones Three, Four, and Five*, premiered in Germany in 1997, and a fourth Robert Wilson collaboration, *Monsters of Grace*, premiered in Los Angeles in 1998. On occasion, Glass's numerous film projects leave this listener doubting just how committed he is artistically to all of the projects he takes on. The music of *Mishima* or *Koyaanisqatsi* could hardly be described as "incidental music"; for the *Candyman* films, however, the description is accurate. Likewise, the more overtly symphonic side of Glass has never appealed to this writer as much as it has to some critics; I appreciate the sentiments behind the Bowie/Eno–inspired symphonies but do not think that the composer is necessarily in his element in the symphonic medium. Glass's writing for the piano, on the other hand, somewhat paradoxically finds him both at his most communicative and his most introverted. Ever since the shimmering piano opening to *Glassworks*, this side of the composer has deeply touched audiences the world over. *Akhnaten* remains, at present, my favorite of Glass's works. This might not always be the case; perhaps there is even an opera or a symphony out there that I have not heard that will displace it from this position. And who knows what Glass has up his sleeve as we approach the new millennium? Of one thing we can be fairly certain, however: Glass is one composer who is unlikely to be troubled by writer's block in the years ahead.

Notes

🦅

1. Oedipus and Akhnaton

1. A slightly less obvious operatic precursor is Giacomo Puccini's "Triptych," itself a trilogy comprising three one-act operas.

2. See Philip Glass, *Music by Philip Glass* [henceforth *MPG*] (New York: Harper and Row, 1987), p. 136.

3. See Andreas Huyssen, *After the Great Divide* (Bloomington: Indiana University Press, 1986), p. 182; see also John Rockwell, "Wagner and Philip Glass: Two of a Kind?" *The New York Times*, 22 November 1987, pp. H27–28, and "Three Philip Glass Operas Become a Sort of Modern 'Ring' Cycle," *The New York Times*, 25 June 1990, pp. C13, C16. In his article "Glass at the Crossroads" (*Opera* 39.11 [1988]: 1278), however, Rockwell refers more aptly to Glass as a "post-Wagnerian, postmodernist" composer.

4. Huyssen, *After the Great Divide*, p. 182.

5. The influence of anti-Semitism on Wagner's music is addressed in a number of recent studies, among them Barry Millington, "Nuremberg Trial: Is There Anti-Semitism in Die Meistersinger?" *Cambridge Opera Journal* 3.3 (1991): 247–60, and Marc A. Weiner, *Richard Wagner and the Anti-Semitic Imagination* (Lincoln: University of Nebraska Press, 1995). There is, of course, a long tradition of similar Wagner criticism, going back all the way to that of his contemporary Nietzsche: e.g., the essays "Nietzsche contra Wagner" (in *The Portable Nietzsche* [New York: Viking Press, 1954], pp. 661–83) and "The Case of Wagner" (in *The Birth of Tragedy and the Case of Wagner* [New York: Random House, 1967], pp. 155–92).

6. Rockwell, "Three Philip Glass Operas," p. C13.

7. Rockwell has voiced such concerns on numerous occasions, particularly with regard to Glass's posttrilogy output: e.g., "Glass at the Crossroads," p. 1280; "A Minimalist Singing a One-Note Tune," *The New York Times*, 4 September 1988, pp. H19, H24; and "Everywhere, Fuel for a Fresh Debate over Glass's Music," *The New York Times*, 19 December 1993, p. H38.

8. In the United Kingdom published as Philip Glass, *Opera on the Beach: Philip Glass, On His New World of Music Theatre* (London: Faber and Faber, 1987).

9. Glass, *MPG*, pp. 136–37.

10. Ibid., p. 29.

11. See Leslie Lassetter, "The Operatic Trilogy of Philip Glass: 'Einstein on the Beach,' 'Satyagraha,' and 'Akhnaten,'" M.M. thesis, University of Cincinnati, 1985.

12. Michael Blackwood, dir., *A Composer's Notes. Philip Glass: The Making of an Opera* (London: Michael Blackwood Productions, 1985).

13. Glass, *MPG*, p. 139.

14. One of the most revealing expositions of Rorty's position can be found in his discussion of the holocaust in the essay "Solidarity" (Richard Rorty, *Contingency,*

Irony, and Solidarity [Cambridge: Cambridge University Press, 1989], pp. 189–98). In this essay, Rorty draws the controversial conclusion that people living in occupied territory during World War II who helped their Jewish neighbors escape Nazi persecution did so not so much because they were fellow human beings but because they were compatriots. This position has been strongly and ably contested recently by Eagleton, who unfortunately uses Rorty's somewhat idiosyncratic assertions as a pretext for his own attacks on postmodernism as a whole (Terry Eagleton, *The Illusions of Postmodernism* [Oxford: Blackwell, 1996], pp. 114–15).

15. Immanuel Velikovsky, *Oedipus and Akhnaton: Myth and History* (New York: Doubleday, 1960).

16. Of his writings, Velikovsky's work in medical psychoanalysis has perhaps achieved the most widespread recognition. His idea that epileptics are characterized by pathological encephalograms has become part of the received wisdom in the diagnosis and treatment of that condition. In addition, many of his controversial theories concerning the gaseous atmospheric constitutions of planets in our solar system have later been substantiated by empirical research, much to the consternation of his critics. Some Egyptologists (e.g., Philipp Vandenberg, *Nefertiti: An Archaeological Biography*, trans. Ruth Hen [Philadelphia: J. B. Lippincott, 1978], pp. 84–87) subscribe to Velikovsky's theory that Akhnaten wedded and impregnated his own mother.

17. For the sake of consistency, my spelling of *Akhnaten* follows that of Glass except when quoting a text by another author. A number of alternative spellings appear in the literature, some of the most common of which are Akhenaten, Akhnaton, Aakhunaten, Ikhnaton, and Echnaton. Some Egyptologists (e.g., Wallis Budge, *Tutankhamen: Amenism, Atenism, and Egyptian Monotheism* [New York: Dover, 1923]) follow the post-Amarna period Egyptian practice in which the name adopted by the king subsequent to his endorsement of Atenism as the sole state religion was deemed unutterable because of the crimes he was perceived to have committed; such studies refer to Akhnaten as Amenhetep IV, Amenophis IV, or some similar variation. The same principle applies to the spelling of other characters, such as queens Nefertiti and Tye, who are referred to by a variety of different names, such as Nefretete, Nefertity, and Tiy, Tiye, and Ti, respectively.

18. Velikovsky, *Oedipus and Akhnaton* pp. 66–72, 86–102.

19. Ibid., pp. 31–35, 36–43.

20. The Amarna period is named after the site of Tell el Amarna, where the ruins of Akhnaten's holy city, Akhetaten, were found. The period includes Akhnaten's reign and those of his immediate successors, Smenkhare, Tutankhamun, and Aye.

21. Velikovsky, *Oedipus and Akhnaton*, pp. 55–58.

22. In *Cosmos* (New York: Random House, 1980), Carl Sagan disputes Velikovsky's theory that a comet, which was later to become the planet Venus, caused the Red Sea to part, thus allowing the Israelites of the Bible to flee in safety from the Egyptian armies that were pursuing them. Regarding this theory, Sagan comments, "these ideas are almost certainly wrong" (p. 90).

23. Glass, quoted in Cole Gagne and Tracy Caras, *Interviews with American Composers* (Metuchen, N.J.: Scarecrow Press, 1982), p. 227.

24. Glass, *MPG*, p. 137.

25. Ibid., pp. 137–38.

26. Ibid., 140.

27. Philip Glass, interview by author, 8 September 1993.

28. Information regarding earlier drafts of the libretto is gleaned from Lassetter, "The Operatic Trilogy of Philip Glass: 'Einstein on the Beach,' 'Satyagraha,' and 'Akhnaten,'" and from my own interviews with the composer.

29. Glass later wrote a trilogy of reworkings of famous films and stage works by

Cocteau; the Cocteau trilogy comprises the films *Orphée* (1991), *La belle et la bête* (1994), and the play *Les enfants terribles* (1996).

30. Foucault's most thorough (and, unfortunately, most unreadable) discussion of the archaeological approach can be found in *The Archaeology of Knowledge*, trans. A. M. Sheridan Smith (New York: Pantheon Books, 1972).

31. Ibid., pp. 138–39.

32. Blackwood, *A Composer's Notes*.

33. Michel Foucault, "Nietzsche, Genealogy, History," in *Language, Counter-Memory, Practice*, ed. Donald F. Bouchard (Ithaca, N.Y.: Cornell University Press, 1977), p. 140.

34. Ibid., p. 142.

35. Paul Ricoeur, *Hermeneutics and the Human Sciences: Essays on Language, Action, and Interpretation*, ed. John B. Thompson (Cambridge: Cambridge University Press, 1981), pp. 182–93.

36. The first chapter of Gary Tomlinson's *Music in Renaissance Magic: Towards a Historiography of Others* (Chicago: University of Chicago Press, 1993), "Approaching Others (Thoughts before Writing)," combines Foucault's methods with those of Gadamer and Bakhtin.

37. Foucault, *Archaeology of Knowledge*, p. 10.

38. Ibid., p. 130.

39. Johannes Birringer has explored some of the implications of recent post-modernist theater's engagement with the past in "Archaeology: Tracing the Ghosts in the Theatre," in *Theatre, Theory, Postmodernism* (Bloomington: Indiana University Press, 1991), chap. 3.

40. See Peter Greenaway, dir., *Four American Composers: Meredith Monk* (London: Transatlantic Films, 1983).

41. *Moses and Monotheism* (*The Standard Edition of the Complete Psychological Works*, ed. and trans. James Strachey [London: Hogarth Press, 1964], vol. 23, pp. 1–37) is an anthology comprising two articles, "Moses an Egyptian" (1934) and "If Moses Was an Egyptian . . ." (1937), both originally published in *Imago*, Freud's psychoanalytical journal, and a third section, "Moses, His People and Monotheist Religion" (1939).

42. Freud writes, "If Moses was an Egyptian and communicated his own religion to the Jews, it must have been Akhenaten's, the Aten religion" (ibid, p. 24). Also: "The great religious idea for which the man Moses stood was, on our view, not his own property; he had taken it over from King Akhenaten. And he, whose greatness as the founder of a religion is unequivocally established, may perhaps have been following hints that had reached him—from near or distant parts of Asia—through the medium of his mother or by other paths" (p. 110).

43. Ibid., p. 29.

44. Ibid., p. 25.

45. Ibid., pp. 8–9.

46. Ibid., pp. 28–29.

47. Ibid., p. 110.

48. Freud's argument has been taken a step further by an Egyptian historian, Ahmed Osman (*Moses, Pharaoh of Egypt: The Mystery of Akhenaten Resolved* [London: Grafton Books, 1990]). Osman's claim that Akhnaten and Moses were the same person has not, however, received widespread recognition, due to the largely circumstantial evidence presented by him.

49. Glass quoted in Robert T. Jones, "Philip Glass: Religious and Musical Revolution Comes to City Opera," *Playbill* 11 (New York State Theater edition, 1984): 4.

50. James Henry Breasted, *A History of Egypt* (New York: Charles Scribner's Sons, 1909), pp. 371–76.

51. Velikovsky, *Oedipus and Akhnaton*, pp. 196–202.

52. Abraham's article, first published in *Imago* in 1912, was republished in English in *Psychoanalytical Quarterly* 4 (1935): 537–69.

53. Velikovsky, *Oedipus and Akhnaton*, pp. 196–202.

54. See Freud, "Totem and Taboo," in *Standard Edition*, vol. 13, pp. 156–61.

55. Velikovsky, *Oedipus and Akhnaton*, pp. 201–2.

56. Glass, *MPG*, p. 29.

57. Glass quoted in Gagne and Caras, *Interviews with American Composers*, p. 227.

58. Glass has stated: "With Akhnaten I would like to suggest a very complicated person. Someone who was capable of [writing] this Hymn to the Sun. . . . He's also capable of destroying this other tradition with as much savagery as any of the other pharaohs. And also capable of having this very romantic attachment with his wife" (Blackwood, *A Composer's Notes*).

2. *Glass's Poetics of Postmodernism*

1. Edward Strickland (*Minimalism: Origins* [Bloomington: Indiana University Press, 1993], p. 204) lists Glass's serial compositions as including a divertimento for flute, clarinet, and bassoon, diversions for two flutes and bass trombone, and a fantasy and a serenade for solo flute.

2. For biographical information on Glass, see, for example, Robert Coe, "Philip Glass Breaks Through," *New York Times Magazine*, 25 October 1981, pp. 68–80, 90; Cole Gagne and Tracy Caras, *Interviews with American Composers* (Metuchen, N.J.: Scarecrow Press, 1982), pp. 210–11; Gregory Sandow, "Philip Glass," in *The New Grove Dictionary of American Music*, vol. 2 (London: Macmillan 1986), pp. 228–30; Dean Paul Suzuki, "Minimal Music: Its Evolution as Seen in the Works of Philip Glass, Steve Reich, Terry Riley, and La Monte Young," Ph.D. diss., University of Southern California, 1991, pp. 509–12; Strickland, *Minimalism* pp. 203–5; and Ev Grimes, "Interview: Education," in *Writings on Glass*, ed. Richard Kastelanetz (New York: Schirmer Books, 1997), pp. 12–36.

3. Glass quoted in David Garland, "Philip Glass: Theater of Glass," *Downbeat* 50.11 (December 1983): 17. In a recent interview, Glass has amended this comment somewhat: "The first problem is to find a voice," he comments. "The second problem is to get rid of it!" (interview with Philip Glass, *The Offline Gallery* website: www.lightlink.com/offline).

4. Glass quoted in Geoff Smith and Nicola Walker Smith, "Twentieth Century Musicians: Philip Glass," *Music Technology Magazine* 1 (1993): 55.

5. For two broader-than-average perspectives on the birth of minimalism, see Tom Johnson, "The Original Minimalists," *Village Voice*, 25 July 1982, pp. 68–69, and Strickland, *Minimalism*.

6. Glass himself has defined minimalism by the presence of tonality, repetitive structures, and "a constant steady beat" (Smith and Smith, "Twentieth Century Musicians," p. 60). One of the most succinct and apt definitions is the five-point formulation given by Dean Suzuki in the sleeve notes to Jon Gibson's recording *In Good Company* (1992), a formulation that is an ellipsis of that Suzuki arrived at in his doctoral dissertation (Suzuki, "Minimal Music," pp. 12–29). Suzuki lists the traits of reductive style, repetition, tonal or modal harmonies, steady pulse ("an unflagging, metronomic beat"), and altered time frame. The use in these two definitions of the word *beat*, a colloquialism whose origins lie in popular rather than high culture, is significant.

7. Glass quoted in Edward Strickland, *American Composers: Dialogues on Contemporary Music* (Bloomington: Indiana University Press, 1991), p. 157.

8. Susan McClary's unpublished paper "Music and Postmodernism," first presented at the New Music America Festival in 1987, was among the earliest discussions of minimalism from the standpoint of cultural theory. See also Linda Hutcheon, *The Politics of Postmodernism* (London: Routledge, 1989), p. 9; and Fredric Jameson, "Postmodernism and Consumer Society," in *The Anti-Aesthetic: Essays on Postmodern Culture*, ed. Hal Foster (Seattle: Bay Press, 1983), p. III.

9. K. Robert Schwarz, "Process vs. Intuition in the Recent Works of Steve Reich and John Adams" *American Music* 8.3 (1990): 270–71; Robert Fink, "'Arrows of Desire': Long-Range Linear Structure and the Transformation of Musical Energy," Ph.D. diss., University of California at Berkeley, 1994, pp. 217–23.

10. Glass interview in Robert Ashley, dir., *Music with Its Roots in the Ether* (New York: Lovely Music, 1976). This passage is quoted also in John Rockwell, *All American Music: Composition in the Late Twentieth Century* (New York: Alfred A. Knopf, 1983), p. III.

11. Coe, "Philip Glass Breaks Through," p. 121.

12. Smith and Smith, "Twentieth Century Musicians," pp. 59–60.

13. Philip Glass, interview by author, 9 September 1993.

14. See Steve Reich, *Writing about Music* (Halifax: The Press of the Nova Scotia College of Art and Design, 1974).

15. Michael Nyman, *Experimental Music: Cage and Beyond* (London: Studio Vista, 1974), p. 119.

16. The term *systemic music* is largely self-explanatory. It was employed first by critics in the United Kingdom in the 1970s to refer to music based on systems worked out in advance by composers. Like the term *minimalism*, however, which was reportedly first used in connection with music by Michael Nyman, the term seems to be have been stolen from the visual arts (see Lawrence Alloway, "Systemic Painting," in *Minimal Art: A Critical Anthology*, ed. Gregory Battock [Berkeley: University of California Press, 1969; rev. ed. 1995], pp. 37–60). The music of Riley, Glass, and Frederic Rzewski has been described as systemic or process music, but the term is applied most aptly to the early works of Reich and various British composers such as John White and Chris Hobbs. See Brian Dennis, "Repetitive and System Music," *The Musical Times* 115.1582 (December 1974), pp. 1036–38.

17. See the discussion on additive procedures in chapter 3.

18. Kyle Gann, "Minimalism vs. Serialism: Let X = X," *Village Voice*, 24 February 1987, p. 76.

19. Ibid.

20. Ibid.

21. Elaine Broad, "A New X? An Examination of the Aesthetic Foundations of Early Minimalism," *Music Research Forum* 5 (1990): 61.

22. Reich quoted in Strickland, *American Composers*, p. 46.

23. Broad, "A New X?" p. 53.

24. Wim Mertens, *American Minimal Music*, trans. J. Hautekiet (London: Kahn and Averill, 1983), p. 17.

25. Paul Ricoeur, "Narrative Time," *Critical Inquiry* 7.1 (1980). Thanks to Anne Sivuoja-Gunaratnam for drawing my attention to this article. For more on narrative and temporality see her *Narrating with Twelve Tones: Einojuhani Rautavaara's First Serial Period (ca. 1957–1965)*, (Helsinki: The Finnish Academy of Science and Letters, 1997), pp. 135–52.

26. See Roland Barthes, *Image—Music—Text*, trans. S. Heath (New York: Hill and Wang, 1977), p. 124.

27. See Susan McClary, "Narrative Agendas in 'Absolute' Music," in *Musicology and Difference: Gender and Sexuality in Music Scholarship*, ed. Ruth A. Solie (Berkeley and Los Angeles: University of California Press, 1993), pp. 326–44;

Susan McClary, *Feminine Endings: Music, Gender, and Sexuality* (Minneapolis: University of Minnesota Press, 1991); Anthony Newcomb, "Once More 'Between Absolute and Program Music': Schumann and Late Eighteenth-Century Narrative Strategies," *Nineteenth-Century Music* 11 (1987): 233–50; Anthony Newcomb, "Sound and Feeling," *Critical Inquiry* 10 (1984): 614–43; and Carolyn Abbate, *Unsung Voices: Opera and Musical Narrative in the Nineteenth Century* (Princeton: Princeton University Press, 1991). Other exponents of the "new musicology" prefer not talk of narrative but use hermeneutic procedures to illuminate discursive levels of meaning. See, for example, Lawrence Kramer, *Music as Cultural Practice, 1800–1900* (Berkeley and Los Angeles: University of California Press, 1990), and *Classical Music and Postmodern Knowledge* (Berkeley: University of California Press, 1995). See also Rose Rosengard Subotnik, *Developing Variations: Style and Ideology in Western Music* (Minneapolis: University of Minnesota Press, 1991); *Deconstructive Variations: Music and Reason in Western Society* (Minneapolis: University of Minnesota Press, 1996).

28. Glass quoted in Gagne and Caras, *Interviews with American Composers*, p. 214.

29. Barthes, *Image—Music—Text*, pp. 179–89.

30. Sally Banes identifies the Greenwich Village community from which Glass and his contemporaries emerged as a Foucauldian "heterotopia." Both utopias and heterotopias are idealistic inversions of the dominant culture—what Foucault calls "Other spaces." What distinguishes the two terms for Banes, however, is that "utopias are fictional not real spaces"; heterotopias, on the other hand, "are real spaces that simultaneously reflect and contest society" (Sally Banes, *Greenwich Village 1963: Avant-Garde Performance and the Effervescent Body* [Durham, N.C.: Duke University Press, 1993], p. 13).

31. McClary, "Music and Postmodernism."

32. Eero Tarasti, "Minimalismin estetiikka," in *Johdatusta semiotiikkaan: esseitä taiteen ja kulttuurin merkki-järjestelmistä*, ed. Eero Tarasti (Helsinki: Oy Gaudeamus ab, 1990), p. 274.

33. Kenneth Baker, *Minimalism: Art of Circumstance* (New York: Abbeville Press, 1988).

34. Barbara Rose, "ABC Art," in Battock, *Minimal Art*, p. 292.

35. Ibid., p. 281.

36. Ibid., pp. 281, 282.

37. Michael Fried, "Art and Objecthood," in Battock, *Minimal Art*, p. 125.

38. The most extreme example of this tendency is the writing of James Boros. Boros is one of a small group of predominantly university-based composers who, revealingly, call themselves "maximalists." These composers reject the music of Philip Glass and John Adams unreservedly, because "having peeked over the fence surrounding this dungheap," they "have determined that shoveling shit is not to be their fate"(James Boros, "Why Complexity? Part 1," *Perspectives of New Music* 31.1 [1983]: p. 7). By "shoveling shit," Boros means "acquiesc[ing] to the culture industry's demand for consumable objects" (ibid.). Boros belongs to a long and distinguished line of twentieth-century composers who, like Milton Babbitt, do not care if anyone listens to their music. (See Milton Babbitt, "Who Cares If You Listen?" *High Fidelity Magazine* 8.2 [February 1958]: 38–40, 126–27.) This is just as well, because very few people *want* to listen to it! For a thorough discussion of the psychology behind assertions such as Boros's, see Susan McClary's seminal "Terminal Prestige: The Case of Avant-Garde Music Composition," *Cultural Critique* 12.2 (1989): 57–81.

39. Jonathan W. Bernard, "The Minimalist Aesthetic in the Plastic Arts and in Music," *Perspectives of New Music* 31.1 (1993): 86–133.

40. Ibid., p. 125.

41. See Gilles Deleuze and Félix Guattari, *Anti-Oedipus: Capitalism and Schizophrenia*, trans. Robert Hurley, Mark Seem, and Helen R. Lane (Minneapolis: University of Minnesota Press, 1983), pp. 1–50. See also Michel Foucault's introduction to *Anti-Oedipus*, pp. xi–xxiv, and Jean-François Lyotard, *The Postmodern Condition: A Report on Knowledge*, trans. Geoff Bennington and Brian Massumi (Minneapolis: University of Minnesota Press, 1984), pp. 3–6. Robert Fink ("Arrows of Desire," pp. 217–30) has ably discussed minimalism's relationship with technology using Deleuze and Guattari's ideas.

42. The term "oppositional postmodernism" is Hal Foster's. See the preface to his *The Anti-Aesthetic* (Seattle, Washington: Bay Press, 1983), p. xi.

43. Sally Banes, *Terpsichore in Sneakers* (Middletown, Conn.: Wesleyan University Press, 1987), p. xv.

44. Ibid., p. xvii.

45. Foster, *The Anti-Aesthetic*, p. xv.

46. Ibid., xi.

47. Philip Glass, *Music in Twelve Parts* (Virgin Records, 1996), liner notes.

48. Glass, *MPG*, p. 37.

49. See Laurence Shyer, *Robert Wilson and His Collaborators* (New York: Theatre Communications Group, 1989), p. 220.

50. Glass, *MPG*, p. 3.

51. Ibid., p. 87.

52. Ibid., p. 88.

53. Note that these are not *true* parents at all. In psychological terms, godparents not only represent both sexes, they play no part in the Oedipus complex.

54. Glass quoted in Gagne and Caras, *Interviews with American Composers*, p. 217, emphasis added.

55. Catherine Clément, *Opera, or the Undoing of Women*, trans. Betsy Wing (London: Virago, 1989).

56. Smith and Smith, "Twentieth Century Musicians: Philip Glass," p. 55, emphasis added.

57. Glass, *MPG*, p. 3.

58. Among the numerous Masonic readings of *Die Zauberflöte* are Jacques Chailley, *The Magic Flute, Masonic Opera: An Interpretation of the Libretto and the Music*, trans. Herbert Weinstock (London: V. Gollancz, 1972) and Howard Landon, *Mozart and the Masons: New Light on the Lodge "Crowned Hope"* (New York: Thames and Hudson, 1983).

59. Suzuki, "Minimal Music," pp. 594–95.

60. Edward Strickland (*American Composers*, pp. 1–2) uses the term *pragmatic* to account for the predominant communicative modality employed in minimal music.

61. Glass, *MPG*, p. 138.

62. Philip Glass, interview by Juhani Nuorvala, New York, 29 April 1987. This interview was published as a Finnish translation in Juhani Nuorvala, "Philip Glassin haastattelu," *Synkoopi* 27.3 (1987): 34–35. The passage quoted is taken from a transcript of the original interview Nuorvala kindly provided to me.

63. The phrase "wheels inside wheels" is from *MPG*, p. 59, where Glass quotes a critic's description of the music of *Einstein*.

64. Ibid., p. 139.

65. Ibid.

66. See Tim Page's discussion of *Akhnaten* in the *New Grove Dictionary of Opera*, ed. Stanley Sadie, (London: Macmillan, 1992), pp. 47–48. In *Satyagraha*, Page observes, Glass developed "his own distinctive mutation of 'traditional'

opera" to which all of the composer's subsequent operas, including *Akhnaten*, are more closely related than to the "sui generis *Einstein on the Beach*" (p. 48).

67. Philip Glass et al., *Akhnaten*, booklet accompanying the compact-disk recording (CBS Records, 1987), p. 16.

68. Philip Glass, interview by author, 9 September 1993.

69. See Winton Dean's review of the English National Opera's production of *Akhnaten* (*The Musical Times* 128.1731 [1987]: 281). The reception of the opera is discussed in more detail in chapter 8.

70. This paraphrases some comments made by Susan McClary in reference to John Adams (*Feminine Endings*, pp. 122–23).

71. See Glass, *MPG*, pp. 3–10.

72. Ibid., p. 6.

73. Ibid., p. 10.

74. Antonin Artaud, *The Theater and Its Double*, trans. Mary Caroline Richards (New York: Grove Weidenfeld, 1958), pp. 89–100, 122–32.

75. Ibid., e.g., p. 125.

76. For a thoroughly and revealing discussion of the genealogy of this idealized view of the ancient Egyptian alphabet, see "The Perfect Language of Images," in Umberto Eco, *The Search for the Perfect Language*, trans. James Fentress (Oxford: Blackwell, 1995), pp. 144–77.

77. Artaud, *The Theater and Its Double*, e.g., pp. 53–67.

78. Ibid., p. 37.

79. Ibid., pp. 37, 76.

80. Ibid., p. 60.

81. Ibid., pp. 74–83.

82. Jacques Derrida, "The Theatre of Cruelty and the Closure of Representation," in *Writing and Difference* (Chicago: University of Chicago Press, 1978), pp. 232–50.

83. Ibid., p. 237.

84. Ibid., pp. 232–33.

85. The second of these tendencies can easily be related to Jameson's comments regarding the emergence of "new kind of flatness or depthlessness" in postmodern art (see *Postmodernism or, the Cultural Logic of Late Capitalism* [Durham, N.C.: Duke University Press, 1991], p. 9).

86. Julia Kristeva, "Modern Theater Does Not Take (a) Place," *Sub-stance* 18–19 (1977).

87. John Rockwell, "Robert Wilson's Stage Works: Originality and Influence," in Robert Wilson, *Robert Wilson: The Theatre of Images* (New York: Harper and Row, 1984), p. 10.

88. The question of androgyny has been exhaustively, if a little one-sidedly, explored by Jean-Jacques Nattiez in his *Wagner Androgyne*, trans. Stewart Spencer (Princeton: Princeton University Press, 1993).

89. Being nonliterary, this kind of theater seems to resist analytical discussion. Some theorizing on the subject has emerged in recent years, however, a good deal of which has been written by people involved on a day-to-day basis with putting on theatrical productions. See, for example, Richard Schechner, *Performance Theory* (New York: Routledge, 1988); Richard Foreman, *Plays and Manifestos* (New York: New York University Press, 1976); Banes, *Greenwich Village 1963*; Shyer, *Robert Wilson and His Collaborators*; Johannes Birringer, *Theatre, Theory, Postmodernism* (Bloomington: Indiana University Press, 1991); and Herbert Blau, *To All Appearances: Ideology and Performance* (New York: Routledge, 1992).

90. I have explored this subject in more depth in an unpublished paper, "Vega Meets Brecht: Alienation Effects and Archaeological Strategies in 'Tom's Diner' and 'Luka.'"

91. A myriad of theoretical discussions concerning Brecht's ideas are currently in circulation. Just about every postmodern theorist has had something to say about him. Those discussions most relevant here include Brecht's own theoretical writings (e.g., Bertolt Brecht, *Brecht on Theatre: The Development of an Aesthetic*, ed. John Willet [New York: Hill and Wang, 1964]), Walter Benjamin's seminal *Understanding Brecht*, trans. Anne Bostock (London: NLB, 1977), and Raymond Williams, *Drama from Ibsen to Brecht* (London: Hogarth Press, 1968).

92. The term Epic Theater was "appropriated" by Brecht from the director Erwin Piscator (see Edwin Wilson and Alvin Goldfarb, *Living Theater: A History* [New York: McGraw-Hill, 1994], p. 407). Kurt Weill also used the term to describe his approach to writing music for the theater, but there seems to have been little agreement between him and Brecht as to how it should be defined, even with regard to projects on which the two collaborated (see Susan Borwick, "Weill's and Brecht's Theories on Music and Drama," *Journal of Musicological Research*, 4.1–2 [1982]: 39–67).

93. Brecht's distrust of unities can be compared easily with Foucault's similar orientation. Compare, for example, Brecht, *Brecht on Theatre*, pp. 37–38, 67–71, with Michel Foucault, *The Archaeology of Knowledge*, trans. A. M. Sheridan Smith (New York: Pantheon Books, 1972), pp. 4–8, and Michel Foucault, "Nietzsche, Genealogy, History," in *Language, Counter-Memory, Practice*, trans. Donald F. Bouchard and Sherry Simon (Ithaca, N.Y.: Cornell University Press, 1977), p. 142.

94. See Brecht, *Brecht on Theatre*, pp. 87, 91.

95. See, for example, Roland Barthes, *Mythologies*, trans. Annette Lavers (New York: Hill and Wang, 1972), pp. 11, 109–59.

96. See Jean Baudrillard, "The Ecstasy of Communication," in Foster, *The Anti-Aesthetic*, pp. 126–34; and Jean Baudrillard, *Simulations*, trans. Paul Foss, Paul Patton, and Philip Beitchman (New York: Semiotext[e], 1983).

97. See Roland Barthes, "Musica Practica," in *Image—Music—Text*, pp. 149–54; and Roland Barthes, *The Pleasure of the Text*, trans. Richards Miller (New York: Hill and Wang, 1975).

98. See Brecht's essay, "On the Use of Music in the Epic Theatre," in *Brecht on Theatre*, pp. 84–90.

99. Glass interview in Michael Blackwood, dir., *A Composer's Notes. Philip Glass: The Making of an Opera* (London: Michael Blackwood Productions, 1985). The composer has also used the term to describe *Einstein* in an interview for *The South Bank Show* (U.K.): "Opera is a species of poetry. It's a poetic image. *Einstein on the Beach* is really a poetic vision of Einstein. We're not really trying to explain his theories; we're not really telling how he lived as a child and how he grows up as a man. We're taking the images of Einstein that we all know and making a kind of poetry out of them. Let's put it this way: the whole of *Einstein on the Beach* could have been a dream that Einstein had" (*The Music of Philip Glass*, on *The South Bank Show*, ed. Melvyn Bragg [London: London Weekend Television, 1986]).

100. Artaud, *The Theatre and Its Double*, p. 38.

101. Ibid., p. 39.

102. Roman Jakobson, "Closing Statement: Linguistics and Poetics," in *Style in Language*, ed. Thomas A. Sebeok (Cambridge, Mass.: MIT Press, 1960), pp. 350–77.

103. Julia Kristeva, *Desire in Language: A Semiotic Approach to Literature and Art*, ed. Leon S. Roudiez (New York: Columbia University Press, 1980), p. 136.

104. Ibid., p. 137.

105. Artaud quoted in ibid., p. 139.

106. See Brecht, *Brecht on Theatre*, p. 192.

107. See Walter Benjamin, "The Work of Art in the Age of Mechanical Repro-
duction," in *Illuminations: Walter Benjamin—Essays and Reflections*, ed. Hannah
Arendt (New York: Schocken Books, 1968), pp. 220–23.

108. See Keir Elam, *The Semiotics of Theatre and Drama* (London: Methuen,
1980), p. 19.

109. See Theodor W, Adorno, *Philosophy of Modern Music*, trans. Anne G.
Mitchell and Wesley V. Blomster (London: Sheed and Ward, 1973), pp. 171–74.

110. Glass, *MPG*, p. 138.

111. See Igor Stravinsky, *Poetics of Music* (Cambridge: Cambridge University
Press, 1947).

112. Aristotle, *Poetics* 12.9.

113. In the *The Theatre and Its Double*, Artaud writes: "The Theatre of Cruelty
intends to reassert all the time-tested magical means of capturing the sensibility.
These means which consist of intensities of colors, lights, and sounds, which utilize
vibration, tremors, repetition, whether of a musical rhythm or a spoken phrase,
special tones or a general diffusion of light, can obtain their full effect only by the
use of *dissonances*" (p. 125). Compare this to Jameson, *Postmodernism*, p. 6.

114. Glass interview in Blackwood, *A Composer's Notes*. It is easy to read a personal subtext into this comment, pertaining to Glass's own difficult position in the
1960s and 1970s and the vilification of minimalism by the modernist establishment.
That Glass identifies closely with the character of Akhnaten I will demonstrate below.

115. Glass, *MPG*, pp. 154–55.

116. Glass interview in Blackwood, *A Composer's Notes*.

117. Ibid.

118. Leslie Lassetter, "The Operatic Trilogy of Philip Glass: 'Einstein on the
Beach,' 'Satyagraha,' and 'Akhnaten,'" M.M. thesis, University of Cincinnati, 1985,
p. 21.

119. Gayanacharya Avinish C. Pandeya, *The Art of Kathakali* (Allahabad:
Prayag, 1961), p. 139.

120. Glass quoted in Strickland, *American Composers*, p. 72.

3. *The Musical Language of* Akhnaten

1. See Dan Warburton, "A Working Terminology for Minimal Music," Intégral
2 (1988): 146–48.

2. Philip Glass, *MPG* (New York: Harper and Row, 1987), p. 59.

3. The rhythmic pattern in question, ta-Ta, ta-Ta-ta, ta-Ta-ta, although an effective core motif in this opera, was to be applied in a somewhat indiscriminate fashion in subsequent works. This motif is now justifiably regarded as one of the most
hackneyed features of Glass's style.

4. Glass, *MPG*, pp. 116–17.

5. The chaconne has throughout the greater part of its history been associated
with a twin musical form, the *passacaglia*. Although the origins of the two are distinct, they became difficult to distinguish from one another in the keyboard variations of Italian composers in the early 1600s. Certain rules of thumb have been invented by musicologists, such as the one that categorizes the chaconne as a
predominantly harmonic and the passacaglia as a predominantly melodic form, but
these formulations are unreliable to say the least (see Thomas Walker, "Ciaccona
and Passacaglia: Remarks on Their Origin and Early History," *Journal of the American Musicological Society* 21 (1968): 319–20; Richard Hudson, "Chaconne" and
"Passacaglia," in *The New Grove Dictionary of Opera*, ed. Stanley Sadie (London:
Macmillan, 1980) pp. 102, 268.

6. Glass, *MPG*, pp. 115–17.

7. In *MPG* (p. 117), the composer combines the harmony of *Satyagraha* with the melodic motif from *Einstein* to demonstrate the relatedness of the two. This ingenious rhetorical flourish gives the impression that the two are related more closely than they in actual fact are.

8. See Richard Hudson, *Passacaglio and Ciaccona: From Guitar Music to Italian Keyboard Variations in the Seventeenth Century* (Ann Arbor: UMI Research Press, 1981), p. 312. Note that the stepwise diatonic ascent from the tonic is a common motif also in *Satyagraha*. The trilogy theme as it is found in this context (e–g–c′–e′; or [5]–6–3–5), although a less convincing example of the chaconne, would be a strong candidate as a passacaglia were it to begin on the first rather than the fifth degree (ibid., p. 269).

9. Charles Jencks, *What Is Post-Modernism?* (London: Academy Editions, 1986), p. 14; Jann Pasler, "Postmodernism, Narrativity, and the Art of Memory," *Contemporary Music Review* 7 (1993): 21.

10. See Ellan Rosand, "The Descending Tetrachord: An Emblem of Lament," *The Musical Quarterly* 65.3 (1979): 345–59.

11. Ibid., pp. 346, 354.

12. Ibid., p. 350.

13. See Susan McClary, *Feminine Endings: Music, Gender, and Sexuality* (Minneapolis: University of Minnesota Press, 1991), pp. 86–90; and Joseph Kerman, *Opera as Drama* (New York: Vintage Books, 1959), pp. 58–59.

14. See Rosand, "The Descending Tetrachord," p. 356.

15. Glass, *MPG*, pp. 115–16.

16. Darius Milhaud, "Polytonalité et atonalité," in *Notes sur la musique: essais et chroniques* (France: Flammarion, 1982), pp. 173–89.

17. Vincent Persichetti, *Twentieth-Century Harmony* (New York: W. W. Norton, 1961), pp. 255–61; Leon Dallin, *Techniques of Twentieth Century Composition: A Guide to the Materials of Modern Music* (Dubuque, Iowa: W. C. Brown, 1974), pp. 132–36.

18. Philip Glass, interview by author, 8 September 1993. In another interview, given two years after the premiere of *Akhnaten*, the composer uses a similar visual analogy: "When I began writing *Akhnaten* . . . I began to think about harmonic language in actually a very different way. . . . It had to do with perspective in a certain way, with point of view. . . . I began to think about polytonality in a very, very different way. I began to think about the ambiguity of polytonality. Not the idea that we simply heard two keys at the same time, but in listening to one piece we could hear it in two keys at the same time—that's not quite the same thing. . . . In other words, if playing the piano, say I play a G major chord in my left hand and an A-flat chord in my right hand, I'm playing two chords at the same time. But I began to wonder about writing a piece which, if you could look at it harmonically, is harmonically ambiguous. And depending on how you looked at it, you heard it as being in a different key at different times" (interview by Juhani Nuorvala, Stockholm, 14 September 1986). See also Kyle Gann, "Midtown Avant-Gardist," in *Writings on Glass*, ed. Richard Kostelanetz (New York: Schirmer Books, 1997), pp. 268–69.

19. Robert Fink interprets the first macrocycle (or "wave," as he terms it) of the funeral, after the entry of the male chorus, in this way ("'Arrows of Desire': Long-Range Linear Structure and the Transformation of Musical Energy," Ph.D. diss., University of California at Berkeley, 1994, p. 255). Leslie Lassetter, while recognizing that there is a strong lydian feel to the scene, interprets the chordal movement as A major to D-sharp diminished ("The Operatic Trilogy of Philip Glass: 'Einstein on the Beach,' 'Satyagraha,' and 'Akhnaten,'" M.M. thesis, University of Cincinnati,

1985, p. 123). On the basis of the written notes, Lassetter's position is certainly defensible. I tend, however, to hear the progression as a tonic to dominant movement in E major and, later in the scene, as a tonic to supertonic in A major (against an implied pedal of E) more strongly than I do as the less conventional tonic to altered dominant (?) movement Lassetter suggests.

20. Fink, "Arrows of Desire," p. 415.
21. Glass, *MPG*, p. 60.
22. Milos Raickovich, *"Einstein on the Beach" by Philip Glass: A Musical Analysis*, pp. 53–67.
23. Gregory Sandow, "The Uses of Structure," *Village Voice*, 13–19 January 1982, p. 95.
24. Ibid.
25. McClary, *Feminine Endings*, pp. 142–42.
26. Raickovich, *"Einstein on the Beach" by Philip Glass*, p. 69.
27. Sandow, "The Uses of Structure," p. 95.
28. Leighton Kerner, "Big Egypt," *Village Voice*, 13 November 1984, p. 80.
29. Glass, *MPG*, p. 174.
30. Ibid., p. 171.
31. Philip Glass, interview by author, 8 September 1993.
32. See Joseph Kerman, "Viewpoint," *Nineteenth Century Music* 2 (1979): 186–91; and Joseph Kernan, *Opera as Drama* (New York: Vintage, 1959), pp. 16–17.

4. Narrating from a Distance

1. Philip Glass, *MPG* (New York: Harper and Row, 1987), p. 159.
2. This opera was written before Wagner had fully formulated his theory on the unified art work, or *Gesamtkunstwerk*.
3. There are no violins in *Akhnaten* because they would not have fitted in the orchestra pit of the Stuttgart Playhouse, where the opera was first performed, and because the composer held the dark timbral qualities of the lower strings to be a suitable medium for its tragic subject matter.
4. In distinguishing an "authorial" from a "narrative" interpretive position, I am borrowing terminology from Peter Rabinowitz. In an unpublished paper on the musical *Showboat*, Rabinowitz uses this theoretical distinction to account for the ways in which contradictory interpretive positions can coexist in a piece of music, often with post-Brechtian implications.
5. See Gérard Genette, *Narrative Discourse*, trans. Jane E. Levin (Oxford: Basil Blackwell, 1980).
6. Roland Barthes, "Structural Analysis of Narratives," in *Image—Music—Text*, trans. Stephen Heath (New York: Hill and Wang, 1977), p. 124.
7. Julia Kristeva, "From One Identity to an Other," in *Desire in Language: A Semiotic Approach to Art and Literature*, trans. Thomas Gora, Alice Jardine, and Leon S. Roudiez (New York: Columbia University Press, 1980), pp. 136–38, 146–47; and Julia Kristeva, "Place Names," in ibid., pp. 280–86.
8. The association of liquid imagery, such as that which I am suggesting in connection with the prelude music, with the feminine, the maternal, and, specifically, the womb is conventional and extremely widespread. Moreover, it forms the foundation of all orthodox ancient Egyptian religious ideas. Conventionally, this association carries powerful misogynistic overtones, but in some of the post-Lacanian "French feminism" of the 1970s, the logic behind the formulation is deconstructed by emphasizing the positive qualities of fluids. See, for example, Luce Irigaray, "The 'Mechanics' of Fluids," in *This Sex Which Is Not One*, trans. Catherine Porter

(Ithaca, N.Y.: Cornell University Press, 1985), pp. 106–18. In *Akhnaten*, the music of the prelude and its reprises is to some extent associated with the womb, in the sense of Kristeva's *chora*, and, much in the manner of Kristeva, this is seen as a site of both rejuvenation and depletion. Kaja Silverman elucidates Kristeva's formulation: "The *chora* is . . . the 'place' where the subject is both generated and annihilated, the site where it both assumes a pulsional or rhythmic consistency and is dissolved as a psychic or social coherence" (*The Acoustic Mirror: The Female Voice in Psychoanalysis and Cinema* [Bloomington: Indiana University Press, 1988], p. 103). This formulation is entirely consistent with the "choric" imagery of the prelude music and, more generally, with the key of A minor: This music is both the wellspring for the protagonist's most inspired ideas and, as Akhnaten's "transgression" theme forewarns us, the site of his annihilation.

9. Lawrence Kramer has explored some of the psychological implications of Wagner's interest in things aquatic in "Musical Form and Fin-de-Siècle Sexuality," in *Music as Cultural Practice, 1800–1900* (Berkeley and Los Angeles: University of California Press, 1990), pp. 135–75.

10. Further evidence that the river is the intended signified is provided by a similar passage in Glass's score to the Godfrey Reggio film *Koyaanisqatsi* (1982), composed immediately prior to *Akhnaten*. The first appearance of similar arpeggios in the film coincides with the first extended shots of a river. The musical textures of the third cycle of the prelude and the river music from the film are a particularly close match; they are even in the same key.

11. It is exactly the kind of writing that characterizes the music of an earlier film version of the Akhnaten story, the Twentieth-Century Fox film adaptation of Mika Waltari's novel, *The Egyptian* (1954). Alfred Newman and Bernard Herrmann's soundtrack to the film (MCA, 1523) is, as one might expect, replete with exotic imagery. Other than the exoticness of the music, however, this score has very little in common with *Akhnaten*. Other scores of Herrmann's, on the other hand, do seem to adumbrate various aspects of Glass's mature style. There are distinct Glassian moments in the Martin Scorsese film *Taxi Driver*, for example, as well as in the Alfred Hitchcock collaborations *Psycho* and *Vertigo*. Similarities between the styles of the two composers include a penchant for parallel voice leading, the extensive use of small, repetitive, rhythmic cells, and a distinctly unromantic approach to tonality.

12. Kurt Honalka, "Wer nicht glaubeb will, shläft ein: Philip Glass' postmoderne Anti-Oper 'Echnaton' in Stuttgart von Achim Freyer gerettet," *Opern Welt* 25.5 (1984): 27–28.

13. Glass, *MPG*, p. 173.

14. Ibid., pp. 155–56, 164–65.

15. See Susan McClary, *Feminine Endings: Music, Gender, and Sexuality* (Minneapolis: University of Minnesota Press, 1991), pp. 11–12. See also Gretchen A. Wheelock, "*Schwarze Gredel* and the Engendered Minor Mode in Mozart's Operas," in *Musicology and Difference: Gender and Sexuality in Music Scholarship*, ed. Ruth A. Solie (Berkeley and Los Angeles: University of California Press, 1993), pp. 201–21.

16. David Lewin, "Women's Voices and the Fundamental Bass," *The Journal of Musicology* 10.4 (1992): 464–82.

17. My thanks to Raymond Monelle for pointing out this association.

18. In speaking of weight, a specifically Russian musical lineage comes to mind that, in addition to Stravinsky, includes composers such as Modest Mussorgsky and Sergei Prokofiev. The catchy vernacular tunes, powerful rhythms, and mystical intensity of Mussorgsky's *Boris Godunov* are certainly valid points of reference when discussing *Akhnaten*. The more modern tonal language of Prokofiev's *L'amour des trois oranges* is closer, however, to Glass's approach in the scenes discussed here. It

is precisely in the weighty, "Russian," side of Stravinsky, as manifest in his early ballets, *The Firebird* and *The Rite of Spring*, that I hear prefigurations of Glass's music. *Oedipus Rex* has this quality, but other stage works, such as *The Rake's Progress* and *The Soldier's Tale*, have a lighter, more playful feel, which is related more easily to John Adams's music than to Glass's. Could it be that "the grandfather of tradition" is making himself heard in passages such as this?

19. As we shall see, the transgression theme is identical also to a prominent theme in Richard Strauss's *Salome*. I consider it unlikely that Glass is alluding knowingly to this theme. I do, however, consider a very general influence more than likely. In other words, the composer might have been trying to connote this kind of early modern music.

20. Pyramids have appeared onstage in various productions of *Akhnaten*. In David Freeman's New York production, regular operagoers were able to recognize pyramids and other items of scenery from the previous season's production of *Aïda*.

21. I will discuss some of the recent debates on androgyny below in my discussion of the representation of Akhnaten's and Nefertiti's religious practices.

22. See James Baikie, *The Amarna Age: A Study of the Crisis of the Ancient World* (London: A. and C. Black, 1926), p. 335.

23. A less likely allusion might be to Sophocles' trilogy of Oedipus plays, *King Oedipus*, *Oedipus at Colonus*, and *Antigone*, all of which were used by Velikovsky in constructing his theory of a correlation between the myth and the life of Akhnaten and all of which are arguably alluded to in Glass's opera.

24. For this to be a geometrically sound pyramid, it would need two more great composers. Monteverdi and Stravinsky would be as good choices as any, given their influence on the music of *Akhnaten*.

25. The musician in question is Juhani Nuorvala. The following is an extract from his interview: "I called it *Floe* because to me it was an obvious quote from Sibelius. To my great disappointment, I found that no one knew the symphony. . . . Now I have to tell you, I've never been to Finland, and I had no idea what you would see there. But I thought, if Sibelius looks out (laughs), what does he see? Maybe he sees an ice floe. . . . And no one has figured out what the damn thing meant! So I guess it didn't make a very good title. I should have called it *Sibelius*, and then everyone would have known" (interview with Juhani Nuorvala, Stockholm, 14 September 1986).

26. The Cocteau trilogy comprises Glass's musical reworkings of the films *Orphée* (1991) and *La belle et la bête* (1994) and the play *Les enfant terribles* (1996); the thus far incomplete Reggio trilogy comprises the films *Koyaanisqatsi* (1982), *Powaqqatsi* (1988), and *Noyaqqatsi*.

27. See Daisetz T. Suzuki, *Outlines of Mahayana Buddhism* (New York: Shoken Books, 1907), pp. 242–76; Christmas Humphreys, *Buddhism: An Introduction and Guide* (Harmondsworth: Penguin, 1951), p. 154; and Lama A. Govinda, *Foundations of Tibetan Buddhism* (London: Rider, 1960), pp. 213–17. Like most Buddhist ideas, these concepts have nothing to do with abstract speculation but rather are planes of experience directly realizable by the practitioner in meditation. For more on Glass's Buddhist orientation see the interview "First Lesson, Best Lesson" from the Buddhist journal *Tricycle*, which was republished in Richard Kostelanetz (ed.), *Writings on Glass* (New York: Schirmer Books, 1997), pp. 316–27.

28. Cited in Govinda, *Foundations of Tibetan Buddhism*, p. 30.

29. Immanuel Velikovsky, *Oedipus and Akhnaton: Myth and History* (New York: Doubleday, 1960), pp. 114–15.

30. Ibid., p. 114.

31. Klaus-Peter Kehr, the dramaturge of the Stuttgart production.

32. Glass, *MPG*, p. 163.

33. Abbate, *Unsung Voices*, p. 62.

34. Ibid., p. 63.

35. Gérard Genette, *Figures III* (Paris: Éditions du Seuil, 1972), p. 256.

36. Leslie Lassetter, The Operatic Trilogy of Philip Glass: 'Einstein on the Beach,' 'Satyagraha,' and 'Akhnaten,'" M.M. thesis, University of Cincinnati, 1985, p. 114.

37. Michel Foucault, "Nietzsche, Genealogy, History," in *Language, Counter-Memory, Practice* (Ithaca, N.Y.: Cornell University Press, 1977), p. 142.

38. Glass, *MPG*, pp. 152–53.

39. See Lise Manniche, *Music and Musicians in Ancient Egypt* (London: British Museum Press, 1991), pp. 74–83.

40. Jean Baudrillard, *Simulations*, trans. Paul Foss, Paul Patton, and Philip Beitchman (New York: Semiotext[e], 1983), p. 19.

41. Glass, *MPG*, p. 154.

42. Ibid.

43. Glass, quoted in Edward Strickland, *American Composers: Dialogues on Contemporary Music* (Bloomington: Indiana University Press, 1991), p. 152.

44. See E. A. Wallis Budge, introduction to *The Book of the Dead* (London: Penguin, 1989 [1899]), pp. xxxiii–xxxiv.

45. Ibid., pp. lxviii–lxx.

46. This was certainly the case for Osiris, whose phallus was lost at the same time as his head was severed from his body and which was the only part of his body never recovered.

47. See Michel Poizat, *The Angel's Cry: Beyond the Pleasure Principle in Opera*, trans. Arthur Denner (Ithaca, N.Y.: Cornell University Press, 1992), pp. 82–84.

48. Velikovsky, *Oedipus and Akhnaton* (New York: Doubleday, 1960), pp. 145–46.

49. Ibid.

50. Cyril Aldred, *Akhenaten, King of Egypt* (London: Thames and Hudson, 1988), p. 298.

51. These wordless passages are highly evocative of Debussy's music, particularly the choral passages sung by the Sirènes in his *Nocturnes*.

52. Glass, *MPG*, pp. 172–73.

53. Glass, quoted in Geoff Smith and Nicola Walker Smith, "Twentieth Century Americans: Philip Glass," *Music Technology Magazine* 1 (1993): 59. See also Glass, *MPG*, p. 138.

54. Philip Glass et al., *Akhnaten*, booklet accompanying the compact-disk recording (CBS Records, 1987), p. 11.

55. Daisetz T. Suzuki, *The Essence of Buddhism* (London: Buddhist Society, 1947), p. 41.

56. Govinda, *Foundations of Tibetan Buddhism*, p. 227.

57. Paul John Frandsen, "Philip Glass's *Akhnaten*," *Musical Quarterly* 77.2 (1993): 247.

58. Ibid.

59. Aldred, *Akhenaten, King of Egypt*, pp. 225–27.

60. See Jacques Lacan, *Écrits: A Selection*, trans. Alan Sheridan (London: Tavistock, 1977), pp. 1–7, 146–78.

61. Glass et al., *Akhnaten*, booklet, p. 15.

62. Philip Glass, interview by author, 8 September 1993.

63. *Jouissance* in the Lacanian sense implies some form of transgression from the highly law-governed and repetitive mode of being he refers to as *plaisir* (see Alan Sheridan's elucidation of the concept in his translator's note in Lacan, *Écrits*,

p. x). Both concepts are influenced strongly by Sigmund Freud's influential essay "Beyond the Pleasure Principle," in which he offers the pleasure-deferring, goal-directed "reality principle" as an alternative to the form of sexually driven psychosis he refers to as the "pleasure principle," which he relates directly to the death instinct (see *The Standard Edition of the Complete Psychological Works*, ed. and trans. James Strachey [London: Hogarth Press, 1961], vol. 18, pp. 9–11). By simply associating the repetition of the death instinct with musical repetition, it is possible, of course, to interpret the whole minimalist movement as a regression toward the pleasure principle and thus toward banal *plaisir*. In one of the boldest interpretations of the subject to date, the Belgian composer Wim Mertens (*American Minimal Music*, trans. J. Hautekiet [London: Kahn and Averill, 1983]) has made precisely this association. Both the Lacanian and the Lacan-influenced Barthesian understanding of *jouissance* suggest a somewhat different interpretation, however. Stephen Heath writes in his translator's note to Roland Barthes's *Image—Music—Text* (New York: Hill and Wang, 1977) that "pleasure (*plaisir*) [is] linked to cultural enjoyment and identity, the cultural enjoyment of identity, to a homogenizing movement of the ego"; whereas *jouissance* is viewed as "a radically violent pleasure which shatters—dissipates, loses—that cultural identity, that ego" (p. 9). In addition, the term carries strong sexual connotations, being derived from the verb *jouir*, meaning "to come" in the sense of "to have an orgasm." In the music of the funeral and coronation (act 1, scenes 1 and 2), the musical discourse of the old order (which seems to be directly associated with musical modernism) is encoded as the stagnant, obsessive, ego-centered discourse of the pleasure principle (*plaisir*) and therefore of the death drive; when appropriated by the crowd, however, in the choral passages toward the end of the scenes, a power rises in the music "from below" and takes it "beyond the pleasure principle" to a place where the identities, the meanings, established in the opening sections are erased, leaving just a powerful—one might even say violent—flow of musical energies. Michel Poizat discusses isolated pockets of such energies in the operatic repertoire in his groundbreaking *The Angel's Cry*. In *Akhnaten*, these energies are extended over extremely long periods of time and reach intensities that threaten to shake the entire discursive fabric of the opera, and sometimes the building in which it is performed, to its foundations.

64. See Michel Foucault, *The History of Sexuality: Volume 1*, trans. Robert Hurley (New York: Random House, 1979), pp. 92–97.

65. Ibid., p. 94.

5. Higher Love

1. Philip Glass, *MPG* (New York: Harper and Row, 1987), p. 156.

2. In Luce Irigaray's *Speculum of the Other Woman*, trans. Gillian C. Gill (Ithaca, N.Y.: Cornell University Press, 1989), pp. 243–364, Plato's myth is deconstructed from the dual standpoints of gender and psychoanalytical theory. The cavern is seen as a maternal place of shelter and nurturing: a womblike environment. In moving away from this shadowy maternal site toward the exterior source of light, the prisoner of the myth is also turning away from the mother—a move that has profound implications for its writer's purported egalitarian vision.

3. See Richard Rorty, *Contingency, Irony, and Solidarity* (Cambridge: Cambridge University Press, 1989); Jean Baudrillard, "The Ecstasy of Communication," in *The Anti-Aesthetic: Essays on Postmodern Culture*, ed. Hal Foster (Seattle: Bay Press, 1983); and Jean Baudrillard, *Simulations*, trans. Paul Foss, Paul Patton, and Philip Beitchman (New York: Semiotext[e], 1983).

4. This notion of subjectivity strongly influenced the ideas of many of the

foremost French theorists, including Roland Barthes, Hélène Cixous, Catherine Clément, Gilles Deleuze, Julia Kristeva, and Luce Irigaray, as well as Anglo-American theorists such as Jane Gallop, Teresa De Lauretis, Jacqueline Rose, and Kaja Silverman, all of whom distance themselves in one way or another from the ideas of Lacan, the "progenitor" of the movement, while still retaining a connection with his ideas. It is in the light of this subsequent body of writing that I read Lacan (much of whose writing I find otherwise unreadable). Julia Kristeva's work has had a particularly strong influence on my interpretations, as have the readings of Lacan by Jane Gallop (*Reading Lacan* [Ithaca, N.Y.: Cornell University Press, 1985]) and Fredric Jameson ("Imaginary and Symbolic in Lacan," in *The Ideologies of Theory* [London: Routledge, 1988], vol. 1, pp. 75–115). I will discuss Kristeva's concepts of "the symbolic" and "the semiotic," which partially overlap with Lacan's categories "the symbolic" and "the real," below. In this specific context, however, I find Lacan's concepts more useful.

5. Quoted in Alan Sheridan, "Translator's Note," in Jacques Lacan, *Écrits: A Selection*, trans. Alan Sheridan (London: Tavistock, 1977), p. x.

6. Ibid.

7. In semiotic terminology, a symbol is a sign which has an arbitrary relationship to its referent; an index is a sign that has a natural association with its referent; and an icon is a sign that has a formal resemblance to its referent. For Peirce's original exposition of these concepts, see *The Philosophical Writings of Peirce*, ed. Justus Buchler (New York: Dover, 1955), p. 102. See also Terence Hawkes, *Structuralism and Semiotics* (London: Methuen, 1977), pp. 123–50. The most thorough discussions of the concepts in the musicological literature are in Raymond Monelle, *Linguistics and Semiotics in Music* (Switzerland: Harwood, 1992), pp. 193–219, and in Eero Tarasti, "Semiotiikan Alkeet" (Foundations of semiotics), in *Johdatusta Semiotiikkaan*, ed. Eero Tarasti (Helsinki: Gaudeamus, 1990), pp. 29–31.

8. Philip Glass, interview by author, 9 September 1993.

9. Ibid.

10. Tavener employs handbells in a number of his compositions (for instance, *Towards the Son: Ritual Procession* [1982] and *Sixteen Haiku of Serefis* [1984]). And the second movement of Górecki's acclaimed *Symphony of Sorrowful Songs* (Symphony no. 3, opus 36 [1976]) begins with a passage played on the piano that is evocative of monotone bell chimes. Other composers who have taken an interest in the bell for similar reasons include two of the more mystically minded modernists, Olivier Messiaen (*Turangalîla-Symphonie* [1946–1984]) and Kalheinz Stockhausen (*Musik im Bauch* [1975]). One of the closest operatic points of reference to the use of bells in *Akhnaten* is Mussorgsky's *Boris Godunov*.

11. Tubular bells are used in a similar way in Glass's score to the Paul Schrader film *Mishima*.

12. Glass, *MPG*, p. 156.

13. Ibid.

14. Ibid.

15. Sigmund Freud, "The Dissolution of the Oedipus Complex," in *The Standard Edition of the Complete Psychological Works*, ed. and trans. James Strachey (London: Hogarth Press, 1961), vol. 19, p. 178.

16. Wayne Koestenbaum, *The Queen's Throat: Opera, Homosexuality, and the Mystery of Desire* (London: Penguin, 1993).

17. Ibid., p. 167.

18. Ibid.

19. The countertenor has reemerged in recent decades as a result largely of the burgeoning interest in historical performance practices. In Britain, this interest can be attributed largely to the influence of two composers, Michael Tippet and

Benjamin Britten, and one extraordinarily talented countertenor, Alfred Deller. (The North American "Oberlin school" exerted a powerful influence on countertenor techniques in subsequent years.) As well as having a strong gendered subtext, particularly in the music of Britten, the interest in the countertenor in the United Kingdom is bound up closely with the search for a "genuinely" British music tradition. The music of Henry Purcell and Handel abounds in parts written for high male voices. While these roles have been performed successfully by women for many years, the use of countertenors offers an alternative means of approximating historical performance practices. Today, there are, arguably, more challenging roles for the countertenor in opera than ever before, particularly in the music of British composers. Noteworthy roles in contemporary British music can be found in Britten's *A Midsummer Night's Dream* (1960) and *Death in Venice* (1973), Peter Maxwell Davies's *Taverner* (1972), and Judith Weir's *A Night at the Chinese Opera* (1987). This tradition could partly explain the extraordinary box-office success of the English National Opera's production of *Akhnaten*. Audiences in a sense knew what they were getting. For more on the countertenor, see Peter Giles, *The Counter Tenor* (London: Frederick Muller, 1982).

20. Joke Dame, "Sexual Difference and the Castrato," in *Queering the Pitch: The New Gay and Lesbian Musicology*, ed. Philip Brett, Elizabeth Wood, and Gary C. Thomas (New York: Routledge, 1994), pp. 139–53.

21. Ibid., p. 142.

22. See Michel Poizat, *The Angel's Cry: Beyond the Pleasure Principle in Opera*, trans. Arthur Denner (Ithaca, N.Y.: Cornell University Press, 1992), pp. 113–19.

23. Elizabeth Wood, "Sapphonics," in Brett, Wood, and Thomas, eds., *Queering the Pitch*, pp. 27–66.

24. Ibid., pp. 32–33.

25. See Georges Bataille, *Erotism: Death and Sensuality*, trans. Mary Dalwood (New York: Walker, 1962).

26. It appears that the idea of taboos and their transgression was an important part of Glass's poetics at the time that he wrote Akhnaten:

I'm interested in the forbidden things. One of the things I've noticed is that the things we make taboos about usually are somehow very interesting. Behind the taboos is something interesting. So, for example, if we have forbidden ourselves certain ideas for long enough then these ideas become interesting again. That was true for the kind of music my generation began writing in the 1960s. (Glass, interview by Juhani Nuorvala, Stockholm, 14 September 1986.)

If it is accepted that Akhnaten and his cohorts are represented in this opera as taboo breakers, it is easy to perceive a link between their ideas and those of Glass and other representatives of 1960s postmodernism, which lends weight to my theory that *Akhnaten* is, on one level of understanding, an autobiographical work.

27. Some nineteenth-century historians speculated that Akhnaten was a woman disguised as a man, a theory to which no contemporary Egyptologist, to my knowledge, subscribes.

28. Glass, in Michael Blackwood, dir., *A Composer's Notes. Philip Glass: The Making of an Opera* (London: Michael Blackwood Productions, 1985).

29. Glass, *MPG*, p. 149.

30. Cyril Aldred, *Akhenaten, King of Egypt* (London: Thames and Hudson, 1988), p. 234.

31. Ibid., pp. 231–32 (emphasis added).

32. Paul John Frandsen, "Philip Glass's *Akhnaten*," *Musical Quarterly* 77.2 (1993): 241–67.

33. Ibid., pp. 248–49.

34. See Susan McClary, "This Is Not a Story My People Tell: Musical Time and Space According to Laurie Anderson," in *Feminine Endings: Music, Gender, and Sexuality* (Minneapolis: University of Minnesota Press, 1991), pp. 132–47.

35. For a discussion of androgyny in heavy metal, see Robert Walser, *Running with the Devil: Power, Gender, and Madness in Heavy Metal Music* (Hanover: University Press of New England/Wesleyan University Press, 1993), pp. 124–36.

36. *The Making of the Representative for Planet 8* and *The Marriage Between Zones Three, Four, and Five.*

37. Carolyn G. Heilbrun, *Toward a Recognition of Androgyny* (New York: W. W. Norton, 1964); June Singer, *Androgyny: The Opposites Within* (Boston: Sogo Press, 1989 [1976]).

38. Wendy Doniger O'Flaherty, *Women, Androgynes, and Other Mythical Beasts* (Chicago: University of Chicago Press, 1980).

39. Julia Kristeva, "Women's Time," trans. Alice Jardin and Harry Blake, in *The Kristeva Reader*, ed. Toril Moi (New York: Columbia University Press, 1986), pp. 187–213.

40. It is my understanding that Kristeva equates the Freudian psychoanalytical concept of "bisexuality" (not to be confused with the vernacular sense of the word: someone attracted to both sexes) more or less directly with what we are referring to as androgyny.

41. See the chapter of Toril Moi, *Sexual-Textual Politics: Feminist Literary Theory* (London: Routledge, 1985) entitled "Rescuing Woolf for Feminist Politics: Some Points Towards an Alternative Reading," pp. 8–18.

42. In the introduction to *Toward a Recognition of Androgyny*, Heilbrun writes: "I believe that our future salvation lies in a movement away from sexual polarization and the prison of gender toward a world in which individual behavior can be freely chosen" (pp. ix–x).

43. See Jean-Jacques Nattiez, *Wagner Androgyne: A Study in Interpretation*, trans. Stewart Spencer (Princeton: Princeton University Press, 1993), pp. 178, 288. By far the most exhaustive typology of androgynies I have seen is in O'Flaherty, *Women, Androgynes, and Other Mythical Beasts*, pp. 283–309.

44. See also Naomi Schor, "Dreaming Dissymmetry: Barthes, Foucault, and Sexual Difference," in *Men in Feminism*, ed. Alice Jardine and Paul Smith (New York: Methuen, 1987), pp. 100–102.

45. Philip Glass, interview by author, 9 September 1993.

46. See Joseph Roddy, "Listening to Glass," in *Writings on Glass*, ed. Richard Kostelanetz (New York: Schirmer Books, 1997), p. 168.

47. Glass interview in Blackwood, dir., *A Composer's Notes.*

48. Ibid.

49. Glass, *MPG*, p. 165.

50. The melodic movement of all three parts is the same in each cycle. Tye's part, for example, is the same in the cycles in which she sings her duet with Akhnaten as when the two are joined by Nefertiti. For this reason, I have given as an example a verse in which all three voices are present. An approximation of the first two cycles can be gleaned by subtracting Tye's and Nefertiti's voices, and of the third and fourth simply by subtracting Nefertiti's voice.

51. See Angus Heriot, *The Castrati in Opera* (London: Secker and Warburg, 1956), p. 30.

52. In the film *Farinelli*, the castrato voice was "reconstructed" by doubling the voice of a male countertenor with that of a female contralto. Glass's doubling of the countertenor with brass instruments, the timbre and register of which are similar to the voice they are accompanying, produces a similar effect.

53. A famous anecdote is reenacted in *Farinelli,* in which the castrato duels with a solo trumpeter to see who can produce the most elaborate musical phrases. To the delight of the audience, Farinelli succeeds in embarrassing the trumpeter with his vocal acrobatics. This kind of trumpet writing is evoked in parts of *Akhnaten,* particularly the hymn to the sun and the duet with Nefertiti.

54. For more on travesti roles, see the editors' introduction to Corinne E. Blackmer and Patricia Juliana Smith, eds., *En Travasti: Women, Gender Subversion, Opera* (New York: Columbia University Press, 1995), pp. 1–19.

55. Glass, *MPG,* p. 170.

56. See Lacan, *Écrits,* pp. 1–7. There is a conspicuous similarity between Lacan's mirror symbolism and that found in Tibetan Buddhism. Buddhists in the Tibetan tradition refer frequently to the "Wisdom of the Great Mirror." According to Lama Govinda, "the Great Mirror reflects the Void *(sunyata)* as much as the objects, and reveals the 'emptiness' in the things as much as the things in the 'emptiness'" (Lama A. Govinda, *Foundations of Tibetan Buddhism* [London: Rider, 1960], p. 131). In both Lacanian theory and Buddhism, the mirror reflects the fundamental alienation of the subject and her or his inability to grasp reality in its totality.

57. See "Jean Genet: A Hall of Mirrors," in Martin Esslin, *The Theatre of the Absurd* (London: Penguin, 1961), pp. 200–233.

58. Mirror imagery also played an important role in ancient Egyptian religious symbolism. The Egyptologist Lise Manniche has, for example, drawn attention to the influence of fifth-dynasty religious practices on Akhnaten's sun cult. One such practice was the so-called mirror dance, in which mirrors that were "identical in shape to the sun disc" were used as accessories. Thus, it is possible that there is some degree of historical accuracy to this element of the staging, which matters little, of course, to the majority of audience members, who will not recognize the possible historical allusion, but does add another layer of interpretive resonance to those in the know (*Music and Musicians in Ancient Egypt* [London: British Museum Press, 1991], p. 87).

59. Glass interview in Blackwood, dir., *A Composer's Notes.*

60. My discussion of this production is based in part on extracts from it that appeared in the documentary *The Music of Philip Glass,* on *The South Bank Show,* ed. Melvyn Bragg (London: London Weekend Television, 1986).

61. Philip Glass et al., *Akhnaten,* booklet accompanying the compact-disk recording (CBS Records, 1987), p. 55.

62. Ralph Lewis, preface to Savitri Devi, *Son of the Sun* (San Jose, Calif.: Supreme Grand Lodge of A.M.O.R.C., 1946), pp. ix–x.

63. The quotations from Abraham's article are taken from its English translation, published in the *Psychoanalytical Quarterly* 4 (1935): 537–69. It was published originally in the first edition of the journal, *Imago,* edited by Freud, in 1912.

64. Immanuel Velikovsky, *Oedipus and Akhnaten: Myth and History* (New York: Doubleday, 1960), pp. 67–68.

65. See Sheridan, "Translator's Note," in Lacan, *Écrits,* p. xi.

66. Wallis Budge, *Tutankhamen: Amenism, Atenism, and Egyptian Monotheism* (New York: Dover, 1991 [1923]), p. 67.

67. Ibid.

68. Ibid. See also Alan Gardiner, *Egypt of the Pharaohs* (Oxford: Clarendon, 1961), p. 212.

69. Budge, *Tutankhamen,* p. 76.

70. Ibid., p. 68.

71. See, for example, Philipp Vandenberg, *Nefertiti: An Archaeological Biography,* trans. Ruth Hen (Philadelphia: J. B. Lippincott, 1978).

72. See Velikovsky, *Oedipus and Akhnaten,* pp. 86–95.

73. Ibid., p. 97.
74. Ibid., p. 91.
75. Glass et al., *Akhnaten* booklet, p. 3.
76. See Velikovsky, *Oedipus and Akhnaton*, pp. 99–100.
77. Ibid.
78. Incest symbolism is common to many religious worldviews. A passage from the Buddhist scriptures, for example, states that "the *Sadhaka* who has sexual intercourse with his mother, his sister, his daughter, and his sister's daughter, will easily succeed in striving for the ultimate goal" (Govinda, *Foundations of Tibetan Buddhism*, p. 101). The "women" in question are, according to Govinda, "the elements that make up the female principles of our psycho-physical personality" (p. 103).
79. See Bronislaw Malinowski, *Sex and Repression in Savage Society* (London: Routledge and Kegan, 1927), pp. 142–43, and Gilles Deleuze and Félix Guattari, *Anti-Oedipus: Capitalism and Schizophrenia*, trans. Robert Hurley, Mark Seem, and Helen R. Lane (Minneapolis: University of Minnesota Press, 1983).
80. One of the most striking examples of the "Oedipus complex" in non-European culture is in Tibetan Buddhism. Buddhists believe that the primary cause of all rebirth, and therefore all suffering, is a fundamental attraction to one of the parents and a corresponding repulsion from the other. When in the passage between births—what Tibetan Buddhists refer to as the Bardo realm—the wandering subject experiences desire for one of the parents and repulsion from the other, and he or she is drawn into the mother's womb, after which birth occurs. The following account is taken from the *Tibetan Book of the Dead*:

You will have visions of couples making love. When you see them, don't enter between them, but stay mindful. Visualize the males and females as the Teacher. Father and Mother, prostrate to them, and make them visualized offerings! Feel intense reverence and devotion! . . . If you enter the womb under the influence of lust and hate, . . . if you are going to be male, you arise appearing to be male; you feel strong hatred towards the father, and attraction and lust toward the mother. If you are going to be female, you appear as female; you feel strong envy and jealousy toward the mother, you feel strong longing and lust for the father. Conditioned by that, you enter the path of the womb. . . . Eventually you will be born outside the mother's womb." (*The Tibetan Book of the Dead*, trans. Robert A. Thurman [New York: Bantam Books, 1994], pp. 184–85)

Freud suggested that the Oedipus complex is formed during infancy (up to age six); post-Freudians such as Melanie Klein and Lacan are both of the opinion that it is established during the first year; Tibetan Buddhism goes further still, claiming that it is the result of the karma (or negative evolution) accumulated in previous lives. (Not all practitioners of Tibetan Buddhism take this idea at face value.) Like Freud, Tibetan Buddhism acknowledges the attraction of the child to one of the parents and his or her aversion to the other, but unlike Freud it sees the condition as a whole as stemming from a more profound psychosis, brought about by the subject's relentless and futile attempts to cling to and ossify life. Glass's cryptic, although seemingly offhand, statement that there is something of Akhnaten in all of us takes on a somewhat different shade of meaning in light of this new piece of information. It could be construed as meaning that we are similar to Akhnaten not only because he is both man and woman but that we all, to some degree, suffer from the same psychological condition as he does—the condition that Freud termed the Oedipus complex but that in another part of the world and at another time became known as samsara, the wheel of becoming.
81. I will not go into Freud's reverse formulation for girls, since it does not

pertain to the specific questions I am addressing here. Suffice to say that Freud conceives of the girl as a rival of the mother for the affections of the father. Female sexuality seems, however, to have been a particularly slippery problem for Freud, one that he grappled with throughout his career without ever feeling that he fully understood it. Most female Freudians and post-Freudians have agreed with him on this.

82. See Freud, "Totem and Taboo," in *The Standard Edition*, vol. 13, p. 17.

83. Freud, "Moses and Monotheism," in ibid., vol. 23, pp. 135–36.

84. Ibid.

85. Julia Kristeva, "Revolution in Poetic Language," trans. Margaret Waller, in *The Kristeva Reader*, pp. 89–136.

86. I refer to the symbolic domain as a whole as phallic with caution and with the knowledge, on the one hand, that the phallus is not directly equitable with the penis and, on the other, that both women and men have equal access to every area of the symbolic domain. This is not to say that I dismiss or resist the argument concerning Lacanian "phallocracy." Unlike Lacan, I do not hold the encoding of the entire symbolic domain as phallic to be an unavoidable state of affairs but instead see it as largely contingent on cultural and individual developmental factors. For the purposes of this scenario, however, I will assume a fairly orthodox post-Lacanian position, as mediated by theorists such as Kristeva, Jane Gallop, and Jacqueline Rose. For various reasons pertaining to the dramatic and cultural issues here as well as the construction of "the composer" I have been and will be to some extent positing, I find the "phallocratic" model quite useful. For more on the argument against Lacanian "phallocracy," see Luce Irigaray, *This Sex Which Is Not One*, trans. Catherine Porter (Ithaca, N.Y.: Cornell University Press, 1985); and Teresa Brennan's editor's introduction to *Between Feminism and Psychoanalysis* (London: Routledge, 1989), pp. 1–23. See also Jane Gallop, "Reading the Phallus," in *Reading Lacan*, pp. 133–56. Lacan's own most direct exposition of the concept of the phallus can be found in "The Meaning of the Phallus," in *Feminine Sexuality: Jacques Lacan and the école freudienne*, trans. Jacqueline Rose (Basingstoke: Macmillan, 1982), pp. 74–85.

87. For more on this subject and its implication for culturally oriented musicology, see Lawence Kramer, *Classical Music and Postmodern Knowledge* (Berkeley and Los Angeles: University of California Press, 1995), pp. 19–21.

88. Kristeva, "Revolution in Poetic Language," p. 93.

89. Kaja Silverman, *The Acoustic Mirror: The Female Voice in Psychoanalysis and Cinema* (Bloomington: Indiana University Press, 1988); David Schwarz, "Listening Subjects: Semiotics, Psychoanalysis, and the Music of John Adams and Steve Reich," *Perspectives of New Music* 31.2 (1993): 24–56.

90. Ivanka Stoianova, "Musique répétitive," *Musique en jeu* 26 (February 1977): 64–74.

91. Wim Mertens, *American Minimal Music* (London: Kahn and Averill, 1983).

92. Ibid., p. 124.

93. A clearly identifiable example of criticism of minimalism that has been fueled by Mertens's critical observations is Wilfrid Mellers's review of Mertens's book, "A Minimalist Definition," *The Musical Times* 125.1696 (1984): 328.

94. The opening passages of *Nixon in China*, for example, contain a quote from *Das Rheingold* very similar to, if slightly more overt than, the one in the prelude of *Akhnaten*.

95. Glass, *MPG*, p. 156.

96. On the phallic implications of the castrato, see Roland Barthes, *S/Z* (New York: Noonday Press, 1988 [1970]), p. 109.

97. For contrasting if partially overlapping views on this issue, see, on the one

hand, Catherine Clément, *Opera, or the Undoing of Women*, trans. Betsy Wing (London: Virago, 1989); Susan McClary, "The Undoing of Opera: Toward a Feminist Criticism of Music," foreword to Clément, *Opera*, pp. ix–xviii; and Susan McClary, *Feminine Endings*; and, on the other hand, Carolyn Abbate, *Unsung Voices: Opera and Musical Narrative in the Nineteenth Century* (Princeton: Princeton University Press, 1991); and Carolyn Abbate, "Opera; or, the Envoicing of Women," in *Musicology and Difference: Gender and Sexuality in Music Scholarship*, ed. Ruth A. Solie (Berkeley and Los Angeles: University of California Press, 1993), pp. 225–58.

98. Nor is there is any sense of the Madonna/whore dichotomy between Nefertiti and Tye. Without Tye's (phallic?) intervention, the Atenist revolution, which we are urged in the music to support, would never have taken place, and Nefertiti's deeply sensual contralto is definitely *not* the voice of an angel. (See McClary, *Feminine Endings*, pp. 114–15.)

99. Glass et al., *Akhnaten* booklet, p. 57.

100. Glass, *MPG*, p. 151.

101. See Alan Gardiner, "The So-called Tomb of Queen Tye," *Journal of Egyptian Archaeology* 43 (1957): 10–25.

102. Glass, *MPG*, p. 184.

103. James Henry Breasted, *A History of Egypt* (New York: Charles Scribner's Sons, 1909), p. 371.

104. Budge, *Tutankhamen*, p. 123.

105. Aldred, *Akhenaten, King of Egypt*, p. 249.

106. Glass, *MPG*, p. 151.

107. Budge, *Tutankhamen*, p. 118.

108. Aldred, *Akhenaten, King of Egypt*, p. 241.

109. See McClary, *Feminine Endings*, p. 37.

110. See Suzanne G. Cusick, "On a Lesbian Relationship with Music," in Brett, Wood, and Thomas, eds., *Queering the Pitch*, pp. 74–78. See also McClary, *Feminine Endings*, p. 37; and Wood, "Sapphonics," in Brett, Wood, and Thomas, eds., *Queering the Pitch*, pp. 36–37, 60.

111. In the Stuttgart production, Tye presumably doubled as Ra.

112. Philip Glass, interview in Blackwood, dir., *A Composer's Notes*.

113. Philip Glass, interview by author, 9 September 1993.

6. The Illusion of Autonomy

1. Theodor Adorno and Max Horkheimer, *Dialectic of Enlightenment*, trans. John Cumming (New York: Herder and Herder, 1972 [1947]).

2. See Fredric Jameson, *Postmodernism or, the Cultural Logic of Late Capitalism* (Durham, N.C.: Duke University Press, 1991), pp. 331–40; Fredric Jameson, "Imaginary and Symbolic in Lacan," in *The Ideologies of Theory* (London: Routledge, 1988), vol. 1, p. 110; and Terry Eagleton, *The Illusions of Postmodernism* (Oxford: Blackwell, 1996). An extremely perceptive post-Lacanian perspective on Glass's *Mishima* score is provided in Robert Burns Neveldine, *Bodies at Risk: Unsafe Limits in Romanticism and Postmodernism* (Albany, N.Y.: State University of New York Press), pp. 106–8.

3. Linda Hutcheon, *The Politics of Postmodernism* (London: Routledge, 1989), p. 50.

4. Teresa de Lauretis, *Technologies of Gender: Essays on Theory, Film, and Fiction* (Bloomington: Indiana University Press, 1987), p. 109.

5. Julia Kristeva, "Modern Theater Does Not Take (a) Place," *Sub-stance* 18–19 (1977): 131–34.

6. Philip Glass, interview in Michael Blackwood, dir., *A Composer's Notes. Philip Glass: The Making of an Opera* (London: Michael Blackwood Productions, 1985).

7. Glass, quoted in Cole Gagne and Tracy Caras, *Interviews with American Composers* (Metuchen, N.J.: Scarecrow Press, 1982), p. 217.

8. See Harold Bloom, *The Anxiety of Influence: A Theory of Poetry* (London: Oxford University Press, 1973). Bloom's theory is pretty much summarized thus:

Poetic Influence—when it involves two strong, authentic poets.—always proceeds by a misreading of the prior poet, an act of creative correction that is actually and necessarily a misinterpretation. The history of fruitful poetic influence, which is to say the main tradition of Western poetry since the Renaissance, is a history of anxiety and self-saving caricature, of distortion, of perverse, wilful revisionism without which modern poetry as such could not exist. (p. 30)

9. Take, for example, the following description by John Rockwell:

As with Cage, the influence [with Glass] was more one of philosophical attitude. . . . The way this Oriental influence most decisively expresses itself in American music of the sixties and the seventies was in a newly meditational mode of perception. Western art music has been built on tension and release, which would be unthinkable without the tonal system, with its balance between consonance and dissonance and its excursions away from and back to a home key. Such music involves considerable variation of dynamics, and rhythmic ideas that, while fairly primitive, still build to an ever more rapid climax. The meditative approach is more quiescent. The listener settles into the flow of a piece rather than tensely awaiting its denouement; a parallel between traditional masculine and feminine love-making suggests itself. Someone accustomed to conventional Western classical music may find this new meditational music uneventful, simplistic and dull; the new listener—and many Orientals—find classical music noisy, clumsy and brash. (Rockwell, *All American Music: Composition in the Late Twentieth-Century* [New York: Knopf, 1983], pp. 112–13)

Susan McClary makes a similar point, that the music of Philip Glass and Steve Reich "suggests the possibility of *being in time* without the necessity of striving for violent control" (*Feminine Endings: Music, Gender, and Sexuality* [Minneapolis: University of Minnesota Press, 1991], p. 122). "Philip Glass," she writes, "often plays with two qualities of motion in his music . . . the cyclical and the teleological" (pp. 122–23). An example of this is his music-theater work *The Photographer*, in which he "repeatedly gives us a typical Mahlerian buildup-to-cadence, only to loop back at the point of promised climax" (p. 123). In McClary's words, "we learn from such passages how very programmed we are to *desire* violent annihilation through the tonal cadence, and our frustration at not attaining the promised catharsis reveals to us the extent to which we are addicts in need of that fix"(ibid.). The example of Glass's music shows, for McClary as well as for Rockwell, that "one need not be a woman . . . to be gravely concerned with getting down off the beanstalk. But the deconstructive methods of postmodernism—the practice of questioning the claims to universality by the 'master narratives' of Western culture, revealing the agendas behind traditional 'value-free' procedures—are also beginning to clear a space in which a woman's voice can at last be heard as a woman's voice"(ibid.). This is not, of course, saying that the voice heard in Glass's music is a woman's voice. It does imply that the postmodern composer does not feel the need to demarcate the boundaries between the masculine and the feminine with the same rigidity as his or her predecessors did; she or he does not feel the same imperative to stay on the right side of the gender-marked musical fence.

10. See Lloyd Whitesell, "Men with a Past: Music and the 'Anxiety of Influence,'" *Nineteenth Century Music* 18.2 (1994): 152–67.

11. In the next scene, the extended self will shrink to encompass only Akhnaten's "inner circle": his family. I will discuss the implications of this below.

12. W. M. Flinders Petrie, *A History of Egypt*, 3rd ed. (London: Methuen, 1924–1925 [1899]), vol. 2, p. 214.

13. James Henry Breasted, *A History of Egypt* (New York: Charles Scribner's Sons, 1909), p. 361.

14. Wallis Budge, *Tutankhamen: Amenism, Atenism, and Egyptian Monotheism* (New York: Dover, 1991 [1923]), p. 112.

15. Donald B. Redford, *Akhenaten: The Heretic King* (Princeton: Princeton University Press, 1984), pp. 234–35.

16. Ibid., p. 234.

17. Ibid., p. 235.

18. Ibid.

19. A large part of the Romantic archaeological literature held Akhnaten to be the first pacifist in history. The writings of Reverend Baikie epitomize this point of view: Akhnaten was, in his words, "the world's first pacifist . . . an idealist dreamer, who actually believed that men were meant to live in truth and to speak the truth" (James Baikie, *The Amarna Age: A Study of the Crisis of the Ancient World* [London: A. and C. Black, 1926], p. 234). Glass does not appear to subscribe to this point of view. Even though Akhnaten's policy of military restraint was "an important part of [the] story" for him *(MPG*, p. 153), he is quick to qualify any misconceptions that might arise in this regard: "This is not," he writes, "to say that he was a pacifist, though some have described him that way, probably incorrectly"(p. 138).

20. For a more detailed discussion, see the chapter "Study and Steal—A Short History of Egyptology," in John and Elizabeth Romer, *The Rape of Tutankhamun* (London: Michael O'Mara Books, 1993), pp. 73–103.

21. For discussions of orientalism in the context of European classical music, see Ralph P. Locke, "Constructing the Oriental 'Other': Saint-Saëns's Samson et Dalila," *Cambridge Opera Journal* 3.3 (1991): 261–302; Richard Taruskin, "'Entoiling the Falconet': Russian Musical Orientalism in Context," *Cambridge Opera Journal* 4.3 (1992): 253–80; Susan McClary, *Georges Bizet: Carmen* (Cambridge: Cambridge University Press, 1992), pp. 29–43; and Philip Brett, "Eros and Orientalism in Britten's Operas," in *Queering the Pitch: The New Gay and Lesbian Musicology*, ed. Philip Brett, Elizabeth Wood, and Gary C. Thomas (New York: Routledge, 1994), pp. 235–56. A valuable early discussion can be found in A. L. Ringer, "On the Question of 'Exoticism' in Nineteenth Century Music," *Studia Musicologia* 7 (1965): 115–23.

22. Edward W. Said, *Orientalism: Western Conceptions of the Orient* (Harmondsworth: Penguin, 1978), p. 3. See also his *Culture and Imperialism* (London: Vintage, 1993).

23. Martin Bernal, *Black Athena: The Afroasiatic Roots of Classical Civilization* (London: Vintage, 1990). For responses to *Black Athena*, both pro and contra, see the debate published in the *Journal of Women's History* 4.3 (1993), and the special review section devoted to it in the *Journal of Mediterranean Archeology* 3.1 (1991).

24. Bernal, *Black Athena*, p. 2.

25. Paul Robinson, "Is Aida an Orientalist Opera?" *Cambridge Opera Journal* 5.2 (1993): 133–40.

26. Edward Said, *Culture and Imperialism*, pp. 133–59.

27. Locke, "Constructing the oriental 'Other': Saint-Saën's Samson et Dalila."

28. Ibid., p. 285.

29. Ibid.

30. Brett, "Eros and Orientalism in Britten's Operas."

31. Baikie, *The Amarna Age*, p. 238.

32. Ibid., p. 239.

33. Budge, *Tutankhamen*, p. 77.

34. Sigmund Freud, "The Dissolution of the Oedipus Complex," in *The Standard Edition of the Complete Psychological Works*, ed. and trans. James Strachey (London: Hogarth Press, 1961), vol. 19, p. 178.

35. I have been unable to trace the origin of this apparent quotation.

36. J. D. S. Pendlebury, *Tel el-Amarna* (London: Lovat Dickson and Thompson, 1935), pp. 14–15.

37. Interpreting woman as "man without a penis" is a classical Freudian move that I do not accept but that does appear to be taken as a given in many discussions of Akhnaten.

38. Alan Gardiner, *Egypt of the Pharaohs* (Oxford: Clarendon, 1961), p. 214.

39. Ibid.

40. Baikie, *The Amarna Age*, p. 375.

41. Cyril Aldred, *Akhenaten, King of Egypt* (London: Thames and Hudson, 1988), p. 283.

42. Ibid., p. 282.

43. Redford, *Akhenaten*, p. 234.

44. Aldred, *Akhenaten, King of Egypt*, p. 297.

45. Redford, *Akhenaten*, p. 211.

46. The title of this section is an intentional misquote of Jean-François Lyotard, who defines the postmodern as "that which, in the modern, puts forward the unpresentable in presentation itself; that which denies itself the solace of good forms, the consensus of a taste which would make it possible to share collectively the nostalgia for the unattainable; that which searches for new presentations, not in order to enjoy them but in order to present a stronger sense of the unpresentable"(Lyotard, *The Postmodern Condition: A Report on Knowledge*, trans. Geoff Bennington and Brian Massumi [Minneapolis: University of Minnesota Press, 1984], p. 81).

47. Glass, *MPG*, p. 158.

48. Edward Strickland, *American Composers: Dialogues on Contemporary Music* (Bloomington: Indiana University Press, 1991), p. 153.

49. Interestingly, Said has argued that the same is true of *Aïda*; that Verdi's extensive use of historical forms in that opera was a means of making the music sound more archaic and therefore more distant (in Brechtian terms) to audiences. The composers' discourse concerning the two operas is, moreover, remarkably similar: Verdi speaks of "making the mummies sing," while Glass refers to his approach as "singing archaeology." (See Edward Said, *Culture and Imperialism*, pp. 133–59.)

50. McClary, *Feminine Endings*, p. 123.

51. One of the more accessible introductions to deconstruction is Jonathan Culler, *On Deconstruction: Theory and Criticism after Structuralism* (Ithaca, N.Y.: Cornell University Press, 1982).

52. See Jean-François Lyotard, "The Sublime and the Avant-Garde," in *The Lyotard Reader*, ed. Andrew Benjamin (Oxford: Basil Blackwell, 1989), pp. 196–211.

53. See Bloom, "Daemonization, or the Counter-sublime," in *The Anxiety of Influence*, pp. 99–112.

54. See Joseph Kerman, *Opera as Drama* (New York: Vintage, 1956), pp. 157–58.

55. See Susan McClary, "Pitches, Expression, Ideology: An Exercise in Mediation," *Enclitic* 7.1 (1983): 76–86.

56. Philip Glass, interview in Blackwood, dir., *A Composer's Notes*.

57. See Freud, "The Ego and the Id," in *The Standard Edition*, vol. 19, p. 33.

58. For example, Redford, *Akhenaten*, pp. 188–93. There is, however, a strong homophobic subtext to Redford's assertion.

59. Little is known about Smenkhkare other than that he took over some of Nefertiti's titles toward the end of Akhnaten's reign. This paucity of evidence might be one rationale for his absence in the opera.

60. Glass, *MPG*, p. 171.

61. There is a musical rationale for this merging as well. With the addition of the full wind section in this part of the hymn, it becomes increasingly hard to distinguish Akhnaten's soft, countertenor voice.

62. Aldred, *Akhenaten, King of Egypt*, p. 51.

63. Glass, *MPG*, p. 186.

64. The German musicologist Michael Altmann has fruitfully explored some parallels between Glass's approach to musical structure in *Satyagraha* and mandala symbolism in his study *Sakrales Musiktheater im. 20. Jahrhundert* (Regensberg: Roderer, 1993), pp. 413–34. German research, as represented by this study and Peter Michael Hamel, *Through Music to the Self* (Shaftesbury: Element Books, 1978), has most fully explored the affinity between minimalism and Central Asian religious thought. A long tradition of mysticism in the Germanic world provides the background to such studies.

65. Glass quoted in Strickland, *American Composers*, p. 153.

66. Breasted, *A History of Egypt*, pp. 371–76.

67. Aldred, *Akhenaten, King of Egypt*, p. 306.

68. See Ahmed Osman, *Moses, Pharaoh of Egypt: The Mystery of Akhenaten Resolved* (London: Grafton Books, 1990), pp. 4–10.

69. Ibid.

70. Strickland, *American Composers*, p. 153.

71. Aldred, *Akhenaten, King of Egypt*, p. 7.

72. The most widely read novel on Akhnaten is Mika Waltari, *The Egyptian* (in the original Finnish, *Sinuhe, egyptiläinen*).

73. Philip Glass, interview in Blackwood, dir., *A Composer's Notes*.

74. Glass, *MPG*, p. 183.

75. See Redford, *Akhenaten*, p. 193; Aldred, *Akhenaten, King of Egypt*, p. 287.

76. Redford, *Akhenaten*, p. 187.

77. See Jacqueline Rose, "Introduction—II," in *Feminine Sexuality: Jacques Lacan and the École Freudienne* (Basingstoke: Macmillan, 1982), p. 51.

78. Ibid.

79. Ibid., p. 50.

80. Ibid., p. 88.

81. Lama A. Govinda, *Foundations of Tibetan Buddhism* (London: Rider, 1960), pp. 238–39; *The Tibetan Book of the Dead*, trans. Robert A. Thurman (New York: Bantam Books, 1994), pp. 30–32.

82. *The Tibetan Book of the Dead*, pp. 31–32.

83. Lawrence Kramer, "Dangerous Liaisons: The Literary Text in Musical Criticism," *Nineteenth-Century Music* 13 (1989): 165. See also Susan McClary, "Narrative Agenda's in 'Absolute' Music: Identity and Difference in Brahms's Third Symphony," in *Musicology and Difference: Gender and Sexuality in Music Scholarship*, ed. Ruth A. Solie (Berkeley and Los Angeles: University of California Press, 1993), pp. 326, 342–44.

84. See the photograph of this scene from the Stuttgart production of the opera in Philip Glass et al., *Akhnaten*, booklet accompanying the compact-disk recording (CBS Records, 1987), p. 78, and in *MPG*, opposite p. 143.

85. Immanuel Velikovsky, *Oedipus and Akhnaton: Myth and History* (New York: Doubleday, 1960), p. 105.

86. Glass, *Akhnaten* booklet, p. 3.

87. Leslie Lassetter, "The Operatic Trilogy of Philip Glass: 'Einstein on the Beach,' 'Satyagraha,' and 'Akhnaten,'" M.M. thesis, University of Cincinnati, 1985, p. 114.

88. Velikovsky, *Oedipus and Akhnaton*, pp. 91–95.

89. Budge, *Tutankhamen*, pp. 89, 92.

90. Velikovsky, *Oedipus and Akhnaton*, pp. 150–60.

91. Glass, *MPG*, p. 188.

92. Velikovsky, *Oedipus and Akhnaton*, p. 102.

93. Baikie is alone in asserting that "Nefertiti was full sister to her husband" (*The Amarna Age*, p. 243).

7. Repudiation and Resurrection

1. Immanuel Velikovsky, *Oedipus and Akhnaton: Myth and History* (New York: Doubleday, 1960), pp. 119–25.

2. The connection between blinding and castration was first made explicit by Freud in a footnote added in 1914 to his discussion of Oedipus in *The Interpretation of Dreams*. See Sigmund Freud, *The Standard Edition of the Complete Psychological Works*, ed. and trans. James Strachey (London: Hogarth Press, 1953 [1900]), vol. 5, p. 398.

3. Philip Glass, *MPG* (New York: Harper and Row, 1987), p. 173.

4. Philip Glass, *Opera on the Beach: Philip Glass, On His New World of Music Theatre* (London: Faber and Faber, 1987).

5. Glass, *MPG*, p. 190.

6. Savitri Devi, *Son of the Sun* (San Jose, Calif.: Supreme Grand Lodge of A.M.O.R.C., 1946), p. 274.

7. James Baikie, *The Amarna Age: A Study of the Crisis of the Ancient World* (London: A. and C. Black, 1926), p. 398.

8. Donald B. Redford, *Akhenaten: The Heretic King* (Princeton: Princeton University Press, 1984), p. 217; Cyril Aldred, *Akhenaten, King of Egypt* (London: Thames and Hudson, 1988), p. 298.

9. Baikie, *The Amarna Age*, pp. 406–10; Redford, *Akhenaten*, pp. 217–18; Aldred, *Akhenaten, King of Egypt*, pp. 297–98.

10. Aldred, *Akhenaten, King of Egypt*, p. 208.

11. The assumption that musical discourse is a pure, monolithic manifestation of the composer's subjective world is widely accepted and only rarely questioned. This view is epitomized in the title of Edward T. Cone's *The Composer's Voice* (Berkeley and Los Angeles: University of California Press, 1974).

12. Glass, *MPG*, pp. 172–75.

13. Ibid., p. 172.

14. Ibid., pp. 173–74.

15. Ibid., p. 193.

16. Ibid., p. 172.

17. Ibid., p. 175.

8. Some Thoughts on the Reception of Akhnaten

1. Philip Glass, interview by Juhani Nuorvala, Stockholm, 14 September 1986.

2. The "young people" in question are now thirty- and forty-somethings, of course.

3. I still notice this distrust among intellectuals when I give presentations on Philip Glass's music in the United Kingdom. It comes both from above and below,

from the right and the left: The left is suspicious of Glass simply because he writes operas but also because they associate his music directly with the "corrupting influence" of North American capitalism; the right because he is reinscribing opera, which they view as their own privileged domain, with values that they find unacceptable. There is also a subtext of cultural chauvinism and domestic insularity in the United Kingdom that underlies many critiques not only of Glass but of North American music in general, the origins of which can be traced to the colonial past. And this chauvinism is definitely not the exclusive property of the political right.

4. Glass, *MPG*, p. 87.

5. John Rockwell, "Opera: Premieres of Two Works by Philip Glass" in *New York Times*, 26 March 1984, p. C20.

6. Ibid.

7. Ibid.

8. Patrick J. Smith, "'Akhnaten'—A Resounding World Premiere," *High Fidelity/Musical America* 34.7 (July 1984): 38.

9. Michael Walsh writes most aptly of this moment in *Satyagraha* that "the purity of its calm resolve has the effect of an emotional tidal wave" ("Making a Joyful Noise," *Time* 125.22, 3 June 1985, p. 76). Thus, one critic's deliquescence is another critic's tidal wave, although both agree that hydraulic forces are at work.

10. Smith, "'Akhnaten,'" p. 37.

11. Ibid., p. 39.

12. Ibid., p. 37.

13. Patrick J. Smith, "New York City Opera: Glass 'Akhnaten,'" *High Fidelity/Musical America* 35.2 (February 1985): 21.

14. Smith, "Akhnaten," p. 38.

15. Ibid., p. 37.

16. Daniel Warburton, "Philip Glass's 'Echnaton,'" *Tempo: A Quarterly Review of Modern Music* 149 (June 1984): 46.

17. Ibid., p. 47.

18. Ibid.

19. Ibid.

20. Tim Page, "Akhnaten," in *New Grove Dictionary of Opera*, ed. Stanley Sadie (London: Macmillan, 1992), p. 48.

21. Horst Koegler, "Reports: Foreign. Stuttgart," *Opera News* 48.17 (June 1984): 36.

22. Ibid.

23. Ibid.

24. See Kurt Honalka, "Wer nicht glaubeb will, shläft ein: Philip Glass' postmoderne Anti-Oper 'Echnaton' in Stuttgart von Achim Freyer gerettet," *Opern Welt* 25.5 (1984): 27–28. A much-abridged version of this review appeared in translated form in *Opera* 35.7 (July 1984): 785–86.

25. Smith, "New York City Opera," p. 21.

26. Gregory Sandow, "Production of Sand," *Village Voice*, 4 December 1984, p. 119.

27. Robert T. Jones, "Philip Glass: Religious and Musical Revolution Comes to City Opera," *Playbill* 11 (New York State Theater edition, 1984), p. 4.

28. Winton Dean, *Akhnaten* review, *Musical Times* 128.1731 (May 1987): 281.

29. Andrew Clements, *Akhnaten* review, *Opera* 38.4 (April 1987): 460.

30. For example, William Mann, *Akhnaten* review, *Opera* 36.8 (August 1985): 958, and Noël Goodwin, *Akhnaten* review, *Opera News* 50.3 (September 1985): 57.

31. Robert Anderson proudly stated in his review of the ENO production of *Akhnaten*: "There was great applause at the end, in which I failed to join, having fallen fast asleep" (*Akhnaten* review, *Musical Times* 126.1710 [August 1985]): 475.

32. Donal Henehan, "City Opera: 'Akhnaten' by Philip Glass," *The New York Times*, 5 November 1984, p. C13.

33. Paul Griffiths, "Opera Glass," *Musical Times* 126.1708 (June 1985): 337.

34. Ibid., p. 339.

35. Ibid., p. 338.

36. According to Gregory Sandow, Glass's home city of New York "hasn't really seen or heard Akhnaten yet" (Sandow, "Production of Sand," p. 119), an opera that critics such as Edward Strickland consider Glass's best (Edward Strickland, *American Composers: Dialogues on Contemporary Music* [Bloomington: Indiana University Press, 1991], p. 152).

37. Glass recently won a sizable monetary settlement after the Honda company used the opening from the *Glassworks* collection without the composer's permission (See Allan Kozinn, "Glass Wins Settlement over an Auto Commercial," *The New York Times*, 17 September 1994, p. 19). This is, however, only the tip of the iceberg. In the majority of cases, it would be virtually impossible to prove that the music had been stolen from Glass.

Index

UNIVERSITY PRESS OF NEW ENGLAND publishes books under its own imprint and is the publisher for Brandeis University Press, Dartmouth College, Middlebury College Press, University of New Hampshire, Tufts University, and Wesleyan University Press.

ABOUT THE AUTHOR   John Richardson is a musician, composer, journalist, and musicologist who has lectured at universities in Finland and conducted research at several institutions in North America. He currently teaches at the Department of Musicology at the University of Jyväskylä, in Finland.

Library of Congress Cataloging-in-Publication Data
Richardson, John, 1964–
    Singing archaeology : Philip Glass's "Akhnaten" / John Richardson.
      p.   cm. (Music/culture)
    Includes bibliographical references (p. ****) and index.
    ISBN 0–8195–6317–X (alk . paper). — ISBN 0–8195–6342–0 (pbk. : alk. paper)
      1. Glass, Philip. Akhnaten.   2. Glass, Philip—Criticism and interpretation.   I. Title.   II. Series.
ML410.G398R54   1999
782.1—dc21   98–19454